Between Ocean and Empire
An Illustrated History of
Long Island

Edited by Robert B. MacKay, Geoffrey L. Rossano, and Carol A.
Traynor

With contributions from Roger W. Lotchin and Gaynell Stone
Partners in Progress by Robert A. Crooke

Produced in cooperation with
The Society for the Preservation of Long Island Antiquities
and
The Long Island Association

Windsor Publications, Inc.
Northridge, California

Between Ocean and Empire
An Illustrated History of
Long Island

Windsor Publications, Inc.
History Book Division

Publisher: John M. Phillips
Editorial Director: Teri Davis Greenberg
Design Director: Alexander D'Anca

Staff for *Between Ocean and Empire: An Illustrated History of Long Island*
Senior Editor: Lynn C. Kronzek
Assistant Editor: Jerry Mosher
Editorial Development: Jill Charboneau, Susan Wells
Director, Corporate Biographies: Karen Story
Assistant Director, Corporate Biographies: Phyllis Gray
Editor, Corporate Biographies: Judith Hunter
Editorial Assistants: Kathy M. Brown, Patricia Cobb, Marilyn Horn,
    Lonnie Pham, Pat Pittman, Lane Powell, Deena Tucker, Sharon L. Volz
Designer: Christina McKibbin
Layout Artist: Donna LaCarra

Frontispiece: Boats dot the dark blue water of Huntington Harbor. Photo by Robert V. Fuschetto

Opposite page: With over 500 acres and numerous man-made lakes, bridle paths, and bicycle paths, Prospect Park represented a new concept in recreation—municipally planned, open spaces within an urban center. Courtesy, The Long Island Historical Society

Page 6: To get around a lack of water power, many millers built tidal mills that twice daily trapped the rising tide water, channeling it over a water wheel to produce power. Photo by Paul J. Oresky

Contents

Introduction

Long Island has always been a land of contrast—of Europeans and native Americans—of Dutch and English—of lords of the manor and tenant farmers—of fashionable watering places and agrarian villages—of suburbia and potato fields. Its rich experience has given it a layering of history comparable to few other regions. Today, Long Island remains a place of many separate realities. There are the Northeast corridor problems of deteriorating neighborhoods, suburban sprawl, and an aging infrastructure, but there is also a strong technology-based economy and an entrepreneurial climate, fostering the growth of hundreds of emerging companies. Long Island also plays host to a significant concentration of institutions of higher learning and remarkable amenities—the great legacy of the Moses parkway system, the estate era museums and preserves, the myriad recreational facilities and, despite the movement of the twentieth-century development, unsuspected natural beauty. Here are found 90 percent of New York's wetlands, its most productive agricultural county, and nineteen state parks.

As Eastern Long Island begins to plan for its 350th anniversary in 1990, we are reminded that our history proceeded apace with the earliest European settlement in North America. Moreover, its habitation by native Americans, which predates the arrival of the Europeans by at least 5,000 years, is at least as noteworthy, since "Seawanhaka" (land of shell beads) was a major center of wampum production for the Algonkian peoples. In the intervening years the history of our Island has been exciting, if often contentious. Positioned in the stream of events taking place between New England and the middle colonies, Long Island experienced just about everything except for the brunt of the Industrial Revolution and it bypassed that era only for the lack of falling water necessary to power mill turbines. Most strikingly, it has been the cradle of so many developments now synonymous with American life. It was here that many of the nation's recreational pursuits, including thoroughbred racing, came of age; that aviation spread its wings; and that suburbia was first realized on a large scale.

Acknowledgments

This project would not have been possible without the initial planning done by William McAllister, vice president of Windsor Publications, Inc., and Russell Bastedo, the former director of the Long Island Historical Society. I would also like to thank Walter Oberstebrink and C. William Gaylor of the Long Island Association for their sponsorship of this publication, as well as Larry Austin of Austin Travel, chairman of the Long Island Association's Identity Committee.

No fewer than nineteen persons have made major contributions to *Between Ocean and Empire: An Illustrated History of Long Island,* making this project very much a team effort. I would like to thank my fellow authors:

Geoffrey L. Rossano, co-editor, author of five chapters and several sidebars, received his Ph.D. in American urban history from the University of North Carolina-Chapel Hill in 1980. One of Long Island's most promising young historians, his special interests include local history and American military history. He has published numerous articles, including "Class and Clan: The Origins and Practices of a Colonial Oligarchy" and "From Colony to Statehood: Some Observations on the American Militia System." Raised in the Huntington area and currently residing in Connecticut where he teaches history and coaches at the Salisbury School, Dr. Rossano remains actively involved in Long Island history. He is currently the director of the Oral History Program for the Nassau County Cradle of Aviation Museum and he will also be working with the Huntington Historical Society on an exhibit to be titled "A Tale of Two Towns: Huntington and Oyster Bay during the Revolutionary Era."

Roger W. Lotchin, author of the chapters on Brooklyn, is professor of history at the University of North Carolina-Chapel Hill. He received his Ph.D. in 1969 from the University of Chicago and his special interests include American urban history and politics. He has written extensively and published numerous articles on these topics and is currently working on a book entitled *The City and the Sword: Urban California and the Rise of the Metropolitan Military Complex, 1920-1953.*

Gaynell Stone, author of the first chapter, received her anthropology doctorate from the State University of New York-Stony Brook. Her special interests include Colonial Long Island material culture and she is currently the editor and a contributor to seven volumes on Long Island Indians, *Readings in Long Island Archaeology and Ethnohistory.*

Robert A. Crooke, author of "Partners in Progress," is an editor with *LI/Business Newsweekly,* a publication for the Long Island business executive. A resident of Northport, Mr. Crooke received his master's degree in English and American literature at Fordham University, New York City. He has edited for *Magazine Age* and *The Gallagher Report.*

Carol A. Traynor, co-editor, picture researcher, and author of several sidebars, also oversaw the production of the book. Currently pursuing her master's degree at the State University of New York-Stony Brook, Ms. Traynor's special interests include Long Island prehistoric and historic archaeology. She has actively participated in excavations on Long Island and was a member of an innovative pilot study of prehistoric sites on Shelter Island. Ms. Traynor joined SPLIA in 1979. She currently serves as the Society's publications coordinator.

I also owe a great debt to our contributing sidebar authors: Councilman Bradley L. Harris of Smithtown wrote the essay on Richard Smythe; Dr. Steven Kesselman, manager of the William Floyd Estate, authored the William Floyd essay; Carolyn Marx, SPLIA's Custom House interpreter and educator, provided the profile on Henry Packer Dering; Robert Farwell, former director of the Whaling Museum in Cold Spring Harbor, wrote the essay on Walter R. Jones; Linda Day, curator of the Black History Museum of Nassau County, authored the essay on Samuel Ballton; Dr. Roger G. Gerry of the

Roslyn Landmarks Society and Anthony Cucchiara, archivist of the Bryant Library, co-authored the sidebar on William Cullen Bryant; Malcolm MacKay, author of *A History of Brooklyn Heights,* wrote the sidebars on Hezekiah B. Pierrepont, Charles Pratt, and Seth Low; Marilyn Oser, director of the Walt Whitman Birthplace Museum, wrote the essay on the poet; John Gable, director of the Theodore Roosevelt Association, contributed the sidebar on our twenty-sixth President; Edward J. Smits, director of the Nassau County Museum and author of *Nassau Suburbia, U.S.A.,* authored the A.T. Stewart essay; Timothy O'Brien, formerly with Long Island Heritage, wrote the essays on Leroy R. Grumman and Robert Moses; and Kimberly Greer of *Newsday* and Stuart Diamond of the *New York Times* co-authored the sidebars on Alicia Patterson Guggenheim, William Levitt, and the Doubledays.

Robert B. MacKay

9

CHAPTER ONE

Long Island before the Europeans

About 12,000 years ago, when the last Wisconsinan Glacier was retreating across the Northeast, it left behind a small lake (now Long Island Sound) and a landmass that stretched from New Jersey to Cape Cod. Except for Long Island, the land mass is presently underwater as part of the Continental Shelf. The Island, residue of two glacial deposits, is itself almost a series of islands. It is nearly cut through at Hashamomuck and Mattituck on the North Fork, at Amagansett and Canoe Place on the South Fork, where the Nissequogue and Connetquot rivers almost meet in mid-Island, and by the Flushing Creek estuary in Queens County.

Thus, native inhabitants of the last 6,000 years had one of the most beneficent environments in the region: a continental humid climate with the Northeast's longest growing season, 220 days, and a landmass warmed by the Gulf Stream. The area contained abundant marine resources—fish, shellfish, waterfowl, seals, porpoises, and whales—as well as animals, fowl, plants, nuts, tubers, berries, and seeds. These resources fell into various ecological niches and weather zones, with the East End—like two fingers poking out into the Atlantic—subject to highly changeable marine weather and heavier snowfall. The coastline is punctuated by innumerable creeks and rivers providing food, transportation, and fresh water for humans and animals. Lakes in kettleholes (a depression remaining after the melting of buried ice) and ponds—strung strategically across the broader parts of the Island and at the head of every estuary—made it a well-watered land. The islands, marshes, and peninsulas evident on early maps illustrate why the Dutch called Long Island "Gebroken (broken) Landt."

The earliest native Americans had crossed the

In 1524 Florentine explorer Giovanni Verrazano described the native Americans in New York as handsome and tall in stature, "clothed with the feathers of birds of various colors," their hair "fastened back in a knot, of olive color." From Adams, History of the Town of Southampton, Hampton Press, 1917

Left: Long Island's first inhabitants hunted caribou, using spears with chipped stone projectile points. Courtesy, New York State Museum/ The State Education Department

Below: Among native American hunting and butchering tools, projectile points are most often used to define cultural periods because of their varied styles. The Wading River (#3) and Orient (#10) points were first found and identified on Long Island. Photo by Daniel H. Kaplan. Courtesy, Nassau County Museum

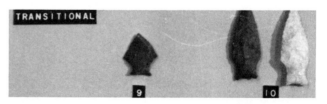

TRANSITIONAL

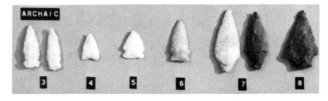

ARCHAIC

Bering Strait land bridge or come by boat or raft from Asia in several migrations more than 12,000 years ago. They followed the retreating glacier across North America and into the Long Island area. In a cold tundra environment, these early peoples hunted animals and gathered plant foods. Indians of the Northeastern United States hunted caribou and elk. Although mastodon and mammoth teeth are still dredged from Continental Shelf waters off Long Island, there is no evidence that these animals were hunted here. As the climate warmed and the glacier retreated, sea levels rose about 350 feet. An evergreen forest slowly developed, then changed to a boreal, or northern zone, parkland. Sea levels 8,000 years ago were about 100 feet lower than they are today, but this later environment was an oak-hickory forest much as we know it today.

A more varied native culture was evolving, but our knowledge of local Indian lifestyles before the seventeenth century (and the availability of written records) is based on information from archaeological excavation. Although abundant wood, bone, and textile products existed from the earliest human life, this material has not survived well in the archaeological record. This is due to a number of factors, including rising sea levels, acid soil, rapid urban expansion, relic-hunting by collectors, and the small number of trained archaeologists active on Long Island.

It is, nevertheless, reasonable to assume that prehistoric Long Islanders had the same needs—food and shelter—and the same preoccupations—

The Pipestave Hollow excavations of 1976 and 1977 uncovered a Late Archaic habitation site at Mt. Sinai on Long Island's North Shore. In addition to studying artifacts and settlement pattern remains, the excavators collected and analyzed over seventy bushels of shell and bone fragments in order to establish an accurate picture of prehistoric life and diet. Courtesy, Gaynell Stone

understanding the unknown and regulating human interaction—that we have today. Human life and culture are a continuous process, but for convenience this long period has been placed in time categories generally based on evidence of technological change. Dating from about 12,000 to 9,000 years ago, the earliest Paleo-Indian period is known on Long Island only from the fluted spear points found scattered from Queens County to Greenport in Suffolk County. No actual Paleo-Indian sites have been discovered here, although there is evidence of one on Staten Island. Any remains of local campsites are now probably underwater on the Continental Shelf.

More types of tools were developed by native inhabitants during the Archaic period, about 9,000 to 3,000 years ago, to meet the expanding subsistence opportunities of a deciduous forest and more temperate climate. Artifacts typical of this era include: new types of spear points and the *atlatl,* which made spear-throwing more effective; more cutting implements and knives; fishing equipment, such as stone sinkers for fishing nets, fish hooks, and harpoon points; and woodworking tools—gouges, axes, adzes, hammerstones, drills, and scrapers. In fact, every type of tool we use today was developed in stone by the Archaic, and possibly earlier, peoples. Dugout canoes, wooden bowls, ropes, and nets of hemp and other fibers, as well as baskets, folded

bark bags, and mats, were made, but generally have not survived. Archaic sites have been studied at Stony Brook, Wading River, Mt. Sinai, Shelter Island, and other spots. These sites provide evidence of a people who lived close to the marine resources available after about 6,000 years ago. According to archaeological excavations, they dwelled around marshes or river estuaries, and had specialized areas for a sweat hut, houses, food processing, and tool-making. Post-molds (remains of saplings in the ground) indicate the Indians lived in round and oval wigwams covered with bark or mats.

Long Island's short Transitional period, about 3,300 to 3,000 years ago, is identified by evidence of a new ritual or religious behavior and is called the Orient Burial Cult. These few ceremonial burials in large pits contained grave offerings such as paintstones, fire-making kits, and tools. The bones, sometimes cremated, were usually covered with red ochre (hematite) powder; this probably meant that the dead enjoyed high status. Period artifacts include pots made from steatite, a form of stone from Connecticut; smoking pipes; and the Orient Fishtail projectile point. Trade networks enabled Pennsylvania jasper, Hudson Valley flint, and Great Lakes and Connecticut copper to be used for Long Island Indian artifacts.

The Woodland period, from 3,000 years ago until about 500 years ago (A.D. 1500), was a continuation

Opposite page: The Island's swamp-like areas provide excellent hiding places for fish and fowl. Photo by Barbara C. Harrison

Below: Long Island Indian groups hunted deer, which can still be found in the Island's state parks. Photo by Paul J. Oresky

Left: As one of the commonest wild geese in North America, the Canada goose is abundant on Long Island's streams and open tundra. It feeds by grazing or by sounding for aquatic vegetation in streams and ponds. Photo by Paul J. Oresky

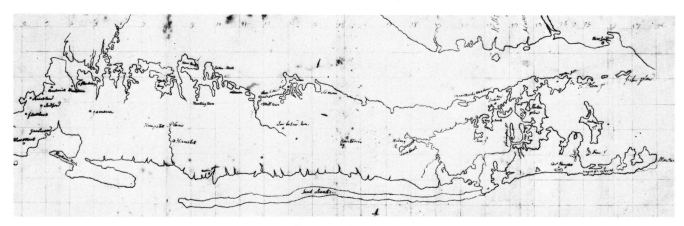

Above: The islands and peninsulas evident on early maps illustrate why the Dutch called Long Island "Gebroken Landt." Courtesy, William L. Clements Library, University of Michigan

At the time of European contact the New England coast was an area of rich and varied resources. These illustrations from a 1502 map of New England, the earliest visual record of the area, depict Indians hunting and smoking meat. Courtesy, New York Public Library

of the diversified gathering, fishing, and hunting strategies of earlier times, augmented by the harvesting of sunflowers, Jerusalem artichokes, groundnuts, and other plants. These plant resources were expanded in the late Woodland with the introduction of cultivated plants—corn, beans, squash, pumpkins, melons, and gourds—from their Central American origins. However, the extent of corn horticulture on Long Island is unknown. Hoes and mortars found on archaeological sites indicate gardening to some degree. The development of pottery at this time also enhanced cooking and storage possibilities.

The development of village sites in the Woodland period possibly reflects trade contact with Europeans as well as increased gardening activity. Since no Long Island Woodland or Contact period Indian villages have been scientifically examined, we have little firm information on this period. Yet Indian villages existed where most of the original Colonial towns were later built. In fact, Indian settlements served as environmental predictors—the best spots for settlers wanting village sites.

The era of contact with Europeans, the Historic period, disrupted the Indians' comfortable subsistence, relatively complex social life, and varied material culture. The Indians adopted iron pots for cooking and guns for hunting. They cut brass kettles into projectile points and tools, adorned themselves with glass trade beads, and chose duffel (blanket) cloth and European clothes over skins. European furniture was added to wigwams, and American wood houses were used by the latter eighteenth century. This radical change took place within 150 years after Giovanni Verrazano's visit to the New World in 1524. After a storm drove the Italian explorer out of New York Bay, he skirted Long Island and Block Island, finally arriving at Newport Harbor. There he found natives, similar to those on Long Island, who

excel us in size; they are of bronze color, some inclining more to whiteness, others to tawny color; the

16

face sharply cut, the hair long and black, upon which they bestow the greatest study in adorning it; the eyes black and alert, the bearing kind and gentle.

Verrazano describes leaders who wore stag skins adorned with colorful embroideries like damask (probably dyed porcupine quills) and broad, stone-encrusted chains of many colors at the neck. In addition, he observed the women to be graceful and comely, similarly dressed, and sporting lynx skins on their arms and pendants in their ears. Both sexes preferred earrings of copper plates to those of gold. They also had a fondness for the colors blue and red. Single women braided their hair on both sides of the head, while married women let their locks—either short or long—hang loose.

Other early observers found that young maidens reaching reproductive age decked themselves in wampum: bands of it circled the head, wampum strings covered the hair, and strands also served as necklaces and earrings. The festively-clad girls positioned themselves in a central point in the village where they might be viewed by all those seeking a wife. Van der Donck noted in the 1640s that "they usually carry small bags of paints with them . . . such as red, blue, green, brown, white, black, yellow, etc . . . that they were generally disposed to paint and ornament their faces with several brilliant colors." Indians of the area also frequently tattooed their bodies and faces, often with the clan totem represented by bears, wolves, turtles, and eagles.

In 1609 Robert Juet, a member of Henry Hudson's crew, described the area's Indians wearing "deer skins loose, well dressed . . . some in mantles of feathers, some in skins of divers sorts of good furs . . . They had red copper tobacco pipes, and other things of copper they did wear about their necks." The first Indian leader they met was Penhawitz or Pennewits, the one-eyed *sachem* of the Canarsies. Although the Vikings may have coasted through Long Island Sound around A.D. 1000, and Europeans had been fishing along the New England coast for several hundred years, the Canarsies were the first Indians documented in regional history to make contact with foreigners from across the sea. This early meeting hastened the swift demise of the Long Island natives through disease, malnutrition, and the effects of alcohol on a people who possessed

no physiological tolerance for it. New World natives also lacked immunity to European diseases such as smallpox, measles, and others. Thus, the Northeastern aboriginal population dwindled to a small fraction of its prehistoric size before the first colonists settled in the region. The Long Island natives had no hinterland to retreat to, as mainland groups had. The settlers' view of this unfortunate situation was characterized in 1670 by Daniel Denton, who felt it

is to be admired, how strangely they have decreast by the Hand of God, since the English first settling of those parts . . . it hath been generally observed, that where the English come to settle, a Divine Hand makes way for them, by removing or cutting off the Indians, either by Wars one with the other, or by some raging mortal Disease.

The inability to tolerate alcohol, exploited by some settlers, led to malnutrition and drunkenness. Rum flowed whenever colonists traded with the Indians or wanted them to sign deeds. Indian leaders requested that no liquor be sold to their people and early town laws prohibited the sale of rum and guns to the natives. Nevertheless, traders and land speculators honored the regulation against weapons better than that against alcohol.

Daniel Denton noted that "in their wars they fight no pitcht fields . . . but endeavor to secure their wives and children upon some Island . . . and then with their guns and hatchets they way-lay their enemies . . . and it is a great fight when seven or eight is slain." Given their traditions, the Indians were amazed by the tactics of the Europeans, who killed everyone, including women and children. Areas of disagreement among tribes were generally resolved not by war, but by protocols of behavior. A Shinnecock leader, for example, stroked the back of a Montauk *sachem* to show obeisance, and an Iroquois family who had lost a father or son often adopted a captive to fill his place. However, the Dutch under Governor William Kieft killed Indians of the area for little reason. Taking peaches from an orchard seemed natural to the communally-oriented natives, but to property-conscious Europeans, this act meant theft. Murder, which was relatively rare among the Indians, could often be assuaged by paying the bereaved family wampum or other remuneration.

Native Americans had no idea they were "selling" their land, but thought that the Europeans were giving them gifts for being allowed to use its resources. Sharing and gift-giving were an integral part of the aboriginal culture, a behavior which enabled groups to survive in times of scarcity. Due to the Indians' communal use of the land, they thought that they would be sharing their territory with the settlers. When the colonists "purchased" Indian lands and developed farms, they removed most of the food sources from the native diet; this created malnutrition, which heightened disease and hastened death. In addition, one regional native American tradition foretold the arrival of a great, white-skinned *Manitto* (Supreme Being) from the East. Verrazano recorded in 1524 that "they came toward us with evident delight, raising loud shouts of admiration, and showing us where we could most securely land . . ." Furthermore, a stone technology, however sophisticated, was no match for the Europeans' "magical" and much more powerful firearms and metal implements.

The settlers actually invaded inhabited land, since the earth was choice wherever the native Americans had settled and cleared gardens. Europeans needed only to push the Indians into less

Long Island Indians befriended the early European settlers, as depicted in this idealized mural of the Hempstead settlement painted by Peppino Mangravite in 1937. Courtesy, National Archives

desirable areas to inherit already cultivated land, multiple food resources, and water for people, animals, and the mills which soon dotted the landscape. Thus, beneath most historical sites on Long Island are prehistoric ones.

There were never "thirteen tribes" on Long Island. Each suitable habitation area had an extended family group or band living there. Each Indian group had a geographically descriptive name for their area; the settlers gave this name for the area to the native group, thereby creating the "tribal name." Thirteen appears to be an average of the numbers of groups named in various historic accounts, which range from two to twenty. Whatever their number, native bands did not constitute separate tribes with different cultures.

Long Island Indian life was fundamentally egalitarian, but an archaeological clue to possible social differentiation is found in the Orient Burial Cult of the Transitional period. This Red Ochre Burial Cult was widespread throughout the Northeast during Archaic times, and occurred during the Paleo period in North Dakota. Performed with red ochre and grave goods for the afterworld, the rites were probably organized by a ritual specialist, such as a *powawa* or *shaman;* his role was essential and, therefore, possibly marked the beginning of social ranking. Although its evolution is uncertain, the *sachem,* another status role, was evident in one form at Contact, where his power was related to his family or band. Aboriginal *sachems* were not absolute rulers in the European sense; rather, they were consensual leaders who emerged by displaying skill. Several accounts report an experienced general leader and a younger coordinator of military activities.

In some cases leadership may have been hereditary, but this interpretation also could be attributed to European misconceptions. Settlers actually fostered a "hereditary ruler" to ensure that property transactions needed to be approved by only one Indian authority. Wyandanch and Tackapausha—historic "leaders" of East End and West End Long Island Indian "confederations"—even signed over lands which they did not actually control. In fact, half of the "Shinnecock"—including the *sachem*—who signed a 1703 deed with the early Southampton purchasers did not appear on the 1698 census.

Long Island's prehistoric artifacts provide some clues to the Indian belief system, as well as to other cultural facets of life. Thunderbird and Great Horned Serpent figures carved on stone, for example, hint at a complex religion and philosophy revolving around and attempting to explain nature. However, descriptions of aboriginal beliefs, especially by the

The outline of a bird figure on this pottery fragment from the Shinnecock site at Sebonac is a representation of the god of the upperworld in the Algonkian belief system. Courtesy, American Museum of Natural History

colonial clergy, proved more subjective, even hostile. The Indians were considered heathens and their actions, illogical. In fact, the "powwow," a gathering which could include healing ceremonies, group dances, trances, and decision-making sessions, was perceived by colonists only as wild, dangerous behaviour. Samuel Taylor, a Quaker traveling on Shelter Island in 1659, observed the ritual:

In came a great many lusty proper men . . . and sat down; and every one had a short truncheon stick in

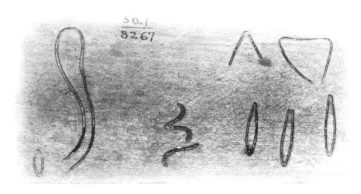

Stone tablets with pictograph symbols found at Dosoris (Glen Cove), the Sebonac Shinnecock site, and Orient provide evidence of a complex comunication system. Early records note that carved wood slabs were used to record a group's family history or a warrior's deeds. Photo by Kay C. Lenskjold. Courtesy, American Museum of Natural History

WYANDANCH

A little known and even less understood commodity was to have a major impact on early relations between the English and the Indians on Long Island during the seventeenth century. Wampum, along with land, was among the chief objects of attraction to early colonial leaders. As sachem of the wampum-rich Montauk Peninsula, Wyandanch played a pivotal role in these complex and often strained relations. Interacting with such prominent colonial figures as Lion Gardiner and Richard Smythe and assuming a strong position of leadership over the other native American groups on the east end of Long Island, he was able to exert a degree of political control unusual for the time—a control that was both shaped and limited by the political and economic climate established by the English.

The production of wampum, or shell beads, can be considered Long Island's first industry. As early as 1633, John Winthrop, governor of Massachusetts Colony, considered Long Island the best place for obtaining wampum for trade. The Dutch even called the Island "Seawanhackey," or "place of shell beads," after the Indian custom. Wampum was produced from two species of shell, whelk and quahog, especially abundant in Long Island waters, but was also produced by other coastal Indian groups as well. The cylindrical beads were fashioned from the

Wampum was used as personal adornment, a unit of exchange in barter, currency in the colonial fur trade, tribute to avoid war, and to ritually finalize agreements. The whelk shells from which it was made were especially abundant on Long Island. Photo by Harvey Weber. Courtesy, Suffolk County Historical Society

shells in a time-consuming process using sharpened stone drills. After contact with the settlers, the Indians were soon supplied with iron drills to speed manufacture. While the Indians had produced wampum before contact and used it for a variety of functions including tribute, ransom, marriage gifts, and adornment, the introduction of Europeans with their different economic concepts caused subtle shifts in the use and value of this commodity. The early colonists began to use wampum as a form of

currency as it was durable, lightweight, fairly uniform in size, and could be grouped in various increments from a single bead to what was called a "fathom" consisting of 540 beads. The Dutch and English traded goods for wampum from the coastal Indians and in turn traded it to inland and northern Indians for furs in a trade network that extended as far as Nova Scotia—a process which amassed a great deal of wealth for the early white traders as American furs had become quite fashionable in Europe. By the 1630s the English and Dutch had established "trade houses" along the trading network and the colonial government attempted to regulate and monopolize wampum production by controlling the areas of production and the Indians who owned and produced it. Wyandanch, as sachem of a rich wampum producing area, was right in the midst of these developments. His backing of the English in their war against the Pequot Indians of Connecticut in 1636-1637 produced a shift in the balance of wampum control and established a new basis for future relations with the English.

Wyandanch was able to exert a great deal of authority over his own group of Montauks, as well as the other eastern Long Island groups of Shinnecocks, Corchaugs, and Manhassets. This authority was based on three factors: the traditional Indian custom of group leaders governing by consensus; the Montauks' apparent strength in terms of numbers; and, most importantly, the influence of the English. It was advantageous to the English in their wampum trading and land deals to negotiate with one individual instead of the whole group. Their influence brought about a shift in power from numerous local "troublesome" sachems, each representing one or a few settlements, to a few "cooperative" chiefs who controlled many settlements. These chiefs became directly responsible for payments of wampum, were the first to be approached in securing land titles, and were often backed by Dutch and English authority in settling disputes. Wyandanch had made no secret of his respect and regard for the Europeans, whom he considered friends, and he was early placed by the English in the role of chief negotiator for the other

By this deed dated East Hampton, July 14, 1659, Wyandanch conveyed as a gift to Lion Gardiner a tract of land in what is now Smithtown. Wyandanch's mark can be seen at bottom right, along with that of his son and his wife, known as "the Sunck Squa." Courtesy, The Long Island Historical Society

eastern Long Island Indians.

Previous to contact, the Montauks had been paying wampum tribute to the stronger and more agressive Pequots across the Sound. After the Pequots' defeat in 1637 Wyandanch petitioned the English through his friend Lion Gardiner and offered to pay wampum to them for protection and trade rights, like the Montauks' previous agreement with the Pequots. In 1644 the four sachems from eastern Long Island requested and received certificates from the English acknowledging them to be tributaries of the English. While this might have been thought to be an astute political move by Wyandanch—a new allegiance for protection and trade with the dominant power—subsequent developments proved otherwise. The Montauks were not completely protected from assaults by other Indian groups and the English were slow to come to their aid. Wyandanch often found himself in conflict with the Narragansetts of

New England and he was now forced to pay tribute to them as well as the English. With his prosperity diminished by these obligations, Wyandanch began to sell Montauk and other Indian land on Long Island to his land-hungry English friends, particularly Lion Gardiner. Gardiner had especially attached himself to Wyandanch through his efforts to ransom the sachem's daughter from the Narragansetts, who had held her captive for a number of years, and Wyandanch showed his appreciation to Gardiner with gifts of land. Gardiner, in turn, sold large parcels to other early settlers, such as Richard Smythe and John Cooper, and it can be questioned whether Gardiner used his influence over Wyandanch to obtain Indian land for others.

Wyandanch was eventually to sell or give away lands occupied by the Shinnecocks, Corchaugs, and Montauks, including areas of present-day Smithown, Huntington, Hempstead, and North Hempstead, as well as much of Montauk. While Wyandanch's authority to dispose of land and wampum for other groups was apparently not questioned in his own lifetime, after his death in 1659 (some claim he was poisoned), many disputes arose over his right to have dealt for other groups and countless lawsuits ensued.

Carol A. Traynor

his hand ... So they began to pow-wow, as they called it ... the sick man sitting up as well as he could, and having a dish or calabash of water ... he supped a little of it ... spirted it with his mouth into his hands, and threw it over his head and naked body ... and beating himself with his arms and clapping his hands till he was all of a foam with sweat and did speak something in his own tongue very loud; and as he spoke they all spoke very loud, as with one voice, and knocked on the ground with their truncheons, so that it made the very woods ring and the ground shake ...

Powwows were banned by town governments, a political act intended to erode the power of the *pow-awa*, the keeper of traditional beliefs.

The Indians also had an effective healing system based on herbs. Indeed, "green medicine" was the only kind known throughout human history until Pasteur proposed the germ theory in the late 1800s. Van der Donck observed of the Indians in the 1640s that "they can heal fresh wounds and dangerous bruises in a most wonderful manner. They also have remedies for old sores and ulcers ... and venereal affections ... All their cures are from herbs, roots, and leaves ..." This aspect of native life received universal admiration from Europeans otherwise critical of this strange, new world and people. The efficacy of the Indian healing methods, including sweat baths, fasting, light-weight rawhide casts for broken limbs, and herbal medicines, was superior to that of the European intruders. Over 75 percent of the U.S. Pharmacopoeia today is still based on these empirically-tested herbal remedies.

Minerals, too, held a special place in the native culture. Paint pots (concretions of red ochre), plus remains of yellow limonite and black graphite found at archaeological excavations, indicate their use for body painting and pictographs. Face and body painting were done daily for both pleasure and for certain ritual occasions, such as war and death.

Historical accounts of mourning practices tell of much lamenting, many visits to the gravesite, and of the family painting their faces black for a year. Ten-day burial feasts cemented ancestral ties and social relations. According to some observers, the dead were buried "sitting up" in a flexed position with the knees under the chin. Christian influence after Contact changed the position to the European style of lying prone. On western Long Island, a small structure of mat-covered saplings was erected around the grave, which was kept free of grass during yearly or more frequent visits. In Montauk territory, mounds of stones marked Historic period graves.

Effigy representations of faces and eyes have been found on rocks and shells. The ritual and religious importance of these objects was noted by Azariah Horton, a traveling Presbyterian missionary to the natives, who wrote in 1741:

This day conversed with a Squaw [Shinnecock], who had the possession of two wooden Gods, but could by no means persuade her to part with them. She said, being askt, that she did not worship them, but kept them, because her father gave them to her.

David Gardiner observed of the Montauk that "they had small idols or images and a regular priesthood ... by whom these idols were consulted." The same effigy faces have been found on some Long Island pots as well. Commemorating their winter Twelve Nights ceremony, Delaware Indians carved similar facial images on the drumsticks and houseposts of the lodge.

Though Indians have generally been thought preliterate, pictographs on Long Island stones give testimony to a complex communication system. Historic records state that men kept visual accounts of their exploits on planks in their wigwams. A wooden slab in the village center documented the group's history and genealogy. In addition, hunting parties left messages along the trail as to their size, destination, and the prey sought. None of these artifacts survived, but early records have preserved this aspect of the area's prehistoric life.

As part of the large body of Indians who lived from Canada to Virginia, Long Island natives spoke variants of the Algonkian language family. If Thomas Jefferson and James Madison had not visited William Floyd in 1791 and documented Poosepatuck words, and if John Lion Gardiner had not recorded a Montauk vocabulary list in 1798, we would not know that Long Island Indians communicated in several closely-related languages. Those of western Long Island spoke the Munsee form of Delaware, as did their neighbors on Manhattan, Staten Island, and New Jersey. These Long Islanders were dispersed

While early missionary efforts were sporadic and largely unsuccessful, by the eighteenth and nineteenth centuries a large number of native Americans had been converted to Christianity. Courtesy, East Hampton Free Library

by colonists before any language was recorded, but it can be recreated from New Jersey linguistic materials. The word lists of the East End Montauk and Shinnecock indicate they spoke a version of Mohegan-Pequot, and the Poosepatuck (Unkechaug), a variant of Naugatuck-Quiripi. It is not known if the Matinecock and other mid-Island peoples used an Unkechaug or Delaware language, but Long Island Indians generally spoke the language of the group directly across the Sound from them. The Sound proved to be a conduit, rather than a barrier, and facilitated linguistic and social interaction.

In addition to cultural remains, the legends and myths of Long Island's natives have survived, often through the recorded history of neighboring Indians. When asked from where his people came, a New Jersey Indian visiting the Flemish Labadist missionary, Jasper Danckaerts, in 1679

took a piece of coal ... and began to write upon the floor. He first drew a circle, a little oval, to which he made four paws or feet, a head and a tail. This ... is a tortoise, lying in the water around it ... This was or is all water, and so at first was the world or earth, when the tortoise gradually raised its round back up high, and the water ran off of it, and thus the earth became dry ... and there grew a tree in the middle of the earth, and the root of this tree sent forth a sprout beside it and there grew upon it

a man, who was the first male. This man was then alone, and would have remained alone; but the tree bent over until its top touched the earth, and there shot therein another root, from which came forth another sprout, and there grew upon it the woman, and from these two are all men produced.

This is the origin myth known by Long Island Indians. All peoples have their own version, just as ours is the story of Adam and Eve.

Life for Long Island Indians was not one unbroken round of struggle for subsistence. Contemporary gathering and hunting groups around the world, for example, spend about twenty hours a week securing food. The longer "workweek" began with an increasing focus on horticulture. Extended family groups on Long Island lived near rivers and estuaries where a wealth of food resources existed throughout the year; they also sought what they needed from various spots as the season permitted. Additional time was spent gathering plants for baskets, clay for pottery, grasses for mats, wood for certain implements, and stone for tools. Toolmaking itself took a great deal of time. The fish trapping season ran from March to May; vegetal foods, as well as berries, tubers, and groundnuts, were collected in spring and summer. Crabs, fish, and shellfish were gathered, smoked, and dried in the summer for winter use. Historic records note that area In-

Left: Because preservation of objects made from materials other than stone or bone is particularly poor on Long Island, the full picture of our prehistoric predecessors' lifestyles is distorted. Leatherworking, textile and clothing manufacturing, basketry, and woodworking frequently produced objects such as these circa 1900 Shinnecock baskets that could be both functional and beautiful. Photo by Kay C. Lenskjold. Courtesy, American Museum of Natural History

Opposite page: The development of fired clay pots around 1000 B.C. was an important technological innovation. This pot was made during the Woodland period, A.D. 1200 to 1500. Photo by Harvey Weber. Courtesy, Suffolk County Historical Society

dians planted corn, beans, squash, gourds, melons, pumpkins, and tobacco in spring and harvested them in summer and autumn. Nuts were collected and stored in the fall. Hunting drives for deer occurred during the autumn, and small game trapping took place throughout the year. The colder seasons also lent themselves to the pursuit of wild fowl, and seals and whales could be harvested in winter. Although there is uncertainty as to the extent of maize horticulture in pre-Contact Long Island, all historic accounts discuss the fields of "Turkish wheat" or "Indian corn"—its amount, storage, and purchase by the traders and colonists. Later, when they became dependent on the European economy, the Indians purchased corn from the settlers. Early records also tell of "Old Fields" in some of the major habitation areas. Planted in "mounds" with bean and squash vines climbing the cornstalks, these Indian gardens were cleared by burning the forests. Settlers invariably saved time and energy by claiming as theirs these already cultivated plots. The hamlet of Old Field, above Stony Brook, is a

reminder of this practice.

Play, sports, and celebrations broke up the seasonal round of work. Children's games, too, fostered practical adult skills such as shooting, weaving, or making pots. Denton (1670) states that the Indians' favorite recreational activities were football and cards. Gaming balls and markers from Mt. Sinai and Nissequogue suggest a form of bowling and "board" games, and a stone puzzle from Montauk sharpened problem-solving skills. Early accounts also refer to seasonal gatherings where matchmaking occurred. At the time of the Winter Solstice, for example, the people held *canticas* or dancing celebrations. Wassenaer found in the 1620s that

the first full moon following that at the end of February is greatly honored by them. They watch it with great devotion, and as it rises, they compliment it with a festival; they collect together from all quarters, and revel in their way, with wild game or fish, and drink clear river water to their fill,

STEPHEN PHAROAH

Stephen Pharoah, a Montauk Indian who was born in 1819 and died in 1879, participated in adapting the Long Island Indians' economic, social, and technological cultures to life in the nineteenth century, and he is certainly one of the most interesting of these native participants. Also known as Steve Talkhouse, Pharoah became a legend in his own time, as well as today, because of his combinations of abilities and strength of character. He had various careers as a whaler, hunter, circus performer, and champion cross-country walker, and was a veteran of the Civil War, serving in the 29th Connecticut Volunteers. This multifaceted figure captured the imagination of the period and stories of his exploits have been passed on to later generations.

Stephen Pharoah lived during an era when life for native Americans was not particularly easy or pleasant. Decimated in numbers by contact with European diseases and the forced migration of many of their groups to other areas, exploited of most of their land through confusing and misunderstood land use rights, and with their former culture and livelihood greatly eroded, the Indians who remained on eastern Long Island survived by adapting their skills to a new lifestyle. These Indians became an integral part of their community and worked in many of the industries of the period, including whaling,

In addition to his other abilities, Stephen Pharoah was a legendary long-distance walker who won a number of competitions across the country. This portrait was taken circa 1875. Courtesy, Smithsonian Institution

craft production, and farming, functioning as agricultural laborers and as noted guides and hunters. As such they contributed to the economic development of the east end of Long Island during the nineteenth century.

Stephen Pharoah was born into this changing environment. He was a descendant of the Montauks (or Meantacuts), one of the Indian groups of the Algonkian culture inhabiting Long Island. Stephen himself was highly regarded in the East Hampton area and the name of Pharoah had a long and important place in Montauk history. Claimed to be descendants of the seventeenth-century sachem of the Montauks, Wyandanch, Pharoahs appear in early documents and town records as active participants in Indian land use disputes involving their property in Montauk. Erroneously called the "King of the Montauks," Stephen's family was considered to be titular leader of that group. Stephen's father, Sylvester, who died in 1870, had reigned as tribal leader, as had other members of his family, and Stephen assumed the role for one year in 1878.

During Stephen's childhood, there is evidence that he was bound out as a farmhand to a Colonel William Parsons. The settlers early encouraged Indians to become indentured servants because of the severe shortage of manpower. As a young man, Stephen, like other Montauk Indians, roamed the Montauk Peninsula hunting ducks and geese to sell to nearby communities. Many of the local Indians were valued for their traditional skills as hunters and fishermen and were employed as guides by wealthy sportsmen who frequented such early resorts as the Southside Sportsmen's Club in Oakdale. Stephen was also known to have participated in the whaling industry for a time, and his son was to follow him in this field. Skilled Indian fishermen were much in demand by whalers as early as the seventeenth century and it is believed that the Indians were the first to teach the settlers the skill of shore whaling. Stephen also worked for wages on nearby farms. Forced off much of their own land due to expansion of the white population, and needing money to purchase the goods and necessities they were now dependent upon, many Indians became wage laborers. Stephen Pharoah was highly regarded as an able and dependable worker by the farmers of his community. He was known to have walked from Montauk to East Hampton, which is quite a distance on foot, perform a full day's work as a farmhand, and walk home again.

In fact, Stephen's walking prowess was legendary in East Hampton and helped to bring him the attention of a larger public than his immediate community. He was a great cross-country walker and was known to walk twenty-five miles to mail a letter, for which he charged twenty-five cents. The year before his death he walked from Brooklyn to Montauk in one day, a distance of over 100 miles. One local story has him refusing a lift in a horse and carriage because he said he was in a hurry to get to town. He participated in several walking races and won one particular race from Boston to Chicago against fifty others. It was through these athletic exploits that P.T. Barnum heard of him, and Stephen was persuaded to join his circus for a time billed as "King of the Montauks."

Stephen died in 1879 and was buried in Indian Field Cemetery in Montauk. A stone monument marks his birthplace and his grave in Montauk contains the only headstone in this traditional Indian cemetery, evidence of his stature in the community. During the year of his death Montauk was partitioned off and sold to Arthur Benson for development, and in 1885 Montauk was closed to the Meantacuts.

Carol A. Traynor

Left: Samson Occum (d. 1792), a Mohegan Indian from Connecticut, came to Long Island in 1759 and was ordained a Presbyterian minister in East Hampton. He ministered to the Montauk Indians for over twelve years and established a school there to teach English. Courtesy, East Hampton Free Library

Opposite page: No longer employed in the defunct whaling industry, the remaining Long Island Indian groups in the latter part of the nineteenth century relied on hunting, fishing, and craft production. Tom Hill, a Poosepatuck Indian, is seen here circa 1890 surrounded by fishing equipment. Courtesy, Smithsonian Institution

without being intoxicated ... this moon being a harbinger of the spring ... they celebrate the new August moon by another festival, as their harvest then approaches.

The prehistoric population of Long Island was probably denser than that of the surrounding region. One scholar believes it to have been around 3,000 people, though other sources set the figure at 6,000 or more. Verrazano noted how populous the area was by the many fires seen along the coast at night. Recurring epidemics which spread across the Northeast around the time of Verrazano's contact, however, rapidly reduced Long Island Indians to less than one-tenth their former number. An estimated 500 survived by 1658. Azariah Horton listed 400 Long Island native Americans in the 1740s, but a 1785 census counted 765, possibly including those who "married in." Some local Indians were made slaves; still more became indentured servants until reaching twenty-one years of age. Daniel Tredwell's early nineteenth-century diary mentions intermarriage between Indian men and local south shore women.

Besides intermarriage with the Europeans, the Indians left other imprints on American culture. The notable surveyor and mediator Cockenoe-de-Long Island also served as the first Indian teacher and translator of Mohegan-Pequot for John Eliot, who later produced America's first Bible. This was written in Narragansett so that the New England tribes could understand it. The Shinnecock, too, presumably helped the Reverend John Pierson prepare his *Some Helps for the Indian,* a Quiripi-language book, just as the Montauk aided the Reverend Thomas James with his *Catechism.*

Samson Occum, the Mohegan-Pequot who married Mary Fowler of Montauk, became that group's teacher and minister. One of the most notable clerics in America and the outstanding Indian preacher of his time, he even traveled to England, raising funds for Dartmouth, the college for Indians he helped to found. The eloquence of the Reverend Paul Cuffee, a Shinnecock who served after Occum and ministered to a Congregational chapel in the Shinnecock Hills during the late 1700s, also was noted by Harriet Beecher Stowe in *Uncle Tom's Cabin.*

In spite of many contributions and the value of their labor, Indians were continually pushed onto smaller plots of land. Since East Hampton Town deported all Montauk who did not marry within the group—a decree which meant limited survival on Long Island—Occum ultimately led many Montauk and some Shinnecock to Brothertown in Oneida Territory in the 1780s. White settlement of the Western New York frontier forced their final migration to Wisconsin.

Early European traders would have perished in New Netherlands without the assistance of local Indians. Generously sharing their food, shelter, and knowledge of local subsistence techniques, the natives added tobacco, as well as the cereal staple, corn, to the European diet. Many Indian words, such as *succotash, squaw,* and *moccasin* have en-

tered our language. And Long Island place names are rich with the aboriginal presence: Peconic, Manhasset, Patchogue, Hauppauge, Rockaway, Connetquot, Merrick, and others reflect the native heritage.

Although the European settlers took their land, Long Island Indians survived because of their flexibility and traditional skills. The eastern end of Shinnecock territory was "bought" by the Southampton Proprietors in 1640; partial use of the western section was restored in 1703, only after Indian protest. As the Long Island Rail Road inched across the land in the 1840s, the Shinnecock were "given" their current 800-acre peninsula reservation in 1859 in exchange for the 3,000-acre Shinnecock Hills tract wanted for the train line. Indians helped to build the tracks across their land, but local land developers became wealthy through the property sales.

The Shinnecock long had harvested the sea; they showed the settlers how to catch whales along the shore and became early members of Colonial whaling crews. This specialty continued throughout the nineteenth century, with an Indian, often a Shinnecock, the harpooner; many served as mates and "exact sailors." A few became captains.

Indian traditional expertise in hunting made them sought-after guides for the late nineteenth-century gunning trade. Charles S. Bunn, a Shinnecock, produced decoys and led members of the Roosevelt, Herter, and Du Pont families on expeditions. Ancient woodworking talents continued with basketmaking and the production of "scrubs," the first scouring brushes in America. The Shinnecock became the original "Fuller Brush" men by selling

their wares from a wagon traveling the length of Long Island.

When the Shinnecock Fire Island inlet closed and fishing and clamming declined, the Indians worked on local farms, and served as plumbers, mechanics, musicians, caddies, and greenskeepers. The women industriously tended gardens and provided the extra hands that enabled Southampton society to lead an elegant lifestyle.

Long Island Indians today are concentrated in state-recognized reservations at Mastic, where about 100 Unkechaug reside at the Poosepatuck reservation, and Southampton, which roughly 350 Shinnecock call home. Descendants of the Montauk dwell in Sag Harbor and East Hampton; more live in Wisconsin, the last stop of the late eighteenth-century exodus led by Samson Occum. Descendants of the Matinecock still live in Nassau County. Other Long Island Indians are scattered throughout the Island, Manhattan, and various parts of the United States.

Shinnecock and Poosepatuck are presently maraculture specialists, clerks, doctors, factory workers, lawyers, teachers, mechanics, students, administrators, craftsmen, housewives, laborers. They have survived by a combination of exogamy (marriage out of the group) and endogamy (marrying within). Today most Shinnecock are multiply related to each other, descendants of their historic four bands through thirteen or more generations. Their family ties remain deep and supportive; their determination to keep their lands is firm (the last challenge was made only twenty odd years ago); and their quest to recover and nourish their ancient traditions, strong.

CHAPTER TWO

New World, New Amsterdam, New York

ong Island's earliest European visitors came searching for gold, furs, and trade routes to the Orient. Italian Giovanni Verrazano first arrived in 1524 while sailing for the king of France. Nearly a century later, in 1609, Englishman Henry Hudson guided his small ship *Half Moon* through the New York narrows and commenced serious exploration. He was soon followed by Holland's Adrian Block and Hendrick Christiaensen, who initiated a series of trading voyages. On one trip in 1613 Block's vessel burned while anchored in New York harbor. Undaunted, he and his crew built the tiny shallop *Restless* and the next year journeyed up the East River, through Hell's Gate, and then eastward down the length of the Sound. They then discovered that Long Island was indeed an island and not part of the mainland. Block later called the fish-shaped landmass "T Lange Eilandt"; the name has stuck ever since.

Explorers and colonial officials described the area in glowing terms. One labeled Long Island "the crown of the province by reason of its ... excellent harbors and bays, as well as convenient and fertile lands ... it is the levelest and finest soil." Another observed, "Oyster Bay ... has on its borders fine maize lands ... the land is situated on such a beautiful bay and rivers that it could ... be converted into good farms fit for the plough."

In 1621 the commerce-minded Netherlands government chartered the Dutch West India Company to oversee New World settlement, and three years later these merchant adventurers established a small outpost of Walloon refugees at the tip of Manhattan island. Their tiny colony of New Amsterdam grew slowly at first. More intrigued with ventures in Brazil, Guiana, and the Caribbean, the

NOVUM AMSTERODAMUM

New Amsterdam, originally a
fur trading center, already
had assumed an air of bustle
and prosperity by the time
Peter Minuit became director
general in 1626. This 1670

view shows the earthen fort
which housed the church, the
governor's residence, and the
prison. From Singleton, Dutch
New York, *1909*

Explorers such as Henry Hudson and Adrian Block sparked Europeans' interest in the New World and its commercial possibilities. Many seventeenth-century books described the land's beauty and fruitfulness. This map appeared in Description of New Netherland *by Adriaen Van der Donck, printed in 1665.*

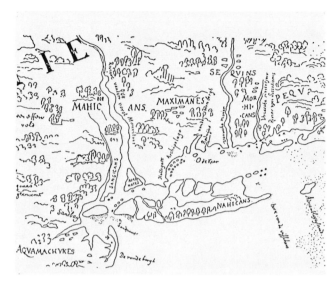

This first map of Long Island, made circa 1616 by Dutch explorer Adrian Block, denotes the names and locations of the area's Indian groups. Block presented the map to the states-general upon his return to Holland, and was one of the first to extol the commercial possibilities of the New World. From Flint, Early Long Island, *1896*

West India Company viewed Manhattan as a fur trading depot, not the seat of a flourishing colony. Luring Dutch settlers to a new and hostile continent also proved difficult. Hollanders at home enjoyed a stable, republican government, religious toleration, and a thriving economy. Well into the 1630s New Amsterdam remained confined to the tip of Manhattan and a few homesteads scattered along the Jersey and Brooklyn shores.

Alarmed at the slow pace of development and the growing menace of neighboring New England, Dutch authorities in the mid-1630s inaugurated a more vigorous settlement program. Officials pur-

chased lands in Brooklyn adjoining Gowanus Cove and Wallabout Bay. Resident Director Wouter Van Twiller and several of his counselors also obtained 15,000 acres in Flatlands from the Canarsie Indians, but home authorities later voided the agreement. Twiller was soon recalled and replaced in 1638 by William Kieft who brought instructions to hasten land acquisition and increase the rate of settlement. As part of his program, the new resident director invited disaffected Englishmen to settle within Dutch territory, providing they would swear allegiance to Holland.

Before the fledgling policies exerted any beneficial impact, however, Indian warfare erupted. In 1643 nervous Dutch militiamen attacked and massacred two bands of friendly Indians camped in Manhattan and New Jersey. This outrage sparked widespread fighting, and many isolated homesteads were ravaged. Over 1,200 Indians and settlers died before calm returned in 1645.

With the resumption of peace, settlement of western Long Island began in earnest. Attempting to impose social order on scattered farmsteads, promote education and religion, and provide for defense, Dutch authorities encouraged the formation of organized townships. Lands across the East River were granted in 1645 to Jan Bout, Huyck Rossun, and Gerritt van Couwenhoven. By December the tiny village of Breukelen, named after a town in Holland, existed. Two years later local farmers began holding market fairs. The community soon maintained a separate church, and the first schoolmaster arrived shortly thereafter. Perhaps eighty adult men lived in Breukelen (Brooklyn) by 1664.

Brooklyn was the first settlement, but efforts to populate the Island gained momentum. Flatlands, farmed sporadically since the 1630s, received a town patent in 1647. Four years later Peter Stuyvesant, the aggressive governor of New Amsterdam, approved a land grant for the region south of Prospect Heights. Colonists called this broad, wooded plain "T Vlacke Bosch" (flat forest), and Flatbush was born. A church was organized in 1654 and a school opened four years later.

New Utrecht became the next Dutch village to spring from the Long Island countryside. In the early 1640s Director William Kieft secured Indian lands stretching from Coney Island to Gowanus Bay. A decade later Cornelius van Werkhoven repurchased that portion abutting Fort Hamilton and the Narrows for a payment of shoes, stockings, shirts, combs, knives, scissors, and adzes. He immediately began developing his site. Though van Werkhoven soon died while on a visit to Holland, his American agent, Jacques Cortelyou, petitioned

New Amsterdam officials to divide the land into small farms. Twenty-one patents were quickly awarded and a town grant proffered in 1660.

Bushwyck, last of the five Dutch towns, was first patented in 1638, but not settled for another twenty-three years. Peter Stuyvesant then took pity on a small group of Huguenot families fleeing French persecution and approved a town charter for them. Twenty-five houses were quickly built; several Dutch farmers joined the settlement. About fifty families resided there in 1664.

While the Dutch and a scattering of French Calvinists populated present-day Brooklyn, other pioneers migrated to western Long Island, too. Among them were dissatisfied Englishmen from Massachusetts and Connecticut who had been alienated by the puritan theocracy.

North and west of Brooklyn lay unoccupied territory in present-day Queens and Nassau counties. Early in the 1640s New Amsterdam officials began

Above: The Dutch Reformed congregation at New Utrecht, formed in 1677 with twenty-seven charter members, erected this church in 1700. Courtesy, The Long Island Historical Society

Left: Dutch houses on Long Island, such as this Flatbush residence, were usually built of wood with a low-pitched gambrel roof. Early Dutch rural farmhouses had no exact prototype in the Old World, but were developed to meet the colonies' different climate and material resources. Courtesy, George B. Brainerd Photograph Collection, Brooklyn Public Library

LADY DEBORAH MOODY

While no longer referred to by its seventeenth-century name, Gravesend's claim to fame for most people is that it contained within its boundaries Coney Island, the most popular seaside resort of the country at the beginning of the twentieth century. However, its history is also closely tied to that of a remarkable woman. Lady Deborah Moody, seventeenth-century civic and religious leader and the only woman patentee in the new colony, was a unique figure in the drama of early colonial history and can be considered Brooklyn's first city planner. Women's participation in the early economy and social life of the colony was crucial, serving as wives, mothers, homemakers, and often as farmhands working alongside their husbands, but few have managed to appear in the colonial records. During a time when women's traditional sphere was the small but important one of home and hearth, Lady Deborah Moody was among the handful of women who participated in a wider circle.

Born at Avedon in Wiltshire County, England, Deborah Dunch married Sir Henry Moody of Garesdon in Wiltshire circa 1605. Both her father and husband were members of Parliament and her own family had a long tradition of devotion to civil liberty. Lady Deborah was an outspoken critic of religious intolerance and early showed great independence of

Before settling in Gravesend, Lady Deborah Moody and her group stayed for protection outside the fort at New Amsterdam. The fort was growing from a crude outpost into a bustling commercial center. Photo by Charles H. Coles. Courtesy, American Museum of Natural History

mind combined with a strong determination. After her husband's death circa 1629 she decided to leave England rather than pay taxes for the support of the established church. Along with others seeking religious and political freedom, she sailed for Massachusetts in 1639 accompanied by her son Henry, and a number of families from her estate in England. First settling in Lynn, she subsequently purchased a large farm called Swampscott on the Essex County coast and settled

there in 1641. However, religious differences were again to determine the course of her life. Attracted to Anabaptism, she was admonished by the Church of Salem in 1643 for her unorthodox views, one of which was her refusal to accept the doctrine of infant baptism. Deciding to resettle in New Netherland with a group of friends and sympathizers who found in her a leader and spokesperson, she and her followers requested and were granted a patent from Governor Kieft to establish the first English settlement in Brooklyn. Gravesend, on the southwest corner of Long Island, became the first colonial enterprise to be headed by a woman.

Surrounded by the Dutch settlements at Flatlands, New Utrecht, Flatbush, and Bushwick, and under Dutch law and governorship, Gravesend was a small English island in a Dutch sea. Dutch was the common language at the time and continued to be long after the Netherlands surrendered their North American possessions to Great Britain in 1664. It is to Lady Moody's credit as an astute and effective leader that she was able to pilot the early settlement of Gravesend through the sometimes strained and uneven English/Dutch relations.

Gravesend did not just "grow" like most other early communities. It was designed according to a coherent plan from its inception as a settlement. Laid out as a sixteen-acre square, it was bisected by two main roads that formed four quadrants. Each of the four squares was divided into equal sections of ten plots, totaling forty, and one section was allotted to each of the initial forty patentees. In the center of each square was a large public yard providing common pasturage for cattle, and eventually space was allotted for a church, a schoolhouse, a town hall, and a burying ground. The village was surrounded by a palisade fence for defense against Indian attacks as well as wild animals. Gravesend Village was laid out using town planning principles that were surprisingly sophisticated for the time, and remnants of this plan are still visible today in the street layout. The farms, or "planter's

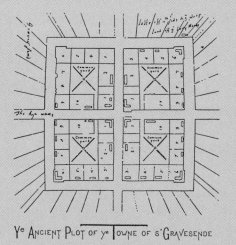

Yᵉ Ancient Plot of yᵉ Towne of s'Gravesende 1645

lots" as they were called, probably consisted of a few acres and were laid out surrounding the village. Lady Deborah Moody was allotted a "bowery" or farm.

Lady Moody took a prominent part in the administration of public affairs. Under her guidance and that of her son and other members of her group, town meetings were instituted and secure titles to the land were obtained from the Indians. The Town Court was established in 1646 and was held at Gravesend for more than forty years before moving to Flatbush. The village grew and prospered and Lady Moody's ability as a town leader won her the respect and friendship of the Dutch governors Kieft and Stuyvesant. In 1654 Governor Stuyvesant appealed to her influence to settle a dispute over his removal of two Gravesend magistrates and finally agreed to let Lady Deborah choose the mag-

Gravesend was laid out as a sixteen-acre village square consisting of forty house plots surrounded radially by forty farms. From Stiles, History of Kings County Including the City of Brooklyn, *Munsell, 1884*

istrates for that year, thus avoiding a potential political dispute.

Lady Deborah's interest in and tolerance of new religious ideas was also apparent in the new settlement. Gravesend was to become the site of the first recorded Quaker meeting in America. In 1657 an English vessel landed in New Netherlands containing eleven Quaker preachers, with two eventually coming to preach in Gravesend at her home. While there is no evidence that she became a Quaker herself, Lady Deborah may have been attracted to this new sect because of the place of equality given to women among its members. Although jeopardizing her good relations with the Dutch authorities, Lady Deborah fostered an environment of religious tolerance, open mindedness, and free discussion. Gravesend soon became a center of Quakerism on Long Island.

By the time of her death in 1659, the young colony at Gravesend was firmly established and would go on to prosper and contribute to the development of Brooklyn.

Carol A. Traynor

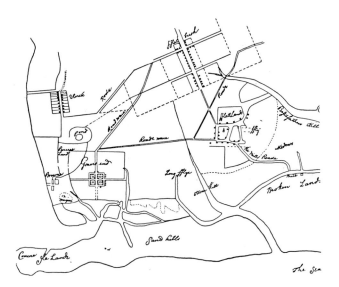

This 1666 map of Brooklyn locates the original five Dutch towns along with the English settlement of Gravesend. Under British rule in 1665, the towns were incorporated into the West Riding of Yorkshire, renamed Kings County in 1685. From Stiles, History of Kings County Including the City of Brooklyn, Munsell, 1884

populating this area with English immigrants as a barrier to further New England incursions. Among the first residents was Reverend Francis Doughty of Taunton, Massachusetts, who led a flock of dissidents to Maspeth/Newtown. During the Indian warfare which soon engulfed the colony, his settlement was destroyed and the villagers dispersed. Ten years later a second contingent from Greenwich, Stamford, and Fairfield, Connecticut arrived, naming their settlement Middleburgh (later Newtown). They elected town officers in the English manner and often conducted local business in the King's name. Never truly content with Dutch rule, inhabitants reacted to unrest in the 1660s by sending representatives to Connecticut's General Court.

Further east another group of non-conformist Englishmen founded Vlissingen (Flushing) under Dutch auspices in 1645. Earlier they had sought refuge from King Charles I by migrating to Holland, then to New England, and ultimately to New Amsterdam. They soon proved receptive to Quaker missionaries, and many converted. George Fox, the great Quaker leader, visited both Flushing and Gravesend in 1672.

Hempstead became still another substantial settlement on New Amsterdam's eastern frontier. The population traced its origins back to early New England, many having arrived in America with John Winthrop and Sir Richard Saltonstall in 1630. These settlers migrated from Watertown, Massachusetts to Wethersfield, Connecticut. By 1640 the church there had fragmented, and a splinter group moved to Stamford. Several restless souls crossed

Long Island Sound in 1643, purchasing thousands of acres from local Indians. After obtaining a Dutch patent, they returned the following year to erect homes. Nearly seventy freeholders resided in Hempstead by 1647 and a church was established in 1650.

Jamaica, after the Indian name Jameco, was the last (1656) English town established in Dutch territory. Originally called Rusdorp, it began as an offshoot of nearby Hempstead. Jamaica had its own minister by 1662 and a meetinghouse was constructed the following year.

By this time, Holland's Long Island empire extended from the East River to the western borders of Oyster Bay. It included a heterogeneous mix of Dutch farmers, English dissenters, and French and Walloon refugees. Relatively broad religious and ethnic toleration, a keen interest in material possessions, and a thriving commercial spirit characterized the region. Jumbled together in a colonial stew were the customs and traditions of rural Holland, bourgeois Amsterdam, the English countryside, and London.

While Dutchmen and their British guests occupied today's Kings and Queens counties, other colonists from New England arrived in eastern Long Island, about 100 miles away. Central to the settlement process was Sir William Alexander, the Scottish Earl of Sterling and a close friend of King Charles. Through his royal patron's influence, Sterling secured a 1636 Plymouth Company patent for all of Long Island and the adjacent territories. Such a patent naturally conflicted with Dutch claims in the region.

Active English colonization efforts commenced in 1637 when Sterling appointed James Farrett as his American agent. The industrious Mr. Farrett quickly began populating Lord Sterling's domain. Lion Gardiner of Connecticut received his famous property in 1639, and Farrett sold Shelter Island to Stephen Goodyear, a New Haven merchant, iron master, and government leader in the same year. Men from Lynn, Massachusetts then purchased lands near Matinecock (Oyster Bay), but the Dutch chased them away. Undaunted, the travel-weary immigrants next obtained property from Southampton's Shinnecock Indians in December 1640. Their first town meeting assembled in April of the following year. Several other Lynn families soon arrived, agreeing to hold power, distribute land, and admit inhabitants, with such rights remaining " . . . at all times in the hands of us . . . and our heirs forever." Boston minister Abraham Pierson and his previously-established church followers exercised considerable influence over the early community. Within twelve months about fifty adult males had moved in and secured Indian lands in exchange for annual payments of corn. English promises to protect the local tribes against Rhode Island's Narragansetts were also part of the bargain.

Settlement at Southold across Peconic Bay preceded even the Southampton migration. Many pioneer residents were natives of Hingham, England and reached Long Island with their leader, the Reverend John Youngs, by way of New Haven. The Connecticut town's officials aided further immigration efforts, helped negotiate the original 1640 purchase, and for some years exercised distant control over the fledgling colony. Such power did not always rest lightly, however. Captain John Youngs, son of the town minister, later appeared before a New Haven court for denouncing the mother colony

as a "tyrannical government." Charged with attempting rebellion, he soon apologized "for his rash and foolish words."

East Hampton, third of the East End villages, was settled in 1648 when a few Lynn residents purchased 30,000 acres for twenty coats, one hundred axes, and twenty-four hatchets, hoes, knives, and mirrors. Local Indians retained the right to hunt and fish. They also received the tails and fins of any whales cast upon the beach. Many original families hailed from Kent, England and they called the village Maidstone after their native hamlet.

As the North and South forks filled, English settlement rapidly shifted westward. In 1655 a group from around Boston settled in present-day Setauket, naming their tiny village Ashford. They obtained a territory of about thirty square miles, running from the Nissequogue River to Mount Misery. Their cost was the usual assortment of coats, hoes,

Above: The English ancestry of eastern Long Island's early settlers is clearly reflected in this house in Southold built by John Budd of Rye, England, in 1649. The four-room, timber-framed structure perpetuates the domestic designs of English yeomen's homes. Photo by James Van Alst. Courtesy, Society for the Preservation of Long Island Antiquities (SPLIA)

Left: New England's influence on eastern Long Island is discernible in the design and decorative detail of this chest made circa 1650-1700 in Suffolk County. (SPLIA)

LION GARDINER

Of all the dreamers and adventurers who settled colonial Long Island, few could match the energy, talents, and accomplishments of Lion Gardiner. Though trained as a soldier, he emerged as a statesman, helping establish the English presence on eastern Long Island while championing amicable relations with the native inhabitants. Along the way he also found time to create a town or two, purchase an island fiefdom, and author a book describing it all.

Gardiner was born in Scotland in 1599, but trained as a soldier and engineer with the Prince of Orange. Gardiner later recalled that both he and Captain John Underhill "had been bred soldiers from their youth." For a time more Dutch than English, he married Mary Willemsan of Waredon, Holland. Later Gardiner served under the English general Fairfax and came to the attention of Lords Say and Brook, who were attempting to establish a colony at the mouth of the Connecticut River. As a result, Gardiner journeyed to America in 1635 to build a fort to protect traders and colonists along the river. The fort was deemed necessary because the region coveted by the English was the traditional realm of the powerful and warlike Pequot tribe.

More a diplomat than a warlord, Gardiner counseled moderation and advised against fighting the Indians. He later wrote that his

Lion Gardiner, soldier, engineer, and statesman, founded the first English settlement in New York State when he acquired Gardiner's Island in 1639. Courtesy, East Hampton Star

duties included "only the drawing, ordering, and making of a city, town, or forts of defense." Fighting erupted nonetheless and Gardiner was soon caught up in it. He and his men endured a perilous winter seige by the aroused natives. Gardiner later recounted his harrowing experiences in his *Relation of the Pequot Warres.* The following spring, Captain John Mason from Hartford and Captain John Underhill from Massachusetts Bay destroyed the Pequots' power, ending the danger.

While at Saybrook fort, Gardiner had exercised his diplomatic talents by securing the release of two women held captive by the Indians. He also met an important Montauk chieftain named Wyandanch. Impressed with the young soldier who counseled peace, Wyandanch sold Gardiner a large island between the north and south forks of Long Island. The price, according to legend, was one large black dog, a gun, powder and shot, some rum, and a few blankets. The natives called the island Manchonake, land of the dead. Gardiner renamed it the Isle of Wight.

To secure his title, Gardiner also purchased the land from James Farrett, an agent of Lord Sterling who held a patent for the entire region from his patron, King Charles I. From Farrett, Gardiner secured permission to create a separate and independent plantation, with powers to control church and civil government. He moved to the island in 1639 with his family and several laborers from the Saybrook garrison.

Gardiner was an energetic and ambitious man, and not content with his island kingdom alone. He continued to amass property and within a few years became one of East Hampton's founding proprietors. By 1653 he had moved to East Hampton with his wife and daughter, leaving his son David

and additional laborers on the island.

Throughout his life Lion Gardiner exercised impressive talents as mediator and peacemaker. On one important occasion he secured the return of Wyandanch's daughter who had been seized by marauding Narragansetts. In gratitude the Montauk sachem granted Gardiner an immense tract of land in central Long Island which he later conveyed to Richard "Bull" Smythe, forming the basis of present-day Smithtown. So favorably was Gardiner regarded by the Indians that they referred to him in one deed as "the most honorable of the English nation here about us."

Gardiner died in 1663, esteemed by his neighbors. He had founded a family dynasty that was destined to play a crucial role in local affairs for generations to come. Gardiner had lived a full life, according to his own lights, and he once confessed that if his comments and actions were occasionally rough-hewn and blunt, it was because he simply could not abide the smoothing plane.

Geoffrey L. Rossano

hatchets, awls, needles, lead, and powder. Nearby Old Field was purchased between 1655 and 1659, and Stony Brook was first inhabited around 1660. Eight families relocated to Wading River ten years later. More southerly Islip, however, was not settled until two or three decades after that.

Neighboring Smithtown was, for most of the seventeenth century, the enormous private preserve of Richard "Bull" Smythe and his family. West of Smithtown and directly across the Sound from Norwalk and Stamford, Connecticut stood Huntington. Its land had been acquired over a decade or more. Governor Theophilus Eaton of New Haven purchased Eaton's Neck in 1646, and seven years later negotiators obtained title to the original town center. Lloyd's Neck (1654), Northport (1656), and Babylon (1657-1659) were soon added.

Oyster Bay, westernmost of the English towns, stood as a sort of no-man's land between Dutch and New England jurisdictions. A 1639 grant from Lord Sterling to Boston seaman Mathew Sunderland was later repudiated. In the late 1640s Robert Williams of Hempstead secured a large tract in present-day Hicksville. Though a formal boundary line between New Amsterdam and New England was established in 1650, a border dispute persisted until 1664. Actual settlement in Oyster Bay began in 1653 with the arrival of families from Hempstead and Sandwich, Massachusetts. Later purchases rounded out the township: Caumsett in 1654, Matinecock in 1658, Musketa (Glen) Cove in 1668, and Glen Head-Jericho in 1685.

The men who founded these English towns were often footloose dreamers and adventurers. A few, like Oyster Bay's Captain John Underhill, were soldiers of fortune, while others, such as East Hampton's Thomas Chatfield, sprang from the minor nobility or gentry. Most, however, were yeoman and artisans, seeking religious freedom, agricultural prosperity, and local autonomy in the face of Tudor/Stuart centralization at home. Having severed ties with families, friends, and communities, and crossed a stormy ocean, they found it very difficult to re-establish roots in the New World.

Typical of these wanderers was the Reverend William Leveredge. A 1625 graduate of Cambridge, he ministered in Dover, New Hampshire; Boston, Duxbury, and Sandwich, Massachusetts; and Oyster Bay, Huntington, and Newtown, Long Island. Joseph

Rogers of Huntington lived successively at Plymouth, Duxbury, Wethersfield and Southampton prior to establishing permanent residency. Thurston Raynor first passed through Watertown (1639), Wethersfield (1640), New Haven (1641), Stamford (1642), and Hempstead (1643) before finally settling in Southampton.

With the exception of Brooklyn's small, quiet communities of Dutch farmers, most early Long Islanders arrived from New England, bringing an intense religious preoccupation with them. A few hoped to find freedom of conscience and practice, while others sought to recreate the tiny puritan republics which defined Massachusetts and Connecticut society. Several communities, Hempstead, Southold, Southampton, and Flushing among them, began life as outposts for specific congregations. Protestant divines like John Youngs of Southold, Abraham Pierson of Southampton, Robert Fordham of Hempstead, Thomas Doughty of Newtown, and William Leveredge of Oyster Bay and Huntington were principal actors in this pioneer drama. For these inhabitants, God was a palpable presence, acknowledged in public worship and incorporated into the fabric of daily life.

Settlers were quite explicit about their intentions. Early on, Hempstead's freeholders noted,

For as much as contempt of God's word and the sabbath is the desolating sin of civil states ... it is therefore ordered and decreed ... that all persons inhabiting this town or the limits thereof should duly resort and repair to public meeting's on the Lord's day ... both on the forenoons and afternoons.

East Hampton villagers agreed in 1653 to "maintain and preserve the purity of the gospel ... and also the discipline of the church." Lofty sentiments often translated into action. Town meetings selected the minister and granted him lands, while local taxes paid his salary, built his home, and erected the meetinghouse. In some villages only church members participated in civil affairs. Attendance at religious services was compulsory and violations of the sabbath were punishable crimes. In 1682 Huntington's Robert Kellam received a twenty-shilling fine for carrying bags of meal on Sunday.

Given the colonists' dissenting background, the

The first Quaker meeting house on Long Island was built in Oyster Bay in 1672; others soon sprang up in Locust Valley, Flushing, and Manhasset. The Manhasset Society of Friends, as the Manhasset Quakers preferred to be called, was founded in 1702 by Thomas Story and William Mott, and this meeting house was erected in 1812. Courtesy, Clarence Purchase Photograph Collection, SPLIA

Church of England aroused deep suspicion and attracted few adherents. Setauket permitted Anglicans to settle but forbade them public worship. When the New York Assembly in 1693 enacted a tax to support Anglican ministers at Jamaica and Hempstead, Oyster Bay voters responded: "This town met together in order to consider a late act of Assembly for settling two ministers in this county, but nothing was done about it, but made return that it was a thing against their judgement ..."

The same villagers who felt God's presence so strongly, also believed that the devil lurked nearby. While no witchcraft hysteria wracked the Island, several incidents betrayed the colonists' fears. Accused of witchcraft in 1657, East Hampton's Goody Garlick was ordered to Hartford for trial. Ralph Hall and his wife were seized in Setauket to be examined by a New York court. Similarly, officials arrested Mary Wright of Oyster Bay and sent her to Boston. Though acquitted of devil worship, she was soon convicted of something equally heinous: Quakerism. For her heresy Wright was banished from the colony.

Holding fast to New England dogma, many Long Islanders opposed those who challenged the established religious order; Quakers seemed the worst offenders. Arriving from Britain in the late 1650s, their missionaries soon held meetings in Gravesend, Flushing, and Oyster Bay. By denying the validity

of puritan church government, infant baptism, oath taking, and public support of religion, the Quakers earned widespread enmity. Peter Stuyvesant, normally tolerant of English Calvinists, actively persecuted them, especially in Flushing and Newtown. Several fled to Oyster Bay.

Transplanted New Englanders further east proved equally hostile. Southold Quaker Humphrey Norton was arrested in 1658 and sent to New Haven to be convicted of blasphemy and heresy. His punishment included a fine, whipping, branding on the hand, and banishment. Hempstead forbade its inhabitants to offer Quakers shelter. When two local women absented themselves from public worship and instead attended a Quaker "conventicle," they were each fined twenty guilders.

Despite continuing harassment, the peaceful Quakers endured, especially in Oyster Bay township. Long Island's first meetinghouse was erected there in 1672 and several influential families converted, including the Wright, Townsend, and Underhill clans. By century's end substantial Quaker communities existed at Westbury, Jericho, Oyster Bay, and Bethpage. They went on to form a permanent, if not always appreciated, element of Long Island society.

Regardless of religion or patriotic allegiance, colonial Long Island was a region of small farms; virtually the entire population depended on the soil

RICHARD SMYTHE

As founder and patentee of Smith-town, Richard Smythe, or Smith as it is now spelled, played an important part in the history of Long Island. Much about Richard Smythe is legendary. Historians are unsure of his ancestry and especially uncertain how he managed to acquire one of the largest proprietary land grants in the New World. Legend has it that Smythe acquired the land that is today Smithtown after making a "deal" with the local Indians to sell to him as much land as he could ride around in one day.

Aside from legends, however, the first record of Smythe on Long Island is in Southampton, where he lived from 1643 to 1656. He was apparently a man of note in this early community; as one of the town's two assessors, he was on the committee to allocate town lands and was appointed constable in 1650. Yet, in 1656 he was suddenly and mysteriously banished from the community. The town records include a charge of "unreverend carriage to the magistrates contrary to the order," and it has been suggested that Smythe converted to Quakerism—an act which his Puritan neighbors apparently could not tolerate.

Smythe sought refuge in Setauket, where he stayed for nine years. He first appears in the town records of Brookhaven as a freeholder in 1661. How he eventually secured title to the lands that make up Smithtown is an interesting part of

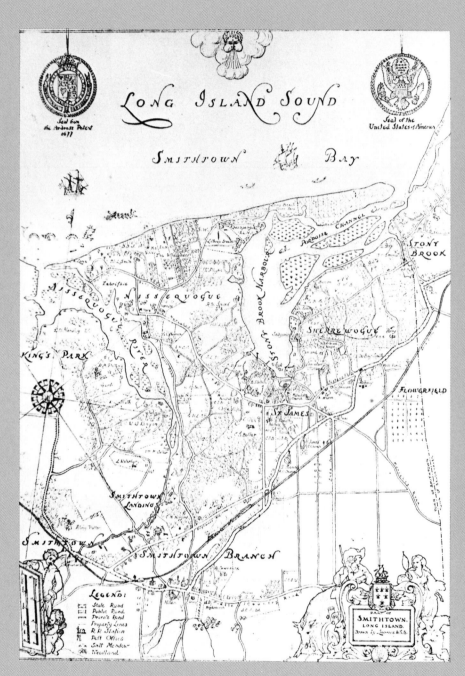

Richard Smythe acquired extensive lands in 1663, including that around Stony Brook Harbor and the surrounding shoreline, which he settled with his sons. The land was subsequently divided among his descendants, some of whose names still appear on this twentieth-century map of the area. (SPLIA)

the development of early Long Island communities. Smythe was a witness to the signing of the deed of gift dated 1659 by which Wyandanch, the sachem of the Montauks, made over to his friend, Lion Gardiner, his title to the land now comprising the town of Smithtown. In 1663, Lion Gardiner deeded the property to his friend, Richard Smythe. While this deed does not survive, a subsequent endorsement signed in 1664 by Gardiner's son, David, does survive. However, this was not the end of Smythe's negotiations for the Smithtown lands. He was eventually to wage twelve court battles to obtain clear title by securing deeds from Wyandanch's descendants, from the Nissequogue Indians who traditionally held and occupied the lands between the Nissequogue River and Stony Brook, and from the towns of Huntington and Brookhaven. In addition, he secured land grants from two English governors and a Dutch governor. In 1677 a final patent was issued by Governor Andros.

Finally securing a patent from the colonial government that stipulated that he had to establish ten families upon the land, Smythe settled with his family and built a house in a little cove in what is today the village of Nissequogue. It was a logical place for Smythe to settle because of its proximity to the river, adequate fresh water supply, and its amenities as the probable site of an Indian village. This would mean that paths led to the area, fields had already been cleared for farming, and the Smythes could more easily establish themselves. Smythe had six sons who would eventually build homes in this area and establish a community in the wilderness. This little settlement, far removed from the present-day Main Street, was the beginning of the town of Smithtown, or Smythefield, Smithfield, or Smith's Fields as it has been variously called. Some of these original houses are still standing and have become part of the Smythe legacy.

By the time of Smythe's death in 1692 he presided over a vast agricultural empire whose livelihood was farming and milling. Through determination, perseverance, and shrewd legal negotiations, Smythe had become the owner of an estate which proved to be one of the largest single estates acquired by an early settler of this country.

Brad Harris

Left: This circa 1675 room in the Jan Martense Schenk house in Flatlands was probably used as the kitchen and all-purpose work and living room. Schenck was a prosperous farmer and miller, and the furnishings reflect his affluence as well as his Dutch ancestry. Courtesy, The Brooklyn Museum

Opposite page: The last of the Dutch governors, Peter Stuyvesant encountered ever-growing opposition from his English constituents and considered Long Island the hotbed of his jurisdictional troubles. From Overton, Long Island's Story, *(1929), 1963*

for its livelihood. Access to land sparked most immigration, and this agricultural preoccupation characterized local society until the dawn of the twentieth century.

Many settlers believed they could not have selected a better spot. Chronicler Daniel Denton observed:

The island is most of it of very good soil, and very natural for all sorts of English grain . . . as also tobacco, hemp, flax, pumpkins, and melons . . . the island is plentifully stored with all sorts of cattell, horses, hogs, sheep, goats, and no place in the north of America better, which they can both raise and maintain by reason of large and spacious meadows.

Denton was especially impressed with the wild strawberry crop,

. . . of which last is in such abundance in June that the fields and woods are dyed red, which the country people perceiving, instantly arm themselves with bottles of wine, cream, and sugar . . . everyone takes a female on his horse behind him, and so rushing violently into the fields, never leave until they have disrobed them of their red colors.

Early farms were necessarily small and crude by modern standards, though Dutch "bouweries" re-

ceived universal admiration for their thrift, cleanliness, and bounty. Production was usually limited to the amount of land a man and ox team could cultivate, plus the level of surplus the farmer could market. Common agricultural products included wheat, corn, butter, cheese, apples, ham, bacon, lard, and beef.

Typical of the broad range of yeoman was East Hampton's Samuel Mulford whose small farm, valued at eighty-three pounds, supported two oxen, seventeen cows, two horses, three pigs, and fifteen sheep. A few men fared much better and acquired substantial estates. Peter Wyckoff's one hundred acres, five horses, two oxen, and twenty-eight cows were worth £304 and ranked him as the second wealthiest man in Flatlands. The much-tormented Quaker John Bowne of Flushing, who was the third richest individual in that village, owned sixty acres, nine horses, four oxen, eighteen cows, and fifty sheep, and was assessed £245. Others were less lucky, or less industrious, and achieved meager results. William Chatterton of Flushing cultivated only nine acres, owned just one cow and two yearlings, and his property was rated at only thirty-five pounds.

Though markets for surpluses were small and the state of technology rather primitive, local settlers refused to endure as hardscrabble rustics. Long Island farms, therefore, were never isolated from larg-

er economic society. Despite the importance of home consumption and self-sufficiency, the profit motive invariably obtained surprising heights. Agricultural fairs became important events in Dutch Brooklyn only a decade after settlement commenced. The eastern towns, too, conducted extensive trade with Boston, Newport, New York, Barbados, and the West Indies. Throughout the late seventeenth century villagers voiced extreme displeasure with the prices of imported goods, actively opposed efforts to control their commerce, and engaged in persistent smuggling—all evidence of their entrepreneurial orientation.

Though economically prosperous, Long Island could not maintain its precarious political balance in the face of larger world events, and tensions generated by the global Anglo-Dutch rivalry were quickly communicated to American shores. Several eastern towns requested aid from across the Sound. Anxious to annex English Long Island, Connecticut proved eager to help, and Southampton joined the mainland colony in 1644-1645. East Hampton followed in 1658, Brookhaven in 1661, Huntington in 1663. Perched on the frontier, Oyster Bay trod a more tortuous path. Settlers first voted in 1654 to unite with New Haven colony. Angry Dutch officials then insisted the land belonged to them and ordered the Englishmen out. Again, Oyster Bay appealed to New Haven. A visit by Peter Stuyvesant

persuaded town fathers to join the Dutch sphere, but nothing concrete developed; in 1660 a town meeting prohibited anyone from negotiating with either political bloc. Two years later Oyster Bay finally swore allegiance to Great Britain. When international tensions reached a critical stage in 1663-1664, East Hampton, Southampton, Southold, Brookhaven, Huntington, Hempstead, and New-town all sent deputies to Connecticut for support.

The colonial pot finally boiled over in 1664 after King Charles II turned the entire region over to his brother James, Duke of York. James quickly dispatched an armed force under Colonel Richard Nicolls, who landed troops at Gravesend in late August. Six days later he accepted Peter Stuyvesant's reluctant surrender and New Amsterdam became New York. All of Long Island was annexed to the fledgling colony, much to the chagrin of expansionist Connecticut and the East End towns.

Most residents viewed the shift to unified rule with relief, and they began to press for their version of local rights modeled after the familiar New England pattern: popular election of town and militia officers, no taxation without a representative assembly, free enjoyment of lands without annual quit rents or patent fees. Colonel Nicolls responded to popular ferment with the Duke's Laws, which he read to a gathering in Hempstead on March 1, 1665. Long Island would henceforth be known as Yorkshire and divided into East Riding (Suffolk), West Riding (Brooklyn and Queens), and North Riding (Queens and Nassau). Towns would be ruled by locally elected constables and overseers. Militia units would be drawn into a colony-wide organization, and the royal governor would appoint sheriffs and justices. Though the Duke's Laws incorporated many common New England and British colonial practices, they did not sanction a representative assembly. As a further irritant, new (meaning replacement) land and town patents were required.

Many resisted such demands, viewing the laws as infringements on their cherished autonomy. As late as 1669, Southold, Southampton, and Oyster Bay had not secured the necessary documents. Southold waited until 1676, Oyster Bay until 1677. Further expressing their displeasure, the three East End towns petitioned the king in 1672 for a return to Connecticut's jurisdiction. A few years later an exasperated Governor Edmund Andros dispatched the

CAPTAIN JOHN UNDERHILL

Boston's Puritan saints labelled him a rogue and an adulterer. To the Indians of New England and New York he was a warrior chieftain. Still others viewed him as a champion of religious freedom, a respected political leader, a town builder, or a chronic malcontent. Undoubtedly Captain John Underhill was, as an early chronicler claimed, the most "dramatic person" in the history of colonial Long Island.

Though his family originally hailed from Staffordshire, England, Underhill was born circa 1597 at Kenilworth Castle in Warwickshire, where his father served as a trusted retainer for Robert Dudley, the Earl of Leicester. When Dudley departed for the Netherlands in 1605, the Underhill family accompanied him, and young John grew up in war-torn Holland. He soon entered military service with the Prince of Orange

and later married a Dutch woman, Heylken deHooch (1608-1658). On a trip back to England in the late 1620s he met John Winthrop, a leader of the restive Puritan faction, and in 1630 departed for Massachusetts Bay as the fledgling colony's military commander.

A distinguished soldier and friend of the powerful Winthrop, Underhill quickly achieved great local prominence. He became a freeman, joined Boston's First Church, and served as a town selectman and a provincial deputy. As Massachusetts Bay's militia leader, he often acted as the strong arm of the Puritan theocracy, leading expeditions to supress Sir Christopher Gardiner, a local Catholic, and free-spirited Thomas Morton of Merrymount, famed for his Maypole frolicking.

Until 1636 Underhill's career proceeded in orderly fashion, but his settled life was soon disrupted,

and he rapidly earned both extravagant praise and heated censure. The praise came first. In August 1636 Underhill led an attack against Block Island's Indians, and during the fighting he was hit in the head with an arrow. His life was saved only by the helmet his wife insisted he wear. The following year Underhill and Captain John Mason of Hartford, Connecticut, commanded an expedition against the warlike Pequots. They stormed the largest Indian settlement, burning it to the ground.

Unfortunately, Underhill's military successes did not protect him from a storm that was brewing back in Boston. Mistress Anne Hutchinson and the Reverend Thomas Wheelwright were challenging the authority of the Puritan ministry, and Underhill had earlier offered his support. Now he was denounced by officials as "one of the most forward of the Boston enthusiasts," disfranchised, and stripped of his military rank. Humiliated, he was also tried for adultery, and soon quit Boston to visit England where he wrote a book describing his adventures.

The New World was in Underhill's blood, however, and he returned to Boston in 1638, where he was again tried for adultery and banished to New Hampshire to serve as "governor" of the Dover and Exeter settlements. Underhill's subsequent return to Boston generated still further turmoil as

In 1638 John Underhill published in London his Nevves From America, *which contained an account of his military exploits against New England Indians. It included this depiction of an Indian fort, or "palizado." Courtesy, The Underhill Society of America, Inc.*

This bronze commemorative plaque erected in 1908 depicts Captain John Underhill receiving peace entreaties from the Indians. During his eventful life Underhill both fought and befriended Indian groups on Long Island. Courtesy, The Underhill Society of America, Inc.

he was twice more charged with adultery. Severely chastened, he was forced to publicly confess his sins and bow to the magistrates' authority.

Underhill and Boston had now tired of each other and in the early 1640s he moved on to Stamford, Connecticut, in a successful effort to recoup his fortune and reputation. There he was selected a deputy to the New Haven assembly. When in 1643 warfare erupted between the Indians and the nearby Dutch, Underhill raised a troop of mercenaries and fought against the Canarsies on Long Island and the Wappingers and Wequasegeeks near Greenwich, Connecticut. The triumphant soldier was rewarded by the grateful Dutch with land on Manhattan, an island in Jamaica Bay, and a seat on the council of New Amsterdam. A few years later he was named Sheriff of Flushing.

But Captain Underhill's allegiance to his new masters only went so deep, and during the 1653 war between England and Holland he was jailed for opposition to Dutch rule. Upon release he journeyed to Newport, Rhode Island, and later to Southold, Setauket, and finally in 1661 to Oyster Bay. Despite his controversial past, Underhill retained popular and official respect, and was selected to attend the famous Hempstead assemblage of 1665. He also served as sheriff of North Riding and surveyor general of customs. In 1666 the former Indian fighter represented the Matinecock tribe in a dispute with Hempstead town. His clients rewarded him with a plot of land which he named Killingworth after his childhood home.

By now an elder statesman known for his Quaker sympathies rather than warlike disposition, Captain John Underhill lived out the remainder of his life on his new estate with his second wife, Elizabeth Feake. His last child was born just five months before Underhill's death in 1671 at the age of seventy-four.

Geoffrey L. Rossano

Responding to demands for self-government on Long Island, Governor Richard Nicolls called a meeting of town deputies in Hempstead on March 1, 1665. The meeting established the basic laws of the province, called the "Duke's Laws," which were based on the codes of older New England colonies. From Bailey, Early Long Island, *1962*

high sheriff to quash such notions.

On several occasions disgruntled colonists sought changes in the legal system, demanding creation of a representative assembly, designation of local free ports, and imposition of fixed prices on imported goods. Colonial governors denied every one of those requests. A special levy for the repair of Fort James in Manhattan and the 1671 decree ordering all trade through New York harbor added to the colonists' resentment. By 1681 some townsmen were

dissatisfied enough to gather at Huntington, where they petitioned redress. Colonial leaders were promptly arrested and thrown into jail.

Protest also assumed less political forms—smuggling being among the most popular. Oyster Bay traders ran afoul of both English and Dutch authorities in the 1660s. Governor Thomas Dongan angrily reported in 1687 that "What is produced of their industry is frequently carried to Boston, notwithstanding the many strict rules and laws made to confine them to this place." A decade later another governor singled out Setauket, Southold, Oyster Bay, and Musketa Cove for their illegal activities. The appointment of Oyster Bay's John Townsend as customs officer was quickly withdrawn, however, after neighbors and relatives threatened him with physical harm.

Political tensions had abated temporarily in 1683 when the Duke of York appointed Thomas Dongan governor. Soon after his arrival in New York, Dongan called a convention which then enacted a Charter of Liberties. This proclamation guaranteed freedom of worship and trial by jury, while also creating an elected assembly. Unfortunately for advocates of colonial self-determination, when Duke James became King James II in 1685, he disavowed the charter. Local disaffection intensified as Dongan demanded that the towns again apply for charters and patents. Many refused, characterizing the entire affair as a transparent scheme to extort money and crush local independence.

Rumors then began to circulate among the suspicious puritan population that Dongan and the King were plotting to impose Catholicism on the colony. Islanders also opposed James' plan to merge them into the recently-formed Dominion of New England under Governor Edmund Andros, who was already heartily detested for his earlier service in New York. Such an explosive situation lacked just one final spark, and it appeared in 1688. The Dutch Protestant monarch, William of Orange, invaded England and overthrew King James. After the news reached the colony in April 1689, a Committee of Safety coalesced in Manhattan to guard against a possible French invasion and prevent any Catholic treachery. Captain Jacob Leisler, a wealthy merchant, emerged as the revolutionary leader. With the assistance of Long Island militia, he captured Fort James and raised the banner of William and Mary.

Leisler's revolt and subsequent assumption of power plunged the entire colony into turmoil. Order was not fully restored until 1693, after Leisler's arrest and summary execution for treason. Despite the disorder, some progress occurred, including creation of the New York Assembly in 1691.

By century's end the economic, social, and political patterns that would dominate Long Island life for the next seventy-five years had been estab-lished. In addition, three rather distinct zones of settlement existed. Brooklyn's small Dutch communities stubbornly clung to their language, faith, and customs; local inhabitants resisted the use of a foreign tongue in official documents and few Englishmen opted to settle there. With the flow of European immigrants cut off by the British conquest, the Dutch towns grew slowly. Emerging labor shortages were usually filled by black slaves. Given its distinctive origins, established patterns of trade, and proximity to New York City, Dutch Brooklyn played little role in the affairs of eastern Long Island.

Stretching across present-day Queens and Nassau counties lay a string of villages generally characterized by religious toleration and ethnic diversity. Several were founded by New England dissenters and offered havens for outcast Quakers and Baptists. Limited Dutch migration into Flushing, Newtown, Jamaica, and Oyster Bay insured that no unified social structure or political view would dominate. Many towns also developed strong links with New York's cultural and economic institutions because they were so close to Manhattan. Both Jamaica and Hempstead became Anglican outposts and home to several royal favorites.

East End communities constituted another world entirely. One governor complained in 1703: "Indeed the people of the East End of Long Island are not very willing to be persuaded to believe that they belong to this province; they are full of New England principles." First populated by Massachusetts and Connecticut migrants searching for land and autonomy, they maintained strong ties of kinship, commerce, and religion with their ancestral communities and perpetually chafed under New York rule. They also attempted to enmesh themselves in virtue and piety, recreating the orthodox New England town, a closed community designed to protect their distinctive church government and unique social vision. That they did not ultimately succeed was not for want of trying.

In all cases the first migration of adventurers, dreamers, and builders had given way to succeeding generations of farmers who cultivated their parents' fields and inherited their gray-shingled homesteads. The meadows, walls, and paths which now defined the landscape gave tangible evidence of sixty years' unceasing struggle with the elements.

Colonial Life and Revolutionary Politics

Eighteenth-century Long Island was a world of small farming villages, large families, solemn religious observance, and oligarchic politics. Scattered sawmills, gristmills, and the elegant manor estates of the politically and socially-prominent gentry dotted the bucolic landscape. A few of the Island's coastal villages supported busy shipyards throughout the century, and trade with New York, New England, and the Caribbean grew steadily. To the casual visitor it must have seemed as if local residents enjoyed all the blessings their ancestors had journeyed so far to find.

But despite the seeming calm and stability, Long Island society was soon plunged into that great cauldron called the American Revolution. The ensuing upheaval divided towns and families, generated hardship and strife, and inspired much of the political and social change which ushered Long Island into the nineteenth century.

Family farms and small farming hamlets lay at the center of colonial Long Island life, much as they had since the first days of settlement. A rapidly expanding population continued clearing the remaining coastal acres and then pressed inland in search of new lands. While citizens might visit the town center for annual meetings, militia musters, occasional shopping, or religious services, most hours were spent on the homestead tending crops and livestock. This was a quiet world where patterns of temperature, tide, and rainfall far outweighed the impact of international political crises or the latest currents in fashion and literature. Even at the end of the century, a visitor could write of many Long Island residents: "Living by themselves, attentive to whatever is their own . . . their views, affections, and pursuits always exist on a small scale . . ."

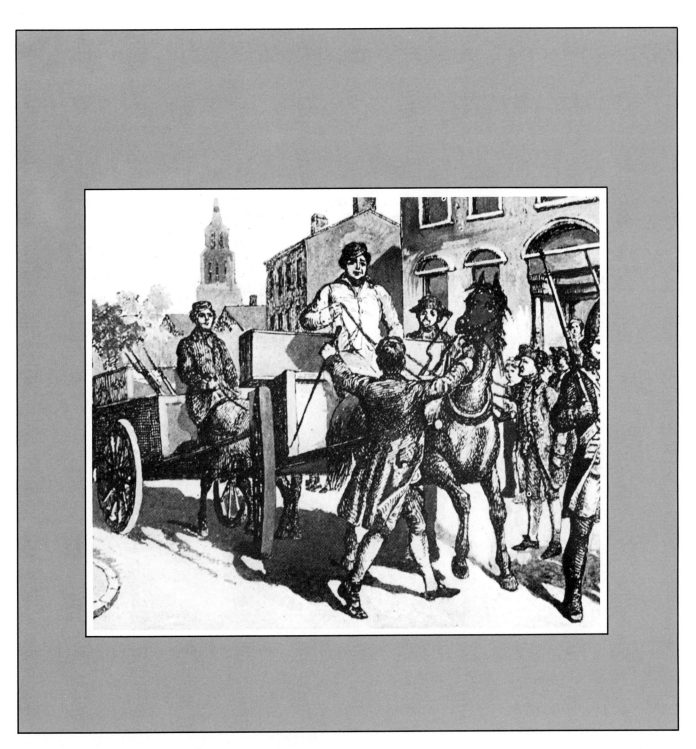

Colonel Marinus Willett of Jamaica, Long Island, halted a British troop shipment of arms. This act and Willett's other exploits during the Revolution earned him the esteem of his country, and he was *appointed sheriff and then mayor of New York City. From Hazelton,* The Boroughs of Brooklyn and Queens, Counties of Nassau and Suffolk, N.Y., 1609-1924, *Lewis, 1925*

In so circumscribed a world the institution of the farm family prevailed. It provided education, entertainment, and economic support, forming the web which held society together. The Englishmen who first settled Long Island retained many Old World family customs. Land in Europe was scarce and large families a burden. As a result, delayed marriages and relatively low birthrates were common. Long Island's early settlers perpetuated these habits. Men usually postponed marriage until their late twenties, and the number of children rarely exceeded six per family.

But as New World opportunities unfolded and the need for more hands to tame the wilderness became imperative, marriage and child-rearing practices shifted dramatically. Men and women began marrying much earlier and the number of their offspring increased markedly. In both Huntington and Oyster Bay the customary age of marriage for men dropped from about twenty-eight to only twenty-four in just two generations. Brides were younger, too, by nearly two years. Births rose to an average of nearly eight per family. With increased childbearing, however, came sharply increased female mortality, and by 1725 nearly four women in ten died before the age of forty. Anna Floyd of Setauket succumbed at thirty-eight, on the same day her daughter Nancy was born, while Smithtown's Susannah Gelson was thirty-two when she died, eighteen days after the birth of baby Hannah. Though not usually as high as some myths would indicate, child mortality also reached shocking levels, at least by modern standards. Isaac and Mary Hedges of

East Hampton lost five of eleven children, and their neighbors, Jonathan and Mehetable Stratton, buried five of seven. By contrast, David and Phebe Miller had eleven children and all survived to maturity.

Around mid-century demographic patterns began shifting once more. The increasing population and frequent subdivision of family lands meant rural overcrowding and reduced opportunities for future offspring. The age of marriage rose, while birth rates dropped nearly 35 percent. After a century of exuberant growth, local society began to replicate the more static Old World patterns.

Although individual farms and families often produced food, clothing, tools, and furniture, artisans occupied essential positions in the local economy. By mid-century a network of craftsmen supplied most villagers with simple manufactured goods. Huntington's 1778 population included numerous

Above: Mourning pictures done in embroidery, such as the one shown here, were made by young women to commemorate the departure of a loved one. Courtesy, The Museums at Stony Brook, Museums Collection

Left: Settled in 1640, Southold's village center grew slowly, as this nineteenth-century illustration reveals. The Presbyterian Church stands on the right, the Academy is in the center, and the brick schoolhouse is on the left. From Pelletreau, A History of Long Island, Lewis, 1903

The importance of mills to the new colony is attested to by the fact that millers were granted free land and guaranteed water rights. Grist mills for flour and animal feed, such as this one built on the Cold Spring Harbor in 1791, were numerous throughout Long Island until the introduction of steam-powered mills in the latter part of the nineteenth century. Courtesy, George B. Brainerd Photograph Collection, Brooklyn Public Library

weavers, cordwainers, coopers, carpenters, smiths, tailors, and papermakers. Blacksmith George Weeks of nearby Oyster Bay was able to open both a general store and tavern, having accrued savings by "shueing a mare," "sherpening sheres," and manufacturing fittings for the local shipyard.

Typical of many artisans were the Hedges of East Hampton, three generations of shoemakers. In 1683 patriarch Stephen Hedges owned the village's largest herd of cattle, and around 1700 the family opened a tanning yard. John Hedges, Stephen's grandson, started shoemaking in the 1720s, mostly in the winter when farm chores were less pressing. Around mid-century his son, Daniel, joined him. A separate shop was erected to house their growing business. Like other nascent merchant/artisans, the Hedges serviced both local and distant markets, including New York, Rhode Island, and Nantucket. Relatives often acted as sales agents, and a brother-in-law, Thomas Chatfield, once advised, "In the future make half pumps and half women's shoes . . . and make them long." Not until the rise of factory production a half century later would local craftsmen retire from the village scene.

Despite generally poor transportation and considerable local self-sufficiency, colonial society occasionally developed ties with nearby cities and the world beyond. Mariners, travellers, craftsmen, and itinerant preachers all played a part in the process. But the most important actors were the country merchants who exported raw materials and farm produce while importing the manufactured goods and tropical Caribbean crops so desired by households of the day.

Throughout the seventeenth century, North Shore settlers exported beef and grain across the Sound to Connecticut. East End villagers, on the other hand, traded with Newport, New Haven, Cape Cod, and Boston. As early as 1668, a group of Rhode Island and Oyster Bay investors erected a sawmill at Musketa Cove so that they could tap the New York City market. Among their Manhattan customers was merchant Jacob Leisler, later leader of the 1689 revolt against the Stuarts. With population and commerce expanding throughout the eighteenth century, country merchants developed extensive trading networks.

Not every Long Islander, however, was a sturdy yeoman, artisan/craftsman, or even merchant/entrepreneur. Scattered across the landscape in Hempstead, Lloyd's Neck, Massapequa, Islip, and Gardiner's Island, lay the manor estates of prominent and powerful families. Here, on private preserves, they built elegant mansions and managed large commercial farms worked by tenants and slaves. Adopting the lifestyle of the English gentry, these aristocrats imported fine clothes and furniture and corresponded with the empire's economic, social, and political leaders. Moreover, they often proved strong supporters of both the Anglican Church and the British throne.

Local magnates included wealthy merchants like

WILLIAM FLOYD

William Floyd, Long Islander, country gentleman, revolutionary, and public figure, typifies a prominent man at the center of local and national events during the hectic and formative years of the young republic. Floyd was an important member of his community, both economically and politically, a major-general in the militia, a representative to the first Continental Congress, a state senator, and the first, as well as the youngest, member of the New York delegation to sign the Declaration of Independence.

The progenitor of the Floyd family on Long Island was Richard Floyd (1620-1690), who came to New England from Wales in 1654. He settled in Setauket shortly after its founding in 1655 and purchased large holdings of land on Mastic Neck, directly across the Island on the south shore. Richard's grandson, Nicoll Floyd (1705-1753), the father of William, was a prosperous farmer on Mastic Neck. William Floyd was born there in 1734 and was only twenty years old at the time of his father's death, when he assumed the responsibility of running the large family farm. Like many of the pioneering South Shore estates it was a "long lots" property, running about six miles north-to-south and about one mile east-to-west. Only the portion closest to Moriches Bay was agriculturally useful. When William Floyd took over the

Above: William Floyd supported American independence and was forced to flee his home at Mastic during the Revolution. Courtesy, Independence Historical Park, Philadelphia

Below: William Floyd was one of three New Yorkers to sign the Declaration of Independence. From Pelletreau, A History of Long Island, Lewis, 1903

estate it was already a large-scale enterprise in commerical agriculture, operated by slave labor, and producing goods—primarily cattle, sheep, grain, flax, and wood—for export to New York City.

Through his aunts and uncles, Floyd had blood and marital connections to the provincial elite, a network that expanded as his seven siblings, whose charge he had inherited, married and moved out. His father had also left a substantial fortune in notes and obligations due on loans made to local residents of all classes. William Floyd's "estate," therefore, con-

sisted of not only the land at Mastic, but social and economic ties to a large segment of the regional population as well.

William Floyd used these ties and expanded them, emerging as a leader in the major social institutions of the area—church, town government, and county militia— in the years leading up to the Revolution. With his brothers-in-law, General Nathaniel Woodhull and Ezra L'Hommedieu, he led the patriot cause in Suffolk County and was sent to represent New York at the Continental Congresses in Philadelphia. After the British won the Battle of Long Island in August 1776, Floyd remained an exile from his home until 1783.

Except for one year, Floyd continued to serve in the Continental Congress and, beginning in 1777, in the new state senate as well, thereby retaining a handle on government at both the national and the local level at a time when it was uncertain which level would attain primacy. The similarity of economic and political interest between William Floyd, the Long Island planter, and his friends Thomas Jefferson and James Madison caused one foreign observer to identify Floyd as a member of the "Southern interest" in Congress. In fact, Floyd sealed the political ties with personal ones, betrothing one daughter to Madison (it was later broken off), marrying another to George Clinton's son, and marrying his son to the daughter of a Jefferson ally in New York City, David Gelston. In 1791, when Jefferson and Madison took the trip that helped create the Democratic-Republican Party, they stopped at William Floyd's estate and solidified their political ties on Long Island. Floyd's personal political career ended in 1795, when he lost the election for lieutenant governor of New York, but he remained a Jeffersonian for the rest of his life.

Floyd's activities went beyond politics and he took part in the general expansion of business enterprise after the Revolutionary War. Like many of the Founding Fathers and other wealthy Long Islanders, Floyd became actively involved in western land speculations. In 1803, he moved to Westernville, New York, on the Mohawk River, where he had amassed large landholdings. Relying more on rents than on personal farm management, Floyd and others like him expanded the sources and nature of their wealth while at the same time forwarding the expansion of the nation itself.

With William Floyd residing permanently on his upstate lands until his death in 1821, the management of the Mastic estate fell to his son, who began the process of shifting the family's interests away from dependence on the land and local lending and into the expanding commercial life of New York City. The Floyds represent a Long Island example of the flowering of major trends in America's future: the combination of wealth based on generations of agricultural pursuits with an entrepreneurial involvement in the growing mercantile and industrial developments during the eighteenth and early nineteenth centuries.

Steven Kesselman

This contemporary view of William Floyd's estate at Mastic shows later additions to the original house built circa 1724. The estate is now a museum operated by the National Park Service. Photo by Joseph Adams. (SPLIA)

Left: Rock Hall in Lawrence, the country seat of prosperous merchant Josiah Martin, is a formal and sophisticated example of eighteenth-century, high-style Georgian architecture. (SPLIA)

Below: Like its exterior, Rock Hall's interior reflects the lifestyle of aristocratic eighteenth-century Long Island. The elegant paneling, oil paintings, and musical instruments show a taste for fashion and cultural pursuits possible for the Island's small group of wealthy families. (SPLIA)

Hempstead's Colonel Josiah Martin (1699-1778) who built Rock Hall, a splendid Georgian home. Further west in Islip town resided the Nicoll and Floyd families. The Nicolls were descended from Mathias Nicoll, first secretary of the colony, mayor of New York in 1674, and a judge of the Supreme Court. His son, William, became Queens County clerk in 1683, acquired a ten-mile square domain in Suffolk County, and married an heiress to the great Rensselaerwyck manor. After a stormy political career, the younger Nicoll was elected speaker of the Assembly in 1702. William's grandson, also William (1702-1768), was similarly voted speaker in 1758.

Closely related to the Nicolls were the Floyds. An original Setauket proprietor, Welshman Richard Floyd also purchased extensive lands in Mastic. His son, Richard, married Margaret Nicoll, Mathias' daughter, while granddaughter Charity Floyd later wed Benjamin Nicoll, one of Mathias' grandchildren. Among the proprietor's notable descendants were Richard Floyd, Suffolk's most infamous tory, and William Floyd, a signer of the Declaration of Independence. Other influential Suffolk clans included the Sylvesters of Shelter Island and the Gardiners, East Hampton's wealthiest family, who ruled a semi-independent island fiefdom.

Also representative of many manor families were the Lloyds of Horse Neck (Huntington). Grizzell Sylvester of Shelter Island inherited the Neck from both her father and a fiance who died. In 1676 she married James Lloyd, a wealthy Boston merchant,

and a decade later he received a royal patent for his new estate, now titled the "Lordship and Manor of Queens Village." Annual quit rent was set at four bushels of wheat. James' son, Henry, also a merchant, was the first Lloyd to actually live on the Neck (1711) where he built an imposing mansion, a granary, schoolhouse, smithy, and barns. Henry later passed the estate to his four sons, Henry II, John, Joseph, and James. Their farms exported large quantities of meat, grain, fruit, and cordwood. Among the family slaves was Jupiter Hammon, who composed religious poetry, an example of which was published in 1760.

Henry Lloyd I (1685-1763), built a mansion in 1711 at Lloyd's Neck, Huntington. His son Joseph Lloyd (1716-1780), erected the handsome Manor House in 1766. Both are still standing. Courtesy, Mrs. Orme Wilson

ton, and 56 percent in Bushwyck. No seventeenth-century town seemed to allow the bottom half of taxpayers to possess more than a quarter of local wealth, and the lower classes usually claimed much less than that.

The passage of time only exacerbated the situation. Forty-seven percent of Huntington's wealth was controlled by the top fifth of ratepayers in 1673. Within a century the figure rose to 56 percent. Powerful clans consolidated their positions through a second and third generation. In Oyster Bay six families amassed 41 percent of all real estate. Four Southampton clans held 25 percent of that jurisdiction's property, and in neighboring East Hampton six families owned one-third of all land and livestock. Extended tenure in office, plural office holding, and dynastic inheritance of offices also characterized oligarchic politics. Between 1690 and 1765 six Huntington clans held nearly 80 percent of all top village posts. Men like Eliphelet Wickes or Epenetus Platt were often elected to five, six, or even seven separate offices, and then re-elected for twenty, thirty, or more terms. Until the American Revolution altered social and political habits, descendents of the original ruling elite dominated the town governments and economies founded by their fathers.

Commencing in 1775, the revolution against Great Britain proved a bitterly divisive struggle. Nowhere was the conflict more intense than on

AN

Evening THOUGHT.

SALVATION BY *CHRIST*,

WITH

PENETENTIAL CRIES:

Compofed by Jupiter Hammon, a Negro belonging to Mr Lloyd, of Queen's-Village, on Long-Ifland, the 25th of December, 1760.

Religious poet Jupiter Hammon was a slave of the Lloyd family and probably received some education in the schoolhouse established near the Manor House. His first poem, "An Evening Thought," appeared on December 25, 1760. (SPLIA)

Although villagers observed many democratic practices and strove to preserve local autonomy, they were not democrats in the modern sense. Rather, between 1690 and 1770 a clannish oligarchy dominated town affairs. Men of merit (generally the wealthy and socially prominent) led, and deference to this elite was an implicit duty for the remainder of society, which accepted the concept of a natural division between the rulers and ruled. Almost all males voted, but restricted their choices to "natural" leaders.

Land distribution patterns reinforced the process. Through luck, hard work, or previous financial status, a few families acquired more and more property, while others made do with smaller portions. Concentrations of wealth developed quite early. By 1683 the top 20 percent of taxpayers controlled 38 percent of all wealth in Flatbush and Brooklyn, 43 percent in East Hampton, 48 percent in Southamp-

Long Island. Families, congregations, and villages splintered as civil war reared its ugly head. Adding to the bitterness were the social, geographic, religious, and political divisions which had first appeared in the seventeenth century and persisted into the eighteenth. Suffolk's parochial villages had inherited the ancient Puritan suspicion of Anglican missionaries and central governments, and feared the establishment of an American bishopric. These East Enders constituted a rather homogeneous society of dissenters, united by their distrust of the outside world.

Far to the west and cut off from the empire's political and social currents, lay overwhelmingly Dutch Brooklyn. Residents remained strangers in an English domain; they proved loyal to their native tongue and employed ministers from their mother country. Long Island's Dutchmen sought no confrontation with their British masters and ignored the revolution as best they could.

Queens County residents followed a middle course. Originally part of New Amsterdam, their area attracted a significant Dutch minority, as well as many Baptists and pacifist Quakers. Close commercial, social, and political ties with New York, rather than New England, predominated. Jamaica and Hempstead were outposts of the established Anglican Church and home to many royal favorites. A rather polyglot society, Queens functioned by championing no one ideology to the exclusion of others.

Long Islanders reacted to the unfolding revolutionary drama in many ways. Oyster Bay patriots protested the Stamp Act in 1766, and the following year Queens voters petitioned their assemblymen to oppose British trade measures. In the aftermath of the Boston Tea Party, Huntington, East Hampton, and Smithtown agreed to cease trade with England.

Queens' residents, reflecting their mixed heritage and outlook, responded ambiguously. While some Jamaica voters protested British actions in Boston and promised to support the new Continental Congress, others argued against any disloyal actions, calling congresses "tyrranical and unlawful." Shortly thereafter, in December 1774, Newtown patriots created a revolutionary Committee of Correspondence, but the entire town soon disassociated itself from rebel measures. Similarly, Oyster Bay voted 205-42 against "having anything to do with deputies and congresses." In April 1775 Hempstead issued a ringing denunciation of all rebel activity, condemning those "threatening this once peaceful and happy land." Instead, villagers wished the union with England to persist "until time shall be no more."

Long Island, however, now was ensnared in events beyond its control. When news of Lexington and Concord reached New York City, patriots paraded through the streets, seized weapons, and occupied the customs house. Suffolk towns responded with nearly unanimous support for the rebel cause, but many citizens of Kings and Queens counties recoiled with outright horror. A loyal militia led by the Ludlow and Hewlett families drilled at Hempstead in expectation of trouble. Only after emissaries were informed that "they (loyalists) would blow out any man's brains who should attempt to take them" did patriot leaders abandon efforts to confiscate their weapons.

In neighboring North Hempstead the Sands and Onderdonk clans opposed the loyalist trend and formed rebel militia companies. Reaction from their southern compatriots proved hostile, and in late September they seceded from Hempstead town because "the behaviour of the majority was inimical to freedom."

As rebel and loyal factions contended for power, Queens freemen gathered at Jamaica in October 1775 and voted 778-221 *against* supporting the revolutionary Congress. New York's patriot leaders were furious, labelling such conduct "inimicable to the common cause of the United colonies and not to be suffered." The Continental Congress, which met in Philadelphia, responded more directly: in January 1776 the assembly ordered Colonel Nathaniel Heard and his New Jersey troops to occupy Queens County, disarm the loyalists, and arrest opposition leaders.

Heard's men advanced quickly through Jamaica, Hempstead, Jericho, and Oyster Bay, forcing 500 tories to sign a loyalty oath. Many others hid in the swamps, and all ridiculed the colonel in song:

Colonel Heard has come to town
In all his pride and glory.
And when he dies he'll go to hell
For robbing of the tory.

Loyalist opposition continued, however, and in

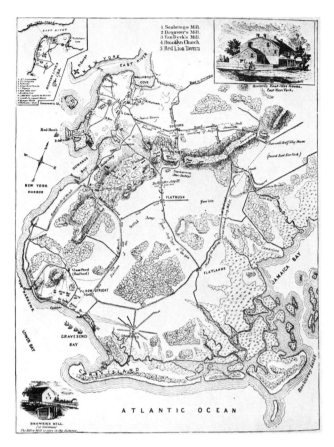

Left: In early March 1776, General George Washington ordered the fortification of Brooklyn against the British forces under General William Howe. The American forces in and about New York has been estimated at about 19,000. From Stiles, History of Kings County Including the City of Brooklyn, *Munsell, 1884*

Below: In this rendering of the Battle of Long Island on August 27, 1776, American forces retreat across Gowanus Creek in the face of a heavy British onslaught. The British landed with 32,000 troops and routed the Americans, who suffered over 1,000 casualties. From Grafton, The American Revolution: A Picture Sourcebook, *Dover, 1975*

March 1776 General Charles Lee, commander of the New York City garrison, dispatched Colonel Isaac Sears to Queens. A patriot zealot, Sears gleefully recalled, "I arrived at Newtown and tendered the oath to four of the greater tories which they swallowed as hard as if it were four pound shot." When George Washington assumed the New York command in April, he became so distressed at tory opposition that he threatened to depopulate Kings and Queens counties. The general quickly ordered Captain Benjamin Birdsall of Massapequa to seize boats suspected of trading with the British fleet.

By late spring a British invasion appeared imminent and Congress took additional steps to shore up local defenses. Militia units were mustered, but only a handful of men from Brooklyn and Queens appeared. Dutch farmers also refused to sell their cattle to the Continental Army or drive livestock away from the coast for safekeeping. Congress retaliated by ordering the animals seized and advising destruction of any grain or forage that could not be relocated.

New York City and its vast agricultural hinterland offered a rich prize to English strategists, but the key to Manhattan was Long Island; extensive American fortifications appeared on Brooklyn Heights during the summer of 1776. Enemy forces began gathering off New York in late June. By early August an armada of 400 ships and 31,000 troops was poised to strike.

The long awaited invasion commenced on August 22 when British and German soldiers came ashore near Gravesend. Though their movements were clearly visible from American lines, little was done to stop them. A Continental officer lamented: "As there were so many landing places, and the people of the Island so treacherous, we never expected to prevent the landing." Unimpeded, enemy troops quickly occupied Flatbush, Flatlands, and New Utrecht.

Britain's hammer blow fell on August 27, 1776, when General William Howe's legions outflanked George Washington's regulars and militia levies, driving them back into their last fortifications on Brooklyn Heights. Under cover of rain and fog, the beleaguered Americans barely escaped across the East River to Manhattan, leaving the rest of Long Island defenseless.

The English General William Erskine, leading nearly 5,000 soldiers, turned eastward on August 29. He called on Suffolk rebels to return to their homes, promising to destroy the property of the disobedient. Two days later General Oliver DeLancey again urged Suffolk to surrender and accept the King's peace. Commissary agents then were directed to seize "all the grain, forage, and creatures you can find" of those remaining in rebellion. Both Smithtown and Huntington capitulated on the fifth of September. For some patriot leaders like John Sands of Cow Neck and John Kirk of Norwich, the British conquest meant arrest and imprisonment. Hundreds of others fled across the Sound to exile in Connecticut. In a mass October display, 1,293 Queens residents took a new loyalty oath to King George III.

By December 1776 royal authorities believed the region calm enough to muster a loyal militia. Governor William Tryon reviewed 820 men at Jamaica and 800 more in Smithtown. Britain's victory appeared complete and the governor informed his superiors, "There is not the least apprehension of any further commotions." But Tryon could not have been more mistaken, and for the next seven years, Long Island was to endure continual strife, conflict, and bloodshed.

With New York now headquarters of Britain's North American war effort, large forces camped in and around the city. General Oliver DeLancey's loyalist brigades were stationed at Lloyd's Neck, Herricks, Hempstead, Flatbush, Jamaica, and Brookhaven. The Queen's Rangers unit of Connecticut tories led by Lieutenant Colonel John Graves Simcoe encamped at Oyster Bay, while Hessian troops bivouacked at Wolver Hollow.

This vast military post required huge quantities of food, forage, and wood, and much of this burden fell on Long Island. In the summer of 1777 General William Howe ordered villagers to provide hay, straw, corn, and oats. Little forage appeared, and in September Howe repeated his orders, adding the threat of confiscation and imprisonment. Colonel Simcoe noted in his diary "I did not give receipts to a great number of people on account of their rebellious principles or absolute disobedience of the general order."

Military occupation spawned continuous outrages against the civilian population, especially in rebel towns. Presbyterian churches were often converted into granaries, stables, or barracks, or simply torn down to provide firewood and building materials. British troops constructed a fort in the middle of Huntington's cemetery, using tombstones for firebacks and bake ovens.

Conflict between civilians escalated, too. In 1779

Opposite page: George Washington directs the retreat from Brooklyn Heights to New York. The successful, massive retreat under desperate conditions is considered one of the most remarkable achievements in the history of warfare. From Grafton, The American Revolution: A Picture Sourcebook, *Dover, 1975*

Left: The British victory at Long Island was announced in London on October 10, 1776, and this cartoon appeared shortly thereafter. It portrays a pleased King George III and other noblemen on the right, scowling commoners who opposed the war on the left, and a tawdry woman with liberty cap and staff weeping in the center. Courtesy, Library of Congress

Below: After the British occupied Long Island, citizens were forced to sign loyalty oaths. From Pelletreau, A History of Long Island, *Lewis, 1903*

I Do hereby certify, that *Elihu Rayner* Aged 26 of Southampton Townſhip, has voluntarily ſwore before me, to bear Faith and true Allegiance to his Majeſty King George the Third; and that he will not, directly or indirectly, openly or ſecretly, aid, abet, counſel, ſhelter or conceal, any of his Majeſty's Enemies, and thoſe of his Government, or moleſt or betray the Friends of Government; but that he will behave himſelf peaceably and quietly, as a faithful Subject of his Majeſty and his Government. Given under my Hand on Long-Iſland this 22 *Sept,* —————— 1778. *Wm Tryon Govr*

fearful tories cautioned travellers about a rebel lair at Bread and Cheese Hollow (Smithtown) where "unfortunate loyalists are greatly exposed to the cruelty of these assassins." On another occasion exiled Major Jesse Brush sent word to a tory farmer occupying his Huntington property. "I have repeatedly ordered you to leave my farm," he wrote. "This is my last invitation. If you do not your next landfall will be in a warmer climate than you have ever lived in yet."

Kidnappings also became popular. General DeLancey warned loyal townsmen to look out for those taking "a leading part in committing scandalous robberies and secretly in the night carrying off peaceable and inoffensive citizens." A spectacular example occurred in May 1779, when the ardent royalist, Judge David Jones of Massapequa, was abducted and spirited across Long Island Sound. He was not exchanged for an American officer until 1780.

With rebel Connecticut so close, cross-water warfare erupted frequently. Privateers, smugglers, and pirates also roamed the Sound, attacking provision ships bound for New York City. Lightning-quick whaleboat raids were common, too. In 1777, 170 men in thirteen boats crossed the Sound to Greenport, portaged to Peconic Bay, and in a fierce assault on Sag Harbor, killed six British soldiers, captured ninety, and burned ten ships. Connecticut-based whaleboatmen also captured Fort St. George, an English outpost overlooking Bellport Bay, and Fort Slongo (Salonga), located between Huntington and Smithtown.

Sometimes the war effort took a more secretive turn. General Washington's acute need to discover British troop movements fostered the creation of an extensive Long Island spy ring. Among its prominent members were exiled Colonel Benjamin Talmage of Brookhaven, Abraham Woodhull of Setauket, and

SAMUEL TOWNSEND

For most of the eighteenth century, country merchants dominated Long Island's economy. Acting as traders, bankers, shipbuilders, and storekeepers, they linked isolated rural farmers with the rising urban centers of London, New York, and Boston. Prominent among local merchants was the Townsend family of Oyster Bay, led by patriarch Samuel Townsend, a fifth-generation Long Islander. Born in Jericho in 1717, he moved to coastal Oyster Bay in 1738 and married shortly thereafter. In partnership with his younger brother Jacob, he built his first trading sloop, aptly named *Prosperity,* in 1747 at a cost of £1,100. From this initial successful investment, Townsend created a small mercantile empire, with ships and cargoes venturing to the Caribbean, Central America, Portugal, and England. With a growing fleet he marketed Long Island's beef, pork, grain, and lumber, and imported molasses, sugar, and rum, which he then exchanged in London or New York City for imported goods to satisfy local customers. His account books bulged with orders for cloth, buttons, nails, coffin boards, paper, rum, and even slaves.

The impact of Townsend's mercantile activities on Oyster Bay was dramatic. Construction and repair of ships and the exchange of varied cargoes employed carpenters, shipwrights, smiths, and

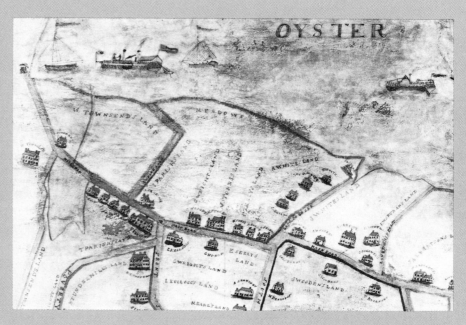

Because of its deep, excellent harbor, Oyster Bay was involved in many aspects of the burgeoning eighteenth-century maritime industry. This 1834 map depicts the wharves, warehouses, and residences surrounding the harbor, including the Townsend family property on the left. Courtesy, Raynham Hall Museum

teamsters. Townspeople not directly employed by Townsend undoubtedly knew him as shopkeeper and retailer, for by the late 1750s he maintained over 275 credit accounts, the majority of the village population.

Much of Townsend's commercial success depended on a talented network of family, in-laws, and business agents. Their discretion in buying, selling, navigating, and negotiating was crucial. Of Townsend's five sons, one labored as a ship's captain and two more acted as business agents. Neighbors like the Lloyd family of Huntington provided valuable banking services and one Lloyd son served as a Townsend commission agent in Jamaica.

The momentous year 1775 found Samuel Townsend a wealthy and respected merchant. He owned extensive real estate, held nine slaves, and served as town clerk. For more than a quarter century his ships had supplied Long Islanders with tropical produce and European imports. Unfortunately his carefully wrought commercial empire could not withstand the damage inflicted by the American Revolution. An important town figure and an active patriot, Townsend was drawn to the center of the military and political storm. His family was separated and his home in Oyster Bay occupied by Loyalist troops. One son became a patriot spy while another sailed under the English flag. British regulations sharply restricted commerce, local business dwindled, and the triangular trade between the colonies, England, and the Caribbean—so integral to Townsend's success—collapsed.

With the triumph of the revolutionary cause in 1783, Townsend regained public respect and political influence. He was elected to the state senate and named a member of the Governor's Council. But his business interests were not so easily revived, and Townsend's advancing age meant that the task of resurrecting the family empire fell to his son Robert. The task proved a daunting one, for Robert Townsend confronted all the debilitating conditions that plagued post-Revolutionary America. Many wealthy merchants and former business associates had fled the country. Trade with Britain's Caribbean colonies was forbidden. No unified American currency existed, severely hampering the task of collecting prewar debts.

Ultimately Samuel Townsend's mercantile business could not be revived. Oyster Bay's small harbor and limited facilities could not hope to compete with the large ports and mercantile elites of Boston, New York, and Philadelphia. Instead, his sons, like so many ambitious young men of their generation, moved to New York to strike out on their own. When Townsend died in 1790, his commercial empire was only a memory, and the age of the independent country merchant died with him.

Geoffrey L. Rossano

Samuel Townsend's 1761 account book records some of his business activities. Courtesy, Raynham Hall Museum

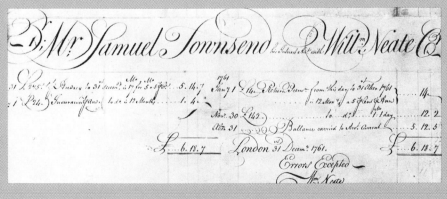

Robert Townsend of Oyster Bay. When enemy troops marched eastward in 1779, agents advised: "Redoubts have been built at Southampton, East Hampton, and are being constructed at Canoe Place." In July 1779 Robert Townsend reported: "The British fleet is arrived and off New York with 7,000 troops . . . the 54th Regiment, the Queen's Rangers, and Lord Rawdon's Corps may also be preparing to embark on ships for Carolina."

But the war could not last forever. After repeated delays, diplomats signed a peace treaty in April 1783; Britain began evacuating Long Island shortly thereafter. Local patriots immediately turned on their loyalist tormenters, and a New York newspaper warned "that the calm the enemies of Columbia have heretofore enjoyed will ere long be succeeded by a bitter and neck-breaking hurricane."

These were not idle threats. In 1779 the state legislature had passed acts of attainder against leading tories, and after the war at least fifty-two loyalist estates were seized in Queens County, as were the Suffolk lands of Richard Floyd, George Muirson, and Parker Wickham. Town officials serving the occupation government also felt their neighbors' wrath. Hempstead and Oyster Bay, for example, turned out all their royalist rulers. Other friends of the King were dragged into court. Oyster Bay's John Luister accused Squire Van Wyck of helping the British seize his horse and wagon. Van Wyck

Above: General William Howe achieved a brilliant victory in the Battle of Long Island, but has been criticized for missing the opportunity to bottle up Washington's troops on Manhattan. From Cirker, Dictionary of American Portraits, *Dover, 1967*

was convicted, fined, and later left the town.

In 1784 the legislature took further revenge when it disfranchised loyalists, cancelled patriot debts to them, and disbarred tory lawyers. Representatives also laid a tax of $100,000 on Long Island "as compensation to the other parts of the state for not having been in a condition to take an active part in the war against the enemy."

Not surprisingly, many loyalists found the local environment extremely uncomfortable, and approximately 6,000 departed for new settlements in Atlantic Canada. Colonel Gabriel Ludlow of Hempstead and DeLancey's Brigade emigrated to New Brunswick in 1783. DeLancey successively became mayor of St. John, judge of the Vice Admiralty Court, a member of the Council, and finally, colonial governor. Others, like Hempstead's Anglican rector Leonard Cutting, quietly moved to Maryland. As American as their neighbors, these unfortunate citizens had chosen the wrong side. One man's liberty was another's mob rule, and for many the blessings of liberty proved very hard to bear.

The Revolution and its aftermath also affected numerous social institutions which had previously defined Long Island life. Local citizens took the ideology of the war to heart and quietly transformed long-established political habits. Most notably, Hempstead and Huntington witnessed an increasingly rapid turnover of elected officials and the practice of plural office holding came to an end. The post-Revolutionary generation feared the concentration of power as corrupting and moved to check the now perceived excesses of oligarchy and privilege. Furthermore, the emerging republican ethos placed less emphasis on family history or economic status. A struggle to defy privilege and overthrow a foreign authority could not help but raise similar questions about political institutions at home.

Religion, a cornerstone of colonial society, was

Sarah Townsend gathered information on British troop movements from her home in Oyster Bay. She passed the information to her brother, Robert Townsend, one of Washington's spies on Long Island. From Pennypacker, General Washington's Spies, *LIHS, 1939. Courtesy, Raynham Hall Museum*

similarly affected by the Revolution. In some places the Anglican Church, tainted with toryism, went into sharp decline as state support vanished and loyalist stalwarts emigrated. Even more important was the war's liberating effect on previous patterns of behavior and belief. The prevalence of one or two denominations was broken, and pluralism became the order of the day. Appealing to the humblest of citizens, Methodists and Baptists attracted the greatest number of converts.

Methodist missionaries were the most active. Circuit riders made fervent exhortations to the common man, who responded with animated hymn singing and extravagant rejoicing. Missionary Phillip Cox described a 1784 meeting held in Searingtown. "Very many attended," he exulted, "until the alarm was sounded that the false prophets

Opposite page: Patchogue was one of the most flourishing villages in Brookhaven during the eighteenth and nineteenth centuries. It served as an overnight stopping place for the stages, which ran from East Hampton to Brooklyn carrying passengers and mail. *From Pelletreau,* A History of Long Island, *Lewis, 1903*

This tombstone erected in memory of Anthony Hannibal Clapp, an indentured servant who died in Setauket in 1816, bears silent testimony to his character and value to his master, as well as to the pleasure he gave to others with his fiddle playing. Courtesy, The Museums at Stony Brook, bequest of Ward Melville, 1977

Rachel Seaman Hicks became a dedicated minister in the Society of Friends. Born in Westbury, she traveled and preached as far west as Ohio and Indiana. From Memoir of Rachel Hicks, *G.P. Putnam's Sons, 1880. Courtesy, Haviland Records Room, Religious Society of Friends*

foretold in scripture had come. The word of truth, however, did not fall to the ground. Souls were awakened." Inspired by the message, Methodist converts gathered at Roslyn and Glen Cove in 1785, Rockville Center in 1790, Patchogue and Brookhaven in 1791. By the mid-nineteenth century, they were Long Island's largest denomination. Having led men to question the old verities, the war also caused them to examine their spiritual lives, which they did with great vigor, casting aside past orthodoxies and embracing new faiths.

The liberating sentiments unleashed in the war years affected local black inhabitants, too, culminating in the Manumission Act of 1799 which set several thousand slaves on the road to eventual freedom. This liberation was a long time coming, for slavery possessed an extensive history on Long Island. Dutch colonists first imported bondsmen around 1626 and shortly thereafter the West India Company promised to "use their endeavors to supply . . . as many blacks as they conveniently can."

Throughout the Dutch period, Brooklyn boweries provided a small but steady market for scores of slaves.

England's conquest in 1664 did not materially alter the institution. Setauket town records mention slave sales in the 1670s, and by century's end slaves resided throughout Long Island. More than one-third of Brooklyn and Bushwyck households contained servants, while half the farms in Flushing, Flatbush, and Flatlands utilized slave labor. Black bondsmen comprised 10 percent of Southampton's population.

Slavery expanded steadily throughout the eighteenth century. There were 1,100 Long Island bondsmen in 1698; 3,400 in 1749; and nearly 5,000 by 1775, when demand and sale prices peaked. During the revolutionary turmoil local whigs worried lest loyalist neighbors induce their servants to flee. When patriot refugees departed for Connecticut in 1776, many took their chattels with them.

Political and social pressures generated by the war dramatically altered local attitudes, and soon conscience-stricken Quakers and New York philanthropists initiated an anti-slavery movement. A society advocating manumission was established in 1785; voluntary emancipations began soon thereafter.

The 1790 census reveals large numbers of freed blacks in several East End towns, and the release of servants accelerated in central Long Island after 1793. Brooklyn, with the highest concentration of slaves (65 percent of all households, compared with 35 percent in Queens, and 15 to 20 percent in Suffolk), recorded its first manumission in 1797, as Quaker John Doughty freed his bondsman, Caesar Foster. But anti-slave agitation really triumphed in 1799, when the state legislature finally passed a gradual emancipation act. By 1827 virtually all slaves had been freed, ending two centuries of bondage.

With the election of presidents Washington, Adams, and Jefferson, Long Island turned away from its colonial and revolutionary path and assumed a place in the new nation. A distance more profound than time separated local society from its recent past. Established allegiances and institutions had been altered, the old orthodoxies challenged. Long Island had taken its first uncertain steps into the modern world.

City and Country Solidified

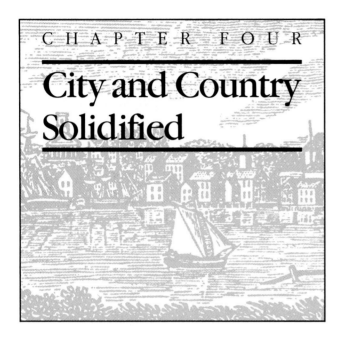

As he travelled through post-Revolutionary Suffolk County in the early years of the new century, Yale President Timothy Dwight described the insularity which pervaded rural Long Island society. "Almost all their concerns," he noted, "are absolutely confined to a house or a neighborhood, and their neighborhood rarely extends beyond the confines of a small hamlet." But as he journeyed westward towards New York City, he watched the quality of life change. Religious observance appeared less strict, agriculture was more commercially oriented, transportation facilities improved, and city manners grew more pronounced. Something exciting was in the air.

A generation earlier the struggle with Great Britain had precipitated a political revolution. Now Long Island stood poised on the brink of a social and economic revolution, as well. Between 1790 and 1850 the population of Queens and Suffolk counties leaped from 32,000 to over 70,000. Farming grew increasingly commercial and city-oriented. Industry, banks, and insurance companies sprouted up, as did dozens of country newspapers. Fleets of whaling ships scoured the seas. Visitors and summer residents swelled from a trickle to a flood. Everywhere rural society felt the approaching hand of its urban neighbor.

It was no wonder. Nearby Brooklyn and New York were mushrooming into a great metropolis, generating demands for agricultural produce, financing industrial development, stoking intellectual ferment, setting the tone in fashion and literature. New York City affected and changed everything it touched. Dramatic transportation improvements facilitated the process. In only thirty years Long Island's oxcarts, sandy paths, and sailing sloops

Just twelve miles from New York City, Jamaica was a thriving and populous Long Island town with a population of over 4,000 in 1850. Its growth was greatly facilitated by the railroad line from Brooklyn, opened in 1836. From Pelletreau, A History of Long Island, *Lewis, 1903*

RUFUS KING

Names such as Gardiner, Floyd, and Lloyd are sooner associated with Long Island history, but perhaps no family was more accomplished than the Kings of Jamaica. They were dominant figures in New York political life for a century, holding such offices as governor and senator.

Rufus King (1755-1827) had represented his native Massachusetts at the Constitutional Convention and had already earned a reputation as a gifted orator before his marriage to Mary Alsop, daughter of a prominent Manhattan merchant, led to his relocation to New York in the late 1780s. King quickly reestablished his political career, first being elected to the New York State Assembly and then in 1789 to the U.S. Senate, where he was to serve a total of four terms spanning three and a half decades. An effective public speaker and an ardent abolitionist, he opposed the extension of slavery to the Northwest Territory and resisted the admission of Missouri as a slave state. A leading Federalist, King was his party's candidate for Vice President in 1804 and again in 1808. In 1816 he ran for the Presidency, losing to James Monroe.

The statesman from Jamaica is probably best remembered, however, as the new republic's ambassador to Great Britain. In a letter to President Washington at the time of his appointment, Alexander Hamilton praised King as a "re-

Rufus King was a prominent American statesman during the nation's early years, and his sons and grandson would continue to play important roles in New York State politics throughout the nineteenth century. From Pelletreau, A History of Long Island, Lewis, 1903

markably well-informed man, a judicious one, a man of address, of fortune and economy." King assumed the post in 1796, succeeding Thomas Pinckney, and quickly became a popular figure in London's social and political circles. With quiet diplomacy, King worked to end impressment of American seamen and to quiet crises while supplying Washington with model correspondence on Great Britain's foreign policy. On learning that the American ambassador (while on a trip to the continent) had passed up an opportunity to be presented to Napoleon Bonaparte to avoid angering the British government, George III is said to have remarked, "Mr. King, you have treated me like a gentleman, which is more than I can say for all of my subjects."

King returned to America in 1803 only to see Anglo-American relations deteriorate. He opposed U.S. entry into the War of 1812, although he supported the government after hostilities had commenced. Perhaps his most famous Senate speech occurred after the burning of Washington, D.C., by the British, when he rose to oppose moving the capitol inland and asked that the outrage be avenged. John Quincy Adams sent King back to London as ambassador in 1825, but illness soon forced him to return, bringing to an end his long career in public service.

On his return from England in 1803, King purchased a farm in Jamaica, which he transformed into his country seat, enlarging the large gambrel-roof house now known as King Manor. City-bound LIRR riders catch a glimpse of this estate every day, just before they pull into the Jamaica station. On his Queens farm, King pursued his deep interest in agriculture and husbandry, developing a model farm that boasted an imported herd of Devon cattle.

Left behind in England in 1803 to complete their education at Harrow, King's eldest sons, John Alsop (1788-1867) and Charles

(1789-1867), returned to New York to lead distinguished careers. Charles served in the state legislature and as editor of the *New York American* before becoming president of Columbia College (1849-1864). John Alsop King, who had been a classmate of Lord Byron at Harrow, followed his father into politics, first serving in the state assembly and senate. He accompanied his father to England in 1825 as secretary to the legation and remained as Charge D'Affairs, when illness forced his father's return. In 1849 the people of Queens elected him to Congress and subsequently he became governor of New York in 1856. For many years Governor King, who shared his father's interest in farming, also served as president of the state agricultural society, and from 1827 until his death in 1867 resided at King Manor.

For a century the Kings of Jamaica represented agrarian Queens in Albany and Washington, D.C. They were among the best educated and most able public servants of their age. John A. King, Jr. (1817-1900), the third generation and the fourth member of his family to serve in the state legislature, bought the land on the tip of one of the North Shore's peninsulas in 1854, which is still known as King's Point.

Robert B. MacKay

were pushed aside by turnpikes, steamboats, and railroads that tied city and country together, broadening the lives and expanding the opportunities of all who used them.

Demands for improved roads dated back to the colonial era, when in 1704 the Assembly authorized a route from Brooklyn Ferry to East Hampton named Kings Highway. Later in the century bimonthly post riders carried the mail eastward, but a stage journey from Brooklyn to Southampton lasted four days, including overnight stops at Hempstead, Smithtown, and St. George's Manor. Such time consuming arrangements proved unsatisfactory, and privately funded turnpikes appeared soon after the Revolution. The first ran from Brooklyn to Jamaica, later extending to Jericho and Smithtown. Other routes fanned out to Williamsburg, Oyster Bay, and Babylon. Wooden plank roads built in heavily trafficked portions of Brooklyn and Queens supplemented the turnpike system. By 1845 a network of roads and stage routes crisscrossed western Long Island, speeding the flow of commerce and passengers. A pleased traveller commented, "Numerous turnpikes present as pleasant journeying for man, and as comfortable travelling for beast . . . in all seasons of the year, as any other equal district in the state."

Improved roads reached eastern Suffolk County much more slowly. As late as 1840 the stage trip from Brooklyn to Orient consumed three days. A weary passenger lamented: "No one was in a hurry to get to his journey's end, and if he was . . . he soon became effectively cured of it." Another be-

moaned that "the roads of (eastern) Long Island are exceedingly numerous and difficult for strangers . . . It is impossible to convey an adequate idea of the inconvenience and obstruction to locomotion which are represented." Not until the railroad arrived would East Enders enjoy truly rapid and reliable transportation.

Advances in waterborne commerce, especially the introduction of the steamboat, also helped unite city and country. Inventor Robert Fulton improved this crude and unreliable conveyance early in the nineteenth century and Long Island Sound's first steamer, appropriately named the *Fulton,* began its New York-to-New Haven run in 1815. Within a few years steam traffic of all descriptions plied the coastal waters, visiting every suitable port, efficiently and speedily carrying freight and passengers. Competition between rival lines grew intense. Races

New Arrangement.
Huntington
STAGE.

THE SUBSCRIBER will hereafter drive his Stage between Brooklyn and Huntington, once a week: Leave Huntington on Mondays at 8 o'clock, A. M., and leave Brooklyn on Wednesdays at 9 o'clock, A. M. Fare, for Passengers, One Dollar. Seats taken at *Richard S. Williams'* store, corner of Fulton and South streets, New York, and at *Isaac Snedicor's,* in Brooklyn.
NATHANIEL RUSCO, Proprietor.
Huntington, Sept. 21, 1826.

Above: In addition to transporting passengers, stage coaches were an important avenue of commerce, carrying mail, newspapers, and small packages. From The Portico, *Huntington, September 21, 1826*

Left: Steamboats provided a rapid and often luxurious mode of transportation. Nearly every North Shore village was served by these boats, some of which were fitted with the finest furniture, carpets, and glassware. (SPLIA)

WINTER ARRANGEMENT.
For New Rochelle, Glen Cove, Peacock's Point, Oysterbay and Cold Spring.
On and after Wednesday, November 20th.

The Steamboat American Eagle,
CAPT. CHAS. B. PECK,

WILL leave New York, every Wednesday and Saturday, at 11 o'clock, A. M. Returning, will leave Cold Spring every Monday and Thursday morning at 8 o'clock, Oyster Bay, 20 minutes past 8, Peacock's Point, quarter past 9, Glen Cove, 10, and New Rochelle, quarter before 11.   November 15, 1839.

THE OLD STONE HOUSE. L.I. 1699.

The earliest Dutch houses on
Long Island were relatively
crude, but by the end of the seventeenth century they attained
greater size and comfort. The
Nicholas Vechte house, a
Brooklyn landmark, was the
only stone house in Gowanus
at the time of its construction
in 1699 and for a long time
thereafter. (SPLIA)

Above: At the beginning of the nineteenth century Long Island Sound was considered to have one of the most well-illuminated coastlines in the U.S., a result of shipping's increasing importance to the Island's economy. This watercolor depicts the 1809 Sands Point lighthouse, which remained in service until 1924. (SPLIA)

Right: In this 1776 view of Brooklyn, the steeple of the Dutch Reformed Church on Fulton Street dominates the surrounding countryside. This peaceful scene would soon be interrupted by British troops, who occupied Long Island during the Revolution. Courtesy, The Long Island Historical Society

Below: British artist Francis Guy painted this Brooklyn winter scene in 1816, looking from the second floor of his home at 11 Front Street. He was particularly intrigued by this intersection at Fulton Street, painting six known versions of it during his stay in America. Courtesy, The Brooklyn Museum

Left: Alden Spooner (1783-1848) published the Suffolk Gazette from 1804 to 1811 and then purchased the Long Island Star, which he supervised until 1840. Spooner also published books on the work of many of Brooklyn's poets, founded his own circulating library, and helped establish the Female Seminary of Brooklyn. Courtesy, The Long Island Historical Society

Above: Born in Setauket, William Sidney Mount spent most of his life on Long Island faithfully recording his observations in portraits, genre scenes, and landscapes like "Flax Pond, Old Field, Long Island." (SPLIA)

Right: An unknown artist captured this view of sperm whaling in the bark Washington of Sag Harbor. The Sag Harbor whaling fleet totaled sixty-three vessels at its peak in 1845. Courtesy, The George Latham Collection, Oysterponds Historical Society

Around 1840 Montgomery Queen established Brooklyn's first effective line of stage coaches, or omnibuses, which spurred the growth of the city's residential neighborhoods. He commissioned painter Henry Boese to depict his new stage, the Sewanhackey, *in front of the new City Hall building in 1852. Courtesy, The Long Island Historical Society*

"Farmers Nooning," painted in 1836, exemplifies William Sidney Mount's concentration on the daily life of his Long Island friends and neighbors as a theme. Courtesy, The Museums at Stony Brook, gift of Mr. Frederick Sturges, Jr., 1954

Left: Brooklyn before the bridge was to a great extent a creature of the ferries—they were the heart of its transportation system until the late nineteenth century. Walt Whitman celebrated their importance in his 1860 poem, "Crossing Brooklyn Ferry." Courtesy, The Long Island Historical Society

Right: In this circa 1840 view from Gowanus Heights, Brooklyn, French painter Victor de Grailly depicted the John F. Delaplaine house (right), noted for its lavish interiors that included frescoes and marble halls. The house stood at the present-day intersection of Second Avenue and 40th Street. Courtesy, The Long Island Historical Society

Opened in 1840, Greenwood Cemetery was conceived as a unique combination of burial ground and park setting. It rapidly became a popular place for outings, and by 1844 one stagecoach company offered several daily stage runs to the cemetery. (SPLIA)

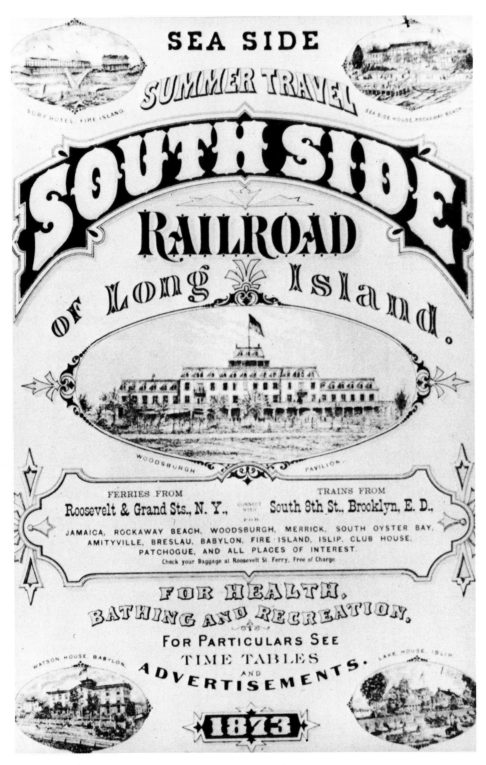

The South Side Railroad was one of the Long Island Rail Road's first competitors, operating as an independent line from 1867 to 1876. The promotional advertisements of both railroads lured thousands to Long Island's summer resorts. Courtesy, New-York Historical Society, Landauer Collection

were common, as were collisions and boiler explosions. One of the worst maritime disasters involved the swift and elegant steam packet *Lexington.* On January 13, 1840, while cruising off Eaton's Point, the *Lexington's* red-hot smokestacks ignited cotton bales stored on deck. Flames quickly engulfed the vessel; panicked passengers swamped the lifeboats, and 120 perished in the icy waters.

Despite periodic mishaps, steamboats forged rapid links to New York and New England's ports. They also proved ideal for conveying city excursioners to country inns, beaches, and picnic groves, remaining an important feature of Long Island life until the twentieth century.

Railroads provided the final component of Long Island's transportation revolution. The flat, sandy landscape proved ideal for railroad construction, and planning began in 1832 for a line from Brooklyn to Greenport. From there, steamers would carry passengers to Connecticut or Rhode Island. Conceived as a through-route to Boston, little heed was paid initially to local needs or sensitivities. Construction commenced in 1833 and the new line reached Jamaica shortly thereafter, pushing on to Hicksville by 1837. That same year Long Island's only two engines, the *Ariel* and *Postboy,* collided near the Hicksville station.

Despite the banking panic of 1837, the line reached Farmingdale in 1841 and Greenport in 1844. There, a great and uproarious celebration commemorated the event. Nathaniel Prime, a prescient local observer, noted: "To a people thus situated, in almost entire seclusion from the rest of the world, a railroad must open new and unconceived facilities ... producing an amazing revolution in manners and habits of the country." Such changes, especially the Sunday trains which disturbed traditional sabbath observance, were not always welcomed, however. Fire posed another problem, since engine sparks ignited vast tracts of Suffolk's Pine Barrens, destroying much valuable cordwood.

Despite the promoters' initial hopes, plans to speed travellers from New York to Boston quickly collapsed after completion of the rival Connecticut Shore Line in 1849. Traffic on Long Island declined precipitously, and by 1850 the railroad was bankrupt. In the reorganization that followed, management decided to encourage local traffic. But while the Long Island Rail Road hesitated, rival lines

known as the North and South Side systems initiated their own construction programs. Rails soon spread in every direction, reaching out to Hunter's Point, Glen Cove, Garden City, Port Jefferson, and Sag Harbor, all by 1872. Three systems vying for limited traffic was a sure prescription for financial disaster, and in 1874 the South Side lines defaulted. A rate war between the surviving companies led to final consolidation of the entire system in 1876.

Although the railroad provided an important tool for hauling farm produce to urban markets, and manure and ashes back out again, the lines' most frequent patrons were the thousands of summer travellers who sought temporary respite from the city's heat and congestion. During the winter, however, management was forced to slash train schedules in an effort to reduce operating losses. Nevertheless, the railroad offered both Island and city residents convenient and speedy access to distant markets, jobs, and resorts. It was the iron pin which united the two halves of nineteenth-century America.

Throughout the first half of the century, Long Island's pleasant weather and attractive scenery tantalized many New Yorkers. Improved transportation also enticed ever increasing numbers to visit and settle there. The precedent was established as early as 1684, when Governor Thomas Dongan purchased a country estate at Hyde Park. Mathias Nicoll, first Secretary of the Province, resided at nearby Cow Neck. Throughout the eighteenth century, traders and royal favorites established Island homes. Antigua merchant Josiah Martin built his Rock Hall mansion in 1767 and Lieutenant Governor Cadwallader Colden lived in Flushing. A visitor to Queens County wrote in 1759, "I took a ride upon Long Island, the richest spot in the opinion of New Yorkers of all America, and where they generally have their villas or country houses."

The post-Revolutionary era witnessed a sharp expansion of this long-established practice. Many, like Newtown's Doctor Isaac Ledyard, "possessed a keen relish for country life ... and was anxious to escape the noise and bustle of the city." Noted politician Rufus King moved to Jamaica in 1805, and five years later it was noted that the village displayed "a polish not visible in towns further eastward, due to its neighborhood to New York and from long having been a resort for the inhabitants of that city."

Transportation improvements further encouraged the flow of suburbanites and by 1840 Hempstead sported a reputation as "one of the most convenient and desirable residences on Long Island." Nearby Jamaica contained "splendid private residences, erected by gentlemen of the city." Blessed with the "great facility of communications with New York," neighboring Flushing boasted some of the "most imposing and splendid residences in that state."

Many other New Yorkers came simply to vacation. Already at the beginning of the nineteenth century, thousands sojourned at Rockaway Beach "in pursuit of pure air and the luxury of sea bathing." City dwellers also visited Long Island to hunt and fish. Timothy Dwight's extensive travels were occasionally interrupted by "sportsmen who come hither to catch trout."

Horse racing attracted additional thousands. Established on Salisbury (Hempstead) Plain in 1665, by the late 1700s racing drew competitors from New

The flat Hempstead Plain made Long Island the home of horse racing from the moment the English settlers had horses to race. In 1821 the Union Race Course was organized; this lithograph shows a trotting match there between Flora Temple and George M. Patchen. Courtesy, The Long Island Historical Society

Jersey, Boston, and Virginia. Legislation permitting "speed trials" was enacted in 1821, and meets were held each May and October thereafter. So heavy did the crush of spectators become that on one day in May 1823, the Fulton Ferry Company collected more than $5,000 in fares. Not everyone, however, waxed enthusiastic about the sport of kings, believing instead that racing was a "principle means of demoralization," fostering gambling, drinking, and swearing.

WALTER R. JONES

Left: Walter R. Jones (pictured circa 1853) and his four brothers were important local businessmen in Cold Spring Harbor. (SPLIA)

Right: Walter R. Jones and Lambert Suydam witness the first experiment made by Captain Douglas Ottinger for throwing a line and sending a "Life Car" to a stranded vessel off the South Shore of Long Island in April 1849. From Overton, Long Island's Story, (1929), 1963

Among the many Long Islanders contributing to New York's development as an artery for maritime commerce, Walter Restored Jones (1793-1855) ranks as a major figure. As an entrepreneur Jones was responsible for the success of such ventures as Atlantic Mutual Insurance, still a major force in marine insurance. Although he spent most of his adult life in Manhattan guiding the fortunes of Atlantic Mutual, Jones also left his mark on his native Long Island. In 1836 Walter, with his brother John and a small group of associates, founded the Cold Spring Whaling Company. Over the next twenty-five years Cold Spring Harbor was the home port of a nine-ship whaling fleet, the third largest aggregation of such vessels on Long Island.

The role played by the Joneses in this endeavor is hardly surprising given their prominence in other aspects of village affairs. The Jones family dominated life in Cold Spring Harbor during the first half of the nineteenth century, operating such businesses as a steamboat company, textile mills, and general store. For the Joneses the decision to enter the whaling trade was based on both local and national trends. The 1830s witnessed severe inroads by foreign woolens into domestic textile markets. Whaling, on the other hand, offered the chance of huge profits and was already dominated by American interests. While the 1830s brought troubles for some domestic manufactures, it also brought burgeoning markets for the oil, candles, and whalebone

was necessary to buy ships and secure insurance. With an active shipbuilding industry and market for used vessels, New York offered Jones and his fellow owners the best opportunity for adding new vessels to the Cold Spring fleet. Walter's position at the helm of Atlantic Mutual put him in an advantageous spot when insurance was required.

The Cold Spring fleet was modestly successful through the 1840s. By the 1850s, however, long voyages and dwindling profits were hurting marginal ports like Cold Spring Harbor. Equally damaging to the local fleet was the loss of both Walter and John Jones within a few years of each other. Walter died in 1855, while John died in 1859. Deprived of their guidance, the whaling fleet slowly broke as vessels were sold and lost to accidents.

The last whaleship departed Cold Spring Harbor in 1858, and was sold nearly four years later. In all likelihood the Joneses and other investors in the Cold Spring fleet realized a modest profit from their investment. For Walter Jones whaling was a venture that fit the pattern of control which his family exerted over the economy of Cold Spring Harbor. That control, like the fortunes of the whaling industry, slowly ebbed and by the 1860s was on its way to disappearing.

Robert Farwell

produced by the whaling industry. When attempts to protect American goods from foreign competition failed, Walter Jones and his kin turned to whaling.

While his brother John served as managing agent of the nine whaling vessels, Walter played an important part in purchasing and insuring these vessels. Although his work at Atlantic Mutual kept him away from Cold Spring Harbor for long periods of time, Walter's position in New York was of considerable advantage when it

Railroads and steamboats further spurred the tourist trade, especially in the summer, speeding visitors to towns and villages scattered across the Island. Distant Oyster Ponds (Orient) maintained a fine hotel, while Patchogue was renowned for its fishing and fowling. Nearby Babylon was a place "much resorted to by travellers and sportsmen." All came searching for a pleasant, rustic diversion from city life.

These suburban residents and throngs of visitors inevitably affected local society. By the early 1800s, Jamaica possessed a noticeable "city air." Straight-laced chroniclers complained that in much of Kings and Queens counties, the sabbath was corrupted by hunting and fishing, visiting and amusement. "Proximity to the city has doubtless increased these evils." Slowly but steadily rural Long Island was being drawn into the urban orbit.

Diversification of Long Island's economy followed quickly upon the heels of improved transportation and increased contact with the city. Though lacking abundant water power or rich mineral resources, the Island was not immune to the stirrings of the Industrial Revolution. Rapidly growing urban markets created new opportunities for rural entrepreneurs, and traditional mills did a booming business. A Cold Spring grist mill ground over 1,000 bushels each week (1792), and when fire consumed Glen Cove's Thorne Mill in 1806, over 10,000 bushels of grain were destroyed.

The early years of the nineteenth century saw new commercial enterprises evolve from the Island's agricultural base. About the time of the Revolution, Hendrick and Andrew Onderdonk constructed a paper mill in Roslyn to supply New York City's book and print sellers. Richard Conklin of Huntington opened another paper mill in 1782. By 1798 a strawboard and wrapping paper factory operated at Patchogue, followed by a twine mill in 1805. Cloth mills were soon started in Babylon, Smithtown, and Patchogue. In 1820 the Jones family erected a larger facility at Cold Spring Harbor which produced 120 pounds of broadcloth and flannel each day. Industrial production was not limited to cloth, paper, or grain. Captain Solomon Townsend, a New York sea captain, merchant, and iron master, built a forge on the Peconic River near Riverhead, and Jeffrey Smith manufactured bar iron in Patchogue. Water power drove most of these establishments, but where stream and tide proved insufficient, enterprising operators at Wheatley Hills and Huntington constructed windmills to saw lumber and spin thread. Although industry and commerce did not replace farming as Long Island's principal occupation, small-scale manufacturing had come to occupy an important niche in the local economy.

Increased business activity naturally generated demands for improved financial services. The Long Island Farmers Fire Insurance Company was chartered in 1833, followed by the Glen Cove Mutual Insurance Company four years later. Suffolk County's first bank opened in Sag Harbor in 1844.

Maritime industries also spurred Long Island's economic development. As available farmlands diminished, men increasingly turned to the sea to earn a living, while successful merchants sought new investment opportunities. Shipbuilding and coastal trading boomed, especially at Huntington, Northport, Port Jefferson, and Stony Brook. But the most profitable venture of all was whaling. From humble, coast-bound origins, it grew into a major industry, with large fleets operating out of Sag Harbor/Peconic Bay and Cold Spring Harbor.

Long Island's first whalemen were Indians who ventured offshore in dugout canoes, armed only with stone-tipped spears. The early English colonists followed their example and soon turned to shore whaling as well. Southampton's original whaling regulations date from 1644, and commercial companies were chartered by 1650. Villagers also manned beach stations at Rockaway, Tobay, and Jones Beach. In both Southampton and East Hampton Indian crews often enlisted for the winter season.

Jealous of their profitable whaling privileges, towns routinely forbid outsiders from invading their territorial limits, and disputes sometimes reached the Governor's Council. Citizens fiercely resisted taxation; smuggling was rampant. Governor Dongan confessed in 1686 that he had collected only ten gallons of whale oil.

Shore whaling was dangerous work. "About the fin," an early (1679) observer noted, "is the surest part for the harpineer (sic) to strike . . . As soon as the whale is wounded it makes all foam . . . so that if the men be not very quick in clearing the ways . . . it is a hundred to one that he oversets the boat."

As the quantity of coastal whales steadily diminished throughout the eighteenth century, sailors began travelling farther and farther in search of their quarry. By the 1780s the Sag Harbor ship *Lucy* had ventured off the coast of Brazil, and early in the next century, Long Island vessels reached Cape Horn and the Indian Ocean. Such extended voyages could last for years. The *Argonaut* departed Sag Harbor in September 1817 for a Pacific cruise and did not return until June 1819. But with whale oil selling at one dollar per gallon, the trips were lucrative indeed, attracting investors and captains from

Opposite page: In 1842 Long Island historian Benjamin Thompson described Montrose as "equally well calculated for a country residence or for manufacturing and commercial purposes." True to its description, the area's water supply attracted mills and factories, and its nice weather lured summer residents. (SPLIA)

Right: Long Island was not completely bypassed by the Industrial Revolution; many local entrepreneurs attempted to apply new manufacturing methods to meet the growing demand for products of all kinds. (SPLIA)

Below: Windmills were often built where water power was scarce. This circa 1826 drawing depicts the mills of East Hampton. From Gillon, Early Illustrations and Views of American Architecture, *Dover, 1971*

HENRY PACKER DERING

In contrast to neighboring villages, a cosmopolitan flavor developed early in Sag Harbor, the community Henry Packer Dering so ably served during its formative years. "Sagg's" deep, well-protected harbor was centrally located on both overland and water routes to New England and New York. Between 1760 and 1770 an active West Indies trade was established and at the end of the century Sag Harbor ranked not far behind New York as a maritime center. In 1789, at the first congressional session under the newly ratified Constitution, Sag Harbor was designated an official United States Port of Entry. Shortly thereafter, Henry Packer Dering was appointed to the prestigious position of collector of the port.

Dering's father, Thomas, had been a prosperous Boston merchant and his mother was heiress to the 1,200-acre Sylvester family manor on Shelter Island. When Thomas Dering took over Sylvester Manor's management, he was appointed inspector of trades and navigation for the Crown, thus becoming an important public figure on Long Island's East End. At the time of the Revolution he espoused the patriot cause and was twice delegate to the Provincial Congress for Suffolk County. Later, he was a member of the state constitutional convention of New York. After the Battle of Long Island in 1776 the Dering family fled to Connecticut

Henry Packer Dering, depicted in a circa 1794 watercolor by William Verstille, held more than ten positions in the Sag Harbor community. (SPLIA)

where Henry Packer Dering spent his adolescence.

After completing his preparatory studies, Henry entered Yale College, graduating in 1784. Following in his father's footsteps, he engaged in a number of mercantile pursuits. By 1790 he had settled in Sag Harbor and in 1793 married Anna Fosdick. Here the couple raised their nine children and Dering took on his role as community leader and public servant. In addition to his position as collector of the port, Dering was appointed United States postmaster, assumed the duties of assistant county clerk, acted as a notary public hearing oaths and arbitrating disputes, and served as a commissioner of highways and of schools. He was the federal agent for the area and as such was responsible for the lighthouses at Little Gull, Cedar Island, and Montauk. Dering issued papers attesting to sworn statements of registry and citizenship which were to serve as precautions against harrassment of sailors in the troubled days preceding the War of 1812. When war appeared imminent, Dering was put in charge of building and managing the Sag Harbor arsenal.

The late eighteenth and early nineteenth centuries witnessed a steady growth in Sag Harbor's importance as a center of trade and commerce. Having been exposed to a more cosmopolitan world outside the agrarian countryside of rural Long Island, Dering's concerns for the development of his home and his devotion to public service influenced the direction this growth would take. He was instrumental in founding schools, a lending library, a literary society, and other cultural organizations, and also attended to the more practical matter of furthering the development of the wharf area and public roads. It was Dering who invited David Frothingham to come to Sag Harbor, where in 1791 Frothingham established Long Island's first newspaper, *The Long Island Herald.* The paper ran articles on both local and international topics of interest and was filled with notices attesting to the variety of Sag Harbor's commercial life. Trading and passenger vessels making frequent trips to Boston and New York were advertised, local craftsmen offered their services, and businessmen of all sorts promoted their wares.

Despite his many roles, Dering's primary occupation continued to be that of a businessman who managed the family estate and engaged in numerous financial ventures. In an attempt to improve the quality of cloth in America, he imported Merino sheep from Spain, bred the animals, and sold the wool. The expanding whaling industry also took his interest and he made several investments in shipping and whaling expeditions, although they proved unprofitable. When Henry Packer Dering did meet with financial difficulties at the end of his life, forty-one prominent men of the area signed a decree releasing him from all debts because of his record of unwavering service to his community.

Dering died in 1822, having promoted the prosperity and sophistication of Sag Harbor, which had become Suffolk County's largest village in the nineteenth century.

Carolyn Marx

Above: Sag Harbor was a flourishing sea-oriented community and a major whaling port. From Hazelton, The Boroughs of Brooklyn and Queens, Counties of Nassau and Suffolk, N.Y., 1609-1924, Lewis, 1925

Blacks had long been active in the whaling industry, supplying a much-needed, skilled labor force. This circa 1912 photograph shows a crew serving on the Long Island-built whaleship Daisy. Courtesy, Cold Spring Harbor Whaling Museum

Suffolk's most prominent families.

An economic boom engulfed the East End. Between 1804 and 1837 Sag Harbor's ships harvested 380,000 barrels of oil and 1,600,000 pounds of whale bone as the village emerged the emporium of Suffolk County. Profits financed the construction of elegant mansions. Shipbuilding flourished; over 1,000 men labored in the fleet, and coopers manufactured 30,000 casks annually. The 1840s were the peak years, with Sag Harbor alone accounting for sixty-three sailings in 1846. Cold Spring Harbor supported a fleet of nine vessels and raucous seamen imparted the name Bedlam Street to its principal thoroughfare. Also active were the Peconic ports of Cutchogue, Greenport, Jamesport, and New Suffolk.

Whaling was not without its risks—storms, accidents, and disease were ever present. The *Governor Clinton* departed Long Island in 1833, but sank in a typhoon off the coast of Japan with the loss of twenty-nine crewmen. Anchored in Tahiti in 1836, the whaler *Telegraph* was struck by a sudden squall and wrecked on the reef. While the crew was saved, the ship and its entire cargo were destroyed.

Development of petroleum products and the American Civil War seriously curtailed the whaling industry, but in its heyday it had brought wealth to many Island families, prosperity to a half dozen communities, and adventure and employment for thousands.

Increasing population and prosperity also created numerous opportunities for Long Island's indigenous craftsmen. In the early years of settlement, wealthy families imported furniture and silver from European or American urban centers, while less affluent farmers made do with simpler country pieces executed by village cabinetmakers and smiths. By the time of the Revolution, however, local artisans had begun to supply the more elegant work associated with shops in New York or Boston. Distant from the city marketplace and patronized by a growing merchant elite, Suffolk artisans were among the most active. The Dominy clan of East Hampton became skilled craftsmen and clockmakers, while Ephraim Byron (1809-1881) of Sag Harbor developed a national reputation for his steeple time pieces and scientific instruments. Southold's John Paine (1737-1815) gained an impressive reputation as a furniture maker, but augmented his income by producing hatblocks, brick molds, coffins, and ropes. Talented silversmiths also flourished. Elias (1726-1810) and John (1755-1822) Pelletreau and John and David Hedges (active 1770-1859) of East Hampton sold their handiwork to leading East End families.

Some businesses grew quite large, benefitting from the prosperity generated by the whaling boom and increased trade. Cabinetmaker Nathan Tinker of Sag Harbor supplied the surrounding communities of Southold, Riverhead, Southampton, and East Hampton. His aggressive competitor, neighbor Henry Byram, even used public verse to attract customers:

From Sideboards of the finest cut
  to workstands for the ladies
And stands whereon your candles put
  and cradles for your babies.

Men like Byram and Tinker made extensive use of the growing number of country newspapers to advertise their wares. A more diverse local economy and society generated increased demands for news,

Above: Nathan Tinker catered to the large and fairly sophisticated clientele of Sag Harbor and supplied a wide variety of furniture items. Unlike their rural counterparts, these well-to-do town dwellers were more aware of changing trends in the decorative arts. Courtesy, Mr. and Mrs. Louis R. Vetault

Right: The Dominy family of East Hampton, successive generations of woodworking craftsmen active from 1714 to 1868, produced many fine pieces of furniture. This case clock was made by Nathaniel Dominy IV in 1790. (SPLIA)

literature, and practical advice. These needs were filled through creation of numerous journals, beginning in 1791 with David Frothingham's *Long Island Herald*. Brooklyn replied with the *Long Island Advertiser* (1799) and the *Weekly Intelligencer* (1806). Other communities also responded, and by the 1850s dozens of papers were doing a booming business, providing clearinghouses for village news, instruction in agricultural techniques, farm market quotations, and word of national and international politics. Newspapers helped to break down the walls of parochialism and drew isolated villages together.

that he constructed a horsedrawn studio with plate-glass windows and a woodburning stove.

A widely-read man, Mount's interests were not limited to art. He achieved proficiency on the fiddle, invented a "hollowbacked" violin, experimented with steamboat propulsion, and studied spiritualism in hopes of contacting deceased relatives. But it was his renderings of country people that made Mount the archetypical American genre painter. An early critic could truly say, "Mr. Mount's pictures are characteristic portraits of American rustic life . . ."

Despite improved transportation, the growth of local industry, and the influx of city residents, Long Island remained at heart a farming society. More, than 80 percent of the population earned its living from the soil, as rural hamlets stood at the center of local life. But even agriculture was beginning to shift its focus. Where once family-oriented homesteads held sway, commercial husbandry now dominated, especially as one neared New York. By 1820 Yale's President Dwight observed that the lands between Brooklyn and Jamaica were owned by farmers grown rich "with the aid of New York, their land under high cultivation . . . resembling a rich garden." From Jamaica to Hempstead cultivation was skillful, produce vigorous, and the influence of New York quite evident. As Brooklyn and Queens farmers held great marketing advantages, Dwight did not wonder "that therefore they are wealthy."

Suffolk County agriculture, distant from the city market and not yet served by the railroad, remained generally backward. Lack of adequate fertilizer was an additional impediment, while hogs often fed at a farmer's doorstep and watering ponds became "corrupted and unhealthy in summer seasons." A bemused traveller wondered in 1840 "in

Genre painter William Sidney Mount continually rejected offers of trips to Europe, staying instead on Long Island to paint its country life. From Cirker, Dictionary of American Portraits, *Dover, 1967.*

Long Island's increasingly complex society could also claim one of nineteenth-century America's greatest artists: painter William Sidney Mount. Mount (1807-1868) spent nearly all his life in Suffolk County. Born of a farm family, he worked briefly for his older brother, a New York City sign painter, and later studied at the National Academy of Design. The young artist exhibited his first genre picture in 1830 and thereafter focused his talents on the country dances and barnyard scenes which enlivened his Stony Brook home.

Mount expressed a mystical concept of nature, observing, "We have nature, it speaks to everyone . . . My best pictures are those which I painted out of doors . . . The longer an artist leaves nature, the more feeble he gets." He also believed an artist should travel to observe ordinary men and women at work and play. So important was this conviction

what manner these people can live comfortably under this embarrassment?"

The arrival of the railroad alleviated many of these deficiencies, greatly expanding the zone of commercial agriculture. Trains provided cheap transportation to urban markets and a more convenient means of importing bone, ash, and manure fertilizers. One writer flatly predicted that "many portions of soil adjacent to the Long Island Rail Road will become highly valuable for agricultural purposes. Villages like Hauppauge, lying astride the line, could anticipate "an increase in population and great improvement in agriculture."

Progressive farmers promoted additional improvements and an exchange of information by creating the Queens County Agricultural Society in 1841. Its Suffolk companion, the Suffolk Society, came along seven years later. Farmers travelled many miles to attend fairs and display their prized livestock and produce. Thus, by disseminating ideas and urging growers to greater efforts, exhibits and societies hastened the shift to commercial agriculture. For another century or more, Long Island would remain true to its farming heritage.

Developments in the first half of the nineteenth century left Long Island a very changed place. Isolated villages and farmsteads were now linked to one another and to the city beyond through a network of rail, coach, and steamboat lines. Newspapers circulated information and advice. Commercial agriculture replaced traditional husbandry even as industry established a place in the local economy. The influx of vacationers and suburbanites was changing the face of village society. By 1860 Long Island was not quite part of the city, but it was no longer apart from it, either.

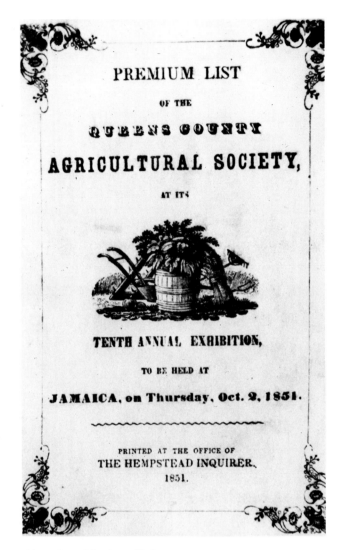

Above: Long Island supplied much of the agricultural produce for the New York metropolitan area during the nineteenth century. According to the New York State census of 1840, the region's greatest crop was corn, followed by potatoes. (SPLIA)

Left: Improved markets and communication fostered development of agricultural societies in the nineteenth century. The Exhibition Hall of the Queens County Agricultural Society stood on its original site until it was demolished in the 1950s. (SPLIA)

SAMUEL BALLTON

One of the village of Greenlawn's most prominent citizens at the turn of the century was a black man named Samuel Ballton. Born in 1838 as a slave in Virginia, Ballton settled in Greenlawn after the Civil War, and though poor and uneducated, helped promote the growth of his adopted community by acquiring and developing property in downtown Greenlawn. Until the opening of the railroad in 1868, Greenlawn had been a quiet farming community known for growing cucumbers and cabbage. But the coming of the railroad fostered the establishment of several pickle and sauerkraut processing plants near the station, and by the late nineteenth century Greenlawn had begun to thrive. Displaying hard work, determination, and good business sense, Ballton tied his own fortunes to those of the town and managed to secure a measure of financial success while at the same time fostering the development of his new home.

Ballton's achievements showed him to be a shrewd man with a strong will to succeed. Ballton had already demonstrated his resourcefulness and determination when as a young man he escaped from a Confederate forced labor detail and managed to reach Northern lines. He even crossed enemy lines twice to see his wife, the second time bringing her with him to the safety of Union-occupied Virginia. He demonstrated a bold and cou-

rageous spirit when in 1864 he enlisted in the Fifth Massachusetts Colored Volunteers to preserve his country and ensure his freedom.

With the war over, Ballton, his wife Rebecca, and their family moved to Greenlawn to start a new life. Ballton's first job in the Greenlawn area was as a farmer for one of the town's wealthiest landowners, Charles D. Smith. There he began to establish a

reputation as a diligent and industrious worker. Later, he was employed as a sharecropper for Alexander Gardiner, who had the largest farm in Greenlawn, and Ballton gained much notoriety by growing record numbers of cucumbers and cabbages. Indeed, he was nicknamed Greenlawn's "Pickle King" as a result of growing 1.5 million cucumbers for pickling in one season.

The Greenlawn Pickle Works was one of several processing plants in Greenlawn. Illustration by June Bassemir. Courtesy, Greenlawn-Centerport Historical Association

Ballton's success in farming was just the beginning of a series of successful ventures. Moving beyond tenant farming, he was able to acquire some capital as a buying agent for a large Boston pickle house. Earning ten cents for every thousand pickles he bought, Ballton started into the business of land speculation. He also acquired some of his capital in the form of personal loans from wealthy local farmers, where his reputation for hard work probably stood him in good stead. With his money Ballton began to buy up valuable property, much of it along the railroad line in the then-growing village of Greenlawn.

Ballton's ventures in real estate demonstrated a creative and systematic method. He borrowed money from local farmers, bought land near the railroad, had houses built on the land, and then sold the houses to other farmers at a small profit. The confidence in his abilities which Ballton inspired is attested to by the long-standing business relationship he maintained with his first employer in the area, Charles D. Smith. Another of Ballton's ideas for Greenlawn's development was to bring laborers up from the South to work on the farms in the summer and build houses in the winter. Ballton did have setbacks, but managed to recover from the misfortune of having two of his houses accidently burn to the ground.

Not only Ballton, but his entire family, displayed the patience, resilience, foresight, and capacity for hard work which make a successful entrepreneur. Both Rebecca and their daughter Jessie worked as laundresses to make extra money for the family. Furthermore, while Ballton and his family were waiting for one of their houses to be built, they had to make do with living behind the unfinished house in a shed so tiny that it was later used as a washhouse.

By the turn of the century, sixteen years after moving to Greenlawn with no money or friends, Ballton had proved himself to be a success by the standards of his community. In spite of never having gone to school, he knew how to read and write. He lived in a home estimated to be worth $5,500. A member of the William Lloyd Garrison chapter of the veterans of the Grand Army of the Republic, and a member of the Greenlawn Presbyterian Church until his death in 1917, Ballton is still remembered as an outstanding founding member of the Greenlawn community.

Linda Day

Brooklyn from First Suburb to Third City

While rural Long Island developed and matured in the first half of the nineteenth century, a great urban metropolis was rising at its westernmost extremity. From a small farming village, boisterous Brooklyn soon grew into America's third largest city. In the process, most vestiges of its earlier Dutch past were erased and, by mid-century, Brooklyn differed as much from its quaint predecessor as it did from its eastern Long Island neighbors. Accordingly, the youthful city faced a new and confusing assortment of distinctly urban problems: explosive population growth; inadequate sanitation, police, and roads; confusing charter reform; and the task of forging a separate identity in the face of Manhattan's persistent challenge. Half a century saw Brooklyn transformed from a bucolic village to an urban giant.

Every American city is a disunited collection of individuals going their own ways; yet each is a community with group loyalties and symbols, also. Many of Brooklyn's popular symbols derive from its nineteenth-century experience. Originally a city of homes and churches, concerned citizens created panoramic open green spaces like Prospect Park and Greenwood Cemetery. The city, too, gained fame for its busy docks, navy yard, Coney Island, the *Brooklyn Eagle,* and the storied Brooklyn Bridge.

Other attributes of Long Island's metropolis, while not so famous, were more distinctive. After the introduction of Robert Fulton's steam ferry in 1814, Brooklyn became the first modern suburb, but it quickly outgrew this role. No other American city ever developed from a suburb into a metropolis, much less in four short decades, and only Brooklyn eventually outgrew the center city that

By the time of this 1840 illustration the small rural community of Brooklyn had been submerged in a mixture of new ethnic groups and commercial activities. Fulton Street appears in the center background and Brooklyn Heights is on the right. From Thompson, History of Long Island, *E. French, (1849) 1918*

initially nurtured it.

Urban historians often speak of a "dual revolution." Originally, several big cities existed but proportionately few people lived in them. Within a comparatively short period of time, however, rural masses were collected in small center-city parcels of land and then redistributed to adjoining suburbs. London housed a million people by 1810 and Great Britain was half urbanized by 1850. Brooklyn experienced both facets of the "urban revolution." From a suburban hamlet of only 1,603 people in 1800, and a town of barely 7,700 in 1820, the Kings County village mushroomed into an "instant city" of 266,000 in 1860. This overwhelming demographic phenomenon dominated every aspect of the city's nineteenth-century development.

Brooklyn's competitive relationship with nearby New York and the struggle to avoid being absorbed by its expanding neighbor provided the second prominent theme of early city history. Throughout the nineteenth century American communities fought tooth and nail for preeminence. New York generally emerged the victor in this contest, besting Philadelphia, Boston, and Baltimore. Meanwhile, Brooklyn gobbled up its own neighbors of Williamsburg and Bushwick, and aggressively jousted with

Manhattan for local dominance. Brooklyn's competitive experience, however, differed in scale from that of most other cities. While all battled for trade, industries, railroad lines, and immigrants, Brooklyn also fought to preserve its very identity and even its continued independent existence. Though Boston and Baltimore might lose some of their commerce to New York, they could not be incorporated into it. Brooklyn could be absorbed and knew it. Therefore, the fight for independence conditioned many facets of local behavior.

Brooklyn's battle to maintain its identity often proved an uphill struggle. Citizens opposed Manhattan's incorporation schemes and fought, instead, to gain control over their own ferries, to achieve separate status as a national port of entry, and to create viable churches, newspapers, and schools. Brooklyn's dynamic neighbor, however, cast a long shadow. Long Islanders often travelled to Manhattan for culture of all shades, work, business, fashion, capital, ministers to man the pulpits, and much else. By the time of the Civil War, at least 19,000 local residents daily commuted to work across the East River, where steamboat service had been established as early as 1814. Brooklyn Heights, home to the city's business and social leaders, looked out

Opposite page: The first ferry between Brooklyn and New York departed from the foot of Fulton Street as early as 1642 and was operated by Cornelius Dircksen. This

1746 view features an old ferry house, with its stepped Dutch roof, built around 1700. From Ostrander, A History of the City of Brooklyn and Kings County, 1894

Above: Built in 1850 and designed by Joseph C. Wells, Plymouth Church had a capacity of 5,000. Brooklyn would eventually earn the title "City

of Churches," and it was during mid-century that the majority of them were established. Courtesy, Library of Congress

HEZEKIAH BEERS PIERREPONT

Above: Hezekiah B. Pierrepont was a leading figure in promoting Brooklyn's potential. From Stiles, History of Kings County Including the City of Brooklyn, *Munsell, 1884*

Opposite page: Brooklyn Heights, seen here from the bluffs of the East River, became New York City's first suburban community. From Hazelton, The Boroughs of Brooklyn and Queens, Counties of Nassau and Suffolk, N.Y., 1609-1924, *Lewis, 1925*

Rare is the man who leaves any lasting memorial behind, much less a living one fully as exciting and impressive 150 years after his death as it was during his lifetime. Hezekiah Beers Pierrepont (1768-1838) was the exception. As the force behind the creation of Brooklyn Heights, one of the most beautiful urban residential areas anywhere, his good works continue to be enjoyed and appreciated by tens of thousands of people each year.

Pierrepont, grandson of the original minister in the New Haven colony, was a natural entrepreneur. By the time he was twenty-five, he had made a small fortune buying up national debt notes and had founded a firm to export goods to provision-scarce post-revolutionary France. He resided in Paris during the Reign of Terror, and saw Robespierre beheaded. In 1795 he bought a ship and sailed to India and China collecting valuable cargo; two years later, with Pierrepont on board, the returning ship was captured by a French privateer and both cargo and vessel were confiscated. Returning to New York in 1800, within two years Pierrepont had purchased a former brewery on the East River in Brooklyn Heights that had been burned during the Revolution, and turned it into New York State's only gin distillery. All these enterprises, however, were only a prelude to Pierrepont's great endeavor in Brooklyn Heights.

While in France, Pierrepont had met Robert Fulton, and he became an active participant with Fulton in establishing the first steamboat ferry between Manhattan and Brooklyn in 1814. Pierrepont realized that, with the inauguration of dependable ferry service across the East River, Brooklyn Heights could become New York City's first suburb, and a very fashionable one at that. He bought up as much of the Heights' land as he could, laid out wide streets, insisted that all new housing be of brick or stone, and in various other ways insured that development would result in a "select neighborhood and circle of society." Perhaps the following 1823 advertisement he placed for "Lots on Brooklyn Heights" best captures what Pierrepont both tried to, and actually did, achieve:

Situated directly opposite the s-w part of the city, and being the nearest country retreat ... the distance not exceeding an average fif- *teen to twenty-five minutes walk, including the passage of the river; the ground elevated and perfectly healthy at all seasons; views of water and landscape both extensive and beautiful; as a place of residence all the advantages of the country with most of the conveniences of the city ...*

... Gentlemen whose business or profession require their daily attendance in the city, cannot better, or with less expense, secure the health and comfort of their families.

Malcolm MacKay

uneasily across the water towards its powerful, prosperous, populous, and ambitious partner.

Nowhere was New York's exercise of power more irksome than in its control of the ferry franchises. Thanks to earlier colonial charters, New York City governed the vital East River right up to the Long Island shore. Under this detested arrangement, Long Islanders actually paid rent to Manhattan for local wharf space, such as the bustling Atlantic Basin docks. Outside control rankled; it sometimes meant poor ferry service to Manhattan, and that, in turn, damaged real estate development and construction activity on the Island in favor of growth in Manhattan. Kings County investors naturally sought to protect their interests, and beginning in 1836 they bought control of the ferries. After 1846 they championed state (outside) regulation. A three-way compromise resulted. By 1860 Brooklynites owned the ferries, New York City granted the franchises, and the state regulated some of their activities. By the era of Lincoln and Walt Whitman, East River vessels, especially Henry Pierrepont's Union Ferry Company, annually carried 32,850,000 passengers, suggesting that Long Island had certainly protected its realty and commuting interests.

It is impossible to say how much this vital transportation link aided Brooklyn's rise, but it is possible to gauge how the steam ferry facilitated the use of Long Island as a specialized part of what historian Edward Spann calls the "New Metropolis." Mid-nineteenth century observers believed that thousands of Brooklynites were no more than

"semidenizens" who spent most of their lives in Manhattan and merely returned across the river to sleep. Indeed, by 1855 Long Island's premier city had already earned the label "New York's bedroom."

The rest of the transit revolution came more slowly, but its impact was equally profound. Stage coaches and urban omnibuses, some capable of hauling thirty or more passengers, serviced the ferry sites by the 1830s, and in 1834 the Brooklyn and Jamaica (later Long Island) Railroad Company inaugurated the steam era. While the railroad exerted only a small impact on intracity commuting, the opening of the Brooklyn City (horsedrawn) Railroad line in 1854 was much more significant. The brainchild of Montgomery Queen, a prominent real es-

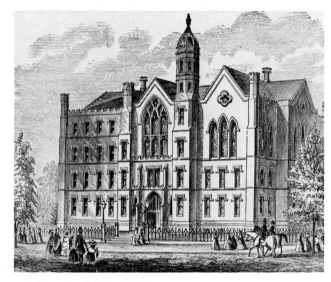

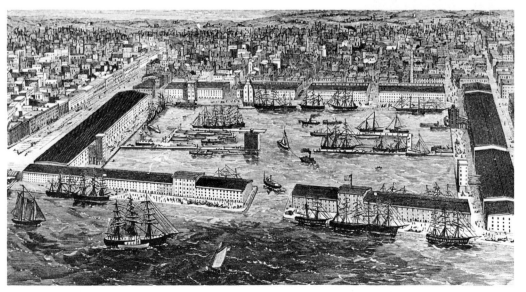

Above: The number of private schools in Brooklyn greatly increased during the mid-nineteenth century. The Packer Collegiate Institute was built in 1854 as one of the state's highest institutions for the advanced education of young women. From Stiles, History of Kings County Including the City of Brooklyn, *Munsell, 1884*

Left: Brooklyn possessed an unrivaled waterfront with great capacity for expansion. The Atlantic Docks were laid out in 1844 on what had been a swamp marsh, and they eventually covered more than twenty acres. From Stiles.

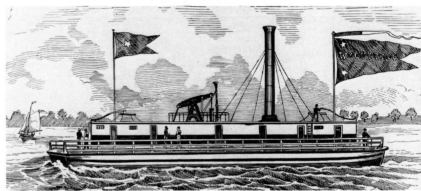

Above: Although still a haven from inner-city congestion in this 1852 view, Williamsburg eventually became industrialized. Courtesy, The Long Island Historical Society

Right: By the 1840s many new ferry lines were opened with new and larger steamboats such as the William Cutting, *named for Robert Fulton's partner. Courtesy, The Long Island Historical Society*

tate developer, the horse cars would dominate local transit until electrification arrived in the late 1880s. Taken together, ferries, horsecars, stages, and steam trains internally and externally integrated Brooklyn into the greater metropolitan areas.

Explosive and unrelenting population growth, aided by the rapid expansion of the transportation network, dominated nineteenth-century Brooklyn life. Local politics accurately reflected this phenomenon. Some leaders tried to stimulate growth through governmental reorganization; others attempted to accommodate the boom by providing streets, health, education, police, and fire prevention; still others sought to avoid the consequences of expansion by opposing taxes. But hardly anyone escaped the issue.

The imperfectly understood "science" of municipal government was barely able to harness such robust development. Like many nineteenth-century cities, the city sought metropolitan greatness. Its large natural hinterland, excellent port, and attractive Brooklyn Heights neighborhood lured many residents. Merchants, lawyers, bankers, and brokers by the score settled near the ferries that carried them to Wall Street every ten minutes. But for its natural advantages to be truly exploited, Brooklyn

would have to provide its new residents with fire protection, clean water, adequate police services, and competent government.

In an effort to bridge the gap between a growing city and a lagging government system, Brooklyn underwent four major and several minor political reorganizations between 1800 and 1865. In 1816 a village charter replaced the old town form of government. Although Manhattan real estate interests fought it, Brooklyn became a city eighteen years later. In both 1850 and 1855, the municipality's law was heavily amended. A considerable minority of citizens consistently favored reorganization by incorporation into New York City, but the Brooklyn-first party always triumphed.

Each charter change increased the range of government power. New municipal departments were spawned and outlying neighborhoods were annexed to the central city. In 1855, Williamsburg and Bushwick entered the boundaries. Brooklyn interests had long taken a jaundiced view of the rapid growth of potentially competitive Williamsburg; and fortunately for Brooklyn, the smaller city refused to raise taxes to fund its own growth. Thus, while evading the clutches of its imperial neighbor, the large Long Island city grasped a few districts of its

own. Its persistent efforts to move its boundary from the beach to the middle of the East River failed, however.

Enhancing the power of government did not necessarily solve urban problems. Most contemporary cities were poorly managed, though it is doubtful that Brooklyn fared worse than others. Moreover, urban developers suffered from unimaginable handicaps, of which unbridled and unregulated growth was the worst. Brooklyn's population doubled every decade from 1810 to 1840, and then tripled each decade thereafter until 1870. Thus, in every decade residents constructed at least one entirely new urban area equal to the one with which they started.

Such rapid development quickly altered the composition of the indigenous population. At the opening of the ferry era, most residents were of either British or Dutch extraction. They were soon joined, however, by tens of thousands of Irish and German immigrants who added a large Catholic population. These migrations created diversity and a cosmopoli-

Above: The first volunteer fire company in Brooklyn was organized in 1785, with firemen chosen annually at a town meeting. By 1869 the first professional department had been established. Courtesy, The Long Island Historical Society

Opposite page, top: The development of pumping engines adequately supplied the city with water for fire, sanitation, and domestic needs. From The Brooklyn Water Works and Sewers, A Descriptive Memoir, 1867

tan air, and in 1860 about one-third of Brooklyn's population was foreign-born. Thanks in large measure to European and New York immigrants, Brooklyn's population was actually growing faster than Manhattan's.

A polyglot city, bursting at every seam, found the exercise in urban growth difficult indeed. Inexperience in everything from police administration to sanitation, a lack of civic loyalty, and an ingrained resistance to higher taxes complicated the process. It is therefore not surprising that the community often found itself only one jump ahead of disaster. On occasion the distance was even shorter. Fortunately, the catastrophes besetting so many other cities seemed rarer in Brooklyn.

Fire was an especially feared menace, and increasingly dense concentrations of tinder-dry wooden buildings frequently erupted in flames. Efforts to combat the danger were halting and usually inadequate. A fire district existed in 1800, but neither imaginary lines nor the fire wardens and citizen bucket brigades mandated by the 1816 charter brought much protection. Regulatory revisions in 1834 replaced primitive firefighting methods with new ones which were both more efficient and more exasperating. Under these arrangements, the city supplied equipment and firehouses, while volunteers provided the labor. Unfortunately, the engine, hose, and ladder companies (of which there were twelve in 1838) were also heavily involved in politics and not subject to strict city control. In 1843 one company refused to help another quench a blaze, resulting in the loss of twelve buildings. On other occasions the "fire laddies" rioted amongst themselves; and on still others they battled the police. With such a department and the absence of adequate equipment, small blazes could easily race out of control. An 1848 fire destroyed eight square downtown blocks. That disaster brought new regulations which were promptly ignored; the threat of large fires persisted until after the Civil War.

Brooklyn obviously required brick buildings and an efficient water supply to effectively fight fires and meet growing domestic demand. As the city expanded, its wells and cisterns were increasingly fouled by sewage and industrial pollution, highlighting the need for a distant source of water. From the time of its incorporation, Brooklyn tried to obtain such a supply, but competing engineering schemes,

rival water interests, and taxpayer opposition postponed the solution. In the meantime, city fathers procrastinated, digging but a few wells. Not until 1859, when the ailing and private Nassau Water Company forced the city to buy it out, did an adequate source appear. Nevertheless, Brooklyn's record was not all that bad, at least in comparison with other American cities. Manhattan did not receive its first Croton water until 1842, and many other urban centers were denied public supplies for a decade or two more.

Inadequate resources inevitably impacted public health, and the sanitary state of nineteenth-century cities is best described as horrendous. Crowded housing, pigs in the streets, sewage seeping into the water table, uncollected garbage and trash, infre-

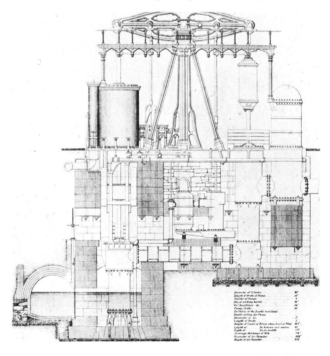

Right: The Kings County Poorhouse was established in 1830 and by the 1850s consisted of a hospital, almshouse, and insane asylum. From Stiles, History of Kings County Including the City of Brooklyn, *Munsell, 1884*

WALT WHITMAN

Above: Walt Whitman's extraordinary poetry spoke for an entire generation growing up with a young, prosperous nation. From Cirker, Dictionary of American Portraits, Dover, 1967. Courtesy, Library of Congress, Brady-Mandy Collection

Opposite page: Poet Walt Whitman was born in 1819 in this Huntington farmhouse built by his father. From the Clarence Purchase Photograph Collection, SPLIA

In 1855, the poet Walt Whitman published the first edition of *Leaves of Grass.* That effort at self-realization, which would take him a lifetime to perfect, forever changed the course of American letters. Without Whitman as forerunner, most modern poetry could not have been conceived and written.

Born in 1819 on a small Huntington farm, Whitman was still a child when his family moved to Brooklyn. Abandoning school in 1830, he worked first as an office boy, and two years later was apprenticed to a journeyman printer. By the late 1830s Whitman had returned to Long Island where he taught at several country schools. From 1836 to 1841 he taught single or double terms in Babylon, Long Swamp, Smithtown, Woodbury, Little Bayside, Whitestone, and Dix Hills. He also took time in 1838 to found the *Long Islander,* a weekly Huntington newspaper.

About 1840 Whitman again moved to Brooklyn and labored for a succession of newspapers, including the *Brooklyn Eagle,* and later in his life contributed historical and reminiscent articles on Brooklyn to the *Brooklyn Standard*. But in the early 1850s he abandoned publishing entirely to devote more time to his personal writings.

"Fish-shape Paumanok," Whitman called Long Island, using the old Indian name. As a small boy, he had roamed the hills and shores in and around Huntington, captivated by the colors, smells, plants, and animals that abounded in rural Long Island. As a young man, he roamed the "populous pavements" of Brooklyn in the same way, revelling in the sharp contrasts, the noise and commercial bustle and the smells of steam and sweat that belonged to the city. All these impressions, as Whitman tells us, became part of him; and out of these he made poetry. Not the carefully controlled and measured verse that was then being written and had always been written in English—but a new creation, entirely bold and free, without regular rhyme, without regular meter, without conventional form.

Whitman was the poet of democracy. He sings of simple people, working people, not just winners, but also "conquer'd and slain persons." Like many of his literary generation, he wanted to produce a truly American literature, one that expressed the values and virtues and wishes and fears of the young American nation. And more than any other poet of his generation, Whitman did speak for us—for all that was brawny and rambunctious, headstrong and open-armed about America in the nineteenth century.

Whitman's mark remains upon Long Island in the *Long Islander,* still published today; and in the old, weathered farmhouse at West Hills, Whitman's birthplace, where visitors cross a threshold and find themselves back in the nineteenth century. And through Whitman, Long Island makes its mark upon the world, as generations of readers absorb the thoughts and images that began there in the mind of one small boy.

Marilyn Oser

quent bathing, faulty drainage, and commerce-borne microbes added up to perennial health emergencies. So did a lack of basic medical knowledge. Doctors bled, cupped, and leeched their patients, were blissfully unaware of the origins of disease, and usually ignored antisepsis.

Brooklyn's residents frequently suffered from these shortcomings, as health precautions were practically nonexistent. Intensified urbanization only heightened the problem of disease communicability; crises multiplied. A cholera epidemic terrorized Manhattan in 1832, causing 100,000 of its 250,000 inhabitants to flee. Its Long Island neighbor also felt the impact of the plague, but apparently not the panic. Historian Ralph Weld called this outbreak "the most terrible experience" in the history of the village. Several additional scourges soon followed. Smallpox struck in 1836 and 1845; cholera returned in 1849 and 1854. Yellow fever, which killed 11,000 in New Orleans in 1853, barely missed Brooklyn three years later, but suburban New Utrecht was hard hit and most of its residents fled.

Mob violence often greeted such epidemics. In fact, yellow fever had come to Long Island in 1856 when an angry crowd drove an infected ship away from the quarantine station at Staten Island. Similar trouble threatened as cases appeared in Brooklyn, but cooler heads prevailed. Several local doctors gave their lives, and Mayor George Hall risked his health by nursing the sick, and confining the disease to New Utrecht.

These periodic scourges, together with more normal urban risks like tuberculosis (the great white plague), eventually generated a growing public health movement. A city-subsidized private hospital appeared in 1839, and Brooklyn's morgue opened in 1842. A public health care facility, city dispensary, and burial regulations followed in 1846, while the collection of vital statistics and control over swill (distillery waste) milk came in due course. After private contractors' neglect had turned the streets into a subject of local scorn and verse, a sanitation department appeared in 1855. Soon storm sewers began radiating outward from the center city. By 1867 demands for better drainage (as well as improved shipping) led to construction of the Gowanus Canal. As yet another cholera epidemic loomed in 1867, the Metropolitan Board of Health assumed sanitary responsibility for both Brooklyn and New York.

Similar fitful progress characterized the local police forces before 1857. Regulations in early nineteenth-century America dated from medieval times and were entirely unsuited to growing cities. In 1829 a modern model of police administration appeared in England, when Sir Robert Peel created London's famous Metropolitan Police Force (the bobbies). Brooklyn and other American cities then looked to Britain for inspiration, but generally evidenced little actual zeal for police reform. A large force was feared as both costly and threatening to American liberties.

Under Brooklyn's old village regime, local officials seemed to devote greater energy to clearing the streets of omnipresent pigs than to running off the criminals. Perhaps that emphasis reflected the large number of pigs and the small number of criminals, but by the 1840s many citizens were alarmed at increasing lawbreaking and violence. These twin threats caused Brooklyn leaders to effect modest reform.

A tiny police force of a dozen men in the 1840s grew to 159 officers in the 1850s, as the city's population mushroomed from 97,000 to 226,000. Officers also began wearing badges, but still resisted uniforms as too military. These limited efforts failed to satisfy the cries for reform; politicians exercised too much control over the force and the police chief, too little. The low level of professionalism was vividly illustrated in 1857, when the disgruntled Albany legislature merged the locals into a state-controlled metropolitan force. In Manhattan that move led to civil war between old and new officers, but Brooklyn apparently escaped the violence. Americans of the Civil War era evidenced a remarkably high tolerance of crime and disorder, and not until the latter part of the nineteenth century would a modernized police force patrol the city streets.

These same streets also acted as the arteries of a dynamic urban organism. Since Brooklyn was, in part, a product of the transportation revolution, it seems fitting that the city fathers spent so much time on street matters. The original town charter offered little guidance for an age of rapid expansion. Later village regulations mandated private maintenance of sidewalks and curbs. Street surveys were begun, as were public contributions towards grading, graveling, and filling municipal thoroughfares. City-sponsored reforms soon included paving, oil lighting, and numbering. Between 1851 and 1854 alone, 192,000 linear feet of streets were upgraded.

Structural improvement was directly tied to real estate development, and there was plenty of that. Tens of thousands of new residents needed homes and shops; the demand for vacant land was enormous. A Gowanus farm worth $18,000 in 1831 sold for $102,000 just four years later. Ex-New York Mayor Phillip Hone called Brooklyn real estate speculation "one of the bubbles of the day." Yet, streets often were laid out haphazardly, and many areas remain unsurveyed. A monotonous square plot governed the plans. Still, given the limited competence of municipal experts and legislators, it is probably well that they did not attempt anything fancier.

By 1861 Brooklyn had laid the foundations of a modern metropolis. Population was booming. Eight miles of commercial waterfront faced Manhattan. Local docks serviced more ships than New York and Hoboken combined. Townhouses and brownstones crowned Brooklyn Heights, radiating in all directions. Local shipyards built elegant clippers and warships for the Czar's navy. Poet Walt Whit-

Opposite page: Born in New York and educated at Erasmus Hall, George Hall was the first mayor of the original city of Brooklyn (1834-35), as well as the first mayor of the consolidated city (1855-57). From Stiles, History of Kings County Including the City of Brooklyn, *Munsell, 1884*

Left: Reflecting its new status as a city, Brooklyn's Borough Hall was originally envisioned as an elaborate marble structure. Public outcry over the extravagance of such a costly design prompted the building in 1846 of this smaller and more subdued version. From Hazelton, The Boroughs of Brooklyn and Queens, Counties of Nassau and Suffolk, N.Y., 1609-1924, *Lewis, 1925*

Above: This mid-century view of East New York, with its newly laid thoroughfares and expanding urban center, would have certainly surprised the area's early Dutch settlers. East New York would eventually grow into a large metropolitan section, spurred by a large influx of German immigrants in the 1860s and 1870s. Courtesy, The Long Island Historical Society

Opposite page: Opened in the winter of 1862, the Union Pond Skating Rink in Williamsburg catered to Brooklyn's growing middle class and their increasing interest in leisure pursuits. Courtesy, The Long Island Historical Society

man sang the city's praises.

In other, less physical spheres, Brooklyn's achievements were, as yet, modest. Modern observers often condemn this record, especially a persistent inability to solve the complex issues of growth. But Brooklyn's urban pioneers labored under burdens inconceivable to today's city managers or critics. The wonder is that Brooklyn kept up as well as it did. No one, rich or poor, wanted higher taxes; and in a political culture which featured annual elections, vigorous party competition, an unbridled press, a weak executive system, and a strong tradition of violent protest, cities had little choice beyond modest, evolutionary change. Republican sentiments were so ingrained that even issues as trivial as the introduction of police uniforms sparked heated controversy. Sheer ignorance also impeded progress. Nineteenth-century physicians knew little about disease and even less about how to eradicate it. Quarantine restrictions often provoked mob violence. Given these facts, one must conclude that Brooklyn did far better than is generally thought.

The Long Island city's animated rivalry with Manhattan abated temporarily with the outbreak of the Civil War. Although Brooklyn voted against Lincoln in 1860, it stood ready to fight for him and the Union in 1861. After the fall of Fort Sumter, a rainbow of flags cloaked the city; 50,000 citizens gathered at Fort Greene to pledge their support; men flocked to the colors; and the sanitary and Christian commissions soon appeared to succor the wounded. A total of 30,000 men served in the Union armies, often in ethnic or vocational regiments like the Schwartze Jaegers, the Irish Legion, or the 173rd Infantry (Brooklyn and Manhattan police). At Bull Run these citizen soldiers fared badly, but at Gettysburg and the Wilderness they fought like heroes.

Also important, though in a less sanguine way, were the efforts of the Greenpoint shipyard, which built the ironclad *Monitor,* and the nearly 6,000 employees of the nearby Navy Yard. Moreover, despite the harsh judgment of some historians that Brooklyn was under-policed, residents proved generally unwilling to join the draft riots that greeted conscription in Staten Island and Manhattan. Its citizens must have enjoyed a good chuckle as their militia set off to squelch New York's upheavals.

The Brooklyn throngs who welcomed the return of peace did so from the streets, neighborhoods, and factories of a now-great American city. The fifty-year odyssey from Anglo-Dutch village to the nation's third metropolis had been astonishing, but the most spectacular era still lay ahead.

CHAPTER SIX

Of Grand Hotels, Great Estates, Polo, and Princes

Benjamin Thompson was so impressed with the then six-year-old Marine Pavilion at Far Rockaway, "a large and splendid edifice, standing upon the margin of the Atlantic," that he made special mention of it in his *History of Long Island.* The novel two-story seaside lodging with "sleeping apartments" for 160 and a 200-foot piazza had been erected in 1833. It was the brainchild of a group of New York investors, headed by Governor Dewitt Clinton's brother-in-law, aiming to accommodate the increasing number of vacationers who wished to experience "fresh inspiration and increased vigor by repeated plunges in the ocean." Longfellow, Washington Irving, and John Trumbull were among the notables who frequented the new watering spot and helped to make Far Rockaway one of the nation's most famous pre-Civil War resorts. The Pavilion burned in 1864, but it was to be the precursor of dozens of seaside hotels, starting at Coney Island and stretching east to the Hamptons and Peconic Bay. On the North Shore from College Point to Wading River, each new resort claimed to be bigger than the last. The Rockaway Beach Hotel, which opened in 1881 near the site of the Marine Pavilion, announced that it was the world's largest hostelry with 1,188 feet of facade, 100,000 square feet of piazza, and a 1,300-foot ocean pier. By the turn of the century, five of these giant havens, the Manhattan Beach, Oriental, Edgemere, Arverne, and Long Beach hotels, could house between 400 and 1,000 guests. Many of the large resorts had their own railroad depots, since convenient transportation links were often the key to success. Not surprisingly, the Long Island Rail Road had a large stake in this burgeoning business. When Austin Corbin, builder of the Manhattan Beach and Oriental, became the

The Marine Pavilion, con-
structed in Rockaway in 1834,
was one of the earliest resort
hotels in the country. Only a
coach ride from New York
City, its country setting and

magnificent beaches attracted
summer inhabitants from
that increasingly urbanized
area until a fire destroyed the
resort in 1864. Courtesy, The
Long Island Historical Society

firm's president in 1881, he revitalized the line and formed the Long Island Improvement Company. The new organization constructed the remarkable Argyle at Babylon, a hotel, cottage, and casino complex in a seventy-acre landscaped park. Under Corbin, the Long Island Rail Road became the principal publicist of the area's resort potential. The annual visitor's guides, produced by the passenger department, were impressive, lavishly illustrated directories which touted this "expanse of ocean-bounded country where beauty of landscape and health go hand-in-hand." Corbin's projects and promotional instincts also helped to keep Long Island in the press. When shore erosion threatened the Brighton Beach Hotel in 1888, the entrepreneur sent his railroad to a much publicized rescue. Laying sections of parallel track, a team of locomotives moved the 500-foot structure to safety.

Despite Corbin's efforts, the new hotels could not begin to fill the need for accommodations during the height of the season. Many of Long Island's eighteenth-century country seats, such as Rock Hall at Lawrence and the Joseph Lloyd Manor House at Lloyd's Neck, were pressed into service as boarding houses. Village residents began taking in boarders. Mrs. J.C. Hawksworth of East Islip, for instance, had room for eight guests in her home during the 1903 season. She charged eight dollars per person

per week. By the turn of the century, the resort business had grown to such proportions that the railroad guides reported accommodations for 24,000 vacationers in Nassau and Suffolk County alone. This represented one room for every five residents in the two-county region, or, by another yardstick, twice the number of lodgings believed available for tourists in 1984.

Proceeding apace with the development of resort hotels was the construction of mansions or country houses for the rich. In this respect Long Island, with its mild climate, had always been a favored locale for country escapes. As previously mentioned, such early notables as Governor Dongan and Mathias Nicoll had established estates as early as the seventeenth century in what is now Nassau County. By the start of the Revolution, Long Island was peppered with the manors and country homes of such city-oriented families as the Martins, Gardiners, Lloyds, Joneses, Coldens, and Smiths. What began to manifest itself in the mid-nineteenth century, however, was an entirely different phenomenon: the establishment of summer retreats on relatively small parcels of land which had no agricultural (i.e., income producing) function. The recurrent warm weather epidemics, increased congestion, and rapid industrialization of New York City had made the prospect of vacationing in Gotham less appealing to many well-healed New Yorkers. Hence, such early summer residents as William Cullen Bryant, who acquired a place in Roslyn on Hempstead Harbor in 1843, and John Banvard, the panorama artist who built a wooden castle in Cold Spring Harbor in the 1850s, pioneered a wave of summer house development which was to begin in earnest during the Civil War—against a backdrop of draft riots, urban tension, and national uncertainty. While Gettysburg was still raging, carpenters in Oyster Bay were putting the finishing touches on Long Island's first sophisticated country house, an architect-designed villa in the Rural Gothic style, for one of New York's most prominent citizens, James W. Beekman. After renting a house in the hamlet of Oyster Bay where his fellow members of the Union League Club also summered, Beekman decided to build.

The factors that transformed this sleepy village into the North Shore's first resort foretold estate development in later decades. As with hotels, the growth of the Long Island Rail Road was the pri-

Above: The Long Island Rail Road helped to popularize the Island's growing resorts and communities. The line published numerous colorful brochures containing photographs and glowing accounts of the Island's attractions. (SPLIA)

Left: Columbia Grove on Lloyd's Neck, depicted in this 1881 painting by Edward Lange, was one of Long Island's resort attractions during the 1880s and 1890s. Courtesy, Andrus T. Valentine

AUSTIN CORBIN

Had Austin Corbin not been killed in a carriage accident in 1896, Montauk might have become a transatlantic terminus for ocean liners, and construction might have commenced on a subway system for New York a generation earlier. Corbin was a remarkable man. An energetic financier with great vision and what his contemporaries termed a capacity for details, Corbin ushered in the age of the resort on Long Island, attracting foreign capital to build huge seaside hotels and reorganizing the transportation system that made it all possible, the Long Island Rail Road.

Born and educated in New Hampshire, Corbin graduated from Harvard Law School in 1849 and first went west, establishing a successful banking business in Davenport, Iowa. Moving to New York City at the close of the Civil War, he established the firm that became known as The Corbin Banking Company and at the same time reorganized the Indianapolis, Bloomington and Western Railroad, earning a reputation as a wizard in railroad affairs. By 1886, Corbin was president of four railroads and had reorganized the Philadelphia and Reading line for J.P. Morgan.

The financier's involvement with Long Island is said to have begun while he was visiting an infirmed son who was recuperating at a small hotel on Coney Island. Walking east on the sparsely settled beach, Corbin sensed the resort potential of Long Island's ocean

The Argyle Hotel in Babylon was one of several large and fashionable summer hotels built by Austin Corbin, a pioneer in resort building. It was completed in 1882 and could accommodate over 700 guests. Courtesy, Vanderbilt Historical Society

frontage. In 1876, Corbin began developing Manhattan Beach, building a rail line to the remote area from Bay Ridge. Corbin's Manhattan Beach Improvement Company then built two immense shore hotels, The Manhattan Beach and The Oriental, as well as a theater, stadium, bandstand, and other amenities. Next came the exlusive Argyle Hotel at Babylon, built by another Corbin enterprise, the Long Island Improvement

Company, in the midst of a seventy-acre casino and cottage complex. In 1885, Corbin added The Long Beach Hotel to his resort empire, acquiring the rail line to Point Lookout and untold property in the process.

Corbin became acquainted with "the slow and uncertain movement" of the Long Island Rail Road while commuting to his summer residence in Babylon near the Argyle. Realizing that a well-run railroad could be immediately profitable and would open up new areas of Long Island for the summer trade, Corbin organized a syndicate of Boston and London capitalists that bought a controlling interest in the LIRR in 1880. As president of the LIRR, Corbin embarked on revitalizing a railroad that was over a million dollars in debt and in such bad shape that one railroad man had called it "two streaks of rust and a right of way." The banker-turned-railroadman replaced the old iron rails with new steel track, built new lines while abandoning unprofitable links, upgraded narrow gauge roads to standard gauge, introduced air brakes and automatic couplers, bought new equipment, built new stations, and within two years had restored the line to profitability. *The New York World* was to hail the LIRR in 1886 "for speed, safety, promptness" which was "unsurpassed on any road."

Corbin was to continue as president of the LIRR until his death, but this man of vision focused his energy on other projects in the late 1880s. He hired an English engineer to design a subway system for New York and proposed the construction of tunnels under the East and Hudson rivers more than a generation before these plans were eventually realized. In 1885, he proposed a scheme which would have shortened transatlantic travel. Corbin wanted ocean terminals constructed at Fort Pond Bay, Montauk and Wilford Haven, Wales. Rail links to New York and London would then have cut hours off travel time to Europe and the LIRR's passenger business would have received a major boost. Corbin made frequent trips to Washington, D.C. to convince Congress of the merits of his plan since federal approval was required to create new ports of entry. Unfortunately, the plan did not survive the visionary's untimely death and the opposition of New York City interests, but Corbin's legacy to Long Island was already in place—a fully developed and completed railway system, the new resort industry, and a large number of investors interested in Long Island's growth potential. Indeed, Austin Corbin did more than almost anyone else in bringing Long Island out of its nineteenth-century agrarian isolation.

Robert B. MacKay

mary determinant; its decision to extend a spur to Syosset in 1854 made Oyster Bay accessible to a rail head for the first time. Surviving papers of the Edward Swan family, among the first summer residents of Oyster Bay, indicate that the train was preferred over the steamship. The vessels were seasonal at best and had trouble running on schedule. So rapid was the railroad, on the other hand, that the average trip made by Caleb Swan in 1854 from the Syosset depot to his lower Manhattan residence was only twenty minutes longer than it is today. When one considers that Swan had to cross the East River by boat and travel to his downtown house by horse-drawn omnibus, the feat seems all the more remarkable. In general, the railroad was making Long Island accessible for resort development in a way that couldn't have been imagined even a generation before. The decision to build a spur to Glen Cove (1867), the projection of the South Side Railroad to Patchogue (1869), the electrification of the Port Washington line (1898), and the completion of the East River tunnels (1910) are among the more notable milestones in the great litany of progressive rail improvements. With the completion of the East River bridges, Long Island's transportation advantages continued to build in the early years of the automotive age. The Queensboro or 59th Street Bridge (1909) was particularly important, since it dramatically shortened the trip from midtown Manhattan to the North Shore via Route 25 or 25A. Extending to the south and east, it also connected to William K. Vanderbilt's new Long Island Motor Parkway, commissioned in 1906. The area's transportation edge over other resort locales

Above: By the 1900s Long Island's two main centers of fox hunting were the fashionable Meadow Brook Club and the Rockaway Hunting Club. This painting depicts a hunt about to begin on the Meadow Brook. Courtesy, Mrs. Betty Babcock

Right: Completed in 1909, the Queensboro Bridge linked Queens and Manhattan, facilitating the spread of population and commerce across the East River. Its influence was immediately felt as many large industrial plants began to seek sites in Queens and Long Island. (SPLIA)

in the tri-state, not to mention more distant watering spots such as Newport, was then considerable. Long Island was a place where the man of affairs could vacation while not losing contact with developments in the city and office.

The development of recreational interests was another factor contributing to the resort phenomenon. Young New Yorkers began renting farm houses in the Oyster Bay area in the 1860s for the sole purpose of participating in the informal sailboat races that took place there every summer. The nation's first open amateur regatta was sponsored by the Seawanhaka Corinthian Yacht Club, organized in Oyster Bay in 1872. Many of the youthful yachtsmen had been among the first undergraduates to participate in intercollegiate athletic contests, deeply believing in the concept of Corinthian (or amateur) sports. They were soon joined by the equestrians, who reestablished on Long Island the late eighteenth-century pastime of fox hunting. The Queen's County Hounds, which gathered at the Garden City Hotel in 1877, were the first pack of drag hounds in the United States, while the Rockaway Hunt, founded in 1878, is believed to be America's oldest such organization in continuous operation, edging out Jericho's Meadow Brook Club by three years. The latter was one of the earliest precursors of this nation's modern country clubs.

Long Island sporting groups did not limit their interests to fox hunting, however. Polo, first played in the United States in 1876, made its local debut at the Mineola Fair Grounds in 1879, and was being played at the Rockaway and Meadow Brook clubs by the early 1880s. Every American to swing a mallet in the twelve international matches against Great Britain from 1886 to 1939 was to be a Long Islander. Golf, a later development, nevertheless, was another pastime in which Long Island made history. Southampton's Shinnecock Hills Golf Club was the first American golf club which owned its grounds, had links laid out by a professional, and a clubhouse specifically designed for the sport. While lawn tennis was also introduced elsewhere in America, the Brooklyn Heights Casino can lay claim to being the country's first indoor club to accommodate that game. The West Side Tennis Club at Forest Hills later became the largest and most prominent tennis club in the United States, holding the U.S. Open matches between 1915 and 1920. After its opening in 1923, the Forest Hills Stadium,

with a seating capacity of 13,000, became the preeminent national tennis arena, hosting both the Davis Cup challenges and the U.S. Open. Even aviation was thought to be something of a gentleman's sport by the New York Aeronautic Society, which had facilities in Mineola as early as 1909. The Long Island Aviation Country Club at Hicksville, which flourished between the two world wars, had no precursors whatsoever. By the end of the first decade of the twentieth century, Long Island had become the cradle of many of America's nascent recreational pursuits, a great national playground where grand prix sporting events were often taking place concurrently. During the 1910 or 1911 summer season, for instance, one could have seen the "Big Four" take on the British for the America Cup, polo's greatest contest, at the new, specially-built, 40,000-seat stadium on the Hempstead Plains; witnessed aerial acrobatics at the first International Air Show at Belmont Race Track where a new

Above: Smartly dressed members of the Meadow Brook Club prepare for a fox-hunting meet at Sagamore Hill circa 1895. Courtesy, Meadow Brook Club Album

Left: Forest Hills Stadium, completed in 1923, and the West Side Tennis Club form a complex that has attracted thousands to its Davis Cup and U.S. Open matches since the 1920s. From Hazelton, The Boroughs of Brooklyn and Queens, Counties of Nassau and Suffolk, N.Y., 1609-1924, *Lewis, 1925*

The Vanderbilt Cup races, held on Long Island from 1904 to 1910, attracted huge crowds. The mounting number of accidents and deaths involving both racers and spectators eventually led its promoters to discontinue the event. Courtesy, Vanderbilt Museum

world altitude record of 9,714 feet was set; thrilled to the maneuverability of the competing speedboats at the International Races in Huntington Bay which could be viewed from such elegant surroundings as the terrace of the new Beaux Arts Casino; observed the spectacle of a great squadron of yachts and America's Cup candidates depart for the annual cruise of the New York Yacht Club from the Club's new "station" at Hempstead Harbor; watched some of the world's greatest drivers tune up their engines at Robert Graves' novel garage-hotel in Mineola before putting their "motors" to the test in the Vanderbilt Cup Races; bet on "Sweep," the winner of the 1910 running of the Belmont Stakes, the greatest prize of the season at one of the most important thoroughbred tracks in America; or one could have attended one of the myriad horse shows, hunt meets, steeplechases, or other sporting events that were focusing national attention on Long Island.

The decision of many of these clubs to establish permanent grounds and facilities for the pursuit of recreational interests became the primary contributor to the later stages of the estate boom. The founding of the Southside Sportsmen's Club in 1865 by frequenters of Snedicor's Hotel at Oakdale, a South Shore hunting lodge, encouraged members to build mansions nearby. The Frederick Bourne Estate (now LaSalle Military Academy), the William K. Vanderbilt Estate (today's Dowling College), and the Bayard Cutting Estate (presently the Bayard Cutting Arboretum), are but three Islip-Oakdale survivors of the phenomenon. So momentous for the North Shore was the decision of the Manhattan-based Seawanhaka Corinthian Yacht Club to build a waterfront facility on Oyster Bay's Centre Island in 1892, that within the next thirty-five years, over forty of its members had built mansions in the vicinity. These individuals, including

Left: Reminiscent of a European cafe with its alfresco dining area and apron-clad waiters, the Beaux-Arts Casino and Cafe in Huntington was an elegant turn-of-the-century gathering spot. (SPLIA)

Below: Many Long Island estate grounds were laid out by well-known architects, and mature trees were imported and transplanted by such nurseries as the Hicks Brothers of Westbury, shown here at the Herbert Pratt estate circa 1912. Courtesy, Hicks Photograph Collection

J.P. Morgan, whose residence was demolished in 1980, and Marshall Field, whose homestead is currently part of Caumsett State Park, had no previous connection to Long Island. A further comparison of construction dates and polo team rosters indicates that almost all the great country estates erected between Old Westbury and North Hills during this period were for aspiring players wearing the sky blue shirts of the Meadow Brook Club. By the turn of the century, sporting interests determined the building sites of mansions. Competition between the organizations was quite real. After continuous boundary disputes, the Meadow Brook Club and the Rockaway Hunt "divided" Nassau County's foxing grounds along an east-west line at Mineola.

So rapid was the pace of mansion construction that in the eighteen years between 1900 and America's entry into World War I, 325 country houses of over twenty-five rooms were constructed east of the Queens line. New York City firms were forced to open Long Island branches in order to handle the volume of business. Many leading contractors spe-

cializing in country houses picked centrally located Hicksville for their headquarters. Lewis and Valentine, the landscapers with offices at 47 West 37th Street in New York, boasted no less than four Long Island nurseries by the 1920s. Architects generally viewed Long Island as synonymous with country house design; 146 firms are recorded to have built mansions in Nassau and Suffolk counties in the eighty years leading up to the Second World War. One company of landscape contractors, the fa-

Left: Built in 1899 by the prominent architect Richard Howland Hunt, William K. Vanderbilt, Sr.'s Idle Hour was an elaborate country estate that included a 110-room mansion, a boat house, coach house, tea house, bowling alley, indoor tennis court, glass conservatory, and a farm complex. (SPLIA)

121

WILLIAM CULLEN BRYANT

Best remembered as a poet and the editor of the *New York Evening Post,* William Cullen Bryant (1794-1878) first received national attention with the publication of the poem "Thanatopsis" at the tender age of seventeen. Perhaps the most famous of his works, this poem's weighty subject, the contemplation of death, caught the attention of nineteenth-century literary notables, including Richard Henry Dana. Surprised at its excellence in expression and style, Dana, then editor of the *North American Review,* published the work, which received wide critical acclaim. It is considered today to be the first significant and true example of American poetry. In addition to his great literary prowess which produced hundreds of published poems, Bryant authored numerous essays and travel books, and even translated such classics as Homer's *Illiad* (1870) and *Odyssey* (1871).

As the editor of the *Post,* Bryant was the first to utilize the editorship of a major newspaper to promote numerous social and political causes. The main issues that placed Bryant in the national forefront were the antislavery movement and the labor movement. In addition, Bryant was the leading proponent of the creation of Central Park, strongly supporting the selection of Frederick Law Olmsted as its landscape architect.

Having been born and raised in

the countryside of Cummington, Massachusetts, Bryant frequently tried to find a country home close to his work in New York City. Drawn initially to the North Hempstead area by a land development promotion in 1837, Bryant subsequently purchased "Springbrook," a simple farmhouse built in 1787, from historian Joseph W. Moulton in 1842. The house, situated in what is now Roslyn Harbor, had been extensively altered by this time to reflect the fashionable Greek Revival style favored by its former owner. Bryant pro-

ceeded in what would be a lifelong undertaking to enlarge and embellish the estate's natural beauty. It was about this time that Bryant changed the name of his estate to "Cedarmere," as it is known today, and altered the structure to mirror his tastes and needs. He enlarged the main house to accommodate the large number of friends and associates who were invited to Cedarmere during his fifty years of residence along the harbor.

Bryant's guest list included many of the nineteenth century's most prominent figures from the world of art, literature, and politics. Among them were actors Edwin Forrest and Edwin Booth, tastemaker Andrew Jackson Downing, and artists Thomas Cole, Asher B. Durand, Daniel Huntington, and Robert Weir. Orville Dewey, probably the most prominent American theologian of the first half of the nineteenth century, was a frequent visitor and his younger sister, Jerusha, later became Bryant's tenant. Bryant continued to write poetry at Cedarmere and this interest attracted Dana and poet Fitz-Greene Halleck, novelists James Fenimore Cooper, Carolyn Kirkland, and William Gilmore Simms, and America's most famous sculptor, Horatio Greenough.

Possessing an almost congenial aptitude for architecture and landscape design, Bryant contributed greatly to the beauty and growth of his newfound community, which he helped rename Roslyn in 1844. As Bryant continued to work on his own house, he also completed or altered a number of other buildings on the estate. Quite early in his ownership, probably in 1844, he built "Golden-Rod Cottage," which served as his house while Cedarmere was being altered. Later it became the home of his daughter Fanny and her husband, Parke Godwin.

In one way or another Bryant participated in the construction or alteration of at least twenty buildings in and around Cedarmere. In 1869 Orville Dewey wrote, "Don't look down from your lordiness, of owning a dozen houses, and three of them you own to live in." Singleton Mitchell's survey of the Bryant property in 1875 recorded fifteen buildings, including two mills. One of these, a board-and-batten structure with superb vergeboards, seems to have been built circa 1860 in large part as a garden ornament, as it is spectacularly sited on a hillside between the pond and the harbor. The architect of this "Gothic Mill" is not known; possibly it was designed by Bryant himself. It is generally accepted today that the estate's dramatic, romantic landscape was designed as well as developed by Bryant. All this activity in the development of the natural and built landscape at the highest possible level contributed immeasurably to the architectural quality of Roslyn and its surroundings, which survives to this day. Happily, most of Bryant's houses still stand. Some, like "Golden-Rod," have been vastly altered, while others like George Cline's "Stone Cottage" have experienced few changes and the superb "Gothic Mill" remains untouched. Cedarmere, now called "Cedar Mere," is owned by the Nassau County Department of Parks and Recreation and plans are being developed for its restoration.

Dr. Roger Gerry
Anthony Cucchiara

Opposite page: William Cullen Bryant (right) confers with Long Island manufacturer and inventor Peter Cooper at Cedarmere in 1875. They discussed Cooper's plans to run for President on the Greenback ticket. Courtesy, Nassau County Museum

Left: Writing to a friend, William Cullen Bryant exclaimed, "At last, I have a house and land on Long Island, a little plain house in a most beautiful neighborhood ..." He continually enlarged and embellished Cedarmere during his lifetime. From the Clarence Purchase Photograph Collection, SPLIA

Left: Pembroke, the home of wealthy businessman J.R. DeLamar (1843-1918), is a striking example of one of the many elaborate mansions and country estates built on Long Island at the turn of the century. From Town & Country Magazine, *December 1921*

Opposite page: Technically innovative and later emulated, the Long Island Motor Parkway was the first limited access concrete toll road ever built on such a grand scale. Its twelve gate houses and inn were designed by architect John Russell Pope. (SPLIA)

Right: Long Island's country estates were the sites of banquets, balls, and weddings, such as this wedding reception for Helen and Ernest Dane at the Pratt estate in Glen Cove. Courtesy, Lawrence and Anne Van Ingen

mous Olmsted Brothers of Brookline, Massachusetts, were commissioned to design the grounds of no less than fifty Long Island estates. Cromwell Childs, in a 1902 *Brooklyn Daily Eagle* article, marvelled at the pace at which these special homes were being built:

No side of the life of New York is more interesting than the splendid way men of wealth and fashion have thrown themselves into making country places. One year a bare hillside, a field, a rugged short front; then rumors of its purchase from the farmers who have owned it for generations go about; suddenly a sale is recorded at the county seat, and the next year a transformation has been wrought where but a few months before there was undeveloped country, now a summer home stands, all but complete.

To agriculturalists, baymen, and merchants the resort boom appeared to be an invasion akin to the coming of the seventeenth-century Europeans. Hundreds of farms were displaced by the phenomenon. When assembling his Manhasset estate, Payne Whitney purchased five such tracts, uprooting families who had owned the land since the eighteenth century. Willie Vanderbilt bought six or seven farms to build his Lake Success place, Deepdale. Perhaps the greatest construction feat occurred when utility magnate John E. Aldred and New York attorney W.D. Guthrie bought up the entire village of Lattingtown, comprising over sixty structures, to build their adjoining estates. The hamlet was then demolished, as Guthrie later told the *World Telegram,* "to get the view we wanted." Westbury nurseryman Issac Hicks wrote in 1900 that the "wealthy ones" were paying more for the land than its agricultural worth. Farming production fell rapidly in the estate areas, and by 1904 *The Long Islander* of Huntington reported that only one packet carrying agricultural produce now made runs to New York in season, where formerly there had been three making trips year-round.

Displacement was not the only effect of the resort boom. Whole industries, such as the Duryea starch works at Glen Cove and the brickyards in Cold Spring Harbor, disappeared due to labor and raw material problems linked to the boom. Bitter shore rights disputes erupted between opulent landowners and town governments. Baymen working the Centre Island beaches cut holes through estate docks which blocked their horse carts. Not even Main Street was pleased with the new realities. In a 1904 editorial, *The Long Islander* expressed the views of many of its merchant subscribers, stating: "When farms have been cut up and sold in plots" for "summer villas" the change had been "beneficial," but "where large tracts of hundreds of acres are monopolized for the enjoyment of a single owner, the change is to be regretted."

In time the estates did win a large measure of acceptance from Long Islanders whose world had been altered by their arrival. Willie Vanderbilt had predicted as much in 1902, when the citizens of North Hempstead had expressed concern that his proposed acquisition of Lake Success would prevent the men who cut ice there from making a living. Didn't they realize, Vanderbilt told the press, how many people would be employed in the castle he planned to build? A staff numbering in the teens was required to run even a modest country house, and fifty was not an uncommon number. Four hundred were allegedly put to work during the heyday of the Pratt Oval, the service complex for the adjoining Pratt family estates in Glen Cove. For many, the estates offered year-round employment at better wages. The brick works in Cold Spring Harbor, for example, is said to have closed after its workers left for better paying jobs on the area's new estates. To agrarian Long Island, which had been in decline since the opening of the Erie Canal and the era when railroads brought cheap western staples to the New York markets, the estates promised increased opportunities. Indeed, Long Island's entire service and transportation infrastructure originated with the resort period. We have already explored

the connection between the expansion of the Long Island Rail Road and the resort hotel. The Vanderbilt Motor Parkway, in which dozens of estate owners held stock, was conceived partially as a commuter road, a precursor of the Robert Moses-era parkways which were heavily influenced by it. Just think of it, noted A.R. Pardington, the chief engineer, in a 1907 article in *Harper's Weekly*:

Think of the time it will save the busy man of affairs, who likes to crowd into each day a bit of relaxation. He will leave downtown at three o'clock in the afternoon, take the subway to a garage within striking distance of the new Blackwells Island-East River Bridge. In twenty minutes a 60 horse-power car will have him at the western terminus of the motor parkway. Here a card of admission passes him through the gates, speed limits are left behind, the great white way is before him, and with throttle open he can go, go, go and keep going fifty, sixty or ninety miles an hour until Riverhead or Southampton is reached.

The Nassau Light and Power Company, the nucleus of what became the Long Island Lighting Company in 1922, began with E.D. Morgan's desire to obtain electricity for his Wheatley Hills Estate in the 1890s. The hand of the seasonal resident is also seen in the spread of telephone service commencing as early as 1884 in the summer community of Glen Cove.

The Nassau Hospital (now Winthrop University Hospital) in Mineola, Long Island's first voluntary,

Alva Vanderbilt Belmont became a leading figure in the women's suffrage movement, implementing an experimen- *tal agricultural school for women on her Hempstead estate in 1911. From Brown Brothers Endpapers*

In cultural life, Long Island's first art museums, the Heckscher at Huntington and the Parrish at Southampton, were the gifts of prominent summer residents. The hand of the estate owners is even seen in the development of Long Island's primary industry of the twentieth century—aviation. When flying was still thought to be something of a daredevil's sport with few practical applications, these individuals invested in aeronautics. Nelson Doubleday's popular magazine, *Country Life in America,* chronicled the leisure activities of the rich and gave monthly coverage to the exciting new pastime of flying. August Belmont, a director of Orville and Wilbur Wright's airplane company, was behind the first international air show at Belmont Park in 1910. Its top prize of $10,000 had been put up by another Long Island millionaire, Thomas Fortune Ryan of Manhasset. The summer community even brought attention to the area through politics. On becoming the Democratic nominee in 1924, John W. Davis of Locust Valley rounded out a quarter of a century of Long Island presidential aspirations begun by Theodore Roosevelt.

In developing new employment opportunities and improved public services, the resort period also put Long Island on the map. A barrier island, this agrarian outpost which had been passed over by the industrial revolution for lack of falling water to power mill turbines, suddenly found itself featured in every periodical in America. By the time "the Gold Coast," as the press began to call the North Shore, was at its height, the editors or publishers of the Brooklyn *Daily Eagle,* and the New York *Sun, Post, World,* and *Tribune* all summered there. Conde Nast, who was to own *Vogue, House and Garden, Glamour* and many more magazines, resided at Sands Point. Ralph Pulitzer and William Randolph Hearst spent the warm months on Long Island for a while, as did various members of the Lamont, Whitney, and Guggenheim families, newspaper owners at one time or another. The heads of publishing houses were also very much in evidence. Ormand G. Smith, of the huge dime novel house of Smith and Street, lived on Centre Island. Not far away was the Mill Neck Estate of Nelson Doubleday, whose Country Life Press was headquartered in Garden City. Great Neck also became the favored world of writers and Broadway luminaries. Ring Lardner and F. Scott Fitzgerald summered

non-profit hospital east of the city line, moved in 1900 from temporary quarters to its first permanent buildings. Located near the railroad tracks, it allowed patients to be brought in from the more distant reaches of Suffolk County. The edifice was designed by no less a figure than Richard Morris Hunt, architect of the Vanderbilt "cottages" at Newport and Oakdale, and Nassau's first wards were named for its major patrons, the Vanderbilts, Harpers, and Belmonts. Estate owners were also involved in the development of community hospitals. Yet, no one did more to establish advanced health care on Long Island than the Whitneys, who largely funded later expansion of the Nassau Hospital and the growth of the North Shore University Hospital at Manhasset.

there, the latter writing much of *The Great Gatsby* in a room over the garage of the Spanish Colonial house at Six Gateway Drive which he and Zelda had rented in 1922. Sinclair Lewis also toured Long Island, as did P.G. Wodehouse and Frances Burnett, who had a substantial estate in Plandome. Many parties were held at both Eddie Cantor's and George M. Cohan's places. Basil Rathbone, Lew Field, Ed Wynn, and Jane Cowl frequented the North Shore, to mention just a few celebrities. Will Rogers hit his head on a rock while diving in the Great South Bay during one of the many summers he resided at the Massapequa estate of vaudeville actor Fred Stone. Some of Stone's other friends who summered in the Freeport and Massapequa areas were Annie Oakley, Eddie Foy, Victor Moore, and George "Spider" Murphy. The Astoria Studios made Long Island an early filming center, and many of the producers, including the president of the American Vitagraph Corporation, Albert E. Smith, lived in Nassau County. Near Smith's Centre Island estate there survives a unique boathouse in the form of a ship's stern, said to have been built as part of a 1914 movie set.

Long Island's varied topography and scenic qualities also attracted the attention of artists. East Hampton on the "East End" of the Island had been an early mecca for a loosely based art colony drawn to sandy beaches, a rural atmosphere, and the ever-changing play of light on sea and dunes. One of the first to arrive and build a studio was the painter and etcher, Thomas Moran. He and his artist wife, Mary Nimmo Moran, were to be followed in the 1870s by other artists including Lockwood de Forest, Winslow Homer, Charles Henry Miller, and Childe Hassam. Wealthy summer residents also encouraged the prominent painter and teacher, William Merritt Chase, to form a studio and art school in Southampton in the 1890s. This group of artists, often collectively called the "American Barbizon," painted the Long Island landscape in a wide range of styles, and the East End to this day has continued to attract contemporary artists and painters such as William de Kooning and Lee Krasner.

Cold Spring Harbor was the site of another type of artist colony, more a retreat than a school, formed briefly in 1920 by Louis Comfort Tiffany at his summer estate, Laurelton. As an artist who worked in many fields, including painting, jewelry, stained

Irene and Vernon Castle were a well-known dance team who popularized the tango and other dances. They had a country home in Manhasset near F. Scott Fitzgerald, and epitomized the glamour and excitment of the 1920s. (SPLIA)

glass, textiles, interior decoration, and landscape architecture, Tiffany conceived and designed this lavish mansion. Both inside and out, it represented his love of the exotic and was greatly influenced by Oriental and Moorish art. Under the aegis of the L.C. Tiffany Foundation, the artist had his carriage

THEODORE ROOSEVELT: LONG ISLAND'S PRESIDENT

Theodore Roosevelt speaks to women suffragists at Sagamore Hill in 1917. Courtesy, Sagamore Hill National Historic Site, Oyster Bay

Theodore Roosevelt, descended from a long line of sturdy Dutch Knickerbockers, was the seventh generation of his family born on the island of Manhattan. He is often called "Long Island's President," however, and rightfully so, because Roosevelt's life since boyhood was linked to Oyster Bay, on Long Island's North Shore.

Cornelius Van Schaack Roosevelt (1794-1871), Theodore's grandfather, is considered the founder of the "Oyster Bay Roosevelts." The old patriarch, who lived on Union Square in New York City, spent summers in Oyster Bay, and he was followed to the North Shore by his sons and their families. Theodore loved Long Island, and after he married he decided to build a home in Oyster Bay. In 1883 Roosevelt, then an

assemblyman from Manhattan, bought land on Cove Neck, a small peninsula to the east of the village of Oyster Bay. The following year he began construction of a spacious house, completed in 1885 and called "Sagamore Hill," after the Sagamore (or chief) Mohannis who had lived with his Indian tribe on the land centuries before. Other Roosevelts, too, built on Cove Neck, and eventually (long before the Kennedy compound in Hyannis Port) there were four Roosevelt

households and sixteen Roosevelt children in Oyster Bay.

Roosevelt took up residence at Sagamore Hill in 1887, after marrying his childhood friend Edith Kermit Carow, who had shared summers with the Roosevelts on the North Shore. At Sagamore Hill, Theodore and Edith raised a lively brood of six children: Alice (born to Roosevelt's first wife in 1884), Theodore, Jr. (born in 1887), Kermit (1889), Ethel (1891), Archibald (1894), and Quentin (1897). When Roosevelt became President in 1901—at forty-two he was the youngest President in history, before or since—Americans for the first time had a "first family," as the nation affectionately embraced the youthful Chief Executive and his winsome family. The Roosevelt family of Sagamore Hill was considered by Americans at the turn of the century to be the perfect model of all that was culturally revered in home life.

Much history was made at Sagamore Hill. There the nation watched the return of the colonel of the Rough Riders, after his Spanish-American War regiment was mustered out at Montauk Point, Long Island. There committees of Republicans came to officially notify Roosevelt of his nomination for governor of New York in 1898, for Vice President in 1900, and, after he entered the White House following the assassination of William McKinley, for

President in 1904. During the Roosevelt administration, 1901-1909, Sagamore Hill served as the "summer White House," the first of the noted presidential establishments outside the nation's capital. Many important meetings and conferences were held there, including the preliminary negotiations for the Portsmouth Treaty, which ended the Russo-Japanese War and earned Roosevelt the Nobel Peace Prize. There, after Roosevelt left the Presidency, supporters and reporters continued to come, day after day, to hear what "the Colonel" had to say about the affairs of the nation and the world. And there, on January 6, 1919, at the age of sixty, Roosevelt died.

The day before his death, Roosevelt had remarked to his wife, "I wonder if you will ever know how much I love Sagamore Hill." Sagamore Hill had a special place in the hearts of many Americans, too, and after Mrs. Roosevelt's death there at the age of eighty-seven in 1948, the house was purchased by the Theodore Roosevelt Association. It opened to the public in 1953. The Association gave Sagamore Hill to the National Park Service in 1963, and the house, one of the most famous in American history, is today probably the most popular public site on Long Island.

The early part of Theodore Roosevelt's life, when he was a summer sojourner on the North Shore, coincided with the rise of Long Island as a popular summer resort area. Roosevelt's adult years, when he made his home in Oyster Bay, witnessed the transformation of Long Island into a land of estates and suburbs. The Roosevelts were among the first to migrate eastward from New York City to enjoy the pleasant Long Island summers, and to take up yachting on the Long Island Sound. And later Roosevelt, who did not have the money to maintain a separate residence in New York City, was part of the first generation of commuters—people who lived on Long Island but worked in New York City or elsewhere. Roosevelt's prominence put Long Island in the public eye as perhaps never before, and his life spanned much of the making of modern Long Island, in which he played an important role.

Theodore Roosevelt's accomplishments, interests, and activities were many and varied; he was a naturalist, historian, hunter, intellectual rancher, explorer, soldier, writer, politician, conservationist, and public official. Roosevelt had a lifetime interest in natural history, and while still a student at Harvard he published a paper, "Notes on Some of the Birds of Oyster Bay, Long Island" (1879), one of the early works on Long Island ornithology. Near the end of his life, in 1915, he was the founder and first president of the Long Island Bird Club. Roosevelt studied, collected, and wrote about wildlife in North America, Africa, and South America. His interest in natural history led to his involvement with conservation; as President, Roosevelt established five national parks and set aside eighteen national monuments, including the Grand Canyon. He increased the federal forest preserves by over 300 percent and created the first federal wildlife refuges, including fifty-one for birds. A man of letters as well as an outdoorsman, Roosevelt wrote histories, biographies and numerous volumes on public affairs and his many adventures.

TR was a major figure in American politics for nearly forty years, and served as New York State assemblyman in the early 1880s; United States Civil Service commissioner, 1889-1895; president of the Board of Police Commissioners of New York City, 1895-1897; assistant secretary of the Navy, 1897-1898; governor of New York, 1898-1900; Vice President of the United States in 1901; and President of the United States, 1901-1909. As President, Roosevelt busted the trusts, built the Panama Canal, and promoted consumer protection and the regulation of big business. Long Island's President was, said the writer Julian Street, "the most interesting American."

John A. Gable

L.C. Tiffany (1848-1933), son of the founder of Tiffany & Company, was an artist who worked in many mediums, most notably stained glass. His eighty-room mansion at Cold Spring Harbor was the scene of many social events; here Tiffany is dressed as an Eastern potentate for one of his elaborate masquerade balls. Courtesy, Mrs. Collier Pratt

house converted into a studio and used his estate to encourage young artists. Although it did not last long for financial reasons, Tiffany's art community was based on a new concept in which artists working in different mediums were brought together to "study decoration from nature." Bellport on the ocean side of the Island also drew its share of artists. From 1907 to 1930 four large summer hotels attracted such visitors as painters Everett Shinn, William Glackens, Ernest Lawford, and John Sloan, as well as such journalists and editors as Walter Lippman, Frank Crowninshield, and Edna Woolman Chase.

By the time *Forbes Magazine's* founder, B.C. Forbes, wrote his 1919 bestseller, *Fifty Men Who Are Making America,* twenty-five titans of American industry and finance either summered on Long Island or had children who owned country houses east of the Queens line. The names of these "movers and shakers" read like a *Who's Who* of the monied communities, and include George F. Baker, Jr., son of George F. Baker, known as the "Sphinx of Wall Street" and President of First National Bank of New York; J.P. Morgan, Jr., heir to the immense banking house; Nicholas Brady, financier and utility magnate who contributed to the formation of Consolidated Edison; Mortimer Schiff, son of Jacob

Schiff, head of Kuhn, Loeb and Company; John C. Ryan, financier Thomas Fortune Ryan's scion; and Howard Gould, son and heir to the brokerage and financial assets of Jay Gould. Among the industrialists were Walter P. Chrysler, founder of the Chrysler Corporation; Henry Ford II; the sons of Andrew Carnegie's partners, Henry Phipps and Henry Clay Frick; and the Graces of shipping line fame. Charles Pratt, of Pratt Institute and Standard Oil, created a unique family compound in Glen Cove that comprised twenty-one estates. As already mentioned, the Vanderbilts, who inherited a transportation empire that included railroads and shipping lines started by Commodore Cornelius Vanderbilt, and four of the seven sons of Meyer Guggenheim, the mining magnate, sometimes called Long Island home. Over 900 mansions dotted the landscape from the city line to Montauk. The area had become the great national playground, "a slender and riotous island," as F. Scott Fitzgerald put it, basking in a visibility it had never before known. Even a future king of England, Edward, Prince of Wales, was impressed when he came to the Island for 1924 polo matches. "My American hosts spared no expense in demonstrating the splendor of a modern industrial republic," he said. Edward was later to note that "compared to the creature comforts Americans took for granted, the luxury I was accustomed to in Europe seemed almost primitive." The Prince saw Long Island as the showcase for "a country in which nothing was impossible." As late as 1946, *Life* was to call it "the most socially desirable residential area in the United States," and *Holiday* reported that "while time is making some changes," it was clear that the "estates of Long Island's North Shore are close to an American ultimate in elegance, exclusiveness and display."

The highlight of the 1924 social season on Long Island was undoubtedly the visit from Edward, Prince of Wales. The prince was feted and entertained on a grand scale *by a number of prominent Long Islanders, including the Burdens and Pratts. From* Spur *magazine, September 1924*

Many of the titans of business and industry summered on Long Island. Pictured from left to right are Matthew S. Sloan, James Cox Brady, Nicholas F. Brady, Thomas E. Murray, Thomas A. Edison, and Walter P. Chrysler. Edison summered in Quoque from 1913-19, and the Sloan estate at Sands Point was the scene of many parties during the 1920s. Nicholas Brady's estate in Manhasset has become a Catholic retreat, while Chrysler's Kings Point estate is now the home of the U.S. Merchant Marine Academy. From Chrysler, Life of an American Workman, *1937*

The factors which were to bring the resort period to a close, however, had begun long before the post-World War II period. In his 1968 treatise, *Dynamics of Community Change,* author Daniel Sobin has chronicled the litany of transformations which ended Long Island's great estate period. Contributing factors included the 1916 appearance of the federal income tax, the establishment of the gift tax in 1932, the 1924 restrictive immigration law effecting servant procurement, the rise in local property assessments, the development of air travel, the construction of the Robert Moses parkway system, and passage of the G.I. Bill. *American Magazine* was informing its readers in 1948 of the great "Bargains in Dream Houses" on Long Island. Henceforth, the most frequent buyers of mansions were to be developers planning subdivisions. The epoch of the great estates was over, but their legacy would continue to shape life on Long Island in the future. Even the majority of the mansions would survive, finding a wide range of adaptive reuses. Largely as country clubs, educational facilities, and cultural institutions, the splendid palaces leave Long Island with a unique architectural heritage and a rich patina of history.

CHAPTER SEVEN

Brooklyn from the Civil War to the Great Renunciation

Nineteenth-century Brooklyn was a city in motion, continually changing from a place that was relatively small, simple, and stable into one that was large, complex, and volatile. With every year that passed, the emerging metropolis grew more like its rival across the East River and less like the surrounding villages and farms of eastern Long Island. Nowhere were the changes more pronounced than in the size and composition of Brooklyn's famous neighborhoods. Way back when Robert Fulton was proposing his first ferry scheme, most Brooklyn residents were of either Dutch or Anglo-American extraction. Beginning in the 1840s, however, large numbers of German and Irish immigrants arrived, and by 1860 just under 40 percent of the population was foreign-born. Over 55,000 Irishmen constituted the largest foreign-born group, while 23,000 Germans added a large non-English speaking contingent. Catholics, once a tiny minority, accounted for about half of all churchgoers. By 1860 Brooklyn was only slightly less "ethnic" than the nearby melting pot of Manhattan and its population was growing even faster than that of New York City.

The astonishing growth of Long Island's major city accelerated after the Civil War as a population of 266,000 quadrupled to over 1,150,000 at the turn of the century. And Brooklyn's population continued changing as it mushroomed. By 1890 the Germans constituted the largest ethnic group, while immigration from southern and eastern Europe brought numerous Jews, Italians, and Slavs. In fact, the number of Brooklyn's foreign-born citizens at the close of the nineteenth century equalled its total population forty years earlier. Valuing mutual support, familiar customs, and the same language, ethnic groups colonized particular neighborhoods:

The Brooklyn Bridge, standing amidst the fireworks on its opening night in May 1883, is still considered to be one of the most beautiful bridges in the world. Its construction sparked the imagination of an entire generation and reflected Brooklyn's potential. Courtesy, The Metropolitan Museum of Art, gift of Edward C. Arnold

Left: Dr. Susan Smith McKenney-Steward (1847-1918) was the first black female physician in Brooklyn and in New York State. Born in Weeksville, she was an important figure in black Brooklyn's intellectual and social circles during the late nineteenth century. Courtesy, The Long Island Historical Society

Below: At one time covering 145 acres, the Brooklyn Navy Yard was kept busy during every major conflict since the Civil War. The Indiana, *part of the U.S. fleet in the Spanish-American War, is depicted here in 1898. Courtesy, The Long Island Historical Society*

the Germans in Williamsburg, the Jews in Brownsville, and the Italians in Red Hook and South Brooklyn. Nearly 19,000 blacks lived in Brooklyn, too.

Underlying such rapid growth, and giving great vitality to the entire Brooklyn experience, was the surging nineteenth-century economic boom that transformed Manhattan's first suburb into a major city in its own right. Like its population, Brooklyn's economy became ever more dynamic. This development owed much to regional and national factors which spurred dramatic urbanization: the transportation revolution, European immigration, the growth of transatlantic commerce, the opening of western lands and resources, the spread of southern cotton culture, the rapid development of technology, and the rise of factory production.

But the Long Island metropolis also benefitted from its closeness to neighboring New York. A direct consequence of this proximity was the explosive growth of Brooklyn's real estate industry, thriving on the population boom and the region's popularity as a residence for middle-class New Yorkers. Brooklyn also controlled Long Island's gateways to Manhattan and flourished with the

trade, transportation, and transshipment functions which occurred at the entrepot. By the same token, Manhattan's commerce soon outgrew its own wharves and spilled across the East River. The Atlantic Docks in South Brooklyn, designed to warehouse grain, symbolized this development. Commerce likewise attracted the resources for manufacturing, and local industry benefitted greatly from these trends. Sugar refining prospered, especially the famous firm of Havemeyer and Elder, which later became Amstar. Brooklyn's shipyards built yachts, cargo vessels, and a host of warships, including the famous Civil War *Monitor.* Though Brooklyn in 1860 trailed far behind New York and Philadelphia in manufactures, it equalled Boston, and led Chicago, Baltimore, and St. Louis.

The same expansive economic trends continued unabated during the second half of the century and by 1900 had transformed Brooklyn into the fourth largest manufacturing center in the United States, a sugar refining giant, and a brewing, warehousing, and meat packing center. Furthermore, local docks handled the bulk of New York's cargo. From an agricultural village in 1800, Brooklyn developed into a commercial and industrial goliath.

Transit construction helped energize and facilitate Brooklyn's economic and population growth. By 1890, 2,500 cars drawn by 8,000 horses served the city, but their days were numbered and that same year the first all-electric trolley line opened to Coney Island. Most other lines were electrified in the next five years. The same era witnessed the introduction of elevated steam railroads (1885), and in 1896 the Brooklyn Rapid Transit Company organized a near monoply of the city's lines to become one of the largest transit companies in the world.

In the pre-automobile age, trollies and elevated trains were indispensable. They not only carried millions of passengers monthly, but hauled freight, removed trash, carted the mail (Brooklyn was the first city to do so), and even hosted parties in special parlour cars which rented for fifteen dollars an evening. These conveyances unfortunately proved rather dangerous for pedestrians, enough to make the "Trolley Dodgers" nickname more than a little grim. Nevertheless, they provided the framework for growth in an interdependent metropolis. Riders increasingly travelled somewhere to play or relax.

Nineteenth-century urban America produced no more profound change than the "Leisure Revolution." By concentrating masses of people and separating them from their former rural pastimes, urbanism both encouraged and necessitated the development of alternate forms of recreation. Brooklyn assumed a leading role in this recreation movement with Prospect Park, the sporting mania, and Coney Island playing the most important roles.

New and better recreational facilities were paramount. Local park reformers expected a lot from their natural settings—an antidote to urban living, encouragement of upright values, and a prestige symbol in the struggle with Manhattan. Early efforts centered on saving Brooklyn Heights as a promenade. This campaign failed; but in the 1830s and 1840s the first city park was built on reclaimed land near Wallabout Bay, and Washington Park

Above: The elevated railroad or "el" greatly improved Brooklyn's rapid transit. It also boosted real estate development, for in the year that it opened 2,000 new houses were built along its routes. Courtesy, The Long Island Historical Society

Left: The E.W. Bliss Machine Shop and Foundry, built in 1879, exemplified Brooklyn's industrial growth during the 1880s. In just a few years Bliss had built up a prosperous business manufacturing iron, brass, and tin for household and commercial use. From Stiles, History of Kings County Including the City of Brooklyn, Munsell, 1884

Above: Frederick Law Olmsted (1822-1903) developed the use of natural landscape resources in the construction of urban parks and recreational grounds. He designed more than eighty public parks in the United States. From Cirker, Dictionary of American Portraits, *Dover, 1967*

Below: Prospect Park's Brooklyn Plaza, later to become Grand Army Plaza, was designed and built in many stages. The park itself had just been completed when this photo was taken circa 1875. Courtesy, George B. Brainerd Photograph Collection, Brooklyn Public Library

opened in 1847. Nineteenth-century urbanites considered rural cemeteries to be parks as well as burial grounds. Creation of Greenwood Cemetery in 1838 put Brooklyn in the forefront of this movement. These initial successes, plus the example of Manhattan's Central Park in the 1850s, led to a decision in 1860 to build a great park system. Designed by Calvert Vaux and Frederick Law Olmsted, the architects of Central Park, Brooklyn's Prospect Park was completed in 1874 and soon became one of the nation's finest pleasure grounds, a fitting tribute to both its landscape architects, park commission president James S.T. Stranahan, and the Brooklyn elite which had espoused parks reform since the 1830s.

The completion of Prospect Park came just in time to encourage another part of Brooklyn's leisure revolution, the rise of participatory sports. Such pastimes existed earlier in the century, but from the 1880s onward a sporting mania developed. As in other cities, local aristocrats fostered the introduction of sports to Brooklyn both individually and through organizations like the prestigious Crescent Athletic Club. While tennis, golf, yachting, and equestrian activities remained upperclass monopolies, baseball, basketball, bicycling, and football soon became popular with middle- and working-class groups. Ethnic fraternities retained their own special activities like the gymnastics of the Germans, the handball of the Irish, and the Highland Games of the Scots. Since Brooklyn enjoyed easy access to nearby open spaces, older rural sports like boating, hunting, and fishing also persisted longer there than in other urban areas.

The original Dutch farmsteads so numerous in Brooklyn were slowly succumbing to urban sprawl by the time of this nostalgic 1864 watercolor by James Ryder Van Brunt. Courtesy, The Long Island Historical Society

In this 1880 watercolor of Smithtown Bay and the mouth of the Nissequogue River, Long Island artist Edward Lange captures nineteenth-century Long Island with picnickers on the beach, horse drawn carriages, and sloops and schooners plying the river. Courtesy, private collection

The completion of the Brooklyn Bridge inspired many artists and writers to celebrate man's triumph over nature. The bridge's towering stature is made clear in this watercolor by Warren L. Harris. Courtesy, National Archives

With over ten shipyards operating at one time, Northport was a busy harbor community through the greater part of the nineteenth century. This 1880 watercolor by Edward Lange depicts Northport's Lower Main Street running eastward from the dock. Courtesy, Mrs. D.C. Bushnell

The interior of Louis C. Tiffany's Cold Spring Harbor estate uniquely expressed his interest in Oriental and Moorish art. The central court featured a crystal water fountain crowned with a dome of Tiffany glass. (SPLIA)

Prominent among the many artists who summered on Long Island, William Merritt Chase (1849-1916) was considered one of the foremost landscape and portrait painters of his day. He painted many views of the Island's East End, such as "Bayberry Bush," which depicts the Shinnecock Hills. Courtesy, Parrish Art Museum, Southampton

Left: Promotional brochures, such as this one issued by the Southampton Chamber of Commerce circa 1917, often touted the recreational opportunities available at Long Island's shorefront communities. (SPLIA)

Opposite page: Coney Island's promoters built several extravagant amusement parks at the turn of the century, attracting a wide audience to the previously upper- and middle-class summer resort. Luna Park featured unique electrical illuminations and exhibits, as seen in this circa 1905 postcard. (SPLIA)

Above: Hunters once gathered at the Southside Sportsmen's Club, which now serves as the superintendent's residence at Connetquot River State Park in West Sayville. Photo by Barbara C. Harrison

Polo developed on Long Island at the turn of the century and continues to be popular today. Here, players from Bethpage (green shirts) and Huntington (yellow shirts) compete at Bethpage State Park. Photo by Barbara C. Harrison

The home of the Brooklyn Dodgers for over forty-four years, Ebbets Field opened in 1913 with a seating capacity of 35,000. Named after Dodgers owner Charles H. Ebbets, the stadium was razed in 1960 to make way for an apartment complex. Courtesy, The Long Island Historical Society

CHARLES PRATT

Horatio Alger had nothing on Charles Pratt (1830-1891). One of eleven children of a Watertown, Massachusetts cabinetmaker, he left home at the age of thirteen to become a clerk in a Boston grocery store. Twenty-four years later, he founded the Astral Oil Works on Bushwick Creek and the East River in Williamsburg (now Brooklyn). Business boomed. Pratt's Astral Oil, a high-quality kerosene used in lamps that was notably less prone to explode than most competing fuels, became a great international success. In 1874, the Pratt combine was acquired by John D. Rockefeller, and Pratt became a major force in the Standard Oil Company. When he died, he was almost certainly the richest man in Brooklyn, and one of the wealthiest in the United States.

There are several explanations for Pratt's success. Astral Oil was, quite simply, a superior product, and the demand for a high-quality yet safe illuminating oil was virtually insatiable. Also, more than most refiners, Pratt found markets for the many petroleum by-products that were separated out during the refining process: varnish, turpentine, naphtha, paraffin, asphalt, and so forth. Perhaps even more important in his success was his creative use of machinery and his emphasis on efficient production. The Astral Oil Works was considered the model refinery in the industry.

Charles Pratt, industrialist and philanthropist, was one of Brooklyn's leading citizens in the late nineteenth century. Courtesy, Pratt Institute

Pratt took his philanthropic concerns seriously. His greatest interest was in what we would today call vocational education. In 1887 he founded Pratt Institute in Brooklyn for the training of skilled artisans, designers, and draftsmen; there were twelve students the first year, over 600 the second year, and several thousand a few years later. Pratt was insistent that the institute serve "all classes of workers, artists, artisans, apprentices and homemakers." Courses would "give every student practical skill along some definite line of work, and at the same time reveal . . . possibilities for further development and study." Admission was open to those of every educational background, and "persons of both sexes." The first black student enrolled in 1888. Tuition, $2.50 per course in the early years, was kept well below cost.

Ever practical, Pratt built the Institute so that it could be converted into a shoe factory if the original purpose was unsustainable; fortunately for hundreds of thousands of students over the last century, this conversion alternative proved unnecessary. Early course offerings included drawing, mechanical arts, and training programs for milliners, tailors, librarians, and kindergarten teachers. Today, Pratt Institute has an international reputation in design, the arts and sciences, architecture, and engineering. Other Pratt philanthropic endeavors included the Astral Apartments, a model worker housing project in Greenpoint near the oil refinery (and still standing at 184 Franklin Avenue), the first free public library in either Brooklyn or New York City, and a savings bank for working class families.

Pratt, like Rockefeller, was a devout Baptist and very much a self-made man, living relatively modestly on Clinton Avenue in Brooklyn. His house, and those of three of his children across the street, still stand. Just before his death, he bought "Dosoris" in Glen Cove, which served until recently as a summer retreat for the Pratt family. From the time of their arrival in Glen Cove, the Pratt family played an active civic and philanthropic role. In addition to employing as many as 400 local residents in the management of the family estates between 1900 and 1935, the Pratts donated land and money for a high school, were instrumental in the founding of the North Shore Community Hospital, and donated the land and architects' fees for the Glen Cove City Hall and Glen Cove Post Office, as well as land for a twenty-five-acre public park.

Malcolm MacKay

Women participated in the sporting boom, too, but were confined to less strenuous activities, such as croquet, bowling, and bicycling. They also participated as spectators in other sports, even the emerging national game of baseball. Invented in New York City, what was to be called "America's favorite pastime" quickly spread to Brooklyn. In 1858 the two cities fielded all-star teams, playing for a mythical world championship. Manhattan won this contest, but Brooklyn dominated the series for the next decade. Professionalism appeared later, and the famous Trolley Dodgers won a pennant and tied for the world's championship in 1889 and 1890. Though baseball went into temporary eclipse in the 1890s, other forms of leisure boomed. Whether it was watching the America's Cup Races which started off from Fort Hamilton, the Battery-to-Coney Island swims, the Trolley Dodgers, or the Highland Games, Brooklynites enjoyed increasingly diverse sports.

Just as the nineteenth century drew to a close, Brooklyn's most famous leisure institution entered its heyday. Coney Island had been used for recreation purposes as early as 1829, when its first hotel was built. Thirty years later, Brighton Beach and Manhattan Beach had developed into pleasure resorts for the more genteel classes, while West Brighton increasingly catered to the masses. At the turn of the century, three new amusement parks—Luna Park, Steeplecase Park, and Dreamland—brought Coney Island its era of greatest fame. An outrageous collection of outsized humans and animals, fantastic rides, never-ending shows, and the excitement of the crowds allowed urban dwellers to experience a world of make-believe. As historian John Kasson described it, the world was turned upside down—class order was disregarded, roles were shunned, mores were loosened, spontaneity replaced regularity and order, and exuberance supplanted cold calculation. Whether to escape the rigors of urban-industrial existence or to enjoy the excitement of modern life to the fullest, millions of middle- and working-class Americans streamed to Coney Island, helping to create what many have termed a new mass culture.

In a similar vein to the leisure revolution, Brooklyn's population growth and economic development were accompanied by an increasingly complex and varied cultural life—churches, schools, and other institutions multiplied to serve the needs of residents and contributed to an emerging sense of community identity. This Long Island metropolis had always claimed its share of small public halls and meeting places, yet nineteenth-century New York City had outshadowed it in terms of more diverse cultural events. However, from mid-century the creation of concert halls, museums, colleges, private clubs, and art associations signified the arrival of the Brooklyn community to full urban status. Many factors contributed to Brooklyn's burgeoning cultural fluorescence: rapid population growth and urban development generated a need for improved educa-

well-known cultural establishment during this period was the Brooklyn Academy of Music (1859). The Academy became Brooklyn's cultural center and most of the great musical artists, actors, and performers in the country (including Edwin Booth and Jenny Lind) were heard under its roof. Performances continue today, attracting not only Brooklynites, but thousands from New York City and surrounding regions.

The mid-1800s also saw the expansion of schools of higher learning and specialized instruction to meet the increasing demand for improved training. Many of Brooklyn's earliest cultural and education-

tional facilities, immigration fostered its own ethnic and cultural diversity; and most importantly, improved transportation enabled people to get around to a degree unimagined in earlier decades.

For most of the eighteenth and nineteenth centuries a secondary education was generally a luxury of the middle and upper classes. As late as 1850, Brooklyn had few secondary schools and no colleges. The apprenticeship system had been one of the most important institutions for educating the young during the previous century, but this type of training had declined with the rise of industrialization. One of the early responses to this change was the founding of the Brooklyn Lyceum in 1833 as part of a national movement to stimulate discussion of science, art, and humanitarian subjects. It offered lectures by Brooklynites on many diverse topics. Speakers included Horace Greeley, Ralph Waldo Emerson, and Henry Ward Beecher, among others. These early cultural institutions continued to grow and expand throughout the century: the Mercantile Library, formed in 1857, was intended for working people and sponsored a library, study classes, and lectures and eventually became the Brooklyn Public Library; The Long Island Historical Society, organized in 1863 by several prominent men to document their city's history; and the Brooklyn Institute of Arts and Sciences (Brooklyn Museum), founded in 1881 and housed in an impressive building designed by the nationally known architectural firm of McKim, Mead & White. Perhaps Brooklyn's most

al institutions were founded by a new breed of residents, self-made business leaders who had come to the city in the wake of its rapid growth and possessed a strong sense of social and community responsibility. Such men as Henry E. Pierrepont, A.A. Low, Charles Pratt, and Isaac Frothingham gave impetus to the movement. Some of the institutions they helped to foster were the Polytechnic Institute (1853), with a curriculum geared to the expanding industrial city; the Long Island College Hospital (1858); St. Francis College (1859), established to serve sons of Irish Catholics; St. Johns College (1871); and Pratt Institute (1887), focusing on manual and industrial training, as well as high school education.

In the area of art, literature, and crafts, Brooklyn during the latter part of the nineteenth century was emerging as a cultural center to be reckoned with—in addition to poet Walt Whitman, its artistic community included Brooklyn native Harry Roseland (1866-1950), who enjoyed a successful career as a portraitist and genre painter. The well-known architect, George B. Post (1837-1913), contributed importantly to the city's architecture, designing the Williamsburg Savings Bank (1875), the Long Island Historical Society Building (1878), and the Hamilton Club (1888). The Brooklyn Art Association was formed during this period as a way for artists to show their work, and private clubs devoted to art and literature flourished, one of which, the Rembrandt Club (1880), is still in operation. In addition, a growing crafts industry catered to the emerging middle class and affluent residents of Brooklyn, producing objects of high quality and artistic value. The Union Porcelain Works at Greenport manufactured ceramic objects that won the admiration of connoisseurs. In fact, as late as 1880, it was the only firm in the country producing such high-grade porcelain. The Flint Glass Works and Christian Dorflinger Greenpoint Glass Works produced everything from fine stemware to street lamps.

Whether for amusement, cultural, economic, or residential pursuits, urban crowds required ever-increasing public works to accommodate them; Brooklyn built several by 1900. Between 1867 and 1873 new docks and anchorages were constructed out of the marshes of Wallabout Bay, and Washington Avenue was built across the wetlands to link Brooklyn and Williamsburg. Prospect Park opened

in 1874, while rapid transit began in 1885. However, the most massive public work of the age was the construction of the "Great Bridge" between 1869 and 1883. Residents had talked of building a structure across the East River since 1800, but costs, engineering problems, and lack of perceived need postponed the work for some sixty years. The technical problems had then been mastered, a substantial population base could bear the cost, and a large commuter group clamored for better service. Steam ferries were crowded, slow, dingy, and sometimes closed due to ice or wind storms. A bridge would eliminate these annoyances and tie the metropolis together, opening new markets for businessmen, making Brooklyn real estate more accessible, and, as usual, allowing the city to upstage New York. These promises, plus a calculated underestimate of the cost, were enough to overcome the opposition of many skeptics: engineers, warehouses, shippers, Navy men, taxpayers, and economizers worried over structural, navigational, and financial problems.

To a later age the conquest of a mere tidal strait may seem inconsequential, but in its day, the

Above: By 1890 Brooklyn had a population of over 700,000, one-third of which was foreign born and hard-pressed to find adequate housing. These tenements were built in the 1870s by philanthropist Alfred T. White in an early effort to provide low-cost, non-profit housing. Courtesy, The Long Island Historical Society

Below: In this early view, ferries can still be seen vying with the Brooklyn Bridge as a means of public transport. In 1920, when pedestrian tolls were discontinued and subways were developed, the ferry industry rapidly declined. Courtesy, The Long Island Historical Society

Brooklyn Bridge was an astounding construction feat. In 1867, when it was chartered, suspension bridges were by no means universally accepted, and for good reasons. One such model over the Ohio River at Wheeling lasted only five years before crashing in 1854; and in 1879 the monumental Tay Firth Bridge (non-suspension) collapsed into the sea during a storm. Though engineer John Roebling had built durable structures at Cincinnati and Niagara Gorge, the public remained anxious all the same.

The East River Bridge did not fall, but it did have numerous crises. Twenty men perished on the span, including John Roebling, the first fatality,

After completing two suspension bridges, German immigrant John Augustus Roebling began work on the Brooklyn Bridge. He died from tetanus in 1869. From Cirker, Dictionary of American Portraits, *Dover, 1967*

vived, but he always considered the political headaches greater than construction difficulties. Cable wire problems illustrate the point. The trustees insisted on giving the contract to a Brooklyn manufacturer, who began supplying defective wire. Roebling later discovered this outrage, but refused to revoke the contract with J.L. Haigh. Fortunately, the chief engineer had built the bridge with a sixfold margin of safety.

The press fully aired these episodes, perhaps too fully. Nevertheless, the bridge soon captured the imaginations of Brooklynites and, indeed, all Americans. The spectacle of hundreds of men working in a pressurized caisson, sinking ever deeper into the earth as the weight of the masonry towers accumulated above them; of the laborers toiling away, with hand picks, shovels, and powder against mud, sand, and boulders; of a specialized machine reeling out fifty miles of wire a day; of two huge, Gothic-arched masonry towers dominating the skyline, all seemed endlessly fascinating to the public. Moreover, the accident victims being carted off to the tenements where they lived and the equally heroic chief engi-

who succumbed horribly to tetanus contracted in a work accident. Several others fell to caisson sickness (bends). Washington Roebling, who succeeded his father and supervised most of the work, almost died from this disease. Bends and accompanying nervous disorders confined him to his house for much of the later stages of construction. Accidents also plagued the project, and on one occasion the heavily timbered roof of a caisson caught fire, requiring massive flooding to extinguish it. Completing the list of disasters and near misses, a sailing ship mast struck the bridge floor while passing beneath. Amidst cheers of the workmen, the suspension structure stood, while the mast went down.

When construction problems abated, political difficulties took their place. Tammany Boss William Marcy Tweed tried to gain control of the bridge and its construction jobs; Boss John Kelly held up New York's share of the funds; the bridge trustees squabbled endlessly; and Brooklyn Mayor Seth Low even tried to fire the chief engineer. Roebling sur-

Above: Difficulties with contracts and expenditures slowed work on the Brooklyn Bridge, and politicians and promoters on both sides of the river constantly bickered. The distant possibility of a completed bridge was a theme of popular songs and newspaper jests, as seen in this 1883 caricature from Puck *magazine. Courtesy, The Long Island Historical Society*

Opposite page: For Brooklyn's poorer residents, the bridge was not only a means of transportation but also a part of their social life. Promenading across the bridge on summer evenings and weekends provided some relief from the heat and offered a chance to watch the city life around them. (SPLIA)

neer fighting the bends, nervous exhaustion, and a horde of politicians as he desperately tried to supervise the work from his house on the Heights via his charts and telescope, gave the bridge a drama shared by few other events of the time.

The bridge also claimed many firsts, not the least of which was the role played by Roebling's wife, Emily, who took over so much of the supervision from her stricken husband that the public often mistook her for the real engineer. Fittingly enough, she and her coachman were the first citizens to ride across the finished structure in the spring of 1883. Brooklyn's celebration of the bridge's opening was outlandish even in a century much more given to urban fanfare. Enormous crowds pressed for admittance on each side, and some enterprising souls rode the ferries back and forth for hours to see the ceremonies.

The completed bridge symbolized many things to many different people. To Henry Cruse Murphy and William Kingsley, who initiated the project in 1866, it was a personal triumph; for realtors it meant increased property values; to immigrants the twin Gothic stone towers represented the gateway to North America; commuters perceived the same landmarks as the entrance to suburbia; to modern historians, the bridge symbolizes the dawning of the age of steel and electricity; and to ordinary citizens of the two great cities, the span offered a release from the confined quarters of the city, a place to stretch the legs, lungs, and soul, and to see the larger community of which they were a part. So popular did the bridge become, and so boisterous were the throngs of eager sightseers, that a tragedy soon resulted. On Memorial Day, 1883, one week after the official opening, twelve people were trampled to death when a crowd of 20,000 pedestrians raged out of control at the steps leading to the bridge promenade. Despite the tragedy, the Roeblings' masterpiece proved itself a hundred times over. Nine million people rode the trains the first year. And the bridge did connect the neighboring urban giants, open the suburban frontier, and bring fame to the city of Brooklyn.

Local politics also brought notoriety to Brooklyn, but of a different kind. During the village and early

SETH LOW

Seth Low (1850-1916), political reformer, college president, businessman, and philanthropist, was perhaps Brooklyn's most outstanding citizen at the start of the twentieth century. A native of Brooklyn and the son and grandson of highly successful China trade importers, Low was valedictorian of Columbia College in 1870, two-term mayor of Brooklyn (1882-1886), president of Columbia College (1890-1901), and mayor of the recently consolidated City of New York (1901-1903). In these difficult jobs, as well as in running his family's importing firm, his performance was exemplary.

As a very young mayor of Brooklyn, he championed various civil service reforms, including the institution of competitive hiring and promotion examinations. At Columbia, he initiated the move from its Forty-ninth Street site to Morningside Heights, personally contributed one million dollars for the construction of the Low Library, forced greater coordination among the various academic departments, created the Columbia Union Press, and brought within the university corporation the College of Physicians and Surgeons. As an anti-Tammany mayor of New York City, he trimmed the city's budget and lowered taxes while strengthening the old departments of health, charities, and tenement housing. Unlike some reformers, however, Low was generally op-

posed to municipal ownership, emphasizing the awarding of city franchises to private companies on a competitive basis. As mayor, Low pushed the planning of the first subway to Brooklyn and the Pennsylvania tunnel to Long Island, as well as the completion of the electrification of the New York Central within city limits.

After being defeated for reelection in 1903 by Democrat George B. McClellan, Jr., the Civil War general's son, Low spent the rest of his life deeply involved with problems involving blacks, labor, and New York City: he served as chairman of the Tuskegee Institute; president of the National Civic Federation; a member of the Colorado Coal Commission, appointed by President Wilson to investigate labor unrest in that state; and president of the New York Chamber of Commerce. The house in which he was born, grew up, and lived most of his life still stands at 3 Pierrepont Place in Brooklyn Heights, appropriately looking out over the harbor and lower Manhattan.

Malcolm MacKay

Brooklyn mayor Seth Low appointed men on the basis of merit rather than patronage and instituted long-needed reforms in the city's administration. From Stiles, History of Kings County Including the City of Brooklyn, Munsell, 1884

city eras, the governing powers initiated paltry efforts to offer basic services, curtail expenses, and regulate liquor licensing. By mid-century, however, Brooklyn's explosive growth came to the fore. Rapid expansion sharpened the conflicts over provision of expensive new services, governmental reorganization, bossism versus reform, and Brooklyn's proper relationship with Manhattan.

Before the Civil War an ineffective city council dominated the local government. Curtailing expenditures remained the prevalent issue, but expenses continued to rise in line with the demands of urban growth. Brooklyn then responded to fiscal woes with a further and counterproductive diffusion of government power. Under the Charter of 1873, local aldermen were given added responsibilities, a move designed to establish checks and balances in a system which already possessed too many. The resulting government lacked cohesion and accountability and was prey to every imaginable kind of corruption. Inefficiencies loomed ever larger because a lack of political responsibility strengthened the hand of Democratic boss Hugh McLaughlin. With easy access to patronage jobs and public works contracts, he was little different from other city bosses who emerged across mid-century America, except that his tenure lasted far longer, from the late 1860s until 1903. Like most of his peers, McLaughlin was not obsessed with tyrannical power, but he certainly wielded more clout than any other Brooklyn politician of his era, and not always in the best interests of the city. In classic machine fashion, he traded favors for votes, jobs for influence, and franchises for cash.

Recent nostalgic writers have invested political bosses with Robin Hood-like qualities—they uplifted the poor, they got things done, they provided illicit but popular services. Perhaps some of these traits are valid. Yet, machine politicians frequently stole vast sums. In Brooklyn's case both the school fund and monies allocated to poor relief mysteriously disappeared. Local citizens finally refused to stomach any further misdeeds, and began protesting these outrages in a series of reform movements. Former Brooklyn mayor Frederick Schroeder initiated the process in 1879 when he secured from Albany a new, "single-head" charter that centralized authority within the city government and enhanced the power of the mayor. This innovation quickly

Brooklyn did not have an organized police department until 1857, when the Metropolitan Police law placed New York City and Kings County under a single system of police enforcement. In 1870 Brooklyn acquired a separate police department and the city was divided into precincts. At the time of this circa 1890 photograph the force consisted of over 700 men. Courtesy, The Long Island Historical Society

*T. McCants Stewart (1854-
1923) was a prominent black
lawyer and intellectual in
Brooklyn. He was appointed to
the Brooklyn Board of Education in 1891. Courtesy, The
Long Island Historical Society*

*The Brooklyn Orphan Asylum
was established in 1833, and
this building was erected in
1872, accommodating 400
children. Courtesy, George B.
Brainerd Photograph Collection, Brooklyn Public Library*

forced reformers to seriously contest the 1881 may-
oralty race, lest the newfound power fall into the
waiting hands of boss McLaughlin. Reformers found
a winning candidate in the popular and aristocratic
Seth Low. As mayor, Low exercised tight control
over his department heads and successfully insisted
on home rule. He proved an energetic reformer as
well. Previously, McLaughlin had kept taxes at a
minimum by selling franchises to private contractors who provided terrible service while corrupting
local government. Not only did Low refuse to cut
taxes, breaking with the more narrow, privileged
view of reform, but he insisted on collecting scan-
dalously large sums of tax arrearages. The mayor
then used the money to provide better health, police, fire, and especially, educational services. He
quickly opened the schools to Brooklyn's Negro
population, ended the practice of looting the education department, and supplied free textbooks to all
children. Low also insisted on competency testing
for office holders, established a civil service system,
and outlawed the custom of squeezing officials for
political contributions at election time. Finally, the
mayor was first and foremost a Brooklyn booster,
favoring development over tightfisted fiscal practices. He was one of the first of a new breed of urban executives who combined sensitivity for the
poor with solicitude for the city's economic welfare.

Low's policies transformed Brooklyn into a model
imitated by reformers across the country, yet he
failed to please all the taxpayers, or even members
of his own Republican party. He retired in 1885, the
Democrats captured the office again, and the duel
between boss and reformers resumed. A new rapid
transit company concluded that it need not pay
taxes and fraudulently escaped with a payment of
only $282,000 out of a $1,500,000 assessment. Such
flagrant abuses soon brought the reformers back
into power in the 1890s, just as the issue of metropolitan consolidation replaced honesty and efficien-
cy as the leading political question.

The concept of a Greater New York had been
discussed for decades, but never caught on, especially in Brooklyn. Rather, Long Islanders had been
busy creating a Greater Brooklyn through the 1894
absorption of Flatbush, Gravesend, and New Utrecht;
the New Lots and Flatlands takeover in 1896; and
consolidation with Kings County the same year.
These and other acquisitions raised Brooklyn's pop-

ulation to more than one million. Manhattan's final push for a Greater New York was simultaneously gaining strength, fanned by the conviction that their city was about to be eclipsed by Chicago and possibly even Brooklyn, itself. In 1888 New York Mayor Abram Hewitt opened the debate. Andrew H. Green, the real father of consolidation, carried it forward. Manhattan elements expected several gains from a massive annexation-control over the entire metropolitan harbor, central public works planning, the prestige of being the world's greatest city, and a chance to implement their good government ideas.

While Brooklyn retained a sturdy sense of its own identity, Manhattan's blandishments nonetheless attracted many local residents. Some citizens hoped that Manhattan's greater wealth might lower Brooklyn's taxes and widen its bonding power, bring a second East River Bridge, hasten growth in the outer neighborhoods, and ease a local water crunch through access to upstate Croton water. Pro-consolidationists included many of Brooklyn's leading citizens: realtors, bankers, insurers, manufacturers, merchants, street railway operators, and builders. In 1892 they formed the Brooklyn Consolidation League to promote their cause. An 1894 advisory referendum favored unification with

Manhattan, but by a perilously thin margin. This election also revealed a curious ethnocultural, class, and partisan split. The pro-unification coalition, embracing wealthier Germans, Irish, Anglo-Americans, and many residents of distant neighborhoods who needed city improvements, won by 277 votes. Opposition forces were led by Brooklyn's Protestant, Republican reform elite, but supported by the normally Democratic German and Irish working-class wards. Out of the referendum of 1894 grew the League of Loyal Citizens who feared that the creation of a Greater New York would destroy Brooklyn's special character. They also predicted a rise, rather than fall, in taxes and fretted over the impact of Manhattan's corrupt Tammany Hall on Brooklyn's good government efforts. St. Clair McKelway and the Brooklyn *Eagle* spearheaded the

Below: Henry Ward Beecher (1813-1887) was the leader of Plymouth Church for forty years. Like his sister, Harriet Beecher Stowe, he endeavored to arouse public awareness of the evils of slavery. From Hazelton, The Boroughs of Brooklyn and Queens, Counties of Nassau and Suffolk, N.Y., 1609-1924, *Lewis, 1925*

anti-consolidation forces. Despite their cause, attitudes and events tended towards merger.

Local forces thereafter lost control of the issue, as New York State boss Tom Platt was not about to let such an important matter pass the legislature without some conformance to his own political needs. In 1896 Platt ramrodded the necessary laws through the senate and assembly. A commission soon drafted a metropolitan charter which took effect on January 1, 1898. Although Brooklyn Firsters lost the larger battle, they obtained several important compromises which guaranteed local autonomy through the borough system. They gained citywide equalization of taxes and maintained control over the school system. Brooklyn now formed the largest part of America's greatest city, brought into being by the most awesome urban consolidation in American history.

The Long Island city's surprising renunciation of independent status was almost unique among nineteenth-century American municipalities. In an age of urban expansion and conflict, these jurisdictions competed in nearly all facets of life: in sports, population growth, industry, culture. Brooklyn was well prepared for the race to urban greatness. Its growth rate placed it among the very largest American cities; Coney Island made it famous; the Brooklyn Bridge loomed as a symbol to all America and even the world; its industry ranked fourth in the United States. Seth Low and his reform colleagues pushed the city to the forefront of American urban reform, and communities all across the nation looked to it for guidance.

Long known as a mecca of churches and homes, Brooklyn's residential neighborhoods were possibly the best in the country, certainly surpassing those of nearby Manhattan. The fame of Brooklyn Heights minister Henry Ward Beecher alone would have been enough to distinguish the city's religious establishment. Beecher helped his congregation accept and understand the urban revolution swirling around them. His popularity was so great that he earned an annual salary of $20,000, preached to audiences of 2,000, and caused the ferries that carried his flock to be dubbed "Beecher Boats."

These varied factors represented just a partial list of Brooklyn's major assets, enough to have given a lesser city delusions of grandeur. Hence, the "great renunciation of 1898" becomes even more mystifying. Just as Greater Brooklyn was within reach, Long Island's own metropolis dropped out of the race.

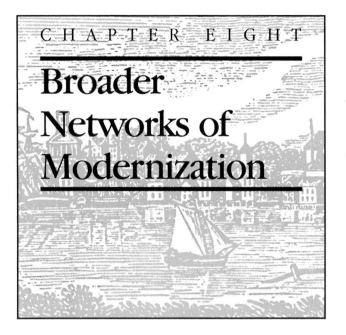

CHAPTER EIGHT

Broader Networks of Modernization

Despite the heavy influx of excursioners and estate owners, turn-of-the-century Long Island retained much of its rural character. Agriculture and fishing flourished, small-town life predominated, and local inhabitants viewed themselves very differently from their urban neighbors. Indeed, their rural state of mind helped foster the creation of a new county, Nassau, formed out of Queens' three eastern towns on January 1, 1899.

Yet, amid the placid landscape change was evident as well. Daily commuters already travelled to New York by railroad and steamboat, and a proposed tunnel under the East River promised to increase the flow. Although farming remained the single most important economic activity, its position on western Long Island had begun to decline. Instead, real estate development accelerated. Within a generation automobiles, trollies, and commuter trains would combine to create the archetypical American suburb.

Suffolk County experienced the same forces, but the pace was slower and the intrusion of modern urban life less persistent. As late as the 1930s, many local farms lacked electricity and running water, and Suffolk's population growth lagged in comparison to that of its exuberant neighbor. Not until after World War II would Long Island's East End fully enter the twentieth century.

Small towns and rural villages, sustained by the agricultural and fishing economy, set the tone for life throughout turn-of-the-century Long Island. Nassau County contained over 1,650 farms spread across 70,000 productive acres. A town like New Hyde Park was termed "rich farming country" by a contemporary guide book, while Syosset was known for "its really good farms and better fruit." Milk,

An old form of horse power confronts a new one on a Port Washington street in 1910. The myriad technological developments of the early twentieth century altered patterns of life on Long Island that had seen little change in over two centuries. Courtesy, Nassau County Museum

Left: The growth of Port Jefferson can be attributed almost entirely to its excellent harbor and to shipbuilding. The Bayles Shipyard (pictured here in 1875) turned out approximately 140 vessels between 1836 and 1917, when it was sold. Courtesy, George B. Brainerd Photograph Collection, Brooklyn Public Library

Below: Like so many other coastal communities, Greenport (depicted in 1879) was adversely affected by the decline of the whaling and shipbuilding industries. Once one of the busiest whaling ports on Long Island, the boats moored at its dock today are pleasure boats, not schooners. Courtesy, George B. Brainerd Photograph Collection, Brooklyn Public Library

potatoes, and vegetables for city tables proved profitable, and in 1898 the H.J. Heinz Company opened a plant in Hicksville to process pickles, sauerkraut, ketchup, and vinegar.

Suffolk County, more distant from New York, was even more agricultural and shipped tremendous quantities of cabbage, pickles, and potatoes to urban markets. Tiny Calverton made a specialty of growing "that indispensable delicacy, the cranberry." Duck farms flourished, too. The first seven "Peking" ducks were imported from China in 1873, and within a generation Long Island and the water fowl were synonymous. Riverhead boasted the world's largest duck farm by 1898.

Fishing and the maritime trades, widely practiced since colonial times, contributed greatly to local economic life and character. Oyster Bay boatmen planted tons of seed oysters every year and South Shore baymen harvested millions of bushels of shellfish annually. Coastal Freeport shipped over one million pounds of fresh seafood to the New York City market. Greenport was Suffolk's fishing leader, supporting scores of processing plants and a large sailing fleet. And Greenport was not alone in its maritime ways. Bridgehampton across Peconic Bay was described by one chronicler as a "rare old town, full of sturdy mariners who wrest a living from the sea." Shipbuilding remained an important industry in Rockaway, Northport, Port Jefferson, Greenport, and additional bay towns.

Other reminders of earlier times were also evident. In many villages gristmills and sawmills, some survivors of the seventeenth and eighteenth centuries, continued to turn. Annual agricultural fairs, dating from before the Civil War, saluted the Island's farming heritage. In numerous one-room schoolhouses, teachers were not only expected to educate, but also to fill kerosene lamps, clean chimneys, carry coal for the stove, and fill the water buckets. Village general stores stocked groceries, dry goods, paints and oils, and hardware, while gaily painted delivery wagons or horsedrawn sleighs carried their wares out into the countryside. Shops for blacksmiths and harnessmakers crowded many streets.

The march towards industrialization, which affected nearby Brooklyn and Queens so heavily, barely touched Long Island. The 1900 census counted only 1,650 employees of 321 small Nassau manufacturing establishments; Suffolk supported even fewer. Though an occasional large firm thrived, such as the Plymouth Lace Mills in Patchogue or the Ladew Leather Works in Glen Cove, they were most conspicuous by their rarity.

As befit their semi-rural ways, Long Islanders generally lived in small villages and towns. Hempstead, Nassau's retail and transportation hub, counted barely 3,600 inhabitants in 1900, and its main street remained unpaved. The size of Suffolk's largest population centers were equally unimpressive: Huntington contained 3,500 residents; Patchogue 2,900; Greenport 2,400. Riverhead, the county seat, numbered but a few thousand, and horses and wagons crowded the central business district. Most Islanders, in fact, resided in even smaller places. Villages like Glenwood Landing, Bellmore, Massapequa, Medford, and Yaphank counted a few hundred inhabitants each. In the words of one observer, Suffolk's Miller Place, Rocky Point, Shoreham, and Wading River all appeared to "have been bodily transported from the Massachusetts shore, so rural and simple are their ways."

Above: In spite of their rural, unassuming character, village centers such as Main Street in Sag Harbor provided a base for the Island's economy. Supplying services and goods to a growing population, each village's cluster of businesses usually included grocery, hardware, and clothes stores, feed dealers, blacksmiths, and ice and coal suppliers. (SPLIA)

Left: While country clubs and sports clubs catered to the wealthy, the circus was for everyone. These boys approach circus tents set up in Jamaica circa 1915. Courtesy, Clarence Purchase Photograph Collection, SPLIA

This rural atmosphere and its accompanying social and political attitudes helped create a new and independent Nassau County. Occurring just before the start of the century, this action ended fifty years of contention among Queens County residents. The differences between the inhabitants of eastern and western Queens ostensibly centered around the location of the county courthouse, but actually reflected the contrasting development experienced by the two regions. Directly adjacent to New York City, the western towns of Newtown, Flushing, and Jamaica had grown increasingly industrial, urban, and Democratic, while the eastern towns of Hempstead, North Hempstead, and Oyster Bay remained largely agricultural and Republican. As a result, the more populous area wished to move the county seat away from rural North Hempstead and closer to its own growth centers.

After more than a decade of political sparring, the state legislature in 1871 selected a new site in Long Island City, close to Manhattan. Resentment in the eastern towns was widespread. A generation later, in 1896, the legislature passed another important bill, this time consolidating several cities, towns, and counties into a unified New York City. The act included Queens' urbanized western towns, but excluded the rural eastern ones. Eastern resi-

dents then faced the unpleasant prospect of being part of Queens County, but not part of New York City. How could their interests possibly be protected? With the encouragement of local leaders, and despite the strong opposition of City and Democratic politicians, the legislature agreed in 1898 to separate the eastern towns and create an independent Nassau County. Henceforth Long Island would be divided into two distinct entities, a New York City portion to the west comprised of Brooklyn and Queens, and a rural component to the east consisting of Nassau and Suffolk counties.

Even as many Long Islanders attempted to preserve their independence from New York City, signs of change rapidly developed, especially in Nassau

Above: Fahy's Watch-Case Factory, built in 1881, was one of the largest manufacturing plants of solid silver and plated ware in the nation. After the whaling industry languished in the 1870s it became Sag Harbor's principal industry, employing over 800 in its heyday. (SPLIA)

Left: Founded in 1855 by Hendrick Vanderbilt Duryea, Duryea's Starch Works in Glen Cove played a leading role in the development of nineteenth-century Long Island industry. It employed hundreds during its peak years, and this 1880 lithograph depicts its bustling activity. Courtesy, New-York Historical Society

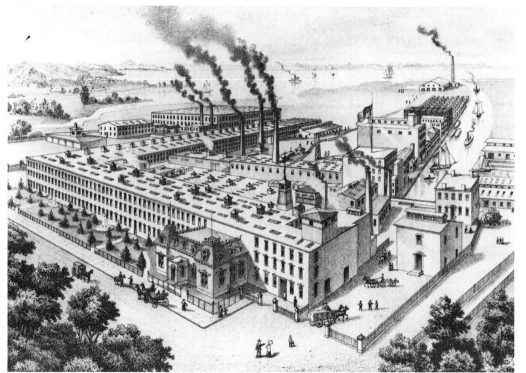

Governor Theodore Roosevelt speaks at the cornerstone laying ceremonies for the first Nassau County Courthouse in Mineola on July 13, 1900. Photo by J. Burt.

At the turn of the century, village social life for most Long Islanders included agricultural fairs, church socials, Sunday outings, and holiday parades, such as this 1916 Decoration Day parade in Jamaica. Concerts and plays were performed at the Huntington Town Opera House and the Music Hall in Riverhead, while vaudeville drew large crowds at the Freeport Theatre. Courtesy, Clarence Purchase Photograph Collection, SPLIA

Opposite page: William K. Vanderbilt, Jr., seen here on the left in 1908, was instrumental in promoting the automobile and auto racing in America. To encourage U.S. auto manufacturers to improve their product and compete with European markets, he instituted the Vanderbilt Cup Races on Long Island. (SPLIA)

County with its close proximity to the metropolis. This phenomenon was especially evident in the realm of modern technology. Telephones appeared in Glen Cove in 1884, and in Hempstead by the 1890s. In 1900 nine Nassau exchanges counted 446 subscribers.

Electric power was another important innovation. Established in 1890 to supply electricity to nearby North Shore estates, the Roslyn Light and Power Company soon combined with similar firms in Floral Park, Oyster Bay, Port Washington, and Glen Cove to form the Nassau Power and Light Company. A growing cosmopolitan element in the local population demanded urban services, and the trend quickly affected Suffolk County, also. Babylon received limited electric power in the late 1880s, and Northport followed less than a decade later. By 1911 several Suffolk firms had united to form the Long Island Lighting Company (LILCO). Under the leadership of financier Ellis Phillips, LILCO then purchased the Nassau-based utilities, creating an island-wide power grid.

Transportation improvements also altered local habits. By 1898 a cross-island trolley sped from Huntington to Amityville in just one hour for a fare of thirty cents. Other lines ran as far east as Patchogue. A similar network appeared in Nassau. After a dramatic political battle, the Mineola, Hempstead, and Freeport Traction Company bested its rivals and commenced service in 1901, running through fourteen towns and villages, with branch lines to Queens. Nassau's second line, serving Roslyn, Port Washington, and Mineola, opened in 1907.

Automobiles began to appear, as well. While only a few thousand vehicles were registered on the Island before 1915, visitors from New York City often travelled eastward. As a result, many county roads were graded or improved. Several resort villages experienced what seemed a never-ending stream of weekend traffic.

Change was also evident on the old Long Island Rail Road. First conceived as a through route to Boston, the line was now almost exclusively an excursion and commuter train. At the end of the 1800s, residents of Garden City, Freeport, and Rockville Centre already rode the morning train to their jobs in the city. Even Huntington Station in Suffolk County serviced about thirty daily commuters.

All these turn-of-the-century changes paled, however, beside the social revolution wrought in

167

the next three decades by the interaction of transportation improvements and intensive real estate development. Between 1900 and 1930, Nassau's population leaped from 55,000 to over 300,000, while the number of Suffolk residents more than doubled from 77,000 to 161,000. The railroad stood at the heart of this boom. Throughout the last quarter of the nineteenth century, the Long Island Rail Road tirelessly promoted the concept of commutation—working in the city and living in the country. But the time-consuming East River ferry crossings discouraged extensive local development. A 1900 edition of *Nassau County Review* noted that "the cool fields, ample beaches, and picturesque hills offer room for tens of thousands of cottages if only people could be assured of rapid transit."

The call was heard, and that same year new railroad management committed itself to "supply swift

express trains to commuters, enabling them to live out on Long Island all year round." Plans were also announced to dig an East River tunnel and build a huge terminal on Seventh Avenue in Manhattan. The railroad kept its promises and New York's Pennsylvania Station opened in 1910. Another new terminal arose in Brooklyn and electrification of the tracks to Hempstead and Babylon began. *Putnam's Magazine* observed, "If Long Island does not blossom like a rose, it will not be the fault of the . . . Railroad." By 1914 the number of daily trains serving growing towns like Freeport, Lynbrook, Valley Stream, and Great Neck had doubled. Even realtors in Babylon, thirty-seven miles distant from the city, touted their lots as "within commuting distance, convenient to the express depot."

Equally important in transforming Long Island from a semi-rural neighbor to a bedroom suburb was the rise of the automobile and construction of a modern road network. First came improved access to Manhattan via three new East River bridges: the Williamsburg, completed in 1903, and the Manhattan and Queensboro, both opened six years later. Farther east, millionaire racing enthusiast William K. Vanderbilt II sponsored a series of highly promoted auto races. Competing for the prized Vanderbilt Cup, drivers from all over America roared through Long Island's country towns, setting records and attracting immense publicity. Between

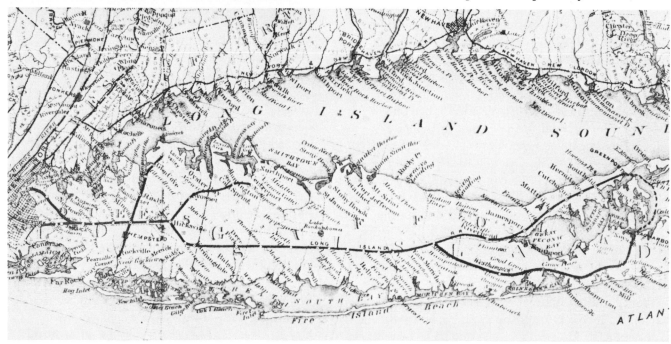

Opposite page, top: Symboliz-
ing Nassau's new status as a
county, the Nassau County
Courthouse was designed by
prominent architect William
Tubby. Courtesy, Nassau
County Museum

Opposite page, bottom: As it
had done for the nation as a
whole, the railroad brought
Long Island together as a cohe-
sive unit, both physically and
ideologically. It also boosted
the Island's economy by lower-
ing the cost of freighting,
opening up previously in-
accessible areas, and encour-
aging settlement. From an
1870 LIRR brochure. (SPLIA)

Above: By 1875 the multitude
of small local railroad lines
was consolidated into three
main lines: the North Side, the
South Side, and the Long Is-
land Central. Austin Corbin
united them under one man-
agement during his presi-
dency of the Long Island Rail
Road in the 1880s. Courtesy,
George B. Brainerd Photo-
graph Collection, Brooklyn
Public Library

1908 and 1914, Vanderbilt and his associates also constructed a modern two-lane motor highway running forty-eight miles from Flushing to Lake Ronkonkama in central Suffolk.

The automobile really caught on after the First World War, and the 1920s witnessed a wide-ranging construction program and an enormous leap in traffic. Older country routes like the Jericho Turnpike and Merrick Road were paved. Along the south shore, a new thoroughfare was laid out atop New York City's old water line right-of-way. Designed to service the rapidly growing commuter villages, the first leg of this "Sunrise Highway" opened in 1928. Under the direction of master builder Robert Moses and his Long Island State Park Commission, modern high-speed parkways were constructed, designed to transport urban residents to new state parks like Jones Beach (1929) and local commuters to their jobs in Brooklyn, Queens, and Manhattan. By 1930

169

ROBERT MOSES

Although never elected to public office, Robert Moses was one of the most powerful men in America, using that power to physically reshape New York's metropolitan and surburban environment to an inner vision conceived of and controlled by him alone. During his forty-four years in public service he personally conceived and carried out over twenty-six billion dollars in public works projects, including the building of bridges, parkways, expressways, state parks, and both private and public housing projects across New York State. Moses was to become famous as America's greatest road builder and the father of the New York State Park system. His influence on Long Island's development was immense.

A look at any current map of Long Island will indicate the impact of Moses' vision, energy, and determination on this relatively small, 120-mile-long strip of land. To cross any bridge, to drive on any parkway or expressway, to swim or boat at any state park on Long Island involves utilizing a project that owes its existence, directly or indirectly, to Moses. Moses was fond of Long Island, summering for most of his life in Babylon. He considered the park and road projects on Long Island as one of his greatest achievements. By the end of his career Long Island had over fifteen state parks and a network of roads,

Above: Robert Moses speaks from the porch of the Taylor Mansion in Islip at the dedication ceremonies of Heckscher State Park on June 2, 1929. Courtesy, Long Island State Park Commission

Opposite page: The Long Island State Parkway system consists of limited access roadways extending from Queens into Suffolk County. Courtesy, Long Island State Park Commission

bridges, and parkways connecting it to the larger metropolitan area. Perhaps more than any other single individual, Moses was instrumental in transforming the physical landscape of the Island. Some of the more famous projects he planned and built on Long Island include the Northern State, Southern State, Wantagh, Sagtikos, Sunken Meadow, and Meadowbrook parkways; a myriad of parks including Jones Beach, Hither Hills, Sunken Meadow, Fire Is-

land, Captree, Bethpage, and Hempstead Lake; and bridges such as Throgs Neck and Triborough, among others.

Born in 1888 into a well-to-do Jewish family, Moses went to Yale and just a few years out of college was appointed to his first state job by Governor-elect Al Smith in 1918. In 1923 Smith did something that would eventually change the direction of park systems throughout America—he appointed Moses as park commissioner and a year later Moses became president of the newly formed Long Island State Park Commission. Moses was far ahead of his time in his ideas about city and urban planning and was one of the few who understood the complexity of the problem posed by the need for parks and the roads to get to them. In the early 1920s, twenty-nine states didn't even have a single state park and road conditions in general verged on the primitive. Moses was quick to notice the beauty of Long Island with its miles of unused beaches and open wooded areas, and he immediately envisioned a sophisticated recreational system encompassing the whole island that would be linked to the city by a network of roads and scenic parkways.

A facet of Moses' personality that to a large extent helped accomplish this grand vision was his willingness, even eagerness, to battle entrenched interests. Moses sensed the difficulty (and the great challenge) in getting groups with vested interests to relinquish any land for the purpose of building public park facilities and connecting roadways. When the report on Moses' plans for Long Island was made public in 1924, he found himself battling the state legislature, town boards, chambers of commerce, civic associations, and wealthy North Shore residents whose estate lands would be disturbed by the building of the

Northern State Parkway. With his vast amount of energy, Moses obtained easements and rights of way, solicited donations from philanthropists such as August Heckscher, negotiated deals and compromises with wealthy landowners such as Otto Kahn, and made sure that friends and allies were appointed as presidents of each of the regional commissions. He discovered estates and searched out abandoned government properties that would make ideal Long Island state parks—600 acres on Fire Island; land in Hampton Bays and at Montauk Point; land on the Sound at Sunken Meadow, Wildwood, Lloyd's Neck, and Orient Point. Moses also eyed, and eventually acquired, two large parcels of land in the center of the Island, the Belmont and Yoakum estates, that would eventually become state parks. In total over 40,000 acres were identified as potential state parks, and an ingenious system of eleven parkways was

designed to joint the parcels together. The "ways to the parks" were designed to portray a rustic look and each had handsome stone overpasses that were deliberately kept low to prevent use by trucks or buses.

When Moses was appointed president of the Long Island State Park Commission in 1924, there was only one 200-acre state park, on Fire Island. By the end of August 1928, Long Island had fourteen state parks. Although Moses' career was not without controversy and his fair share of critics, his legacy to Long Island is best exemplified in these public parks that provide oases of unspoilt woodland and beachfront and hours of recreational pleasures for millions of people every year. In 1964 the creation of Robert Moses State Park and the Robert Moses Causeway paid homage to the man called America's greatest road builder.

Tim O'Brien

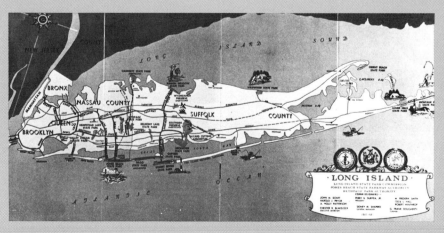

Long Island Highways

JERICHO TURNPIKE

MOTOR PARKWAY

NORTH HEMPSTEAD TURNPIKE

MONTAUK HIGHWAY—SHINNECOCK HILLS

ROUTE 25—COLD SPRING HARBOR

Rapid technical improvements and lower prices after World War I had transformed the automobile from a rich man's toy to a transportation necessity. This change *required highways such as those in this 1931 view to be continually enlarged and improved. From* Long Island: The Sunrise Homeland, *1931*

*The Motor Parkway was begun
in 1906 by William K.
Vanderbilt, Jr., and other
wealthy Long Island residents
to facilitate their love of auto
racing and touring. Running
from Lake Ronkonkama westward to the metropolitan area,
the toll road operated until the
public parkway system developed in the 1930s. (SPLIA)*

Nassau's auto population surpassed 110,000, up from only 8,800 just fifteen years before. Such dramatic changes in transportation were intimately linked to the burgeoning real estate boom then altering the very face of the Island.

Real estate development on Long Island had extended antecedents. As early as the 1840s, immigrant entrepreneurs Frederick Heyne and John Heitz purchased 1,000 acres of Hicksville farmland and attempted to settle fellow Germans there. After the railroad reached Rockaway in 1869, Thomas and Samuel Marsh began laying out building lots. So did brothers Alfred, George, and Newbold Lawrence; one South Shore town still bears their name. Retailing magnate A.T. Stewart created a model community in central Nassau and called it Garden City. At Breslau (later Lindenhurst) Thomas Welwood and Charles Schleier formed the Breslau Cooperative Building Association and during the 1870s marketed thousands of small house lots. But until direct routes to Manhattan were completed, growth remained relatively slow. Nassau's popula-

tion increased by a modest 8,500 in the 1880s and again by 9,500 in the 1890s. Suffolk County expanded only slightly more rapidly, adding 24,000 residents in the same period.

After the opening of the New York City bridges and tunnels, the picture changed entirely and the human floodgates opened. Railroad suburbs soon sprouted everywhere. Promoters called Floral Park an ideal spot for commuters "where short travel hours and good train service are the essence." Hempstead was only thirty-eight minutes from Manhattan via electric express. Even towns in Suffolk County boasted of their excellent rail connections.

The villages closest to New York, such as Great Neck, Port Washington, Valley Stream, and Freeport, naturally attracted much of the initial influx. One Port Washington resident soon noted, "Our population is largely made up of New York businessmen." Every developer was selling the suburban dream. Builder John Randall asked, "Why pay rent in a crowded city when you can secure a beautiful

ALEXANDER TURNEY STEWART

The history of Garden City is closely tied to the unique vision and force of one individual. Alexander Turney Stewart (1801-1876), known as the "merchant prince" of New York, was an immigrant of Scotch-Irish heritage who arrived in New York City in 1818. After teaching for a year he started a small retail dry-goods business. Through unstinting labor and astute management practices (he was the first to advertise "fire and remnant" sales), Stewart became an undisputed leader in merchandising and one of the world's wealthiest men. His famous six-story "iron store" on Tenth Avenue, the largest retail store in the world at the time, and his mansion at Fifth Avenue and Thirty-fourth Street, called the "Marble Palace" by New Yorkers, were designed by John Kellum, a native of Hempstead. Stewart had a plan to build a model suburban community, a relatively new idea at the time, and it was probably Kellum who informed Stewart in 1869 that the residents of the town of Hempstead were willing to sell a large area of the unused Hempstead Plains. A special town meeting was called on July 17, 1869, to consider Charles T. Harvey's bid of forty-two dollars an acre, but Stewart's last minute cash offer of fifty-five dollars and his willingness "to expend several millions of dollars in improving the Plain land" received an overwhelming vote. Some 7,170

acres of town land and an additional 2,000 acres purchased from individuals that extended from Floral Park through Bethpage became Stewart's, and the history of Garden City began.

Stewart immediately had Kellum prepare plans for a model village of 500 acres to provide a beautiful suburb of "pleasant and reasonable" housing on a rental

Above: This circa 1860 painting is the only known portrait of Alexander T. Stewart. Courtesy, Garden City Archives

Opposite page: These simple and austere wood-frame residences, Garden City's "Disciple" homes, were built for the working classes. Courtesy, George B. Brainerd Photograph Collection, Brooklyn Public Library

basis for the executives and clerks who worked in his stores. The village proper was laid out on an orderly geometric pattern of wide streets with houses, stores, and other public buildings. Stewart's own home would double as a small hotel. To make it a real "garden" city, the entire village and park were planted with thousands of trees and shrubs, most obtained from Prince's Nursery in Flushing. As part of his grand plan, Stewart also built the Central Railroad Company to connect the village with existing railroad lines, and a brickwork at Bethpage to supply building material for the developing community.

By 1874 the four-story hotel and a dozen large, mansard-roofed houses known as "The Twelve Apostles" were built in the latest Victorian style. Smaller houses, called "The Disciples," stores, a huge brick stable, and the largest well on Long Island created a semblance of a community. Stewart, however, was not to live to see his model village completed. His death in 1876 ushered in a period of faltering development. In 1885 Garden City had a total population of only 550 and was mocked as "Stewart's Folly."

Perhaps the most impressive building projects of Garden City were constructed not by Stewart, but by his wife, the former Cornelia Clinch. The Cathedral of the Incarnation was designed by architect Henry G. Harrison and completed in 1885 as a memorial to Stewart from his wife, who provided a permanent endowment for its maintenance. The cathedral, the seat of the Episcopal bishop of Long Island, is an impressive example of Gothic revival architecture and is considered Harrison's finest ecclesiastical work. Before her death in 1886, Cornelia Stewart was instrumental in developing plans for an entire ecclesiastical complex including the twin cathedral schools, St. Paul's and St. Mary's, and the bishop's residence.

In 1893, prospects for the growth of Garden City began to improve. In that year, Stewart's lands were acquired by several companies, including the Garden City Company which had been formed by a number of Stewart's heirs, and vigorous development of the village began. Previously, houses and stores had been available for rent only; now Garden City would develop like other communities. With its new hotel, designed in 1894 by Stanford White, husband of one of the heirs, and its casino and golf and gun clubs, the village became a center for fashionable New Yorkers and Long Islanders to gather for sport and recreation. In 1907 a large tract of the original Stewart holdings was sold to a separate company that developed what is now known as Garden City Estates. While Stewart's vision of an ideal suburb was not realized in his lifetime, his imaginative plan laid the basis for one of America's finest suburban villages.

Edward Smits

cottage with all the improvements?" Each town and village seemed to have an eager promoter. As late as 1906, Nassau Boulevard was a mile-square expanse of open fields. Then the Garden City Development Company stepped in, building streets, parks, and homes, all converging on a central railroad station. In 1912 nearby Malverne was a rural hamlet. That same year Alfred Wagg organized the Amsterdam Development and Sales Company, bought up eight farms, and began building. By 1920, 100 homes had been erected and a newly incorporated village was born. This story was repeated a dozen times.

Some men even created entirely new cities. William Reynolds and others spent over four million dollars to develop the Atlantic Ocean resort of Long Beach. At times 1,500 workers and a herd of elephants dredged channels, stabilized beaches, and erected boardwalks, apartments, and houses. The

cumulative effect of all this real estate activity was dramatic. By 1920 Nassau's population had more than doubled from its 1900 base to 125,000, surpassing geographically larger Suffolk County for the first time.

The outbreak of war in 1917 did not materially affect the social and economic trends already underway, but did impose a temporary moratorium on the rising level of activity. Instead, local energies were directed towards the great military bases situated on the Island. At Camp Mills in Garden City, the 42nd Rainbow Division trained for duty overseas. Nearby Mitchell and Roosevelt fields constituted the largest flying center in the East. Out at Camp Upton in Yaphank, the 77th Infantry Division practiced with broom handles instead of rifles, while clearing stumps and brush and struggling to erect shelter. Among Camp Upton's most illustrious

THE MEADOWBROOK MODEL

THE Meadowbrook is a favorite Bossert design offering an amazing number of ingenious variations both in plan and design, all of which are most economical, because, the building being square, the greatest amount of floor space is enclosed with the least amount of wall area.

The front entrance can be on the side or on the gable end of the building.

Porch is of ample size and is made unusually attractive with pergola beams and flower trellises. From this porch handsome double French doors open directly into the spacious well-lighted living

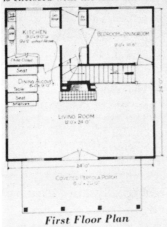

First Floor Plan

READY-CUT OR SECTIONAL
FLOOR PLAN

1. Width, 24 ft.
2. Depth, 24 ft.
3. It has five rooms and bath, with a dining alcove.
4. The porch is 20 x 8 ft.
5. Living-room, 24 x 12 ft., with a dining alcove 6 x 9 ft. and space provided for fireplace.
6. A dining-room or bedroom on first floor is 9 x 10 ft.
7. The kitchen is 9 x 9 ft.
8. A china-closet is provided in the kitchen.
9. A butler's pantry and rear entrance, 5 x 9 ft., with ample space for ice-box and stores with door to kitchen and dining-room and entrance to cellar.
10. Second floor, two bedrooms, each 9 x 12 ft.
11. A bath 6 x 5 ft. 6 inches.
12. From each bedroom are two large closets for storage.
13. Each bedroom has four windows.

Second Floor Plan

There Are Hundreds of Short Cuts in the Building Game and We Know Most of Them

BOSSERT HOUSES

Opposite page: Camp Mills in Garden City, like Camp Upton in Yaphank, was a military training center during World War I. It became a principal embarkation center for troops going to Europe. Courtesy, Garden City Archives

Left: Firms like Louis Bossert & Sons, Inc. offered simple design and inexpensive prices while providing a variety of choices to new suburbanites. From Louis Bossert & Sons, Inc., Bossert Houses, 1926

residents was a young soldier named Irving Berlin who was inspired during his stay to write "Oh, How I Hate to Get Up in the Morning."

With the return of peace, local energies turned away from military requirements and resumed, instead, the great peacetime activity of growth and development, setting the stage for the fantastic decade still known as the "Roaring Twenties."

The impressive development activity of the prewar years only anticipated the fabulous 1920s when Nassau became America's fastest growing county. National prosperity, ever-improving roads, slick advertising, and continually expanding rail service all combined to create a land boom of feverish proportions. Almost 200 companies and 16,000 construction workers labored mightily to meet the demand for new housing. One outfit, the Zenith Land Corporation of Hicksville, auctioned 242 building lots in October 1923 on "the day of days for all those who believe in the future of Long Island." Apparently, there were many believers. The population of

Floral Park quintupled to 10,000. Lynbrook added 7,500 new residents and Garden City, 5,000 more. Total Nassau population surged to over 300,000 before the great stock crash.

The number of commuters rose also, as Nassau was truly transformed into a bedroom suburb. Perhaps 75 percent of the local labor force worked outside the county. By the end of the decade, nearly 110 daily trains stopped at Valley Stream, eighty at Mineola and Rockville Centre, seventy-six at Lynbrook, seventy-two at Babylon. George LeBoutillier, a senior vice president of the Long Island Rail Road, proudly noted in 1925: "Fast, clean and adequate railroad services for more than a generation is primarily responsible for the marvelous growth Long Island has enjoyed for many years."

Such voracious development naturally required extensive acreage, and many farms were quickly converted to building lots. Although the amount of agricultural land had been slowly shrinking since the 1870s, the decade of the 1920s was one of espe-

Opposite page: Immigrants farmed, built roads, worked in early industries, and served as domestic servants and gardeners on the large estates. These men worked at the Hicks Brothers Nursery in Westbury circa 1900. Courtesy, Hicks Photograph Collection

Above: A growing suburban population imposed considerable land requirements during the twentieth century, causing farm acreage to drop. Views such as this lone farmer on his land circa 1920 would all but disappear. Courtesy, Clarence Purchase Photograph Collection, SPLIA

cially swift conversion: total Nassau farmland diminished by almost two-thirds to about 25,000 acres. Operators of the county fair noticed the difference. Visitors seemed less intrigued by agricultural exhibits and showed far more interest in simple entertainment.

Though somewhat removed from the frantic Nassau scene, many Suffolk communities also felt the quickening pace of development, especially those North and South shore villages along the railroad right of way. Population, while not growing as swiftly as in Nassau, still jumped by 50,000 to 165,000 during the 1920s, the largest increase in Suffolk's history. Clusters of new homes appeared. Promoter T.B. Ackerman converted a "Bay Shore gentleman's estate into a high class suburban residential park where those of modest means may enjoy all the advantages." Realty Trust of New York City actively developed properties in Babylon, and in Brightwaters "choice 100' X 150' plots" sold for as little as $500. Villages like Amityville, Lindenhurst, Babylon, Patchogue, Islip, Bay Shore, and Huntington all experienced significant growth. Even some newspapers got into the act. The New York *Daily Mirror* offered eighty-nine-dollar lots in Rocky Point for less than five dollars down. They also threw in a free six-month subscription.

Further east at Montauk Point, brash promoter Carl Fisher promised something much grander. Fisher had previously built the Indianapolis Speedway, backed coast-to-coast motor highways, and earned a quick fortune developing Miami and Key West real estate. Turning his attention to eastern Long Island, he purchased 9,000 sandy acres for $2.5 million and dredged Lake Montauk to create a deep water harbor. Fisher then erected a seven-story office tower amidst the dunes and built the huge $1 million Montauk Manor hotel. On one summer day in 1927, over 25,000 visitors in 10,000 cars came to watch. Fisher's great scheme, however, ended in failure, for the Depression soon intervened. Land values plummeted, his companies went bankrupt, and when the super promoter died in the late 1930s, his real estate empire was only a tattered memory.

Long Island in the boom years attracted more than just commuters who shuttled daily to city offices and factories. A colorful and flamboyant show business colony of considerable proportions also developed, drawing strength from the Broadway stage and the motion picture studios in nearby Astoria, Queens. Performers, producers, writers, and directors like Fanny Brice, D.W. Griffith, W.C. Fields, Paulette Goddard, Ring Lardner, and Groucho

Marx clustered along the North Shore, especially in Great Neck. The Long Island Rail Road even ran a special late evening train to accommodate homeward-bound entertainers.

When the Vitagraph Company of Brooklyn opened a studio at Bay Shore in 1915, an artists' colony blossomed there too, including Marie Dressler, Norma Talmadge, and Fatty Arbuckle. Long Island's geographic diversity also provided varied backdrops for many on-location films. Much shooting was conducted at Roosevelt aviation field, while Rudolph Valentino's "Sheik" galloped across the dunes at Montauk Point.

Even more colorful than the movie stars who es-

Opposite page: Great Neck played summer home to many celebrities of the New York entertainment and publishing industries. W.C. Fields, who lived on Long Island, is depicted here in 1925 touring with director D.W. Griffith. From the Film Stills Archives, Museum of Modern Art

Above: Long Island's landscape began to change drastically in the 1930s as an unprecedented influx of suburban dwellers beseiged the area. Some Island communities, such as Baldwin in Nassau County (depicted circa 1931) clustered the new homes around small industry. Courtesy, Baldwin Historical Society and Museum

Left: Glenn Curtiss' experimental flights at Mineola in his "pusher plane," a small biplane looking somewhat like an enlarged box kite, helped make Long Island the center of aviation development. It continues to be one of the Island's largest industries. Courtesy, Nassau County Museum

THE DOUBLEDAYS

As with the great painters, it is perhaps best to describe the Doubledays through the breadth of their work. This three-generation book empire, headquartered in Garden City, introduced to the annals of literature works by W. Somerset Maugham, Rudyard Kipling, Daphne du Maurier, Joseph Conrad, H.G. Wells, Theodore Dreiser, Norman Mailer, and Alex Haley.

Without the support and guiding hand of the Doubledays, the world might never have had *Rebecca, A Tree Grows in Brooklyn,* and *Roots.* Indeed, the contributions of what became the world's largest book publishing firm are hard to overestimate. There are fifteen book clubs, including The Literary Guild. There are 600 new titles a year. There were, at times, 30 million books printed annually.

Like many of today's Long Island residents, the Doubledays came from New York City and migrated out to the country east of the Queens County line. Frank Nelson Doubleday, the founder of the book dynasty, was the son of a poor Brooklyn hatter and began his book career as a three-dollar-a-week staffer at Scribner's in 1881 at twenty-three years of age.

Eight years later, Doubleday struck out to form his own company, publishing some of Kipling's first works and forming a lifelong friendship with the author. Kipling had nicknamed Doubleday "Ef-

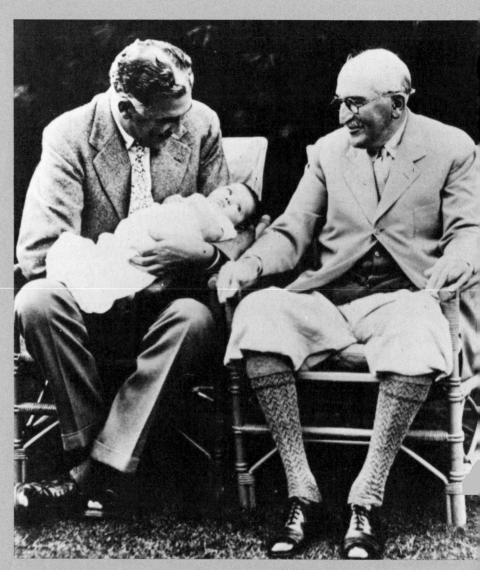

fendi," a Turkish title of respect and a play on the book magnate's initials, F.N.D. The city, however, could not provide the quiet and open spaces to which the publisher was suited, so in 1910 he moved the entire operation to a forty-acre site in Garden City.

Many of Doubleday's workers

Three generations of Doubledays established and maintained a book empire: Nelson Doubleday, Sr., holds Nelson Doubleday, Jr., as patriarch Frank Nelson Doubleday looks on. Courtesy, Doubleday & Co., Inc.

first came out on the Long Island Rail Road, and their special train stop, Country Life Press, exists today. By 1930 the plant was producing 40,000 books and 150,000 magazines a day.

Doubleday's sensibilities attracted a continual stream of talented writers and famous admirers. Formal garden parties at the exquisitely landscaped Garden City headquarters attracted the likes of industrialist John D. Rockefeller and President Theodore Roosevelt. Doubleday and his wife, Neltje De Graff, an author of nature books, and their two children, Nelson and Neltje, made their home in Mill Neck on Long Island's famed Gold Coast.

In the 1920s Nelson began assuming increasing amounts of responsibility in the firm and in 1928, at the age of thirty-nine, became president. He became chairman of the board in 1934 when his father died at the age of seventy-four. Nelson Doubleday was a shrewd and innovative businessman, developing the idea of selling month-old, high-quality magazines at half price. He started a mail-order book business and in 1929 bought the fledgling Literary Guild, then two years old. Nelson helped start a Canadian branch of Doubleday and revolutionized book publishing by striving to print large numbers of books at ever-lower unit costs. He often transacted business at his home on Long Island and at his plantation in Yemassee, South Carolina.

But Doubleday remained a product of Long Island and New York City, having been educated at Friends School, Holbrook Military Academy, and New York University. In 1932, after his first marriage ended in divorce, he married Ellen McCarter, daughter of Thomas N. McCarter, the president of the Public Service Company of New Jersey.

Nelson Doubleday died in 1949 at the age of fifty-nine, and his son, Nelson Jr., took over the business. Educated at Princeton, the younger Doubleday wrote his senior thesis on paperback books. While some of Doubleday's main offices have moved off Long Island, its Garden City building remains as the accounting division and Nelson Jr. remains active in Long Island affairs. Much of the Doubleday family still lives on Long Island, from East Hampton to Glen Cove.

Kimberly Greer
Stuart Diamond

The Doubleday headquarters in Garden City, designed to resemble England's Hampton Court by the firm of Kirby and Petit, was dedicated by Theodore Roosevelt in 1910. Courtesy, Doubleday & Co., Inc.

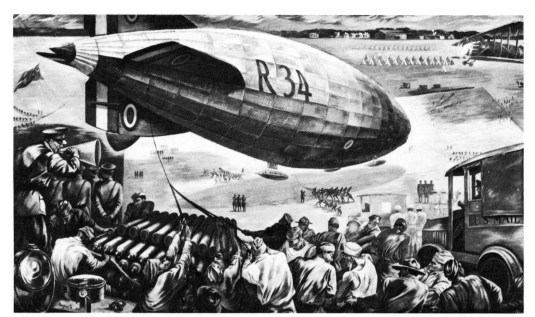

Painted in 1937 for the Hempstead Post Office, Peppino Mangravite's mural was commissioned through the Works Progress Administration's effort to counteract severe unemployment during the Depression. In addition to working on art-related projects, Long Islanders built roads, drainage systems, and county facilities such as Bethpage State Park in Nassau. The mural illustrates the arrival of the first airmail by the British dirigible R34 in 1919. Courtesy, National Archives

tablished homes on Long Island were the intrepid aviators who made the flat, open landscape their own. Aviation first reached the Island in 1908 when the infant New York Aeronautical Society purchased one of Buffalo inventor Glenn Curtiss' rickety pusher biplanes. In June 1909, after first rejecting a Bronx site, Curtiss surveyed the broad Hempstead Plains of Nassau and liked what he saw. He quickly commenced a series of exhibition flights, and soon Mineola and Garden City buzzed with the sounds of young adventurers trying to emulate his feat.

The following summer witnessed the great international air meet at Belmont Park. Twenty-five French, British, and American aviators competed before a huge audience, seeking fame and $75,000 in prize money. One of the most dramatic events was a race around the Statue of Liberty. That same year air mail service was initiated between Minoela and Garden City, a distance of about six miles. Shortly afterward the New York Aeronautical Society established a 1,000-acre flying field, complete with grandstand and twenty-five hangars. By 1916 Nassau was the undisputed leader of East Coast aviation. The First World War provided further impetus when the Army Air Service constructed huge complexes at Roosevelt and Mitchell fields, while naval aviators and flying boats were stationed at Far Rockaway and Bay Shore. A host of aircraft manufacturers also began production, spurred by wartime demand.

Though the postwar years were strewn with cor-

porate bankruptcies caused by the collapse of military orders, they were also the most exciting in the history of Long Island flight. In 1919 a Garden City-built Curtiss flying boat travelled to England by way of the Azores and Portugal. That same year Roosevelt Field hosted Britain's huge R-34 dirigible after a 108-hour non-stop flight from Scotland to New York. During the early 1920s, the Curtiss Company developed several record-breaking racing planes which dominated international competition. Among the most successful Curtiss pilots was James "Jimmy" Doolittle, later to win further fame for his "Thirty Seconds Over Tokyo."

Roosevelt Field, by now converted to civilian use, thronged with weekend crowds who came to watch assorted daredevils, wing walkers, and parachute jumpers, or to experience a thrilling ten-minute "joy ride." Roosevelt Field also became a take off point for several transatlantic expeditions, the most famous being Charles Lindbergh's epic 1927 hop from New York to Paris. Out east lesser known pilots used their fragile planes for less newsworthy missions, like the bootlegging of illegal whiskey from Canada.

America's Great Depression sharply affected the suburban boom. Land speculation virtually ceased, while homebuilding slowed to a trickle. Perhaps one worker in six was laid off. Unemployment soon stalked the Island, and federal, state, and local governments eventually responded with a variety of programs. Emergency work bureaus hired tens of thousands to perform a wide range of assignments: traffic accident surveys, road sign installation, historic surveys, adult education courses. Major public construction projects (including courthouses, post offices, roads, and military buildings at Mitchell Field) were also initiated. For those unable to work, home relief often helped put food on the table.

Despite the suffering and drastic slowing of the local economy, some growth continued. By 1940 Nassau's population had swelled to 400,000. Depression or not, Nassau County was no longer a sleepy neighbor or even a country retreat for the urban masses. It had instead become a bedroom community for the New York metropolis. Everywhere new houses, roads, schools, and shops appeared, while farming and all the old ways that went with it contracted dramatically.

One measure of the changes wrought was a comprehensive governmental overhaul instituted at the county level to address modern problems of explo-

sive growth. After a struggle lasting two decades, antiquated county institutions were replaced in 1938. Local voters adopted a new charter which created the centralized office of County Executive, a unified budget, a county welfare department, a remodelled Board of Supervisors, and a countywide tax assessment board.

Suffolk County, still relatively isolated from New York City, also succumbed to the economic collapse. The impact was especially severe where agriculture and fishing predominated. Several older communities like Port Jefferson, Greenport, and Southampton actually lost population and the overall county growth rate plummeted 50 percent. Despite the heightened real estate activity of the 1920s, Suffolk remained essentially agrarian in outlook, decentralized in government. A new and even more dynamic brand of post-World War II suburbanization would be required to wrest the county from its nineteenth-century past.

Charles Lindbergh and his Spirit of St. Louis captured the wonder and imagination of a generation of Americans when he flew from Long Island on May 20, 1927, and landed in Paris 33½ hours and 3,640 miles later. Courtesy, Nassau County Museum

185

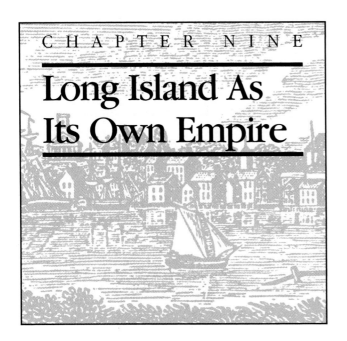

CHAPTER NINE

Long Island As Its Own Empire

The decades which followed World War II witnessed Long Island's greatest and most rapid transformation, as a tidal wave of suburban growth overwhelmed Walt Whitman's Paumonok, leaving no aspect of the local landscape untouched. Nassau County, greatly developed in the 1920s and 1930s, rapidly assumed a role as one of America's leading suburbs. Population spurted from approximately 400,000 in 1940 to over 1,300,000 by 1960. The often cantankerous Long Island Rail Road truly earned its nickname as "The Route of the Dashing Commuter." Suffolk, still largely rural at war's end, experienced a somewhat delayed, but equally energetic, surge that carried local population from 275,000 in 1945 to 1,125,000 in 1970.

Both counties confronted similar challenges: explosive expansion and all the pressures which accompanied it, followed almost immediately by the very different dilemmas which characterized consolidation, aging, and sharply curtailed growth. In only two decades vast housing developments, hundreds of new schools, dozens of retail shopping centers, and miles of highways opened. So did major universities, cultural institutions, and a host of recreational facilities. Surprisingly, within just a few years, some of those very same schools bolted their doors for lack of students, and foreclosure signs dotted certain subdivisions.

Farming, long an economic mainstay, virtually disappeared in Nassau and fell under increasing pressure in its eastern neighbor. In place of agricultural activities came a host of manufacturing and financial pursuits, led by giant aerospace corporations. Industry finally took root in the Long Island economy. Along the way, the area's relationship with New York City changed from nearly complete

Cold Spring Harbor Labora-
tory, founded in 1890, stands
at the vanguard of cancer
research and molecular genet-
ics, preserving its historic
buildings while accommodat-
ing the needs of modern sci-
ence. Photo by Dave Mikloso.
Courtesy, Cold Spring Harbor
Laboratory

dependence to far greater autonomy. As the *New York Times* rightly concluded: "From behaviour to politics, ecology to economics, there is virtually nothing this outward migration has not changed."

Triggering the postwar suburban phenomenon was a fantastic housing boom generated by the pent-up demands of millions of ex-G.I.s. Both the depression of the 1930s and stringent wartime priorities combined to limit home construction in the metropolitan area. But now the vets were coming home, clamoring for houses with which to shelter their new families. Sensing the opportunity, developer Abraham Levitt and his son, William, announced plans in May 1947 to build hundreds of small, inexpensive homes on a tract of farmland in central Nassau County. The response was overwhelming. They received 6,500 applications within a few weeks, and the first houses were completed by October. Plans to sell the small capes and ranches—originally designed as rental units—were facilitated by the growing availability of veteran's financing and long-term mortgages. Terms were easy: ninety dollars down and fifty-eight dollars per month purchased a $7,000- to $10,000-domicile. When construction ceased in November 1951, over 17,440 houses had been sold and a new community born. In 1940 Levittown counted only a few hundred residents, but by 1955 the population had reached 56,000, including 19,000 schoolchildren.

As other developers quickly emulated Levitt's methods, the remaining farmland of central and southern Nassau County rapidly gave way to homes, streets, and playgrounds. Potato and vegetable fields in Hicksville, Plainview, Syosset, Massapequa, and elsewhere soon sprouted capes, ranches, and colonial-style houses. East Meadow quadrupled its population to 57,000 in only six years. In the same period, Hicksville added 30,000 residents, Massapequa, 25,000. There seemed no end to the demand for housing, as the stream of new homeowners from Brooklyn and Queens became a flood. In just ten years Nassau welcomed 650,000 new citizens.

Such explosive expansion, however, could not possibly be sustained indefinitely. As the quantity of easily developed land diminished, so did the rate of construction and population growth. The peak occurred in 1958 when 7,200 new homes were built. Thereafter volume slipped to 4,160 dwellings in 1960, 3,000 in 1965, and barely 1,000 by 1970. Pop-

ulation trends mirrored the construction slowdown. After spurting by nearly 100 percent in the 1950s, Nassau grew by a much more modest 10 percent in the 1960s.

Yet even while Nassau's expansion slowed, nearby Suffolk's accelerated. In the first burst of postwar energy, the county's population jumped by 75,000 in the late 1940s and by almost 400,000 more within the next decade, as Nassau's frantic economic activity spilled across the border into the westernmost towns. By 1960 Suffolk's own boom was roaring along and the number of county residents leaped from 667,000 to more than 1,125,000 in the next de-

Art lovers enjoy the Huntington Art League's annual summer show held on the historic village green. The exhibits display a wide range of media and attract over 5,000 visitors. Courtesy, Huntington Township Art League, Inc.

Coney Island continued to draw huge summer crowds after World War II, as seen in this view from the parachute jump at Steeplechase Park in 1950. Courtesy, National Archives

WILLIAM J. LEVITT

His name is identified with the quintessential suburb and with America's first great post-World War II community. Like Henry Ford with cars, he revolutionized the building of houses and, perhaps more than any other individual, he gave Long Island its modern identity. He is, of course, William J. Levitt, the builder of Levittown. "Any fool can build houses," Levitt said as his community neared completion in 1948. "What counts is how many you can sell for how little." In 1950, *Time* magazine called Levitt "the most potent single modernizing influence in a largely antiquated industry."

Born in 1907 in Brooklyn, William Jaird Levitt, one of two sons of attorney Abraham Levitt, dropped out of New York University after his junior year and started building homes. "I wanted to make a lot of money," he said. His father started Levitt and Sons builders in 1929, and in the 1930s Bill Levitt and his brother, Alfred, an architect, were building custom houses for the upper middle class on the North Shore of Nassau County. These early communities included the Strathmores in Manhasset, developed between 1933 and 1949 on former Frank Munsey and Virginia Graham Vanderbilt properties, a Strathmore community in Rockville Centre, and a development in Roslyn. But the move that would lead to fame occurred during World War II when

In 1946, William J. Levitt became a household word when he converted a Hempstead potato field into a sprawling community of 17,447 Cape Cod houses. Courtesy, Newsday, Inc.

Levitt learned Navy techniques of quickly building identical slab houses as an officer in the Seabees.

Departing from the age-old and costly technique of crafting each house individually, Levitt divided home building into twenty-six separate steps and trained teams of workmen in each step so the houses could be built in assembly-line fashion. For each working day over a three-year period, an extraordi-

nary average of thirty homes were finished. The four-room expandable homes sold for $6,990 each—$2,000 below those of competitors. None had basements, another feature that enabled the homes to be built more quickly and more cheaply, but all had a complement of appliances, including refrigerators, ranges, and washing machines. Levitt also planted more than 500,000 trees that would grow along with young families. And eventually there were swimming pools, ballfields, shopping centers, churches, schools—a complete suburban community.

The Levittown formula has been transferred to many places, both in the United States and abroad. Not only have replicas of Levitt's models been built throughout Long Island, but there are senior citizen Levittowns in Florida and Levitt communities in France, Puerto Rico, Nigeria, and Venezuela; in all, there are more than 140,000 of his homes. There was even to be a Levittown in Iran, called Levittshar, but the property was taken over by the revolutionary government when the Shah of Iran fell, prompting a still-pending thirty-four-million-dollar lawsuit by Levitt in international court.

Although the houses in Levittown have largely been modified and expanded by their owners so that they no longer look alike, the imprint of Levitt endures. So valuable has this imprint become that when the company, Levitt & Sons, was sold to International Telephone and Telegraph Corporation for ninety-two million dollars in 1968, Levitt was barred for a time from using his own name on his new projects.

Kimberly Greer
Stuart Diamond

Levittown, depicted circa 1948 before lawns and trees were planted, began a unique episode in the development of American communities. Courtesy, Newsday, Inc.

cade.

Real estate developers began looking eastward after the end of the war, and shortly thereafter new or enlarged communities appeared at Huntington, Islip, East Northport, and Lindenhurst. Speculators then snapped up nearby farmland, anticipating the same growth then transforming neighboring Nassau. Their predictions were correct. A farming hamlet like Centereach counted only 628 residents in 1950. Ten years later there were tracts of development homes, new schools, and modern shopping centers, as the population reached 6,700. By 1980 it topped 30,000. The same story was repeated throughout western and central Suffolk County. Brookhaven Township, the county's largest, jumped from 44,000 residents in 1950 to 365,000 two decades later. Huntington, Babylon, and Islip all quadrupled in size. Smithtown grew by 475 percent in twenty years.

In contrast to Nassau, where space was the only factor limiting construction, Suffolk's red-hot expansion was cooled by man-made events. The 1973-75 recession and inflation caused high interest rates and slow economic growth, consequently ending the era of cheap mortgages and homes. OPEC's oil embargo and the resulting high gasoline prices also made long-distance commuting prohibitively expensive. Bank foreclosures mounted; Suffolk's impres-

sive growth rate skidded from 10 percent annually in the 1960s to only 1.5 percent in the 1970s.

Holding the burgeoning communities together, indeed, making so much of the growth possible at all, was the tremendous expansion of Long Island's transportation network. Whereas Long Island's first land boom in the early twentieth century was based on the railroad, the suburbs of the 1950s and 1960s depended entirely on the automobile.

Well into the mid-century, many of Long Island's principal thoroughfares were tree-lined, two-lane affairs. Adequate for the traffic of the 1920s when they were first paved, they became increasingly overburdened with each passing year, however. State parkways on the North and South shore counted only two lanes in either direction, excluded commercial traffic, and barely penetrated Suffolk County. Yet, the volume of vehicles soared without precedent. Nassau auto registrations jumped from 210,000 in 1950 to 700,000 in 1970; Suffolk experienced identical growth. And so construction of new roads and improvements of old ones commenced. A Suffolk extension of the Southern State Parkway opened in 1946. Nine years later the route was widened to six lanes, invigorating older South Shore villages like Islip, Patchogue, and Bay Shore. New roads, including the Sagtikos Parkway, Meadow-

Opposite page: Southampton is one of the most famous and fashionable summer resort villages in the United States. Surrounded by summer cottages, exceptional recrea- *tional facilities, and natural beauty, this small village attracts hundreds of thousands of visitors each year. Photo by Joseph Adams. (SPLIA)*

Above: During World War II women comprised more than 40 percent of the production force in Long Island's busy aviation and military support industries. At Grumman Air- *craft, women worked as draftsmen, riveters, sheet metal workers, and mechanics. Courtesy, Grumman Aerospace Corporation*

Left: Built in 1930-1931, The Big Duck in Flanders is a Long Island architectural landmark. Containing a poultry store, the huge duck symbolizes the poultry industry's importance on the Island. Photo by Harvey A. Weber. (SPLIA)

Opposite page: Nassau County's school age population greatly expanded in the 1950s, and Suffolk County experienced the same growth a decade later. These schoolchildren are walking home from Lloyd Harbor Elementary School. Photo by Harry Haralambou

brook Parkway extension, and Seaford Expressway, improved north-south access. The old Sunrise Highway was enlarged as an expressway all the way to Southampton.

But of all the transportation projects, the most important was the (in)famous Long Island Expressway, a new six-lane concrete spine running down the center of the Island. Construction of the region's first high-speed commercial highway began in 1955, intending to facilitate commuter traffic into New York City and service Long Island's expanding industries. Road crews reached central Nassau in 1958, touched the Suffolk border in 1962, and pressed on to Riverhead in 1972. The new road lured commuters and businesses ever deeper into Nassau and Suffolk counties. In fact, it proved so popular that almost from the start, huge traffic jams developed. "The Longest Parking Lot in the World" often seemed the kindest epithet uttered by frustrated motorists.

Almost as important to Long Island's growth as the construction of modern highways was the emergence of the aerospace industry. Looking back over recent history, a local newspaper observed in 1965, "When Long Island's economy was in its prime in the 1940s and 1950s, the base of the boom was high-paying employment at five giant defense contractors." Clearly the growth of the aerospace industry contributed to the Island's transformation into a

heavily settled region of urban and suburban areas supporting a diversified manufacturing complex. Yet such a result was by no means preordained, since Long Island aircraft manufacturers had earlier endured decades of frustration and defeat.

Shops building one- or two-seater airplanes appeared during aviation's pioneer days, but fared poorly in securing investment capital and adequate sales. World War I altered the picture and a number of modern factories emerged: LWF and Chance Vought in Queens, Curtiss in Garden City, Breese in Farmingdale. Despite such progress and glittering growth prospects, the Armistice in 1918 triggered the near-complete collapse of American military aviation. Government contracts evaporated and surplus aircraft flooded the market.

The reviving civilian economy in the 1920s and epic achievements like Lindbergh's great flight rekindled interest in the industry. A new crop of inventors and manufacturers led by Igor Sikorsky and Sherman Fairchild entered the field. Their plans received a sharp setback with the onset of the Great Depression, however. Soon Sikorsky, Vought, Fairchild, and Curtiss moved away, and despite the Island's topographic advantages and nearby New York City's financial and industrial strengths, aviation's overall impact remained quite limited.

Gathering war clouds in Europe and the Orient changed all that, with firms like Grumman, Repub-

lic, and Sperry spearheading the shift to military production. Grumman began operating in a rented garage, but soon moved to larger quarters in Valley Stream and then Bethpage, where workers specialized in building fast, tough fighters for the Navy. The guiding spirit at the Seversky (later Republic) Aircraft Corporation was Major Alexander DeSeversky, an expatriate Russian naval officer who dreamed of building the world's fastest, strongest fighters. Many of his 1930s creations were flown to racing victories by aviatrix Jackie Cochran. Sperry, founded in Brooklyn at the turn of the century to produce naval navigation systems, entered aviation in a big way during World War I and thereafter became a world leader in aircraft instrumentation.

America's prewar rearmament effort led to rapidly rising employment and production levels, and Pearl Harbor triggered full-scale mobilization. Long Island's growing aviation industry responded heroically. Grumman increased its workforce from 1,500 to 25,000 and produced more than 17,000 airplanes. Bethpage-produced Wildcats and Hellcats played a dominant role in America's Pacific victory. Republic at Farmingdale exerted similar efforts, as a work-

force of 23,000 manufactured 16,000 aircraft, most notably the rough, tough P-47 Thunderbolt. Moving to Nassau in 1942, Sperry employed 32,000 men and women who turned out mountains of navigation and guidance equipment. Every Long Island garage and factory seemed to resound with the chatter of riveting hammers.

Victory in World War II led to temporary disaster on the shop floor. Washington cancelled most contracts and 80 percent of the 100,000 wartime workers were laid off. It appeared likely that the dismal post-World War I story would be repeated again. But aviation had become too important a part of national defense planning, and Long Island's firms were now too large to languish for long. Introduction of jet aircraft, especially Republic's F-84 Thunderjet and Grumman's F9F Panther, revived local industry. With the outbreak of fighting in Korea, new orders skyrocketed and employment jumped again. Republic hired hundreds weekly; the workforce peaked at 30,000 in 1954. Grumman, Sperry, Fairchild, and Arma enjoyed a similar upsurge, at the very moment the Long Island real estate boom was in full swing. As some of the largest employers in the New York metropolitan area, local aerospace firms provided high-paying jobs for thousands, subcontracts for hundreds of smaller firms, and an enormous ripple effect throughout the civilian economy. Within a few more years these same firms would be building guided missiles, satellites, and lunar landers. Suburbia armed was suburbia transformed.

The frantic postwar construction boom, while creating new homes, communities, and employment opportunities, spelled the final demise of Nassau agriculture and greatly altered the course of Suffolk farming. A socio-economic activity which dated back to the Indian era and the first days of colonial settlement was drawing to a close. Predictably, the impact was most severe in Nassau, where any available land sold at a premium. As late as 1945, the county retained 650 farms on 27,000 acres of cropland. Villages like Plainview, Woodbury, and Jericho remained overwhelmingly rural. But by 1954, with housing growing in the potato fields, cropland had already dropped to 13,000 acres. Small agricultural hamlets like Syosset, in the words of a local guidebook, "felt the pressure of home development . . . large tracts of farmland are reluctantly giving

LEROY R. GRUMMAN

Leroy Randle Grumman was one of aviation's early pioneers in America and founded an aircraft company that grew and expanded into one of the nation's largest. This company was to become world famous as the designer of the Apollo Lunar Module.

Leroy Grumman was born on January 4, 1895, and was raised in Huntington, Long Island, attending Huntington High School where he graduated second in his class. His father, Tyson Grumman, was a carriage shop owner and later a postal clerk. As a youth, Grumman

developed a fascination for the budding field of aviation by watching early Long Island aviators take off and land on the dirt strips near his home. Long Island, in the early days of aviation, was an exciting and stimulating place generating an abundant cross-pollination of ideas. Most of the early pioneers flew their experimental biplanes, monoplanes, and pusher planes from the flat plains of Hempstead. In 1910 the first international Aviation Tournament was held at Belmont Park, where speed and altitude records were set. Glen

Curtiss, the aviator and inventor, thrilled thousands with his exhibitions of aerial feats in his "Gold Bug," an early pusher plane. Curtiss operated an aviation school near Mineola in the early teens and eventually headed the Curtiss Aeroplane and Motor Company. From 1909 to 1929, the activities of experimental fliers on Long Island fields made the Island world famous as "the cradle of aviation," culminating in the famous Charles Lindbergh flight across the Atlantic in the *Spirit of St. Louis.*

When Grumman left Huntington, he went to Cornell to study engineering, graduating in 1916. During World War I he became a Navy test pilot. After the war he worked in a Philadelphia Naval aircraft factory and then with Loening as general manager of its Long Island plant.

Grumman Aircraft Engineering Corporation got its start on January 2, 1930, in a Baldwin garage. Leroy Grumman, Jake Swirbul, and Bill Schwendler, along with former colleagues from Loening, opened the small company with a lot of ideas and spunk, but little capital. However, in the 1930s Grumman forged a strong relationship with the Navy developing naval aircraft, fighter biplanes, and amphibious aircraft. In 1937 the company constructed its first civilian aircraft, the twin-engine Grey Goose amphibian. The company was soon selling amphibians to a clientele that included Marshall Field, Henry S. Morgan, and Lord Beaverbrook. With war looming in 1939, the production of military aircraft became a priority. The fighter planes that Grumman designed during World War II were revered by pilots and were reported to have shot down more than 60 percent of the enemy aircraft destroyed in the Pacific. Vice Admiral John McCain said that "the name Grumman on a plane or a part is like sterling on silver."

Leroy Grumman's talents were legendary around the company. His sight had been damaged due to an allergic reaction to penicillin and he relinquished the role of president in 1946, but remained as chairman of the board for the next twenty years. A quiet man who did not go in for the showier side of

business, he steered his company to success with a combination of exceptional executive leadership and an outstanding staff. In 1968 he was awarded the first Hunsacker Medal from the National Academy of Sciences for his contributions to aeronautical sciences. Grumman died in 1982 and the flags at the Grumman plants were lowered to half-staff.

From his boyhood days watching the daring pilots take off from local dirt strips to the engineering genius who led the development of the Lunar Module used in the 1969 Apollo 11 moon landing, Leroy Randle Grumman was a major force in developing Long Island into the "cradle of aviation."

Tim O'Brien

Opposite page: Leroy R. Grumman sits at his desk at the Grumman Aerospace Corporation. Courtesy, Grumman Aerospace Corporation

Above: Grumman's main plant at Bethpage features an air strip used for experiments. Courtesy, Grumman Aerospace Corporation

FINE ARTS CENTER

way to the march of the homeseeker." Barely 7,500 acres of open land remained in 1960, just 1,500 by 1980, mostly located on scattered North Shore estates. Only a dozen small vegetable farms survived.

Suffolk agriculture rested on a firmer foundation and for a time successfully resisted suburban encroachment. The county's 2,100 farms contained 120,000 acres in 1950 and produced 15,000,000 bushels of potatoes and 5,000,000 ducks. A Long Island Rail Road brochure called the region an "Agricultural Paradise." But soon there was trouble in this agricultural haven, too. Financial pressures mounted and within a generation extensive residential and commercial construction nearly ended farming in Suffolk's western towns. The populations of formerly rural villages like Medford, South Huntington, and Hauppauge leaped from a few hundred to 15,000 or 20,000. Total county cropland fell by a quarter. Presented with the opportunity to sell out at high prices, many growers turned off the tractor and retired. Hundreds of farms were converted to homes and shopping malls, and by 1980 only 160 acres of cropland remained in Islip and just 74 acres were left in Babylon.

Further east, development proved less intense

and farming persisted, even flourished. Brookhaven, Riverhead, Southampton, and Southold continued producing potatoes, vegetables, and fruit. When older staples like potatoes and ducks declined, new ones, including fine wine grapes, replaced them. Surprisingly, with 50,000 acres in production and its 1980 crops valued at $100 million, heavily-settled Suffolk still stood first among New York's agricultural counties.

Realizing the great changes taking place in land use patterns, and hoping to preserve open, agricultural spaces, Suffolk's Planning Commission in 1960 recommended that at least 30,000 acres be saved from the bulldozer. As the problem grew even more acute, the county legislature responded in the early 1970s by enacting a fifty-five-million-dollar program to acquire farmland development rights, thus preserving the countryside's pastoral character. By 1980 about 7,500 acres had been reserved under this and a related New York State Agricultural Districts Law. It remains to be seen, however, whether these programs can maintain additional amounts of open space, especially as demand for summer homes soars and the price of land rockets upward on the vacation-oriented East End.

Opposite page: Established on land donated by philanthropist Ward Melville, The State University of New York at Stony Brook is considered one of the nation's best state

universities. Its Fine Arts Center offers residents and visitors an extensive schedule of performances. Courtesy, SUNY at Stony Brook

Above: The Health Science Center at the State University of New York at Stony Brook is one of the world's most sophisticated medical centers. Its schools of medicine, dentistry,

nursing, allied health professions, and social welfare are all linked to the dark glass towers of the 540-bed University Hospital. Courtesy, SUNY at Stony Brook

Above: Jones Beach was opened in 1929 and has received worldwide recognition for its beauty and outstanding recreational facilities. In the background is Jones Beach Theater, constructed in 1952 and known for the music concerts once conducted there by band leader Guy Lombardo. Courtesy, Long Island State Park Commission

Opposite page: Eaton's Neck Lighthouse and Coast Guard Station is one of many lighthouses guiding ships away from Long Island Sound's coastline. Photo by Robert V. Fuschetto

Above: Father and son feed the ducks at Heckscher Park in Huntington Village. Photo by Robert V. Fuschetto

Left: A mute swan and her cygnets glide through the waters of Connetquot River State Park. Photo by Barbara C. Harrison

Below: Freshwater fishing is a popular Long Island pastime for young and old alike. Photo by Paul J. Oresky

Right: Bicyclists enjoy the beauty and breeze of Cold Spring Harbor. The harbor town, with its impressive whaling museum, is listed on the National Register of Historic Places. Photo by Robert V. Fuschetto

Left: Children enjoy horseback riding at West Hills County Park in South Huntington. Photo by Robert V. Fuschetto

Long Island's tree-lined country lanes turn to gold during autumn. Photo by Harry Haralambou

Above: Scenic wetlands display their autumn colors around Huntington. Photo by Harry Haralambou

Right: Long Island has had considerable fishing, oystering, and clamming industries since its first settlements appeared more than 300 years ago. (SPLIA)

Beautiful, untouched vegetation can still be found in Long Island's state parks. Photo by Paul J. Oresky

*A Huntington pond begins to
show signs of autumn. Photo
by Harry Haralambou*

One of Long Island's many modern recreational facilities, the Nassau Veterans Memorial Coliseum opened in 1971 and features a wide range of events. It is the home of Long Island's major league hockey team, the Islanders. Courtesy, Nassau Veterans Memorial Coliseum

Long Island in the days of the great land rush and corresponding baby boom saw much more than just home construction and the disappearance of ancient farmland. An entirely new society was taking form, a family-oriented community larger than all but a handful of American cities. Young, affluent, mobile residents demanded services and amenities to fit their lifestyle, and nowhere was this more obvious than in public education. Nassau's school age population leaped from 70,000 in 1947 to about 330,000 in 1964, while Suffolk's crested about a decade later. Hundreds of new schools were built, tens of thousands of teachers were hired, and property taxes were raised again and again. No matter how high the cost, Long Island's parents seemed willing to pay it.

Nor was education expected to cease after high school graduation, for the Island's middle-class population placed great emphasis on college, as well. In the early years, returning veterans provided the bulk of new students. Adelphi College, a school for women in Garden City, consequently went coed after the war. Within a few years, however, the children of the suburbs added to the collegiate throngs. Hofstra University in Hempstead counted 3,500 students in 1950 and more than 12,000 two decades later. C.W. Post College opened in 1955 with 121 undergraduates on a site donated by heiress Marjorie Merriweather Post. Over 15,000 attended classes a generation later. Nassau County organized a community college from scratch and eventually enrolled over 16,000 young men and women, while the state university built or expanded campuses at Farmingdale and Old Westbury. As Suffolk County grew and matured, it too received new facilities, notably the large community college at Selden, and even more significantly, the State University at Stony Brook which held its first classes in 1962. One of New York State's four university centers, Stony Brook attracted thousands of students, and within a decade a major teaching hospital was under construction there.

Retail services were a prime consideration of local residents, also. It often seemed that land not covered with homes, schools, or parks supported the new suburban mecca, the shopping mall. The first mall opened in Manhasset in 1945 and eventually grew to encompass 182 stores. During the next decades, huge retail complexes followed at Roosevelt Field in Garden City (148 stores), Green Acres in Valley Stream (100 stores), Mid-Island in Hicksville (159 stores), Walt Whitman in Huntington (125 stores), and Smithaven on the Smithtown-Brookhaven line (127 stores). Situated near the highway and designed to accommodate auto shoppers, these re-

Above: The H. Lee Dennison Building (center) in Hauppauge was named after Suffolk County's first execu- *tive and houses the district courts and the traffic courts. Courtesy, Aero Graphics Corporation* *Opposite page: Grumman has become Long Island's largest private employer. Best known as a manufacturer of military aircraft and aerospace systems, its other products* *include computer services, boats, truck bodies, and emergency vehicles. Courtesy, Grumman Aerospace Corporation*

tailing palaces utilized generous parking, air conditioning, and tremendous variety to draw customers away from the older village centers.

Still another component of the suburban dream was sufficient recreational facilities for the growing crowds. During the 1920s and 1930s the Long Island Park Commission, headed by Robert Moses, had given the region a fine start with recreational facilities at Jones Beach, Fire Island, Bethpage, and Orient Point. Visitation at existing installations increased rapidly after 1945, and several layers of government actively intervened to develop additional parks. Nassau County created a large recreational complex at Salisbury Park and later constructed a modern indoor arena for basketball and hockey. Nature preserves were set aside in Massapequa and Roslyn. Local governments developed beaches and built pools and playgrounds.

Suffolk County, with 75,000 acres of recreational lands, actively participated in this movement, too. State, county, and town parks were established at Captree, Wildwood, Nicolls Point, Smith Point, Sunken Meadow, Shinnecock Inlet, and Hither Hills. The magnificent beaches and open lands that had attracted so many excursioners in years past were thus preserved for future generations, despite the fantastic development pressures all around them.

Modern suburban life also required important changes in the political and governmental system. Nassau first came to terms with the processes of centralized management through its charter reforms of 1938. More rural Suffolk did not fully address the issue for another generation. Instead, the somewhat rustic county remained a rather loosely governed confederation of towns and incorporated villages, overseen by a Board of Supervisors. The challenge of coordinating the unprecedented regional growth of the 1950s called for expert and permanent leadership, however. In 1958 Suffolk followed Nassau's example with a major governmental overhaul. Lee Dennison, a Democrat in a largely Republican electorate, became the first County Executive. Also created were effective county agencies and a unified police force for the five heavily populated western towns. Hauppauge, located closer to emerging popu-

ALICIA PATTERSON GUGGENHEIM

The wealthy and socially prominent Alicia Patterson Guggenheim, founder and editor of Newsday, *was the driving force behind what was to become one of the nation's largest evening newspapers. Courtesy,* Newsday, Inc.

Few newspaper ventures in modern history have succeeded as well as *Newsday.* Started in a drafty Hempstead garage in 1940, *Newsday* is now the nation's largest evening newspaper and tenth largest overall, with 539,000 copies circulated daily and 602,000 on Sunday. Its profit statements are envied throughout journalism. Both the birth and growth of *Newsday* bear the mark of one woman, Alicia Patterson. Miss Patterson began her undertaking with $70,000 from her third husband, millionaire Harry F. Guggenheim, the major

benefactor of the Guggenheim Museum in New York City. The first day's sales on September 3, 1940, were 15,000 copies of a thirty-two-page tabloid printed on second-hand presses. With what she called sheer guts, Miss Patterson built the paper into a lively, irreverent, prize-winning venture of national reputation. Perhaps the pinnacle of her career came on September 13, 1954, when she appeared on the cover of *Time* magazine with the caption "Publisher Patterson. On Long Island, big city ways."

Born in 1906 into a fifth-genera-

tion newspaper family, Alicia Patterson did not have to work for a living. Her father, Joseph Medill Patterson, owner of the New York *Daily News,* was the grandson of the publisher of the *Chicago Tribune.* She spent her early years on an isolated Libertyville, Illinois, farm, her teenage years at a succession of private schools, and her leisure time at society parties in Manhattan and at Long Island's "Gold Coast" mansions. She also spent time big game hunting, riding to hounds, and setting an aviation speed record flying solo from

New York to London. After two marriages, she wed Harry Guggenheim and in 1940 started her own newspaper, holding a contest to name the new paper. She commuted to Hempstead from "Falaise," the thirty-room mansion she shared with her husband at Sands Point, now a museum owned by Nassau County. Despite her earlier, rather aimless life, Patterson had always wanted to be a newspaperwoman. "I have been in love with newspapers since I first learned to read," she said. "I've always had a passion for having a paper. I don't want to make money. I don't want political power. I just want a good newspaper." Guggenheim was *Newsday's* president, owning 51 percent of the stock; Miss Patterson, called "Miss P" by the staff, was the editor and publisher. They frequently disagreed on editorials: Guggenheim was much more conservative, resulting in signed editorials. *Newsday* grew along with Long Island, with Levittown and the Long Island Expressway, with the young families and the shopping centers and the problems of a burgeoning suburb. By 1957 *Newsday's* daily circulation was 130,000, as the paper mixed readable animal and crime stories with tough investigations. Miss Patterson's maxim was "Never let go, once you have sunk your teeth into a good story." "We have never succumbed to the stuffed-shirt approach to life; we have never been scared of

a fight," Miss Patterson wrote in 1959, as the paper crusaded against local real estate and political corruption that won it fame while it occasionally lost subscribers. "The paper is like me, for I am a temperamental person, with violent likes and dislikes." Her fervent support of President Franklin D. Roosevelt, in fact, led to an estrangement from her father, who changed his will in 1946 to leave control of the *Daily News* to his widow in trust for his son, James.

When she died at age fifty-six on July 2, 1963, following surgery for a stomach ailment, the paper's circulation had reached 370,000 daily, its weekly ad lineage topped every other New York newspaper, and *Newsday* had a Pulitzer Prize and four Polk Awards to its credit. Letters of condolence arrived from all over the country, including one from President John F. Kennedy, who praised her "initiative and leadership." Perhaps the most eloquent eulogy came from Adlai Stevenson, her childhood friend, who said: "Her memory will refresh and liven and stimulate. ... The newspaper she created was a reflection of a genius that she inherited and enlarged ... this remarkably vital woman who thought and lived with purpose, conviction and courage."

Kimberly Greer
Stuart Diamond

Above: Brookhaven National Laboratory is considered one of the world's foremost institutions for research in the fields *of physical, biomedical, and environmental sciences. Courtesy, Brookhaven National Laboratory*

Opposite page: Local art leagues offer classes and workshops for adults and children in addition to lectures, symposiums, demonstra- *tions, and exhibitions. Photo by Lisa Lewicki. Courtesy, Huntington Township Art League, Inc.*

lation centers, became an important hub of government activity. In 1965 the Long Island Regional Planning Board was established, and a few years later Suffolk created a countywide legislature.

Increased governmental capabilities and sophistication soon proved vital as the suburban experience took an unpleasant detour. By the early 1970s the Long Island Regional Planning Board was chronicling the impact of two decades of unrestrained growth: crowded beaches and parks, polluted waters, declining village centers, frustrating travel on clogged highways, and undependable trains. Suddenly, the suburban dream seemed in grave peril. The passing of the baby boom in the late 1960s and early 1970s, coupled with a dramatic decline in the

number of young families moving to the bi-county region, created problems that officials rarely contemplated in earlier, expansionary times.

But growth did end. The society which blossomed overnight now began to age, a process first reflected in Nassau County, which witnessed a decline in elementary school enrollments in the 1960s. The number of births fell by half and the average age for the entire populace rose sharply. In fact, significant out-migration commenced in the 1970s, as Nassau's population fell by 100,000 (8 percent), the first decline ever recorded.

Suffolk felt the same forces, but a decade later, reflecting its more recent suburban boom. Births decreased by 20 percent, while the proportion of

children in the community fell at twice that rate. Residential construction expenditures dropped by two-thirds, and the number of building permits fell by 90 percent. Only on the East End, where second homeownership gained strength, did earlier growth patterns persist.

The great slowdown spawned a host of new problems for governments, businessmen, and local residents. The prevalent boom psychology gave way to pronouncements of limited choices and scarce resources. No longer were neighborhoods concerned about where schools should be built, but rather which ones to close in the face of declining enrollments. In many cases education budgets were defeated and austerity measures imposed. The question of teacher layoffs divided many communities. Some schools, built at great cost in the 1950s and 1960s, were converted to alternate community uses. Others were boarded up or torn down, even before the mortgages had been paid off.

A shortage of affordable housing developed, proving especially troublesome to young couples just starting out and to retired citizens who no longer required the large homes they had purchased twenty or thirty years earlier. Many suburban villages

exacerbated the problem by opposing construction of multiple dwellings and two-family houses. Yet high costs and even higher interest rates demanded modification of established patterns. Between 1945 and 1956, fewer than 7,000 apartments were built in Nassau, yet the Levitts alone constructed more than 17,400 homes. During the 1960s, however, the balance began to shift. For the entire decade, apartment starts outnumbered detached home permits. By 1980 Nassau's 90,000 rental units comprised one-fifth of the local housing stock. Suffolk also increasingly turned to rental housing, and during the 1970s built about 30,000 new apartments. Despite intense opposition by many property owners, several towns eventually accepted the presence of two-family homes, as well.

The aerospace industry which achieved such prominence in the 1950s and early 1960s could not carry the Long Island economy alone. Despite their size, corporations like Grumman, Republic, and Sperry remained subject to the ebb and flow of Pentagon procurement policies. When Republic failed to secure a follow-on contract to the successful F-105 "Thunderchief" fighter-bomber, its fortunes rapidly turned downward. Thousands of

Left: The Island's own philharmonic orchestra, seen here in a 1982 performance of Handel's Messiah, *joins a host of other notable cultural institutions that offer a wide range of performances and exhibits throughout the year. Photo by Charles Abbott. Courtesy, Long Island Philharmonic*

Pages 218-219: One of Long Island's major challenges is to balance its expansion and growth while preserving aspects of its history and architectural heritage for future generations. Here, the 1767 Joseph Lloyd Manor House, now preserved as a museum, provides the background for a colonial muster and encampment performed by the Huntington Militia, Queen's Rangers, and the 3rd New York Regiment. Photo by Joseph Adams. (SPLIA)

employees were laid off, and the company was eventually sold to Fairchild-Hiller. Although the new corporation remained a major Long Island employer with thousands of workers, it retained only a portion of its earlier economic clout.

In an effort to avoid a similar fate and reduce the overwhelming dependence on military orders, state and local officials backed programs leading to the construction of industrial parks specializing in diversified, non-defense, precision manufactures. Private industry also branched out into many technology-oriented fields: computers, guidance systems, communications, space exploration, radar. Though the Island's industrial sector remained heavily committed to military production, civilian efforts gained importance. Between 1964 and 1976, Nassau and Suffolk counties added 45,000 new manufacturing jobs and thirty-two million square feet of plant space, as Long Island industry acquired a marked high-technology orientation.

Equally important in sustaining the local economy as the 1970s progressed was the increased impact of white collar employment and related office construction. As late as 1965, Nassau contained less than two million square feet of commercial office

space in only fifty large buildings, while Suffolk supported barely half that amount. Most white collar workers still commuted to New York City. In the next few years, however, the rate of local construction increased, and by 1970 the volume of available office space had doubled. This was only a prelude to the 1970s, when New York banks, insurance companies, and brokerage houses finally discovered Long Island. The region's emerging computer and research firms also augmented the demand for commercial space. Major new office centers soon emerged at Melville, Lake Success, Jericho, and Garden City. Construction totalling over 3.5 million square feet was proposed for Mitchell Field in central Nassau, and a single complex containing over one million square feet arose adjacent to Hofstra University. By 1980 over twenty million square feet had been built, with much more underway. The result was a marked re-orientation of working patterns. In both Nassau and Suffolk, the number of locally employed workers increased rapidly, while the proportion of railroad commuters dropped sharply.

The growth of economic independence, the passage of time, experience with community-based organizations, and a growing appreciation of the region's unique past all combined to create a new sense of Long Island identity. Designation as a federally recognized metropolitan area in its own right aided the process. Despite their urban origins, local residents grew more distant from their New York City roots with each passing year. A new generation was raised on Long Island and knew no other home. More regional employment meant fewer commuters and greater interest in local economic affairs. Actively promoting a separate Long Island spirit were giant corporations like Long Island Lighting Company and Grumman; universities like Hofstra, Adelphi, the State University of New York, and C.W. Post; and a vigorous community press. These efforts often found expression in cultural groups like the Eglevsky Ballet, or athletic teams like the Islanders hockey club, both of which played to packed houses.

As development engulfed many vestiges of local history, preservation and museum groups moved to save and interpret what remained. A major outdoor historical museum opened at Old Bethpage, while a growing collection of vintage airplanes at Mitchell

Field saluted the Island's aviation heritage. Several Gold Coast mansions have been preserved as museums, schools, or conference centers, including properties once belonging to the Vanderbilts, Coes, Guggenheims, Chryslers, Pratts, Posts, and Phippses. Preservation societies have restored architectural landmarks, while maritime museums at Sag Harbor, Cold Spring Harbor, Sayville, and Amagansett highlight the Island's fishing and whaling past. In some cases entire downtown districts have been refurbished, as in Sea Cliff, Roslyn, Sag Harbor, and Greenport.

And so, more frequently and more insistently than at any time since the colonial era, Long Islanders of the seventies and early eighties viewed their towns as something special and apart from the surrounding cities. Slowly at first, and then with accelerating vigor, a new society of 2.6 million inhabitants

took shape. The colonial outpost, the vital breadbasket, the urban playground, and the bedroom suburb had all come of age.

Long Islanders at the beginning of the 1980s look both to their past and to the uncertain future. Faded downtowns are being revived, older homes renovated, historic sites preserved, some farmland saved. Current residents are attempting in many different ways to reach out to those who have passed before. At the same time, planners, business people, officials, and ordinary citizens address the evolving and troubling questions of modern suburban life: a dearth of clean water, affordable housing, adequate social services, effective transportation, rational planning, and good schools. The dual focus of preservation and development should come as no surprise, however, for Long Island society has always accommodated a generous measure of tradi-

tion and growth, steady habits and social revolution.

In its three and one-half centuries, the area has seen a world of change crowded onto its finite acres. The Island has borne the tread of Indian hunters and warriors. It has hosted settlers from other continents, and witnessed religious conflict and the clash of empires. In the compressed space of a few generations, Long Island experienced the political upheaval of the American Revolution, followed quickly by the social transformation of the Industrial Revolution. More recently the suburban explosion swept away many relics of earlier times, reshaping the landscape to suit its fancy.

Yet the Island remains, stretching eastward to the morning. Ocean tides still bathe its fragile, but enduring, shores. Baymen search daily for clams and oysters, fishermen challenge the deep, and

farmers till the fertile soil and send their produce to market. On a crisp fall day, irridescent waterfowl wing their way southward across the marshes.

A century ago Walt Whitman, Long Island's poet laureate, hiked the country paths and shoreline dunes; he rode the trains and ferries, prowled the Brooklyn streets, and described what he saw and felt. His powerful words, though written so far in the past, could easily address today's audience. In a moment of vision, he said of his beloved Paumonok:

See, vast trackless spaces
As in a dream they change, they swiftly fill,
Countless masses debauch upon them,
They are now cover'd with the foremost
* people, arts, institutions, known.*
See, projected through time,
For me an audience interminable.

219

Partners in Progress

As perhaps the definitive suburb, Long Island is the product of meshed contradictions. Increasingly self-sufficient in its professions and service industries, yet as dependent on international markets as on New York for its major industries, it is actually more city-state than suburb.

The Indians were Long Island's first baymen, harvesting rich bundles of scallops and clams from inland waterways, from coves along the Sound facing Connecticut, and from the Great South Bay at the edge of the Atlantic. They ventured into the vast ocean to hunt great whales, which seventeenth-century English explorers dubbed "royale fish."

But if raging ocean shore and swelling leeward pools attracted Dutch and English explorers in the 1600s, Long Island's acres of sunken meadows, wooded hills lush with game, and rolling farmland kept them coming shipload after shipload from Europe. Farming remains a staple of Long Island commerce, though cabbages, potatoes, pumpkins, and sod acres gave way to horses and vineyards.

As Long Island fishing and farming prospered into the nineteenth century, shipbuilding, banking, publishing, and spectacular feats of engineering appeared at its westernmost end in Brooklyn and Queens. In 1834 the railroad came. Today the Long Island Rail Road, America's oldest operating under its original name, is the nation's largest business commuter line.

The twentieth century dawned, and Long Island was the cradle of American aviation. However, real cowboys were still driving herds from Montauk to the Riverhead rail junction.

Suddenly, Long Island was the home of major military suppliers even as the Depression began. Today Long Island remains the base of many important contractors to the nation's defense and aerospace segments.

The world grew smaller, and the universe closer, as the technology that revolutionized communications, and sent Americans to the moon, was born and developed on Long Island.

Today Long Island ranks with "Route 128" in Massachusetts and with the "Silicon Valley" in California as a seminal high-technology center. Business publications and government statistics rank Nassau County third among all United States counties in production of electronic equipment, fourth in book publishing, and fifth in aircraft manufacturing. Suffolk County ranks sixth in production of radio and television communications equipment, and tenth in aircraft manufacturing.

Still, Long Island remains synonymous with the terms "bedroom community" and Manhattan "satellite." The ubiquitous 1955 Levitt home is still many people's idea of the place. Ironically, British occupying forces, bivouacked on Long Island's western shore to hold Manhattan against George Washington's Continental Army, were even earlier commuters. Old notions die hard.

The organizations whose stories are detailed on the following pages have chosen to support this important literary and civic project. They illustrate the variety of ways in which individuals and their businesses have contributed to the area's growth and development. The civic involvement of Long Island's businesses, institutions of learning, and local government, in cooperation with its citizens, has made the community an excellent place to live and work.

During the latter part of the nineteenth century Brooklyn's docks absorbed Manhattan's expanding trade, benefitting local industry and providing jobs for workers such as these at the Lawrence Paper Box Company on Atlantic Avenue. Courtesy, The Long Island Historical Society

SOCIETY FOR THE PRESERVATION OF LONG ISLAND ANTIQUITIES

The Society for the Preservation of Long Island Antiquities is a non-profit organization devoted to the preservation and interpretation of Long Island's past. SPLIA pursues this goal through the maintenance of historic house museums, educational programs, the publication of studies on Long Island's history and material culture, and through its preservation services program. Organized in 1946 by Howard C. Sherwood, SPLIA was formally incorporated in 1948. Suffolk County executive Kingsland Macy, Sperry Gyroscope president Preston R. Bassett, Ward Melville of Stony Brook, George Latham of Orient, Henry Francis du Pont of Southampton, and Allen L. Woodworth of Huntington were among the society's founding trustees who were collectively concerned about the effects of post-World War II development on Long Island's fragile historic resources.

To address this threat, the society acquired a number of Long Island landmarks that were restored and opened to the public as historic house museums. Among the houses now owned by or under the aegis of the society are the Custom House in Sag Harbor, the Sherwood-Jayne House in East Setauket, the Thompson House in Setauket, the Joseph Lloyd Manor House at Lloyd Neck, Rock Hall in Lawrence, and the Wyckoff House in Flatbush. In recent years the society has broadened its programming to include educational programs at its historic house museums for elementary and secondary school students, a publication program focusing on salient aspects of Long Island's interesting history, architecture and decorative arts heritage, and a preservation services program that offers advice to individuals, local officials, organizations, and communi-

ties on landmark ordinances, building conservation, and actions to save threatened structures.

Current projects at the society include four publications under way simultaneously: *Long Island Country Houses and Their Architects, 1860-1940,* a veritable encyclopedia of information on the region's mansions on which the society has been working for seven years; *Useful Art: Long Island Pottery,* a ninety-page catalog documenting the history of the major stoneware potteries at Greenport, Huntington, and Brooklyn; a black history manual offering self-contained topical units on the black experience in Suffolk County through 1860; and a chart entitled *The Style of Long Island: 300 Years of Architecture and Decorative Arts.* In addition, preservation advocacy continues to be one of the most important functions of the society. Through its biannual periodical, *Preservation Notes,* the society alerts the public about landmark crises and appears at hearings all over the island in support of endangered landmarks.

The Society for the Preservation of Long Island Antiquities publishes a wide variety of pamphlets, flyers, and books.

Under the leadership of director Dr. Robert B. MacKay, the society's various functions are coordinated by a full-time staff of seven, a part-time staff of ten, a 26-member board of trustees, and an annual operating budget of approximately $.5 million. The activities of the 1,400-member society are administered from offices in a restored early nineteenth-century house at 93 North Country Road, Setauket.

The Thompson House in Setauket, built c. 1700.

LONG ISLAND ASSOCIATION

In 1922 a group of Long Island businessmen, led by Frank G. Holly of Hewlett, formed a kind of regional chamber of commerce with offices on Fifth Avenue in Manhattan. Though little record of their activities survives, their basic idea lives today as the 2,000-member Long Island Association.

Headquartered at 80 Hauppauge Road in Commack and under its twenty-seventh president, James L. Larocca, the LIA addresses many of the same issues it did when Holly's informal group was incorporated as the Long Island Chamber of Commerce on July 1, 1926. Highway, waterway, rail, and air transportation; energy; taxes; and land development/conservation remain central concerns.

The chamber's first managing director was Meade Dobson, and until 1930 his offices were at 20 West Thirty-fourth Street in New York City. During these years the group had an annual budget of about $40,000 and slightly more than 800 members.

In 1930 the chamber and the Long Island Rail Road discovered their common interest in south shore Long Island housing development, and a friendly relationship ensued with the railroad providing the chamber free office space in Pennsylvania Station for the next nineteen years.

Through the late 1920s and into the 1930s the chamber championed the completion of Horace Harding and Queens boulevards, Sunrise Highway, and Jericho Turnpike on Long Island, as well as the Triborough Bridge and Queens Midtown Tunnel.

By the time the chamber changed its name to Long Island Association on August 4, 1936, it had helped improve the Rockaway and Fire Island inlets, Shinnecock Canal, and the Patchogue to Pe-

conic Bay inland waterway. Meanwhile, Long Island's fishing and farming industries received attention, and light industry was being lured to the region.

The 1939-1940 World's Fair at Flushing, Queens, was a major event for the LIA, which had been one of its most instrumental fund-raising agents. Four million visitors filed through the LIA's Long Island exhibit.

Long Island became the LIA's home for the first time in 1949 as the group took executive offices at the Garden City Hotel and opened a satellite Suffolk office in the Patchogue Hotel. That same year legendary banker Arthur Roth began a three-year LIA presidency.

Roth's first major accomplishment was the successful October 1949 parlaying of Nassau County's Golden Jubilee Celebration with a Long Island Industry Exposition. The success of the five-day gala at Roosevelt Field spawned another LIA Industry Exposition in 1951 and served as prototype for the Long Island Association Business Showcase.

In 1959 the LIA moved to 320 Old Country Road, a few miles from the Garden City Hotel. The Patchogue office moved to Smithtown the next year, while plans for the 1964-1965 World's Fair in Queens were already under discussion.

During the 1960s the LIA pushed for Long Island defense contract procurement, Mitchel Field development, the opening of the Throgs Neck Bridge, a cross-sound bridge, and the formation of the Long Island Industrial Job Development Corporation. In 1965 the LIA became the Long Island Association of Commerce & Industry and moved to Jericho the following year.

As the 1960s drew to a close, the

Long Island Association championed Nassau Coliseum construction and became an increasingly effective government liaison force under president William J. Casey.

The chamber moved to Melville in the late 1970s, and in 1982 was fully accredited by the U.S. Chamber of Commerce. In 1983 the organization merged with the Long Island Action Committee, changing its name back to the Long Island Association, and moved to a new building in Commack.

In addition to its lobbying efforts, the expanded resources available to the association allow it to present meaningful programs, workshops, seminars, and publications to provide members with the knowledge to help manage their own businesses more efficiently and profitably. Some of the services of the association include a Business Help Hotline (499-4400), business referral service, low-cost group health insurance, member discounts, conference rooms, speakers' bureau, export certification, and notary public. In addition, as an associate office of the U.S. Department of Commerce, the LIA provides an on-site senior trade specialist from the department to assist members.

As Long Island's largest business organization, the LIA continues to work to maintain and improve the economic well-being and quality of life of the entire Long Island region.

RECKSON ASSOCIATES

Reckson Associates creates working environments for people. By approaching all construction design from the standpoint of corporate needs, within twenty years this company has become one of the region's foremost developers of industrial, high-tech, and white collar office space. In the process, Reckson, with its twelve million square feet of developed space, has also been in the vanguard of those companies that have changed the face of the economy of Long Island.

Roger and Donald Rechler founded Reckson Associates as a full-service development firm in 1968. Prior to the advent of Reckson Associates, says Donald Rechler, companies constructing industrial work space "just built a square brick building." The brothers identified a growing market for space designed for the very specific needs of industrial and high-tech tenants and they set out to meet that need.

The now three-generation Rechler development history began with father William Rechler and his brothers who, in 1958, developed New York City's first major industrial park at Newtown Creek in Brooklyn. Even then the family goal and philosophy was clearly evolving. The norm in industrial development at that time was spot buildings. The Rechlers departed from that norm by creating logically grouped buildings that met an industrial need.

In 1962 "out east," at least in terms of industrial development, still meant Nassau County. William Rechler, along with part-

Roger and Donald Rechler survey the progress of their Melville site, home to the full-service real estate development firm. It is staffed by sixty employees who are specialists in architecture, construction, financing, and management.

ner Walter Gross, dared to purchase 600 mid-Suffolk acres in Hauppauge, expanding the frontiers of Long Island's industrial community. The result—Vanderbilt Industrial Park—was the state's largest industrial campus and, due primarily to its innovative use of trees and open-space landscaping, became the trend-setting model for future industrial parks.

Roger and Donald Rechler brought their father's concept to its next step of development and, in doing so, confirmed the family conviction in eastern Long Island's ability to attract and retain new industry. After completion of the newly formed Reckson Associates' first project, 125,000 square feet of industrial space in Islip, the Rechler brothers began new construction on a 200-acre site in Bo-

hemia. It was this project that set the future pattern for Reckson and for Long Island. Called Airport International Plaza, the park, located near MacArthur Airport, was designed to accommodate the region's infant research and development industry.

A 2.5-million-square-foot complex with thirty-two buildings, AIP, called New York State's prototypical high-technology park, has earned Reckson wide industry

Before and after news of the Archi Award-winning North Shore Atrium, formerly a Davega Store (inset) in the 1950s. This was the site for the building of the lunar module by Grumman in the 1960s, and Long Island's first conversion in the 1970s.

recognition with many awards for design, landscaping, and economic development.

The successful AIP pattern was replicated further west in Melville with the one-million-square-foot County Line Industrial Center. With its high-tech industrial parks firmly in hand, the growing Reckson organization next turned its efforts toward filling what it saw as a void of quality office space to combine with the high-caliber white-collar labor force on Long Island. In cooperation with B&W Enterprises, the Rechlers purchased a vacant 120,000-square-foot industrial building on Jericho Turnpike in Syosset. The building had been a Davega Discount Store in the 1950s and in the 1960s served as the site for Grumman to build the historic lunar module. Its new incarnation, the North Shore Atrium, was to be no less historic. Reckson's retrofit, one which almost doubled the building's size to 205,000 square feet, included amenities unheard of at the time: health clubs, atriums, racquetball and tennis courts, sundecks, and restaurants. This total working and leisure environment earned Reckson the coveted American Institute of Architect's Archi Award for excellence in design.

The project paved the way for the ambitious Huntington/Melville

The 500,000-square-foot Omni Building facing Nassau Coliseum (last of the three-building Nassau West Complex) plays a major role in transforming Mitchel Field into Long Island's Midtown Financial District.

Corporate Center Complex on a 32-acre tract at Route 110 and Pinelawn Road. Completed in 1980, the two-story, 100,000-square-foot Corporate Center I was followed by the Archi Award-winning Corporate Center II in 1983, the area's first "smart" building with a totally computer-controlled environment. Melville Corporate Center and Huntington/Melville Corporate Center III appeared soon after, with a fifth building now in the design stage.

The development of almost one million square feet of prime office space on forty acres at Mitchel Field's core represents what is perhaps Reckson's most ambitious

The Archi Award-winning Huntington/Melville Corporate Center II reflects the old and the new. It was the first "smart" computer-controlled building of its kind on Long Island.

project to date. The Nassau West Corporate Complex, planned for three major structures surrounding Mitchel Park, will be an integral component in Long Island's increasingly important Midtown Financial District. Nassau West I, completed in 1983, was followed by Nassau West II the next year. The third building, to be called Mitchel Field Corporate Center Omni and to face Nassau Coliseum, will be one of the island's largest office buildings designed to meet the most advanced technology of the future.

Today over sixty employees comprise Reckson Associates. On staff are specialists in architecture, construction, management, real estate, financing, and engineering. The Reckson range of services remains rare among companies in the real estate field. Each of the firm's projects has the benefit of on-site management.

The "people-consciousness" of Reckson's buildings is a reflection of a corporate climate that encourages teamwork and growth. The company sponsors an annual Corporate Center Run for the benefit of community-related charities.

Accounting for the remarkable track record of Reckson Associates in anticipating and meeting the needs of Long Island business and industry, a record that parallels the region's growth, Roger Rechler notes: "We're closer to the needs of the market. Because everybody involved in our projects including the architect, is part of the staff, marketing has always had a significant input in our organization."

MILTOPE CORPORATION

In May 1975, one month after a major computer company (Potter Instrument Co.) declared bankruptcy, its former military products division rose from the ashes of Chapter 11 as Miltope Corporation. This new, fifty-employee entity was headed by engineer Richard Pandolfi, who is still the firm's president, and who was the military products manager at Potter.

Backed by several former Potter Instrument executives, as well as by a major new stockholder introduced to Pandolfi by Miltope's first chairman, Stuyvesant Wainwright III, the new enterprise would grow in ten years to become the largest military computer peripheral equipment manufacturer in the United States.

This quick growth was due to several factors, not the least of which was a limited, though well established, background of Potter Instrument defense contract work during the 1960s and 1970s on the Polaris, Poseidon, and Trident nuclear submarine projects.

Wainwright is the grandnephew of famed World War II General Jonathan Wainwright and was himself Long Island's First District U.S. Congressman for four terms from 1953 to 1961.

Beginning in a 25,000-square-

foot section of a plant once owned by its former parent company on Broad Hollow Road in Melville, Miltope Corporation, with its 250 employees, moved in 1977 to a Plainview building that was more than three times as large.

Finally, in 1981, the firm purchased its present 1770 Walt Whitman Road headquarters—a sprawling, 170,000-square-foot office and manufacturing complex about one mile from its birthplace. Today there are 600 Miltope employees on Long Island, supported by offices and industrial facilities in Alabama, California, England, Israel, and West Germany.

As a military subcontractor through major government vendors such as Sperry, IBM, and Honeywell, Miltope Corporation provides equipment for United States Army, Air Force, Navy, and Marine projects that include the Trident and new Trident II nuclear submarines, the Pershing cruise missile, and the AWACS reconnaissance aircraft.

Miltope also contracts with overseas armed forces, including those of West Germany, Israel, Singapore, Switzerland, and the United Kingdom. As such, the firm is a rarity on both Long Island and the East Coast, since the computer technology it provides generally

Miltope Corporation's computer technology and peripheral equipment is used by the U.S. Armed Services and many NATO countries in missiles and planes such as the AWACS reconnaissance aircraft shown here.

originates in California's famed "Silicon Valley" region.

The company's computer peripheral equipment line includes tape transports, high-speed printers, cartridge recorders, magnetic disk systems, terminals, video disk players, portable military computers, and other information storage and retrieval devices. Besides its delivery of this equipment to military and other rugged applications, such as the oil rigging industry, Miltope maintains nearly 100 percent of the commercial market for ACARS cockpit printers used by TWA, American Airlines, PSA, Air Canada, and many other carriers.

Most of Miltope Corporation's fifty engineers and technicians were educated in nearby engineering and technical colleges in Brooklyn and Manhattan, while the international presence of the firm is largely due to its cadre of Long Island employees, many of whom have been together for twenty years.

HAZELTINE CORPORATION

Professor Alan Hazeltine with his invention, the Neutrodyne receiver, which is now on display at the Smithsonian Institution.

The Hazeltine story began in the 1920s when professor Alan Hazeltine of Stevens Institute, New Jersey, designed a "neutralizing" circuit allowing commercial production of the first truly practical home radio receiver. On February 1, 1924, Hazeltine Corporation was formed to license the professor's Neutrodyne patent.

Over the next sixty years Hazeltine became synonymous with landmark radio, television, and defense electronics technology. The firm also expanded into microwave landing systems and computer-based training systems. But Hazeltine is still best known for its ongoing developments in electronic identification systems and display technology.

By the 1930s Hazeltine Corporation had moved from the professor's original Hoboken lab to a converted house in Bayside, Queens. The Hazeltine imprint was standard in the patents acknowledged on all major radios.

In 1939 the firm moved to a Little Neck, Queens, lab where Hazeltine created the equivalent of a complete television studio, transmitter, and several television receiver models. One year later discussions began with the U.S. Navy, and Hazeltine was called upon to organize the larger radio manufacturers for a major electronics development and production program for the war effort.

Hazeltine's staff of thirty-five engineers began to adapt a British Navy identification system for U.S. use. The resulting technology is still central to the Identification Friend or Foe (IFF) system used by all U.S. armed forces.

After the war Hazeltine produced Navy, Air Force, and Army radar displays and developed underwater-to-surface-to-air sound detector/transmitters called "sonobuoys."

During the postwar years several Hazeltine engineers made basic inventions that were central to the success of color television receivers produced throughout the world. Licensing of these patents was a significant worldwide service carrying on the tradition of Hazeltine's first activities.

By 1949 the firm's military work progressed to the development of the display system for the Airborne Early Warning Radar System, a forerunner of the now-standard AWACS system. The Mark XII identification system Hazeltine developed is still the U.S. and NATO standard IFF system, while sonobuoy technology has been updated to the nuclear submarine and satellite communication levels.

In the early 1950s, with former chief engineer William MacDonald as president and chairman, Hazeltine Corporation developed innovative distance-measurement equipment for the Federal Aviation Administration. The firm subsequently built VHF "omni-ranges" and is now producing the FAA's newest microwave landing system for use at airports across the country.

After a Riverhead production plant opened in 1957, Hazeltine commenced a steady Suffolk County growth by purchasing a former Republic plant in Greenlawn in 1959. Two plants were added to that site in 1962.

David Westermann led the firm from 1966 through 1980, and continued the concentration of operations in Suffolk County. In 1978, the corporate headquarters was moved to a newly acquired building in Commack.

Sal Nuzzo became president and chief executive officer in 1980. Another building was added in Hauppauge in 1982 for a major communications program. Today Hazeltine Corporation is a $175-million, 2,500-employee firm.

The Hazeltine operations moved in 1930 to a converted house in Bayside, Queens, which is in marked contrast to the current headquarters building in Commack.

AUSTIN TRAVEL

Austin Travel was established in 1955 at 7 West Marie Street in Hicksville, Long Island, by Larry Austin and Jules Mirel. The two gentlemen owned and operated an advertising agency overlooking Madison Avenue from 1951 to 1955. In 1955 they decided to move their company east to Long Island, where most of their accounts were located. When the realtor arrived with a list of choice Long Island locations, he offhandedly "suggested" they consider opening a travel agency in conjunction with the advertising company. Austin's first reaction was, "What's a travel agency?" But they went ahead with the realtor's suggestion, and Austin Travel was born that same year.

Originally known as Hicksville Travel Corp., the office moved to a two-story freestanding building on South Broadway in Hicksville in 1961. This remained the headquarters until 1982, when the company moved to a 22,000-square-foot facility on the Long Island Expressway in Plainview.

As the years passed, Austin Travel's growth in the regional business community and its president's personal involvement in that community became steadily intertwined. Austin is recognized both as a Long Island business leader and a driving force in the travel industry. Since 1975 he has served as vice-president of the Long Island Association of Commerce and Industry, and in 1976 he was elected president and chairman of the fledgling Long Island tourism and convention commission and served in those roles through 1982. In 1984 Austin was elected to serve a second term as chairman of Hickory Travel Systems, a multibillion-dollar worldwide travel consortium, which he co-founded in 1976. Other travel-

Larry Austin (bottom, in dark suit) in 1968 with his staff of forty-one, many of whom are still with Austin Travel.

related positions held by Austin include board member of the Association of Retail Travel Agents (ARTA), 1974-1981; and president and chairman of the Long Island Travel Agents Association (LITAA), 1966-1971.

Austin continues to serve as president of the corporation, as he has done since 1964. In 1981 Austin's two oldest sons, Jeffrey and Jamie, officially joined the company as vice-president/general manager and director of marketing, respectively. Austin's youngest son, Stewart, is a senior at Hofstra University.

During the first year of operation in 1955, Austin Travel had one employee on its payroll, with total sales amounting to $25,000. Today Austin Travel employs a staff of 200 people, and is projecting sales of $50 million in 1985.

In addition to the executive headquarters in Plainview, where the main corporate reservation center is located, Austin Travel has thirteen offices on Long Island—Albertson, Hauppauge, MacArthur Airport, Hicksville, Garden City, Syosset, Brookhaven, and the newest offices in Great Neck, Stony Brook, Woodbury, Oceanside (two), and Levittown. All offices are open to the public and sell both corporate and vacation travel.

Austin Travel is the largest producer on Long Island for every major airline serving the New York metropolitan area, and handles the travel arrangements for over 1,000 companies on Long Island and in New York City, New Jersey, and Connecticut. Austin Travel is completely automated with American Airlines' Sabre, Eastern's System I, Delta's Datas II, and TWA's PARS.

ALEXANDER & ALEXANDER

In 1971 Alexander & Alexander established its Long Island office. The foundation for the firm's success on Long Island dates back to 1887 when Silas Goldberg, a young immigrant from Lithuania, settled on a farm in Brookville, Long Island. He and his brother ultimately opened a clothing/dry goods store in Glen Cove, and in 1903 operated a real estate and insurance agency there.

Eventually, the clothing business was discontinued and the agency became a sole proprietorship under Silas Goldberg following his brother's death in 1924. In 1946 it became a partnership trading as Silas Goldberg & Son when Lionel M. Goldberg returned to Glen Cove after four years of military service in the U.S. Air Force. In 1953 the firm was incorporated as Silas Goldberg & Son Inc., until it was acquired in 1971 by Alexander & Alexander.

At that time Alexander & Alexander also acquired the firm of Mollod & Berkowitz, established in Great Neck in 1967. This was a firm whose antecedents were established in 1920 in New York City and subsequently moved to Long Island following World War II. When the Long Island office of Alexander & Alexander was established, the combined staff of both firms consisted of thirty people in its first office at 280 Northern Boulevard, Great Neck. These facilities were quickly outgrown and the office moved in 1973 to its present location at One Huntington Quadrangle in Melville. Three smaller firms were acquired over the next few years, further expanding the Long Island office. In 1977 Riscom Organization Ltd. was added, providing an expertise in self-insured risk-management services.

The most recent acquisition, ef-

fected on January 1, 1985, added the facilities and staff of American Coverage Corporation of Great Neck, the second-largest firm on Long Island, creating an office with a staff of 250 in some 70,000 square feet in the Melville complex. This office also houses the Northeast regional director of Alexander & Alexander and his staff. Through these acquisitions and consequent growth, A&A is now by far the largest insurance agency/brokerage firm on Long Island, with a full range of insurance products and financial services available to its many clients.

Backed by the resources of its international parent, the Long Island office provides all forms of general insurance, human resources management, risk analysis, and management and financial services. This level of insurance service sophistication began more simply in West Virginia during the 1880s, when brothers Charles B. and William F. Alexander opened a small agency and ultimately acquired a deserved reputation as insurance brokers to the transportation industry.

Alexander & Alexander went

Brothers Charles B. and William F. Alexander (left to right), who founded the original Alexander & Alexander insurance agency in Clarksburg, West Virginia, in the 1880s.

public in 1969 with about 300 employees and offices in fewer than twenty U.S. cities. By 1985 it was part of the world's largest retail insurance brokerage and financial services group, Alexander & Alexander Services Inc., a multi-million-dollar international entity employing some 16,000 people in nearly 100 U.S. cities and over forty-eight countries.

The Baltimore & Ohio (B&O) Railroad was the first major client of Alexander & Alexander.

DALE CARNEGIE & ASSOCIATES, INC.

Dale Carnegie was only twenty-three years old in 1912 when he started teaching adult public speaking at Manhattan's 125th Street YMCA for thirty dollars a night. The young Missourian, with a state teacher's college degree and collegiate debating team experience, had already been a successful Armour Meats salesman in the Dakotas.

But now he was about to launch one of the most successful avocational training programs of the twentieth century. From a night course in confidence building through effective public speaking, Dale Carnegie, and later his wife, Dorothy, built an educational network that today has fourteen regional offices, 250 employees, 128 licensees, and 2,500 part-time instructors.

Dale Carnegie courses are now taught in 68 countries worldwide and are accredited by the Council for Noncollegiate Continuing Education. The American Council on Education also recommends various Carnegie programs for college transfer credits. There have been nearly three million Dale Carnegie graduates since 1912 and over eight million dollars in Carnegie course scholarships have been awarded to 17,100 young people.

Always based in the New York metropolitan area, the Dale Carnegie international headquarters has been located at 1475 Franklin Avenue in Garden City since 1964. This Tudor-style building, which houses executive and administrative offices and the Dale Carnegie Department of Instruction, also serves as the Nassau County regional office. In 1983 the firm's international distribution operations moved from Mineola to a new 43,000-square-foot Motor Parkway, Hauppauge, facility which also houses the Suffolk

J. Oliver Crom, president of Dale Carnegie & Associates.

County office.

But things were more informal in 1912. After commencing the YMCA public speaking course, which had been rejected by several New York college business departments, Carnegie set up offices as a professor of speech in Carnegie Hall. One day in 1914 a Princeton University speech instructor named Lowell Thomas read Carnegie's name among the lobby listings and called on him.

Lowell Thomas, on his way to international fame as an explorer and news correspondent, had just returned from Alaska and wanted help booking a photo/lecture tour detailing the trip. Carnegie became what amounted to Thomas' business agent as well as a close colleague.

Their most successful collaboration was done just after World War I when they toured the United States, Canada, and Great Britain with a lecture series about Lowell Thomas' wartime experiences with legendary British officer Thomas Edward Lawrence, known as Lawrence of Arabia.

During the 1920s Carnegie, who always considered himself primarily a writer, began a book about his personal hero, Abraham Lincoln. He also traveled widely in Europe and Asia and perfected his public speaking course. In 1926 he published his first book, *Public Speaking: A Practical Course for Business Men.*

By 1931, with the United States slipping into the depths of the Depression, Carnegie worked on a series of projects that combined his commitment to public speaking as a method of self improvement and confidence building, his view that success is possible under the most trying of circumstances, and his patriotic belief in the basic American values of competitive achievement and enterprise.

That year his revised *Public Speaking and Influencing Men in Business* appeared, followed in 1932 by his first truly popular book, *Lincoln the Unknown.* The Carnegie penchant for seeking out telling details in the lives of famous individuals—making their qualities and success stories accessible to the general public—was

Dale Carnegie with his dog, "Tippy."

clear in this work.

In the early 1930s Carnegie brought this concept to radio with a series of popular interviews with the likes of New York City Mayor Fiorello LaGuardia and Eleanor Roosevelt. At one time or another Carnegie interviewed virtually every well-known actor, explorer, politician, and religious leader in the country.

From 1935 through 1945 Dale Carnegie's "Little Known Facts About Well-Known People" radio program was among the most popular shows on the air. During much of this time, he also wrote a daily syndicated newspaper column.

Finally, in 1936 the culmination of twenty-five years' work came in the successful publication of his book *How to Win Friends and Influence People.* With a modest first printing of 5,000 copies, the book was soon selling 5,000 copies a day and it took up residence on the *New York Times'* best-seller list for a decade. To date it has sold over fifteen million copies in virtually every known language.

In 1943, at the height of his national radio popularity, Carnegie published a book version of *Little Known Facts About Well-Known People.* Five years later his book *How to Stop Worrying and Start Living* appeared.

Meanwhile, the work of organizing the Dale Carnegie philosophy into a substantial network began in 1945 with the help of Dorothy Carnegie, whom Dale had married two years earlier. During this time the Dale Carnegie Sales Course was added to the original course. Together with Dorothy, who became and remains the company's chairman of the board, Carnegie wrote a course for businesswomen in 1946.

When Dale Carnegie died in

International headquarters of Dale Carnegie & Associates, located at 1475 Franklin Avenue, Garden City.

1955, the work of organization had progressed. Dorothy declined several offers by groups of businessmen to buy the company, and in 1957 Dale Carnegie & Associates was still a course licensor with about twenty full-time employees.

In subsequent years decentralization and growth led to the opening or expansion of Dale Carnegie offices in Nassau and Suffolk counties, New York City, Houston, St. Louis, Atlanta, Jacksonville, Syracuse, Albany, Salt Lake City, Westchester, San Diego, Allentown, Washington, D.C., and Puerto Rico.

The Dale Carnegie curriculum now also includes the Dale Carnegie Customer Relations Course, Personnel Development Course, Management Seminar, and Professional Development Series.

J. Oliver Crom, the firm's current president, entered that position in 1978 after joining the firm nineteen years earlier and playing a major role in its expansion and solidification. Only the third president in the history of Dale Carnegie & Associates, Inc., Crom oversees an annual enrollment of more than 100,000 people in courses, and is at the center of plans for expansion that include the imminent opening of two to three new Long Island sites.

Dale Carnegie's NBC radio program was among the nation's most popular in the 1930s and 1940s.

CHEMICAL BANK

Chemical Bank was founded on February 24, 1823, in lower Manhattan as an adjunct to a small chemical manufacturing firm in Greenwich Village. From its beginning wealthy New York families, such as the Roosevelts and Goelets, were important investors and officers, and Chemical's story is a central part of banking history itself.

From its genesis at the dawn of American banking, through directorship by Theodore Roosevelt's grandfather, Cornelius, Chemical Bank weathered depressions in 1857, the early 1860s, the 1870s, and the 1930s, and grew to be the sixth-largest bank in the United States with total assets of fifty billion dollars and 20,000 employees worldwide.

But Chemical's presence on Long Island was largely due to two post-World War II developments. One was the growth of larger banks through acquisition of local banking institutions predominantly in the suburbs.

The other was a drastic change in both the financial standing and the spending habits of middle-class Americans, which greatly altered retail banking practices. This, again, was largely a suburban phenomenon.

Thus, as postwar suburban demographic shifts led Manhattan-based banks inexorably to Westchester and Long Island, Chemical acquired or merged with eight different banks between 1951 and 1972. These acquired institutions were themselves the results of more than thirty-four other bank mergers that had occurred since 1900 mostly on Long Island.

Chemical's 1954 merger with the then-101-year-old Corn Exchange Bank Trust Company increased its presence in Queens since Corn Exchange had itself acquired the Queens County Bank in 1899. The

Harold Helm, Chemical chairman from 1954 to 1965, engineered the bank's first important Long Island inroads including the opening of Nassau County's first Chemical branch in Massapequa in 1961.

bank's acquisition of the prestigious New York Trust Company in 1959 increased Chemical's reach in both Queens and Brooklyn.

The bank's first Nassau County office opened in Massapequa in 1961. Acquisitions of the Bank of Rockville Centre Trust Company in 1963 and Bensonhurst National Bank of Brooklyn in 1964 further strengthened this regional expansion.

But the single most important Chemical move on Long Island was its merger with the already established Long Island network of Security National Bank. This acquisition, masterminded by Chemical's renowned chairman Donald D. Platten (1972-1983), brought Chemical ninety Long Island branches, some dating back to before the turn of the century.

Long Island has also been the setting for several Chemical Bank "firsts" in expanding service. For example, the bank's first automated-teller machine was installed in the Rockville Centre branch in 1969. The new "Pronto" home TV/telephone banking service, now being sold nationally to other banks, was successfully tested in 1982 on Long Island. Long Island is also the location of unique Chemical services such as the summer "boat banking" ferry which sails round trip to and from Fire Island and Bay Shore six months each year.

The Nassau-Suffolk headquarters, directed by regional chief executive officer Frank Lourenso, has been located at 115 Broad Hollow Road in Melville since Chemical acquired the site from Security National in 1975. With 2,695 Long Island employees, Chemical has thirty-two branches in Nassau and fifty-three in Suffolk, plus an additional twenty-one in Queens and nineteen in Brooklyn.

A rare look at the early twentieth-century days at the Chemical Bank.

GRUMMAN CORPORATION

On July 20, 1969, Neil Armstrong landed his Grumman-built Lunar Module in the "Sea of Tranquility," taking a giant leap for mankind and another step in an ongoing Grumman journey that had begun in a drafty Baldwin garage during the early days of the Depression.

In 1929 several top engineering talents from famed Loening Aircraft decided to stay on Long Island when the firm moved to Pennsylvania. The men included a Cornell- and MIT-educated World War I Navy flier named Leroy Randle Grumman.

With former Loening manager Jake Swirbul and engineer Bill Schwendler, as well as investors such as Clinton Towl, Leroy Grumman formed the Grumman Aircraft Engineering Company which opened on January 2, 1930. Almost immediately they won a $33,700 Navy contract for prototype aircraft floats fitted with an innovative retractable landing gear designed by Roy Grumman. By year-end the company was $5,476 in the black and had twenty-three employees.

While building a successful line of aluminum truck bodies for working capital, Grumman won its first contract to build a new plane in early 1931. The XFF-1 two-seat fighter was the first Navy aircraft to use a retractable landing gear.

By the mid-1930s the firm had moved to an abandoned Navy hangar at Curtiss Field in Valley Stream, and then to its first real factory in Farmingdale. In 1937 Grumman made its final move, to Bethpage.

During World War II Grumman's all-metal, single-wing Wildcat fighter and its Hellcat and Avenger relatives were introduced. Between December 7, 1941, and August 14, 1945, the firm delivered 17,013 planes to the Navy, whose records show that Grumman aircraft accounted for two-thirds of the enemy planes destroyed in the Pacific.

The F9F Panther jet fighter began service in 1947. The innovative, carrier-based Panther and its swept-wing Cougar version, Grumman's first supersonic design, would soon dominate the skies during the Korean War.

By the mid-1950s Grumman's Albatross amphibian line was the standard Navy, Air Force, and Coast Guard rescue plane, while its S2 Tracker, Trader, and Tracer line was state of the art in detection aircraft. This line culminated in the Navy's current Hawkeye early warning aircraft.

Also in the mid-1950s the high-performance F11F Tiger set speed and altitude records and appeared at popular air shows with the Navy Blue Angels precision teams. During the late 1950s Grumman designed and built several turboprop and corporate jet aircraft, while the Mohawk surveillance aircraft, soon to be important in Vietnam, was introduced in 1959.

The 1960s were years of transition for the company, which became known as Grumman Corporation in 1969. In 1962 the firm won NASA's Project Apollo Lunar Module development contract.

Grumman was awarded the important Navy F-14 Tomcat fighter contract in 1972. Increasing international aircraft sales to countries

Grumman's World War II effort made world history. Roy Grumman, Bill Schwendler, and Jake Swirbul (left to right) confer on designs in the early 1940s.

including Japan and Israel, and developments in electronics systems brought Grumman into the 1980s as one of Long Island's great national success stories and largest employer.

Roy Grumman died in 1982. In 1984 Grumman's forward swept-wing X-29—the first government-funded experimental aircraft to fly in a decade—began its flight test program in California. Grumman continues to grow on Long Island with an expanded headquarters building in Bethpage and new facilities in Melville, Woodbury, Bohemia, and Holtsville. Today Grumman has 31,500 employees—21,000 of them on Long Island. The company's chairman is John Bierwirth; the president is George Skurla.

The Grumman-designed and -built Apollo Lunar Module made six earth-moon round trips.

UNDERWRITERS LABORATORIES, INC.

Underwriters Laboratories was founded by engineer William Henry Merrill in 1894 after he had been called upon to investigate electrical fires at the 1893 Chicago Columbian Exposition. Because of Merrill's success in that capacity, he obtained National Board of Fire Underwriters backing to start the first three-man Underwriters Laboratories office.

Today the firm has 3,000 full-time and 300 part-time employees working at four major U.S. locations—Melville, Long Island; Northbrook, Illinois; Santa Clara, California; and Tampa, Florida—as well as in sixty-three other countries.

Though born in the Midwest, UL's East Coast presence dates to 1911 when an old Edison building on Van Dam Street was converted into a UL electrical testing facility. Headed by regional vice-president and engineer Dana Pierce, this New York lab and nearby office were created because of the firm's growing relationship with the predominantly East Coast-based wire and cable industry.

Since the East abounded with telephone wires, trolley cables, and other newfangled electrical systems, the company flourished. By 1914 Pierce had combined the Manhattan lab and office on one floor of the old New York Evening Mail Building.

By 1932 these operations had expanded to four floors at a site on Leonard Street just off Broadway. Pierce was president of UL nationally, and was leading the firm into automobile, building, and aeronautic testing.

Pierce died in 1935 and was succeeded by Alvah Small, who registered UL as a not-for-profit corporation operating in the area of public health and safety in 1936. The Manhattan office expanded

Underwriters Laboratories' Melville facility is located on Walt Whitman Road.

several more times during the 1930s and by mid-decade was moved onto a single, custom-designed floor of the Butterick Building at 161 Sixth Avenue.

UL's World War II effort involved explosion and combustibility testing, which brought Army and Navy commendations in 1946. The 1950s saw Underwriters move to the suburbs. UL's Chicago headquarters moved thirty miles northwest to Northbrook in 1954, while a year later a new UL center was opened just outside San Francisco in Santa Clara.

This trend hit the Manhattan office in 1963, when it was moved to 1285 Walt Whitman Road in Melville. The Melville site remains UL's East Coast headquarters and is second in size only to the Northbrook center within the UL network.

Under vice-president/officer-in-charge Howard Reymers, this 700-employee office is committed to full-service UL activities and is now the control center for all East Coast and European factory follow-up inspection. The largest of any UL engineering department, the Melville electrical unit tests the complete range of electrical products including wires and cables, switches, fuses, appliances, and medical equipment, and has recently begun robotics and elec-

tromagnetic interference testing.

Today more than one-third of UL's staff is devoted to engineering services, while 500 inspectors support ongoing work for 35,000 clients in 69,000 product tests and 318,000 factory follow-up inspections annually. The UL symbol now appears on 2.5 billion products each year, and most state, county, and city safety inspectors in the United States rely on the Underwriters Laboratories standard of safety inspection.

Modern robotics testing is done in large part at the Melville office of Underwriters Laboratories.

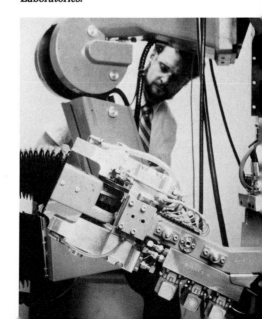

HARTMAN SYSTEMS/A FIGGIE INTERNATIONAL COMPANY

In 1951 Waldorf Instrument Company, renowned for its work with Werner Von Braun's V-2 rockets, moved from Manhattan to Park Avenue in Huntington Station. Sixteen years later this firm would be known as Hartman Systems, but the Hartman story actually began eighteen years earlier when Helmut Waldorf founded Waldorf Mechanical Laboratories in 1933.

During World War II the firm, then known as Waldorf and Kearns, attained prominence manufacturing precision devices for General Electric and the Army Ordnance Department. But by 1948, known to that point as a hydraulic and pneumatic device manufacturer, Waldorf Instrument Company was about to enter the space age.

In one of many occasions where the government or a major contractor would call on the company for emergency help, the Army commissioned Waldorf to duplicate precision bearing and hydraulic parts for German V-2 rockets captured during the war. Dr. Von Braun commended Waldorf for the successful completion of a job he thought impossible, and the firm had launched itself into the country's infant missile, space, and jet programs.

During the early 1950s a small electronics division of Waldorf began producing instrumentation devices. Gradually the firm's electronics work would supersede its mechanical product lines. In fact, the Huyck Corporation of Rensselaer, New York, acquired Waldorf in 1956, seeking to apply this growing instrumentation capability to automation of the paper industry.

Waldorf met another emergency in 1956, this time for Sikorsky Aircraft, which needed deadline delivery of specially manufactured

hydraulic parts to perform a government test of its then-newest helicopter.

During this period the corporation received multimillion-dollar contracts from the likes of Lockheed, Sperry, and the Navy for electronics systems, navigational computers, instruments, and displays. In the 1960s several innovative antisubmarine navigation and display systems for aircraft and surface ships were produced by the firm, whose evolution from mechanical to electronic parts manufacturer was nearly complete.

The Hartman name entered the company lexicon in 1966 when Ohio-based Mid-Continent Manufacturing acquired it and phased in the name of its Hartman Electrical subsidiary. Under Mid-Con, Hartman gained a reputation with the military for design and production of increasingly complex computerized navigational systems, many of which are still in use.

On June 30, 1967, Hartman-Huyck Systems, a 385-employee entity, changed its name to Hartman Systems Company. In 1973 its current president Peter Barry entered the executive offices.

In 1969 Hartman became part of A-T-O Inc., and four years later

Hartman executive Charles Poppe accepts Navy congratulations in June 1960 on delivery of the firm's first major U.S. Navy contract.

acquired A-T-O's International Engineering Company of Springfield, Virginia. This acquisition enabled Hartman to procure well-known telemetry product lines. In 1982 A-T-O Inc. became Figgie International. Today Hartman Systems Division, a Figgie International Company, employs over 400 people at its Huntington Station headquarters, and is a major supplier of electronics to all branches of the military, both in this country and abroad.

The March 1912 test of a hand generator and portable radio built by National Electrical Machine Shops (Washington, D.C.). They were the forerunners of Hartman's telemetry product line.

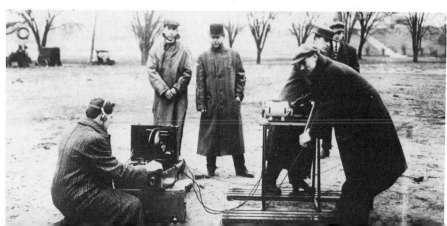

ALLSTATE INSURANCE COMPANY

One fall morning in 1930, two bridge players on a Chicago commuter train hatched the idea of mail-order automobile insurance. Some might have viewed a new method of selling auto insurance as ill advised, given that the Depression was beginning in earnest. But the more Sears & Roebuck president Robert E. Wood listened to his friend, Carl Odell, the more he liked the idea.

Apparently Sears' board of directors also liked the idea since it approved General Wood's proposal on November 17 with a $700,000 capitalization. The name "Allstate" was borrowed from the well-known trademark of Sears' tire line. On April 17, 1931, the Allstate Insurance Company was officially founded as a Sears subsidiary, which it remains to this day. The first office was a 1,500-square-foot room in the retailer's west side Chicago headquarters.

The Long Island roots of Allstate Insurance began in Manhattan in 1936 when, soon after the firm was licensed in New York State, a branch office was opened at 71 West Twenty-third Street in an old Masonic Temple. A sales office was opened in Jamaica, Queens, as well.

By 1939 Allstate was undergoing a full-scale decentralization program. In New York this resulted in the merger of several metropolitan area offices into a single New York metropolitan branch with headquarters at Twenty-third Street and seven sales agents servicing the region's customers.

Decentralization was successful in creating strong regional identity for each branch office, including New York. Still, daily communication with the home office was a must. To do this the New York branch brought its mail to Penn Station every morning at six

Allstate Insurance agents discuss their sales strategies with regional vice-president Vincent J. DeLuca (left, center).

o'clock. From there it began a twelve-hour rail trip to Chicago.

General Robert Wood retired in 1943 quite satisfied that Allstate had made a good start toward permanent, national acceptance. By 1947 the firm changed the designations of its local branches to "regions." Thus, the New York branch, which served Long Island, was now the New York Metropolitan Region.

In 1950 employees in New York were informed that a new Long Island regional office, serving Brooklyn, Queens, Nassau, and Suffolk, was being planned. Soon afterward a tract of land in the Melville-Huntington Station area was picked as the site of the new headquarters.

In 1953 Allstate's 500 Long Island Region employees won the first in an unprecedented string of four Chairman's Awards For Excellence signifying best annual performance among all the company's

regional offices. That year the Long Island Region serviced some 200,000 customers, generating three million dollars in written premiums.

Meanwhile, Allstate was successfully expanding its basic line of auto insurance products while bringing several innovations to the industry. One of these was the 1947 landmark "Illustrator" policy, simply written and illustrated without legal jargon, making it easier for consumers to understand the policy coverages.

Allstate ventured beyond its automobile specialty for the first time in 1952 by introducing personal liability coverage. This was followed in 1954 by its first residential fire insurance policy.

By the late 1950s Allstate had

Employee training is continuous and uses advanced office technology.

become a full-circle insurer, offering commercial fire, personal theft, and homeowner coverages. Life insurance protection was offered by the newly formed Allstate Life Insurance Company in 1957. A year later personal health and commercial liability products were added. Then, in 1959, group life and group health were added together with boat owner insurance, a development that was popular on Long Island.

Naturally, Allstate continued to provide auto coverage and to earn the reputation of an industry maverick. When introduced in 1956, Allstate's "Crusader" policy offered the broadest coverage of any single policy in the history of auto insurance.

In 1959 the company strengthened its reputation for keeping pace with consumer needs by becoming the first major insurance firm to offer premium discounts specifically to owners of the then increasingly popular small cars.

Meanwhile, while waiting for its new Huntington Station facility to be built, three portions of the Long Island regional office moved to three temporary Huntington sites in 1957. The main administrative office was located next to a dairy farm on Park Avenue. Another Huntington office was set up in a former village dress shop, and the claims department worked out of an office building on Old Country Road. A truck shuttled back and forth among these small offices serving as a kind of mobile record and file department.

In September 1958 the Long Island Region moved into its new two-story, 83,000-square-foot office building on Old Country Road in Huntington Station. Robert Leys was regional vice-president. By 1961 this office boasted 1,000 employees. That year it won its sec-

ond Chairman's Award with six million dollars in written premiums and 400,000 policies in force. In 1969, with 500,000 policies, Allstate's 1,400 Long Island employees won their third Chairman's Award.

The Long Island regional employee base grew beyond the 2,000 level until finally, in December 1975, the Westchester, Putnam, Bronx, Staten Island, and Manhattan offices, then part of Allstate's Harrison Region, were merged with the Long Island Region.

Under regional vice-president Daniel Begley, this New York Metropolitan Region office moved from Huntington Station to its present 200,000-square-foot headquarters on Allstate Drive, Farmingville, in November 1977. One year later the office won its fourth Chairman's Award. In 1983 the office of Allstate Life of New York opened in Melville.

Today the New York Metropolitan Region of Allstate has 2,200 employees and serves all of Long Island, New York City's five boroughs, and Westchester and Putnam counties. On Long Island alone Allstate has over forty sales offices and six claims offices. The Farmingville regional office, headed by vice-president Vincent DeLuca, is Allstate's largest among twenty-five nationwide.

Allstate is Suffolk County's eighth-largest and Long Island's seventeenth-largest employer, and is New York State's largest insurer. Allstate insures 16.3 percent of the cars and 11.7 percent of all the

homes in New York State.

The famed slogan, "You're in good hands with Allstate," which has become one of the best-known advertising themes in American business history, was the brainchild in 1950 of national general sales manager Davis W. Ellis. Ellis borrowed a phrase his wife had used when assuring him that their sick daughter was "in good hands" with the family doctor.

Founded at the national level in 1952, the Allstate Foundation makes regular regional and community service grants each year in nine categories: charitable, civic, urban affairs, education, culture, nursing scholarships, health, youth, and safety. On Long Island Allstate consistently supports United Way, the March of Dimes, and many other charitable and community causes.

Allstate has come a long way since that morning commuter train bridge game, and a long way since insuring its first car—a $530, 1930 Studebaker—for a $48 premium. Allstate's "Audatex" automated auto-repair-estimate system, its "AFIS" paperless record-keeping system, and its satellite communications ensures the firm in its role of insurance innovator.

An artist's drawing of Allstate's New York Metropolitan Region office in Farmingville, New York.

APOCA INDUSTRIES

On February 4, 1974, Santos T. Abrilz, Jr., and eight partners founded a small technology company called APOCA Industries. It was so small, in fact, that, for the first several months after its creation, it had no permanent address other than a suite in the Pickwick Motor Inn that Abrilz maintained at a day rate of $12.50.

In May 1974, when APOCA Industries finally moved into its first real office—a 5,000-square-foot building at 467 Brook Avenue in Deer Park—it was still basically a one-man operation.

Today the 140-employee APOCA Industries is a growing manufacturer of electronic and telecommunications equipment and systems for both commercial and military markets. Headquartered at 10 Connor Lane in Deer Park, APOCA also maintains facilities at 127G and 65-15 Brook Avenue. The three contiguous locations, which total 26,000 square feet of office and manufacturing space, will be consolidated under a single company-owned roof by 1988.

But in 1974 APOCA was still the barely realized boyhood dream of 37-year-old, Brooklyn-born Santos Abrilz, whose Spanish and Puerto Rican ancestry included an electronics engineer father who moved the family from Brooklyn to Westhampton Beach when Santos was in his early teens.

After graduating from Westhampton Beach High School, Santos Abrilz, Jr., entered the U.S. Navy as an electronics technician. Between the ages of twenty-one and thirty-six, he worked for several technology firms until he saw the chance to head up a group of investors and create APOCA as a telecommunications equipment manufacturer and supplier predominantly to the U.S. Air Force.

Three years of agonizingly slow growth elapsed until APOCA hired its first employee in 1977. Just one year later the company boasted fourteen employees, and Abrilz was beginning to gain the recognition of the regional business community. The Long Island Association gave him its Long Island Leadership Award in 1978.

The following year APOCA moved to 10 Connor Lane in a 17,200-square-foot unit. The firm had acquired its first million-dollar contract, employed forty people, and had added significant amounts of U.S. Army work to its ongoing Air Force business.

In December 1982 APOCA was ranked ninety-seventh among *INC.* magazine's 500 fastest-growing private companies in America. At that point the firm had 119 employees and Abrilz, its president, was earning national stature as an advocate of government assistance to the development of small businesses.

Abrilz became especially known for his work with U.S. Congressman Thomas Downey, and with the late singer-songwriter-social activist Harry Chapin. In particular they addressed corporate social consciousness and the business advancement of women and minorities.

Abrilz had been a member of Congressman Downey's small business advisory council in 1978, and soon thereafter was representing the Long Island District in the Small Business Administration under President Jimmy Carter. Abrilz was also a prominent figure in President Carter's White House Conference on Small Business in 1980.

In December 1983 APOCA was ranked eleventh on *INC.* magazine's list of 500 fastest-growing private firms. As part of that listing it was reported that the company's 1978

Santos T. Abrilz, Jr. (right), APOCA founder and president, with his wife, Patricia, who is a board member and corporate secretary.

sales of $107,000 had jumped to $5.4 million in 1982. That was a five-year increase of nearly 5,000 percent at an annual compound rate of 167 percent.

Hispanic Business magazine ranked APOCA second in 1984 among its annual top 400 fastest-growing Hispanic-owned U.S. firms. That same year the *Journal of Electronics Defense* gave APOCA's in-house advertising agency two separate awards for creative excellence for its "Communicating with the Future" and "Advanced Technology Today" campaigns.

In June 1985 APOCA was ranked thirteenth among the top 500 fastest-growing Hispanic-owned U.S. firms by *Hispanic Business* magazine.

Still mainly a supplier to military markets, APOCA Industries has met its greatest success recently with its PP-7286 battery charger.

APOCA remains well known for its official policy of hiring women, veterans, minorities, and senior citizens to responsible positions on all levels—from drivers and shipping clerks to corporate officers, directors, and board members. Today about 75 percent of the firm's 140 employees are women.

Besides Santos T. Abrilz, Jr., who maintains the title of president, important APOCA functions are handled by executive vice-president Carl Barbuscia, vice-president of engineering Richard Gucciardo, vice-president of operations William Hassis, vice-president of personnel Genevieve Bolletino, and production department chief John Hahn. Patricia Abrilz serves as vice-president of procurement

and is an APOCA Industries board member and corporate secretary.

Today Abrilz continues his work as a self-described corporate citizen, working for continued technological development at SUNY/Stony Brook while working with Southside Hospital in Bay Shore, the United Way, the Suffolk Coun-

ty Boy Scouts, and as a member of the New York State Business Council.

He is a founding and current director of the Long Island Philharmonic, past president of Long Island Forum for Technology, and a member of the Amos Tuck School of Business Management

Program at Dartmouth University. Suffolk County executive Peter Cohalan recently reappointed Abrilz to the post of County Human Rights Commissioner and appointed him to a new blue ribbon executive committee studying the future of Suffolk County Community College.

NATIONAL WESTMINSTER BANK USA

Unlike several major banks that came to Long Island from a Manhattan base of operations, the NatWest story began on Long Island and grew beyond this region into a tale of international proportions.

What is now known as National Westminster Bank USA began in 1949, when two small Long Island banks joined forces to form Meadow Brook National Bank. This new institution operated from just two Long Island offices, Freeport and Merrick, and had only about twenty-two million dollars in assets.

Today National Westminster Bank USA employs 4,300 people in the greater New York area, with 2,285 of them on Long Island, and has assets of almost nine billion dollars. There are more than 150 branches in the five boroughs of New York City, Westchester, and Long Island. More than half of these are in Nassau and Suffolk counties. National Westminster Bank USA ranks in the top thirty among the more than 14,000 commercial banks in the United States.

Regional executive vice-president L. Douglas O'Brien heads NatWest's Community Banking Group and oversees its Long Island territory, which is headquartered at 60 Hempstead Avenue in West Hempstead. The bank's Long Island operations center is located at 3 Huntington Quadrangle in Melville.

All of this began almost forty years ago because Long Island was the fastest-growing population center in the United States during the post-World War II period, and smart Manhattan-based banks were seeking a strong suburban foothold. The Meadow Brook National Bank was able to expand rapidly because it was already established on Long Island.

The Merrick office of Meadow Brook National Bank, 1963.

In 1950 Meadow Brook acquired West Hempstead National Bank, and over the next decade became a major Long Island financial institution through mergers, acquisitions, and the construction of new branches.

By 1960, at a time when New York City banks were still competing heavily for the lucrative suburban market, Meadow Brook went in the other direction and became the first Long Island bank to establish a Manhattan beachhead by acquiring Colonial Trust Company and Queens National Bank.

Then, things got even bigger. In 1965 Meadow Brook was itself acquired by the multiline financial services organization called C.I.T. Corporation. In 1967 the bank merged with the Bank of North America, which was a thriving commercial institution with sixteen offices, fifteen of which were located in New York City.

At this point Meadow Brook changed its name to National Bank of North America (NBNA). Through the 1970s NBNA made

The 60 Hempstead Avenue (West Hempstead) office of Meadow Brook National Bank (pictured here in 1961) was acquired by Meadow Brook in 1951.

significant moves in Westchester, with acquisition of the eleven-branch First National Bank of Yonkers, and in the Manhattan textile, precious metals, and entertainment industries. This was done through the acquisition of the six-branch Trade Bank and Trust Company, which was already established in those business lines.

Finally, in 1979, National Westminster Bank PLC of London, England, bought NBNA from C.I.T. Corporation. The British institution, known familiarly as "NatWest," is among the world's top five banks, and has more than

ninety billion dollars in assets and over 90,000 employees in 3,900 offices worldwide.

During 1980 and 1981 the benefits of international NatWest ownership became apparent within National Bank of North America in the New York and suburban areas. First, the parent infused NBNA with seventy-five million dollars in new capital. Then, sixteen branches of Bankers Trust Company were purchased in Westchester, making NBNA's reach in that county even stronger.

By 1982 the new strength produced by acquisitions, new funding sources, and overall NatWest management permitted NBNA to specifically target four distinct business markets: consumer, middle market, large corporate, and international. In September 1983 National Bank of North America changed its name to National Westminster Bank USA in order to stress its alignment with the parent company to domestic and international customers and new markets.

That same year a new corporate headquarters building was built at 175 Water Street in the heart of lower Manhattan's traditional financial district. This thirty-story tower, known as National Westminster Bank Center, houses over 900 employees and serves as the parent's North American headquarters.

A National Westminster Bank USA office of the chairman is composed of chairman/chief executive officer William T. Knowles, president/chief operating officer

On July 1, 1934, Gus Weller (seated, center) assumed the presidency of First National Bank of Merrick, which merged in 1949 with Freeport Bank to form Meadow Brook National Bank.

In 1957 bank president Gus Weller and his wife greeted U.S. Vice-President Richard M. Nixon at the Theodore Roosevelt Centennial Celebration held at the old Garden City Hotel.

Robert F. Wallace, and senior executive vice-president/chief administrative officer John Gale.

Growth through new business lines and expanded services continues on Long Island. During 1983, for example, NatWest USA's first Long Island office for trust business development was opened in Jericho, while a new Brooklyn branch office was acquired that year as well.

Long Island is also central to the bank's 24-hour "Teller Beam" automated-teller machine program,

which has about 100 in place in the New York metropolitan area. National Westminster Bank USA is now installing ATMs in major corporate locations, and is test marketing free-standing ATM kiosks in large Long Island shopping centers.

NEW YORK ISLANDERS

On May 19, 1984, the New York Islanders lost in the Stanley Cup finals to the Edmonton Oilers but in so doing, entered a realm where "failure" is judged in Herculean terms. They had failed to match the epic record of five straight Cup championships set by the fabled Montreal Canadiens of the 1950s. But the "Isles" already possessed four consecutive Cups, plus a twelve-year record most National Hockey League teams envy.

The Islanders were born on June 6, 1972, when the NHL accepted Connecticut businessman Roy Boe's $6-million bid for a new franchise to play in the Nassau Coliseum in Uniondale. The team also paid the New York Rangers a $4-million "territorial indemnification."

The following October 7 at the Coliseum the Isles played their first game before 12,221 spectators. Eddie Westfall scored the team's first goal in a losing effort. In fact, during that first season the team set NHL records for most defeats (59), fewest wins (12), fewest points (30), and most goals allowed (347).

However, the second season was better. They finished fifteenth out of sixteen teams and reduced their goals allowed by 100. After two head coaches the first season, Al Arbour took command in the second, and was joined by rookie defenseman Denis Potvin. This was the Isles' last season in which they failed to make the championship playoffs.

The 1974-1975 season greeted rookie goaltender Glenn "Chico" Resch, and the team's first amateur draft pick of the year, forward Clark Gillies. The Isles finished third in the Patrick Division and seventh overall, but lost in seven games to the eventual Cup-winning Philadelphia Flyers in the playoff

semifinals. They hurdled a magic milestone in defeating the rival Rangers in their first playoff series.

Rookie forward Bryan Trottier helped the Islanders win forty-two games to finish second in the Patrick Division behind the Flyers and fifth overall during 1975-1976 regular season before losing in the Cup semifinals to the Canadiens. In 1976-1977 the Isles lost only two of their first nineteen games and ultimately won forty-seven for a fourth place finish in the sixteen-team league. But they still finished just behind the Flyers in the Patrick Division, and lost again to the Canadiens in the Cup semifinals.

In 1977-1978 rookie Mike Bossy joined the forward line with Gillies and Trottier, and the Isles won forty-eight games to beat Philadelphia in the division and post the NHL's third-best overall record. Bossy scored a goal in the first period of his first game and set an NHL rookie record of fifty-three goals. However, the Isles lost in seven games of the Cup quarterfinals to the Toronto Maple Leafs.

In 1978 the team was nineteen million dollars in debt, largely due to its original $10-million obligation. Boe was relieved of his ownership, and minority partner John O. Pickett, Jr., saved the team from bankruptcy, encouraged by general manager Bill Torrey. The two reorganized the debt, negotiated several lucrative cable television

contracts, and now direct one of the NHL's most successful organizations. Pickett also promoted Torrey to the team presidency.

By 1978-1979, with Bossy scoring sixty-nine goals including an NHL record of ten consecutive games with at least one goal, the Isles won fifty-one games and finished first in the league. But the Rangers eliminated them in the Cup semifinals, and many people wondered what was keeping the Long Island team out of the Stanley Cup finals.

However, the turnaround came the following season, and they went on to win four consecutive Stanley Cups in the 1979-1980, 1980-1981, 1981-1982, and 1982-1983 seasons. In this period they finished first twice and second twice in their division, and twice posted the NHL's best season record.

During those years forward Butch Goring joined the team, and Resch was traded as Bill Smith became a premier NHL goalie. Coach Al Arbour remained a constant as did his team's apparent love of drama, perhaps best exemplified by Bob Nystrom's electrifying overtime goal at the Coliseum on May 24, 1980, which beat the old nemesis Flyers and gave the young Isles their first Stanley Cup.

Bobby Nystrom reacts to his 1980 Stanley Cup-winning goal.

HOFSTRA UNIVERSITY

The story of Hofstra University began fifty years ago when it opened as a small liberal arts college in 1935, with a single building and about 159 day students. The original fifteen-acre Hempstead campus was an endowment from William S. and Kate M. Hofstra, for whom the school is named.

Today Hofstra, with a total enrollment of 11,500, has grown in size and reputation to the level of a nationally prominent university. Hofstra is now a complex of seventy buildings on 238 acres both north and south of Hempstead Turnpike in the heart of Long Island's historic Mitchel Field area.

This area, with Hofstra University as its focal point, is regarded as one of Long Island's most important and active cultural and academic centers. National and international endeavors in the arts, law, business, the sciences, athletics, communications, and government originate there.

Remarkably, a large part of Hofstra's growth has come in the past ten years, especially since the university board of trustees' approval of a five-year plan for growth instituted by Dr. James M. Shuart following his 1976 appointment as university president.

After this substantial enlargement and improvement of the school's resources was begun during the late 1970s, Dr. Shuart and the board instituted a second five-year plan in 1981. At a time when many American colleges and universities began retrenching as a reaction to declines in enrollment, Hofstra continued to build.

Since 1982 Hofstra has added seventeen new dormitories to its campus, as well as an indoor Olympic-standard swimming pool and natatorium center, the largest of its kind in the New York metro-

politan area. The university has also added a new student center, a new computer center, and has five new dormitories under construction in 1985 to accommodate record student enrollments.

During the 1984-1985 academic year Hofstra achieved a record full-time undergraduate enrollment of 6,600. This figure represents a 6.5 percent increase over the 1983-1984 full-time undergraduate enrollment of 6,200. It is also higher than the university's previous all-time enrollment record of 6,410 in 1971.

The faculty profile has changed, as well. From a staff of about 560 some twenty years ago, Hofstra's total faculty is now over 660. That includes a 35 percent increase in full-time faculty. In 1965 about 60 percent of the full-time faculty held the highest degree in their

Hofstra Hall, built in 1904, was the original home of William S. Hofstra, for whom the university was named.

fields compared with 80 percent today.

As Hofstra University celebrates its fiftieth anniversary in 1985, it remains positioned among the nation's top 10 percent of universities according to *Barron's Profiles of American Colleges.*

Having come a long way in fifty years from its birth on the old Hofstra estate, Hofstra University now boasts an award-winning library containing more than one million volumes, the only nationally accredited school of business on Long Island, and the only chapter of Phi Beta Kappa at a private school in Nassau and Suffolk counties. Construction was completed recently for the Hofstra Television Institute, which will be the most advanced educational, noncommercial television production facility in the East.

Hofstra University's million-volume, award-winning library.

AVIS RENT A CAR SYSTEM

In 1963 Avis Rent A Car System won the attention of American consumers with ads boldly proclaiming its "underdog" status and challenging its number one competitor to watch Avis catch up. "We Try Harder" became not merely an advertising classic but a company ethos and helped make Avis the number one vehicle renting service outside the United States.

Today Avis is a nearly $900-million company. At its 430,000-square-foot world headquarters at 900 Old Country Road in Garden City, it employs 1,000 of its 11,400 worldwide corporate staff. Together with over 9,000 licensee employees, they represent Avis at 3,500 locations, including 1,200 airports, in 135 countries.

The Avis story began in 1946 when ex-Air Force officer Warren E. Avis, then a Ford dealer in Detroit, recognized a market potential for linking air travel with the infant car rental business. He opened the country's first airport car rental counter at nearby Willow Run Airport in December, calling it Avis Airlines Rent-A-Car System.

Soon Avis was franchising independent rental operations at other airports across the country. In 1948 the word "Airlines" was dropped from the corporate name as Avis began opening additional outlets in downtown locations.

In 1954, after eight years of steady growth, Warren Avis sold his interest in the firm to Richard S. Robie, who owned the U-DRY-VIT Corporation in Boston. With a car and truck rental, car leasing, and parking network spread throughout New England, Robie was the country's single largest Hertz System franchisee at the time.

As a result of his purchase,

When you're only No. 2, you try harder. Or else.

Avis can't afford to relax.

Little fish have to keep moving all of the time. The big ones never stop picking on them.

Avis knows all about the problems of little fish.

We're only No. 2 in rent a cars. We'd be swallowed up if we didn't try harder.

There's no rest for us.

We're always emptying ashtrays. Making sure gas tanks are full before we rent our cars. Seeing that the batteries are full of life. Checking our windshield wipers.

And the cars we rent out can't be anything less than spanking new Plymouths.

And since we're not the big fish, you won't feel like a sardine when you come to our counter.

We're not jammed with customers.

© AVIS RENT A CAR SYSTEM, IN

An early advertisement exemplifies the Avis philosophy.

Robie became part of the Avis System, which had corporate operations only in Detroit and Chicago, while the rest of its national system was franchised. Soon new corporate locations were opened in New York City, St. Louis, Cincinnati, Pittsburgh, and Houston.

Suddenly, by 1956 there were sixteen corporate city offices in the Avis System, which was now producing four million dollars in revenue on an average of 1,200 vehicles operated. At that time Avis launched a revolutionary charge card distribution campaign. The first working national one-way car rental plan was also established.

Ironically, the fast growth created severe capital drains, and Robie was forced to sell U-DRY-VIT, including his Avis interest, to a Hertz affiliate in September

1956. The affiliate sold Avis to a group of Boston investors, and William M. Tetrick, who had succeeded Robie as president in June, continued in this position under the new owners.

The new group formed Avis, Inc., and incorporated it in Maine. This holding company proceeded to acquire all outstanding Avis System assets while the new owners incorporated Avis Rent A Car System, Inc., in Delaware to conduct operations. In 1957 Frederick C. Dumaine became the firm's president.

Over the next five years Avis, Inc., established corporate operations in San Francisco, Seattle, and Denver. Meanwhile, the firm entered the field of truck and car leasing, and the Avis licensee operation was significantly expanded both nationally and overseas.

By March 1962, when it was acquired by the Manhattan-based international banking firm of Lazard Freres & Company, Avis was a $25-million, 7,500-vehicle company. That year unorthodox executive Robert C. Townsend was named Avis president. Townsend was a moving force behind the bold "We Try Harder" ad strategy.

On July 16, 1962, the firm's headquarters was moved from Boston to Garden City, and by 1965, with the addition of corporate operations in Mexico, Italy, and France, Avis corporate sales had reached $74.5 million.

In July 1965 Avis was acquired by International Telephone & Telegraph for a value of fifty-one million dollars. Robert Townsend left the company, and Winston V. Morrow became chief executive officer. Avis also began a major international marketing effort and in some cases, was spectacularly successful.

In Spain, for example, Avis went from "zero" to being the country's largest car rental company in just over one year. Similar growth occurred in other European countries, and by 1973 Avis had surpassed Hertz for control of the continent.

Meanwhile, in 1971 European regional manager Colin M. Marshall had moved to the Avis world headquarters in Garden City as executive vice-president responsible for all line operations. By 1975 he was president and two years later was named chief executive officer.

Late that year the Avis world headquarters took a brief hiatus from Garden City, relocating in Manhattan, though the firm's North American operations remain

Avis' 430,000-square-foot world headquarters is located at 900 Old Country Road in Garden City.

based on Long Island. At that time Avis was a $433-million company.

Growth continued due to steady increases in daily truck rentals and long-term car and truck leasing. By 1977 the Avis system's combined corporate and licensee operations boasted the world's largest car rental fleet—112,000 vehicles. In July of that year consumer products giant Norton Simon, Inc., acquired Avis.

During the 1970s Avis introduced "Wizard," the industry's first totally computerized real-time reservation and rental processing system. The firm has remained at the forefront of the entire self-service rental market, which has included such industry trends as the air flight computer terminals known as Rapid Return and the Rapid Rental machines. Some 300 of the 1,000 Avis Garden City employees operate the world headquarters computer center, which links all worldwide Avis locations.

In 1982 Avis updated its revolutionary slogan: "Trying Harder Makes Avis Second To None." The firm remains the number one car rental company outside the United States and is second among those

represented at United States airports.

Since mid-1984 Avis, Inc., of which Avis Rent A Car System is a wholly owned subsidiary, has been a part of Beatrice, the international food and consumer products marketer. J. Patrick Barrett, who came from the Norton Simon organization, is now chief executive officer of Avis, while Joseph V. Vittoria is president/chief operating officer.

Avis' worldwide business interests now include car rentals and leasing, vehicle retail sales, chauffeur drive service, and luxury car rentals.

Besides its own amazing growth, Avis has been the driving force in the opening and expanding of two particular markets: the airport car rental business, and the non-U.S. car rental market, where Avis was literally the first of such companies, particularly in Europe. Its next major market push is under way in the Far East and the Pacific area generally.

MONITOR AEROSPACE CORPORATION

After working in World War II as a machine shop instructor at Brooklyn Navy Yard, Joseph Monitto decided that he wanted a ship repair business of his own. In 1948 he borrowed $10,000 from his family and opened a 2,500-square-foot shop called Monitor Machinery Corporation. This first shop, on Shore Parkway in Brooklyn, was the genesis of Monitor Aerospace.

Ultimately the ship repair business faded. But, as Monitor-Boxart Corporation and finally Monitor Aerospace, Monitto's little machine shop grew into one of the world's most sought-after machining and assembly manufacturers in the aviation and aerospace industry.

Today Monitor Aerospace Corporation is a $40-million entity with over 400 employees performing major contracts for Avco, Boeing, Grumman, Kaman, Lockheed, McDonnell Douglas, Martin Marietta, Northrop, Republic, Rohr, and Rockwell International in the United States, as well as Embraer in Brazil, Saab in Sweden, and British Aerospace in England. The firm is headquartered in a new 240,000-square-foot building on twenty-five acres at 1000 New Horizons Boulevard in Amityville.

Until 1950 small ship repair contracts were the corporation's staple. Gradually contracts for Grumman aircraft parts helped Monitor Machinery Corporation grow to ten employees.

In 1959, when current Monitor Aerospace president Guy Lepore joined the forty-employee firm as a toolmaker, it was well on its way to becoming a precision airplane parts manufacturer. Monitor grew in direct response to the growth of the aerospace industry.

In 1961 Monitor Machinery Cor-

The Brooklyn headquarters of Monitor Machinery Corporation in the 1950s.

poration and Boxart Machine Company left Brooklyn for Farmingdale where Monitto set up his 100 employees in a 25,000-square-foot facility on Milbar Boulevard. Meanwhile the company expanded because of a flexibility that allowed it to accommodate the rapidly changing technological demands of the aerospace industry it served.

In June 1963 the firm underwent its first name change, to Monitor-Boxart Corporation. Monitor had purchased the formerly Brooklyn-based Boxart Machine Company in 1959. Among the benefits of this purchase were thirty skilled employees and Boxart's long-term relationship with Republic Aviation.

As Monitor-Boxart's reputation grew among the prime aerospace manufacturers, the Farmingdale headquarters also grew, to 60,000 square feet. In 1968 the 200-employee firm acquired its first numerically controlled hydrotel, used for manufacturing components on Grumman's F-111 aircraft. At this time Monitor was also working for

Grumman on the LEM lunar module.

Monitor-Boxart began work on the famed Boeing 747 in 1970. One year later Monitor acquired its first numerically controlled gantry system and, as a result, was able to win substantial contracts from McDonnell Douglas beginning in 1972.

On September 6, 1975, Monitor-Boxart's guiding force and founder, Joseph Monitto, died. He had seen his small machine shop, underwritten by $10,000 in family funds, grow to become a $6-million company working for every major aircraft firm in America.

At this point Guy Lepore, who had been named vice-president in 1966, assumed the presidency of Monitor-Boxart Corporation. Joe Monitto's son, Douglas, employed by the firm since 1968, was named executive vice-president. Lawrence Goldberg joined the company in 1976 and serves as vice-president/

treasurer.

Meanwhile, during the 1970s, major contracts had developed into long-term relationships with aviation technology giants such as Northrop, Saab, and Rohr Industries. Monitor-Boxart leased an additional 60,000 square feet of production space in other buildings along Milbar Boulevard until its total Farmingdale capacity was in excess of 120,000 square feet.

By 1980 it became clear that the firm needed more room than the small acreage in Farmingdale and the neighboring leased buildings provided. A single, new facility would unify the company's inner structure while reflecting the stature it had achieved within the industry. It was finally decided that Monitor's needs would be best met by building on land at the former Zahn's Airport in Amityville, which the Town of Babylon was converting to a business and industry park.

Monitor-Boxart bought twenty-five acres and broke ground for its new office and plant complex on August 28, 1980. In the beginning of 1982 the process of moving 325 employees from Farmingdale to Amityville began.

In June 1982 the firm's name changed again, to Monitor Aerospace Corporation. By the end of that year the major part of the move was complete. This transition cost a total of twenty-eight million dollars and was highlighted by the addition of eight new gantry systems at a cost of fifteen mil-

Monitor-Boxart's president and founder, Joseph Monitto (right), confers with the company's then vice-president and current president Guy Lepore during the early 1970s.

lion dollars.

During the early 1980s important parts of the aerospace industry, Monitor's prime market, underwent a retrenchment. To combat this, Monitor management diverted engineering and production expertise to new endeavors, such as the building of assemblies and subassemblies for Boeing Corporation and the negotiation of its first major international contract.

Monitor Aerospace survived and prospered. The firm carried into the 1980s the same production creativity and flexibility that kept it abreast of aviation's transition to an aerospace industry in the 1950s and 1960s.

The firm's most recent accomplishments include its work on a subcontract to Martin Marietta for the United States Space Shuttle program, and a new contract to produce substantially all machined parts for the Brasilia, Embraer of Brazil's new commuter aircraft.

A thirty-employee engineering department directs the Monitor Aerospace manufacturing process from blueprint and computerized design to finished product. This includes methodizing, tool design, cutter selection, numerically controlled programming, and part prove-out.

The company's specialized manufacturing capability is highlighted by twenty five-axis and three-axis numerically controlled gantry mills, and thirty other multi-spindle numerically controlled profilers and machining centers. The firm also designs and manufactures its own custom cutting tools.

Now performing at the rate of forty million dollars in annual sales, and contemplating expansion in the next five years on the unused 19-acre part of its 25-acre Amityville property, Monitor Aerospace Corporation remains the kind of family-run business in which a toolmaker can become its chief executive.

Monitor Aerospace Corporation's new 240,000-square-foot office and manufacturing facility in Amityville's New Horizons Business Center.

LONG ISLAND TRUST COMPANY, N.A.

In late 1922 prominent Garden City businessman George L. Hubbell raised $150,000 to capitalize what he viewed as a necessity for local residents as well as a personal dream. This vision, the beginning of the Long Island Trust story, opened for business on July 23, 1923, as the Garden City Bank. There were two employees in two rooms of the Hubbell Realty Building at 59 Hilton Avenue, and Hubbell was its first president.

Apparently Garden City residents were tired of banking in Mineola and Hempstead, because they deposited more than $100,000 in their new community bank on its first day. By August 15 that figure had reached $281,000, and by mid-1924 deposits reached one million dollars. The institution's services then were largely savings and checking accounts, letters of credit, and travelers checks.

This little bank would ultimately grow to be the region's largest. Today, as Long Island Trust Company, it is a 47-branch, 1,150-employee subsidiary of North American Bancorp, Inc., which is itself a subsidiary of Banca Commerciale Italiana of Milan. NAB deposits are more than $1.3 billion, and its assets are $1.5 billion.

But this took more than sixty years to happen. On June 26, 1926, Garden City Bank moved to a new building on Seventh Street around the corner from its Hubbell Realty birthplace. Three years later it attained trust powers, and Garden City Bank and Trust Company ended the 1920s as a fourteen-employee institution with $2.6 million on deposit.

The 1930s were hard times for all financial institutions, but Garden City Bank and Trust kept its deposit level over two million dollars and ended the Depression years with a staff of twenty-five

Gathered on November 14, 1983, for Long Island Trust's sixtieth anniversary were (left to right) Arthur Hug, Jr., chairman; James Dinkelacker, consultant; Frederick Hainfeld, Jr., director emeritus/former president and chairman; George Hubbell, Jr., director emeritus and the founder's son; David Darcy, vice-chairman; and Mario Arcari, president/chief executive officer.

and $4.2 million in deposits. The 1940s were a healthy decade for the bank, which saw 1943 assets of $5.6 million grow to $18 million in 1949 and the staff grow to sixty-five.

Meanwhile, a $140,000 expansion of the Seventh Street headquarters was the big event of 1947. Originally limited to the building's ground floor, the bank now took over its mezzanine, second, and third floors, giving it a total of 17,000 square feet and making it Nassau County's second-largest bank building.

Real growth began in the 1950s, a decade in which banks in the New York area sought increased presence in the developing postwar suburbs. Of course, Garden City Bank was already on Long Island.

In January 1951 Hubbell became chairman of the board and was succeeded as president by Edward A. Nash, who had joined the bank as a cashier in 1926.

In 1954, under its president, Frederick Hainfeld, Jr., the Garden City institution acquired the old-line Bank of Great Neck, which had been founded in 1906

by Joseph Grace. The board of directors saw a need to make the Garden City Bank's name more descriptive of its widening area of service; thus, Long Island Trust Company was born. The staff now topped 100, and on November 10 the East Garden City branch on Stewart Avenue was opened.

In July 1957 Long Island Trust acquired Freeport Bank, which had been established in 1892. The headquarters at Seventh Street was expanded to a total of 26,000 square feet by breaking through to an adjoining A&P store in 1958.

New branches were opened in Stewart Manor in 1956, South Farmingdale and Garden City Park in 1958, and Nassau County Center in 1959. By the end of the decade

Today the firm's headquarters is located at 1401 Franklin Avenue in Garden City.

Long Island Trust was a 250-employee, eight-branch network, boasting $87.9 million on deposit. The $100-million level in resources was surpassed for the first time in 1960.

In January 1961 the Lindenhurst Bank, founded in 1929, was acquired, and six months later four headquarters departments with sixty staff members moved from Seventh Street Doubleday & Company. By 1963, with $155 million on deposit, Long Island Trust was the country's 218th-largest bank and the largest state-chartered institution in Nassau and Suffolk.

The first Suffolk County branch opened in Melville in 1960 together with new branches in Levittown and South Freeport that same year, followed by branches in West Hempstead (1961), Copiague (1962), East Farmingdale (1963), Syosset (1964), Deer Park (1966), Hauppauge (1967), and North Lindenhurst (1968).

On August 1, 1968, Arthur Hug, Jr., was named president. The following year a new 33,000-square-foot, three-story granite and glass headquarters building opened at 1401 Franklin Avenue. This design-award-winning structure remains the bank's headquarters today. Meanwhile, by the close of the 1960s there were twenty Long Island Trust branches, employing 575 and holding $235 million on deposit.

Seaside Bank and the four-branch Bank of Westbury were acquired in 1970, while new branches in Bohemia, South Melville, North Patchogue, Smith Haven, and Port Jefferson South were open by 1973. Soon there were two branches added in South Hauppauge, and one each in Bethpage and Huntington. Since then, Long Island Trust branches have been opened or added in Hicksville, Jericho, Plainview, Commack, Greenlawn, Farmingville, and Westhampton Beach, as well as in New York City and Queens.

By October 1971 the bank's data-processing and installment loan departments were moved to a facility on Kellum Place behind the Franklin Avenue headquarters. These two buildings represent a $5-million investment and together form an 86,000-square-foot operations center for Long Island Trust in Garden City just blocks from its birthplace.

By the end of 1972 there were 715 employees in twenty-nine offices with $463 million on deposit. In 1972 the directors formed

LITCO Corporation of New York as a holding company, and by June of that year Long Island Trust was ranked 189th among U.S. commercial banks.

In 1982 LITCO was acquired by Banca Commerciale Italiana, enhancing Long Island Trust's international trade presence and giving the Italian parent an important addition to its New York office and its Chicago and Los Angeles facilities. In 1985 the LITCO name was changed to North American Bancorp, Inc.

A five-year, $30-million computerization upgrading of Long Island Trust began in 1983, while on April 2, 1984, the Third Avenue office of Dime Savings Bank of New York, FSB, was acquired.

Commercial lending and other services to middle-market Long Island firms remain Long Island Trust's prime business line, but consumer banking, trust, and international services are also strong.

The corporation is headed by Hug, who is chairman of Long Island Trust Company, N.A., and North American Bancorp, Inc. Alberto Abelli serves as president/chief executive officer of Long Island Trust and as NAB president. Long Island Trust remains ranked among the top 200 commercial banks in the United States.

The Hubbell Realty Building on Hilton Avenue, circa 1900. Twenty-three years later the first Garden City bank office was installed on this site.

TAMBRANDS INC.

In 1936 an investment of $200 would have bought 100 shares of Tampax common stock. In late 1984, after stock splits, those 100 shares had become 3,600 shares with a market value of more than $200,000. In addition, dividends on those shares during the intervening forty-eight years had totaled over $135,000. How did a $200 investment grow to over $335,000? This is a brief history.

The Tampax tampon was invented by Denver physician Earle C. Haas in 1931. He was certain he had developed a product that would be liberating for women and would have mass-market appeal. He was right on both counts.

Since the mid-1930s more than eighty billion Tampax tampons have been sold in 130 countries. Yet the product's amazing acceptance was accomplished only after a difficult educational, marketing, and advertising effort to overcome resistance to the product and ignorance of its benefits.

The company founded on Dr. Haas' invention is today known as Tambrands Inc., headquartered at 10 Delaware Drive in Lake Success. Here, Long Island's third-largest profit producer has embarked on a growth and diversification strategy.

After Dr. Haas was granted his patent, he found that major manufacturers like Johnson & Johnson, Kimberly-Clark, and Bauer & Black were not interested in tampons. Thus, he sold his patent for $32,000 to Denver businesswoman Gertrude Tenderich, who immediately directed engineer Joseph Voss to create a machine that would produce 1,100 tampons per day.

Tampax Sales Corporation began selling tampons in pharmacies in Colorado and Wyoming. But the *Denver Post*'s reluctance to run a product advertisement reflected a

A 1949 Tampax board of directors meeting with Earle Griswold (left), Ellery Mann (fourth from left), and Thomas Casey (fifth from left).

common misunderstanding of the new item. Finally, by 1935, blind ads succeeded in encouraging women to contact an address for information and samples. Sales started to increase in the two target states. Then Gertrude Tenderich met Ellery Mann.

Mann was a marketing and advertising genius. He had been vice-president at McCann-Erickson advertising agency, had started the Zonite Company, whose antiseptic was a popular 1930s product, and had launched a successful trade magazine called *Drugstore Selling*. Mann became president of the newly formed Tampax Incorporated.

Mann immediately hired several key Zonite employees. Financial expert Thomas Casey helped him issue shares of Tampax stock, registering 300,000 shares with the Securities and Exchange Commis-

sion in 1936. Earle Griswold was hired as production engineer. Griswold came from a family involved in the cotton-processing business, and his knowledge of cotton led him to the vital discovery that heating the material as it fed through the compressing machine ironed each tampon into shape without destroying its absorbency or wasting expensive cotton.

On July 27, 1936, the first Tampax tampon dropped off the compressor onto the conveyor belt at a leased plant in New Brunswick, New Jersey. It had been seven years since Dr. Haas had begun making tampons by hand in the cellar of his Denver home.

Griswold searched from the

United States to the Far East for the most absorbent cotton fiber he could find. In 1937 the firm began buying custom-processed cotton from Kendall Mills in Massachusetts, and soon Tampax was using twenty million pounds of cotton per year.

In Manhattan, working with his former employer, Harrison McCann, Mann created an advertising campaign to reach what he saw as Tampax's three major audiences: drugstores, the medical profession, and female consumers.

The first Tampax ad for a general audience appeared in *American Weekly* on July 26, 1936. This ad was joined by others in Sunday supplements and in large-circulation women's magazines and home publications. In the first nine months of operation, the firm's total expenditure was $218,000, half of which was for advertising. A net loss of $157,000 was incurred, and by March 1937 wholesalers returned more product than they

sold. The message was clearly ahead of its time.

But slowly the ingeniously written ads began working. Sales for 1937 were 171 percent better than the previous year's figures. Losses for 1937 were only $27,000. The advertising and educational effort intensified.

As early as 1937 some Tampax sales were being recorded in thirty-four countries. Today the product is a leader in the $1.3-billion U.S. market for feminine hygiene, and Tampax tampons are sold in more than 125 countries worldwide.

Tampax now has seventeen plants throughout the world, including facilities in Canada, England, France, Spain, Ireland, Mexico, South Africa, and Japan, with discussions under way for production in the People's Republic of China. The firm has domestic plants in Massachusetts, Vermont, New Hampshire, Maine, New York, and Nevada.

In 1956, following Mann's death,

The Palmer, Massachusetts, Tambrands Inc. plant began operations in 1942.

Casey assumed the firm's top position, and he moved the headquarters to Lake Success in 1969. Casey retired in 1980, and Russell Sprague, who had been president since 1976, also became chairman, a position he still holds. Edwin Shutt joined Tampax in 1981 and is now president and chief executive officer.

In 1980 the board of directors decided the company should become a diversified consumer-products operation in the years ahead. The successful 1981 launch of the new "Maxithin" external pad freed the firm of its one-product image, and products other than tampons now account for over 25 percent of total volume. In April 1984 the shareholders approved changing the company's name to Tambrands Inc. to reflect its diversification.

THOMSON INDUSTRIES, INC.

When NASA's Apollo 15 moon photo mapping made history in 1971, Thomson Industries' precision linear-motion bearings allowed the lunar camera to deploy accurately and smoothly. Formed in 1945 by engineer/pilot John B. Thomson because the Army sought to perfect a variable-pitch, constant-speed propeller, Thomson Industries today supplies its patented bearings to commercial, industrial, and consumer, as well as aerospace and military markets.

Thomson Industries' three facilities employ 660 people, 500 of them at the 165,000-square-foot Port Washington headquarters. The Thomson Corporation division in Lancaster, Pennsylvania, employs 130 in a 77,000-square-foot manufacturing facility. And the firm's ABEK division in Bristol, Connecticut, produces precision balls for Thomson's bearings.

This all began in 1930 because Flushing native John Thomson loved aviation so much that he enrolled in flight school at nearby Flushing Airport when he was fourteen years old. A year later he was the youngest pilot ever licensed there.

After earning a mechanical engineering degree in 1938 from Pratt Institute, Thomson became East Coast sales representative for the Spartan executive aircraft. By flying the models around the country in demonstrations for potential customers, he sold most of the thirty-eight planes Spartan had built.

In 1939 this job abruptly ended as World War II began in Europe and the U.S. Navy ordered Spartan to cease making private planes in favor of Navy trainers. However, a steel company president to whom Thomson had sold a Spartan hired him to fly to California and secure an option on the vari-

able-pitch propeller just invented there.

Meanwhile, Thomson's brother-in-law was head of Long Island City-based Zimmer Manufacturing Company, the chief producer of the Allies' battlefield stretchers. An agreement was reached for Thomson to use the Zimmer plant to perfect the propeller, and on November 7, 1940, the Zimmer-Thomson Corporation was formed.

By 1942 Thomson was spending most of his time on the propeller, which the Army Air Corps wanted for a flying bomb similar to the V-1 "buzz bomb" the Germans were developing. At the Wright Field Development Center in Dayton, Ohio, Thomson met civilian engineer Bob Magee who was a project engineer in the Propeller Laboratory. The pair discussed a "governor" Magee had developed for the propeller.

Thomson and his associates received military contracts for a prototype just as German V-1s began hitting England, making the U.S. Army's plans obsolete. But the Zimmer-Thomson contracts were honored in that the propeller could be used on trainers and drones. The prototype, however, had problems meeting military performance standards due to friction in some of the sliding governor parts.

Finally, engineer H.K. Ferger offered a solution: a ball bearing to support linear—straight line rather than rotary—motion. This suggestion led to the innovative "Ball Bushing," an oval circuit raceway bearing that greatly reduces metal-on-metal friction in reciprocating motions.

As this idea grew closer to reality in 1944, Thomson was now president of Zimmer-Thomson. But the war—and demand for the firm's specialized medical supplies—was ending. In a hail of cancelled

In 1932 sixteen-year-old John B. Thomson was one of America's youngest licensed pilots.

stretcher contracts, Thomson Industries was formed on March 12, 1945, with a $500 investment, some loans, and the former Zimmer-Thomson plant. Six months later Magee came to work full time with Thomson, and he suggested an economical way to make Ball Bushings by punch-press stamping rather than machining—but it needed much development.

By 1947 Thomson Industries faced difficulties making its payrolls. The Long Island City plant was sold for cash, and in May the six-employee company moved to a small administrative office in Manhasset supplemented by a little machine shop leased in one corner of Hangar F at Westbury's Roosevelt Field.

Meanwhile, the propeller was sold to Fairchild Airplane Company, and in April of that year a successful drillhead manufacturing business was split off as Thriftmaster Products Corporation and

In 1948 Thomson Industries ran this initial ad in Product Engineering *magazine for the patented Ball Bushing. The ad clearly explained the then-innovative Thomson principle of using a ball bearing for linear motion.*

moved to Lancaster under H.K. Ferger.

In 1948 the company's first Ball Bushing ad in *Product Engineering* magazine indicated a strong interest in the item, and by 1950 Sperry Corporation at Lake Success was a substantial user, particularly for its bombsight.

Roosevelt Field was being cleared for a major shopping mall in 1951, and the 25-employee Thomson Industries moved again to a 10,000-square-foot New Hyde Park facility. The Korean War increased Thomson's production in 1952-1953, and during this decade the firm's employee base grew to 170.

The product base was also increased during the 1950s. The special steel shafts on which Ball Bushings roll had been the customers' responsibility until Thomson created its "60 Case Shafts" and began mass production at the Thriftmaster building.

During this time "Nylined plastic bearings" were invented with Thomson's patented compensation gap that prevents locking of these nonrusting bearings on the shaft. Nyliners are now integral parts of the "big three" automakers' brake systems, Xerox copiers, IBM printers, and many home appliances.

In 1963 the firm moved to new 52,000-square-foot quarters at Shore Road and Channel Drive in Port Washington. Through three subsequent expansions tripling the original space, this site remains the Thomson headquarters.

The company developed a linear-motion roller bearing during the 1970s. Resembling a heavy-duty bicycle chain, the "Roundway bearing" carries more weight than the linear ball bearing because it distributes the load along a broader contact surface.

With the development of the "Mill Drill table" accessory for reproducing sophisticated parts on drill press and milling machines, Thomson had his sixth major patent. By the time he died in 1978, work had progressed on a new series of linear ball bearings composed partly of plastics and other inexpensive alternatives to steel.

John B. Thomson, Jr., had started with his father's firm in 1960 at the age of sixteen. After experience in the research and development department, John Jr. moved into the sales division with Fred Klein in 1964 while studying mechanical engineering at New York Institute of Technology. In 1973 he started full time with the firm, and two years later he became executive vice-president.

In 1977 he received a patent of his own for a twin-block, double-length bearing that was derived from his solution of a slip-stick problem on the traveler block of his racing yacht. John Jr. became the firm's chairman and president when his father died, and named Magee vice-chairman. In the years since, John Thomson, Jr., has guided Thomson Industries' transition from an entrepreneurial company to a market-driven, professionally managed operation.

Today Thomson bearings are found in aerospace and military applications such as tanks, spacecraft, missiles, and flight simulators. Grumman, Fairchild, and Hazeltine are among its largest Long Island users.

However, chief Thomson applications are found in consumer, industrial, and medical markets including IBM data-processing equipment, Westinghouse robots, industry machinery of all types, CAT scanners and X-ray machines, heart pumps, orthotic devices, physical fitness machines, and everything from sliding subway doors and food processors to automated-teller money machines at banks.

In September 1984 *Power Transmission Design* magazine placed Thomson Industries' Ball Bushing among the past quarter-century's forty most important technological developments.

COMPUTER TERMINAL SYSTEMS, INC.

On May 28, 1968, the day of its incorporation, Computer Terminal Systems, Inc., occupied 1,000 square feet of space rented from a friend, and employed five people. By 1985 the company had become a $12-million firm, employing 180 people. Its new 56,000-square-foot semiautomated office, engineering, and manufacturing facility occupies five acres of the Hauppauge Industrial Park at 89 Arkay Drive. With over 77 percent of the U.S. market for its principal products, Computer Terminal Systems is the leading designer and manufacturer of label, form, and ticket printers and printing terminals for the airline, transportation, and entertainment industries.

In 1972 Gerald H. Schoenberg joined the firm as executive vice-president. With degrees in me-

---

Computer Terminal Systems, Inc., is the leading designer and manufacturer of label, form, and ticket printers and printing terminals for the airline, transportation, and entertainment industries. Shown is the firm's Blue Wiz® theater ticket printer.

chanical and electrical engineering, as well as proven expertise in electromechanical technology, manufacturing, and marketing, he helped design many of the company's products. By then, Computer Terminal Systems had begun to manufacture printers for its first big customer, General Computer Systems, which bought hundreds of its early one-line printers. Soon thereafter, Diebold Company and Docutel Corporation placed significant orders for more advanced two-line printers, for planned application in the banking industry. That same year two significant contracts also arrived. New York City Off-Track Betting Corporation placed an order for 200 highly specialized employee time clock terminals, and Raytheon Corporation ordered the development of a boarding-pass printer for use by major airlines, including Eastern, American, and British Caledonia. By 1973 the company was in production of its first airline boarding-pass printer, an unqualified success, and Raytheon placed an additional order for airline ticket printers. By 1974 Computer Terminal Systems had made significant inroads in the production of theater ticket printing systems.

Gerald Schoenberg was elected president and chairman of the board of directors in 1980. At that time the firm was grossing $3.7 million in sales. As chief executive officer, Schoenberg soon identified two serious problems—the firm's product line was obsolete, and Computer Terminal Systems was entirely too dependent upon its two major customers, which accounted for 80 percent of its total production. A crash program of research and development was instituted, and by 1982 this program culminated in the creation of vital new microprocessor-based product

lines, which the company markets under five trademarks for different market segments: BLUE MAX® (Airlines), BLUE WIZ® (Entertainment), BLUE STREAK® (Transportation), BLUE BIZ® (Business), and BLUE CHIP® (Securities and Gambling). During its 1984 fiscal year the publicly owned, NASDAQ-listed, over-the-counter company (stock symbol CTML) racked up $8.7 million in sales. The following year saw an increase in sales to $10 million. Most important, dependence on any single customer was virtually eliminated, and the firm now has a diversified product line and a vastly expanded customer base, including original equipment manufacturers (OEMs) and end-users.

In the United States some 85 percent of all airline industry ticket, boarding-pass, and baggage-tag printers are Computer Terminal Systems' products, as are 90 percent of all ticket printers used by the AMTRAK System. A large number of the printers used to produce computerized entertainment tickets are printed using the company's products. Computer Terminal Systems also holds substantial shares of the domestic betting ticket, passport, and production control label printing markets. The firm has received contracts from the New York Stock Exchange and the Chicago Board Option Exchange for printers used to implement the trading of securities on the exchanges' trading floors.

Computer Terminal Systems has seen its customer list grow to include Telex, Kodak, Sperry, IBM, and NCR. With NCR, Computer Terminal Systems, Inc., also has an exclusive international agreement providing for the servicing of its products and worldwide stocking of spare parts.

CABLEVISION OF LONG ISLAND

Cablevision, the country's largest privately owned cable company, located at One Media Crossways in Woodbury, presently employs some 2,600 people—over 1,000 in Long Island.

Founded in 1973 by Charles F. Dolan, Cablevision has grown from a ten-employee office in Jericho, Long Island, with a 1,500-subscriber base, to become one of the nation's largest cable companies. Cablevision's Long Island system is the second largest in the country, now serving over 240,000 subscribers throughout Nassau and Suffolk counties.

Cablevision operates cable systems in six states and provides programming to cable subscribers across the nation. Its cable operation is expected to reach nearly 1.3 million subscribers by 1990 through systems in Nassau, Suffolk, and Westchester, New York; Bergen County and Bayonne, New Jersey; suburban Chicago; Fairfield County and Bridgeport, Connecticut; Boston and Brookline, Massachusetts; and suburban Cleveland, Ohio. In 1983 Cablevision was awarded the largest franchise agreement in cable TV history, winning the right to wire a potential one million subscribers in Brooklyn and the Bronx. A franchise for the London suburb of Croydon, England, is Cablevision's first international venture.

Charles Dolan's successful pioneering efforts in the development of the Cablevision systems operations paralleled his successful ventures into the field of programming. His early successes—serving as president of Sterling Movies USA, establishing Manhattan Cable TV in 1961, creating Home Box Office, and being the first to offer professional sports on cable television—resulted in the founding of Rainbow Programming Services in 1980, the programming arm of Cablevision.

Rainbow Programming Services markets and distributes pay cable services such as Bravo and American Movie Classics to cable subscribers across the country, as well as regional sports services such as PRISM (in the Philadelphia market) and SportsChannel (in the New York metropolitan area). Bravo offers international award-winning films and performing arts, while American Movie Classics presents the finest in American film from the 1940s through the 1970s. The Yankees, Mets, Islanders, and Nets are available to SportsChannel New York subscribers, while cable viewers receiving PRISM, SportsChannel New England, and Sportsvision Chicago can see their own home teams in action.

In addition to Rainbow's programming services, Cablevision systems offer subscribers other high-quality pay cable services including The Disney Channel and The Playboy Channel.

Cablevision provides this alternative programming to subscribers through a sophisticated system of transmitters and receivers. On Long Island, satellite, microwave, and broadcast signals are transmitted to Cablevision at its headend, or receiving/distribution, center

Chairman of the board John Tatta (left) with Charles F. Dolan, general partner, who founded Cablevision, the country's largest privately owned cable company, in 1973.

atop the Nassau County Medical Center in East Meadow. These signals are then sent to subscribers' homes through an elaborate network of over 5,000 miles of cable.

Cablevision's locally produced programming reflects a commitment to community and local interests. On Long Island, Cablevision has developed and produced such shows as the nightly Cablevisionews, the tutorial Extra Help program, and the Long Island Sports Network to meet the special interests of local viewers. Mobile production facilities, community programming studios, and local special events coverage are large elements of the company's daily operation. This commitment to quality programming designed for different individual tastes is the key to Cablevision's success.

Cablevision's corporate headquarters at One Media Crossways in the Crossways Industrial Park in Woodbury.

TOUCHE ROSS

Accounting came into being as an organized profession during the 1850s in Scotland. And when the ancestor firm of what is today Touche Ross was founded in Detroit on August 20, 1947, as Touche, Niven, Bailey & Smart, it had strong Scottish and British roots. At the same time Leo Spandorf, a New York City accountant, was beginning to look at Long Island as a new frontier for his practice. Touche Ross Long Island had its roots.

Touche, Niven, Bailey & Smart began with thirty-three active partners, operating from its Detroit headquarters and in nine other U.S. cities. In 1960 the firm underwent a name change to Touche, Ross, Bailey & Smart when Harold Ross joined the firm and then, on September 1, 1969, the name Touche Ross was adopted.

The youngest of the "Big 8" accounting and management consulting firms, Touche Ross is an international affiliation of firms, with 7,000 professionals operating from 83 offices in the United States, and 22,000 professionals in 430 offices in 90 countries worldwide. The executive offices of Touche Ross, U.S., are located at 1633 Broadway in New York. The firm's international headquarters is located in New York City as well.

On Long Island, Touche Ross is represented by a well-established office of sixty-five professionals and support staff at Two Jericho Plaza in Jericho. Under the direction of partner-in-charge Richard A. Kron, the office combines the full resources of an international organization with the local presence and knowledge of the marketplace that began with Leo Spandorf and his partners on Long Island.

As far back as the mid-1940s Spandorf was aware of a market

The Touche Ross Long Island partners include (standing, left to right) director of tax operations Eric H. Hananel; Leonard J. Smith; David W. Kirchenbaum; and Dennis E. Mulvihill. Seated is partner-in-charge Richard A. Kron.

for the traditional tax and auditing services of an accounting firm on Long Island. From his Manhattan office, he began regular sojourns to Riverhead where he served several trucking companies and farmers as well as other agriculture-related clients. Commuting in those days was a planned excursion, especially traveling to eastern Suffolk.

On September 1, 1951, he joined forces with fellow Manhattan accountant Sid Kohleriter to create the four-partner firm of Kohleriter & Spandorf. Though the office remained in Manhattan, Spandorf solidified the Long Island practice together with Leonard Goldschmidt, one of his partners who worked for several years from an office in his Bay Shore home.

K&S grew during the 1950s into one of Suffolk County's most respected accounting practices, providing "urban-style" professional services to potato farmers, auto dealers, trucking firms, and several common carriers. Then, as the 1950s drew to a close, an office was opened in Babylon, and a true physical presence of the K&S firm

was established on Long Island.

During the early 1960s the K&S client base expanded into areas that are still solid markets for Touche Ross Long Island today, including real estate and construction, high-technology, and a cross section of emerging companies looking for private or public financing. In 1968 K&S opened a larger office in Huntington at the Old Colonial Building on Route 110. At that point the firm was a thriving accounting practice of sixty individuals, twenty of whom worked on Long Island in Huntington.

Thus, when K&S merged into Touche Ross on April 1, 1970, Touche Ross acquired a developed, experienced, and well-known practice with more than twenty years in the Long Island market. Says

Richard A. Kron, partner-in-charge, "Touche Ross saw an opportunity to impact a new marketplace and to provide "Big 8" professional services to the Long Island community." By 1972 this new Long Island office of Touche Ross was moved a few miles south on Route 110 to the Huntington Quadrangle. In those days Route 110 was still bordered by farmland. The "Quad" was the first major modern office building on the strip.

Throughout the 1970s Touche Ross established itself as one of the most respected accounting/ management consulting firms in the region, creating a substantial presence, in the face of growing competition, in vital Long Island markets such as health care, real estate and construction, retailing, high technology, aerospace, and electronics.

As the Long Island business community continued to grow in complexity, the full-service capabilities and sophistication of "Big 8" accounting firms became a necessity. As more companies grew in size, many raising capital through public offerings, and as more companies evolved into multilocation operations, both nationally and internationally, Touche Ross' services were increasingly sought after.

Touche Ross moved into its new Jericho headquarters in 1983. Under the direction of its Long Island partners, Touche Ross has maintained its expertise in the traditional areas of auditing and taxation that made it, and its predecessor, prominent. Meanwhile, the firm has transitioned into a diverse area of business consulting that includes computer and systems consulting, troubled company restructuring, market research and competition evaluation, business interruption services, and litigation support.

Touche Ross employs one of the largest tax departments in the accounting profession, boasting more tax professionals with law degrees than any other "Big 8" firm. These resources are made available in the Long Island office under director of tax operations/partner Eric H. Hananel. The Touche Ross management consulting practice on Long Island, headed by partner Dennis E. Mulvihill, is part of the firm's national management consulting operation, which employs 600 professionals nationwide.

Among the Long Island companies served by Touche Ross are Bulova Watch Company, Nikon, North Shore University Hospital, Vanguard Ventures, Patient Technology, Fortunoff's, Aeroflex Laboratories, the Town of North Hempstead, Quantronix Corporation, and Health Extension Services.

The firm's Washington, D.C., Service Center and its Financial Services Center on Wall Street act as a liaison between all Touche Ross clients, the federal government, and the investment community.

The Long Island partners of Touche Ross, including David W. Kirchenbaum, director of the office's high-technology practice, and Leonard J. Smith, director of health care, continue the responsiveness to the local business community begun by Kohleriter & Spandorf. Among organizations where they are, or have been, active officers and board members are the Long Island Association and its committees, the Long Island Forum for Technology, the Nassau Citizens Budget Committee, the Long Island Philharmonic, the United Fund, and the YM and YWHAs of Suffolk County. Says Richard Kron, "Our commitment to Long Island is strong. We have focused resources in what we believe will be one of the country's fastest-growing business communities during the rest of this century."

The home of Touche Ross' client, Bulova Watch Company. The Long Island landmark is situated in a 24-acre parklike setting that has been the company's home since 1952.

ADELPHI UNIVERSITY

Long Island's oldest liberal arts college was born in 1896 when sixteen prominent American educators led by Charles H. Levermore founded Adelphi College. At the beginning there were fifty-seven students and 8,000 books in the library.

Adelphi University has a nearly 100-year history of preparing young people to meet the demands of world involvement through individual achievement. America's first licensed female pilot, Ruth Nichols, was an Adelphi graduate who launched the college's flying program in 1939, and alumna Sally Knapp became a World War II flight instructor on aircraft carriers and wrote several aviation books.

Today Adelphi University has 11,000 students—60 percent of them female—attending classes in seventeen campus buildings on seventy-five acres on South Avenue in historic Garden City. But for over thirty years Adelphi prospered as "Brooklyn's college for Brooklyn girls" though its New York State charter was always coeducational.

It was in 1927, during the administration of Frank Dickinson Blodgett who had assumed the presidency in 1915, that school officials raised the issue of moving east on Long Island. At first a twenty-acre Roslyn site seemed attractive for its proximity to the Pratts, longtime Adelphi supporters. But a 65-acre site on Garden City's Hempstead Plain offered more room for growth.

On October 8, 1928, Adelphi's new Garden City cornerstone was laid. The noted architectural firm of McKim, Mead & White designed the first three buildings on the basis of a 625-student enrollment with capacity for 1,000.

Classes began on September 30, 1929. The following June 7, during

Adelphi's first commencement week, the original three buildings were dedicated. These were the arts building (now Levermore Hall), the sciences building (now Blodgett Hall), and the recreation building (now Woodruff Hall).

In May 1937 Dr. Blodgett retired and was succeeded by Paul Dawson Eddy under whose 28-year presidency Adelphi would grow to national prominence. One immediate result of Dr. Eddy's tenure was the institution's de facto resumption of coeducation.

In 1938 famed dancer/choreographer Ruth St. Denis initiated America's first collegiate department of dance at Adelphi. Eleanor Roosevelt dedicated two nursing buildings as America's first college unit of the U.S. Cadet Nurse Corps on May 6, 1944. This soon led to creation of Adelphi's renowned Marion A. Buckley School of Nursing. During the 1940s and 1950s the schools of education and social work grew to national stature as well.

During the 1960s, under Freud disciple Theodore Reik, Adelphi's Institute of Advanced Psychological Studies earned international renown that continues to this day. Adelphi was granted university status by the state in 1963, and two years later Dr. Eddy retired.

Under president Timothy W. Costello, Adelphi University, which now includes schools of business

On May 6, 1944, Eleanor Roosevelt dedicated Adelphi's first two nursing buildings. Present were (left to right) Ruth S. Harley, dean of women; Thomas Parran, U.S. Surgeon General; James E. Stiles, Adelphi board of trustees' chairman; Mrs. Roosevelt; Paul Dawson Eddy, then Adelphi president; and Lucille Petry, U.S. Nurse Corps director.

administration, banking and money management, the University College for adults over twenty-one, prelaw and premed programs, and a joint dental degree with Georgetown University, continued as an educational innovator.

The "Adelphi on Wheels" program during the early 1970s offered the country's first university credits on a speeding commuter train. And the Institute for Teaching and Education Studies at Adelphi University is making history by literally guaranteeing that its students will pass the professional section of the New York State Teachers Certification examination.

Adelphi University's present 75-acre, 20-building campus.

NEC AMERICA, INC.

Federal deregulation made it possible to market private telephone systems in 1963. Immediately, NEC Corporation of Japan established NEC America as its first wholly owned U.S. subsidiary. From a small Pan Am Building suite in Manhattan, NEC America ultimately moved in 1977 to 532 Broad Hollow Road in Melville with about 100 employees.

Today NEC America is still headquartered at Melville but in a new three-story corporate office and warehouse complex at 8 Old Sod Farm Road. Under president and chief executive officer Dr. Ko Muroga, NEC America is a $600-million telecommunications product manufacturer with 450 of its 1,800 employees on Long Island.

NEC America's story is marked by prescient reactions to the rapid evolution of twentieth-century communications. In 1968, for example, further U.S. government deregulation opened the first market for interconnect products.

NEC America took advantage of that event by creating a small customer equipment group that began successful marketing of crossbar PBX telephone systems. In 1970 it sold one of the first privately owned network tandem switches to the OLIN Corporation. And by 1972 sales volume increased sufficiently to require formation of the important NEC Telephones subsidiary.

But this penetration of a vital new U.S. phone market was prefigured in the early 1900s when the engineering and sales of telephones and switchboards was already a staple for the Japanese parent, Nippon Electric Co. (NEC).

Nippon Electric Co., which is currently called NEC Corporation, was founded in Tokyo on July 17, 1899, as history's first Japanese/American joint business venture.

The partner was Western Electric Company. Today NEC employs 80,000 people worldwide in more than thirty countries including the United States.

Prior to its 1963 American incursion, NEC initiated the research and development of transistors in 1950, of computers in 1954, and of electronic switching systems in 1956. In 1963 the firm entered satellite communications.

During the late 1970s a corporate philosophy known as "C&C," the integration of computers and communications, was established. Under Dr. Muroga, NEC America's three operating groups address their markets with this company credo.

The Switching Group, of which Melville-based NEC Telephones, Inc., is one part, also includes a

Dr. Ko Muroga, president of NEC America.

switching systems division and the Dallas plant. The Radio and Transmission Group includes radio and transmission, mobile radio, and broadcast equipment divisions. The Special Products Group includes Melville-based facsimile division, new products and electromechanical device departments, plus the data communications products department and export division.

NEC America is also represented by offices in or near Boston, Atlanta, Chicago, Dallas, Los Angeles, San Francisco, and Washington, D.C. In addition to Dallas, there are manufacturing plants in the suburbs of Los Angeles and Washington, D.C., and a new one is under construction in Hillsboro, Oregon.

Consumers for NEC America products include the Bell operating companies; major independent phone companies; satellite communications, broadcasting, and film production companies; hospitals; universities; hotels; banks; the U.S. government; and many *Fortune* 500 firms.

NEC's Dterm® executive work station telephone features appointment scheduling, electronic mail message center, directory service, voice message memo, wireless keyboard, world clock, call forwarding, and even printer capability.

KNOGO CORPORATION

Long Island's Knogo Corporation, started by Arthur J. Minasy, created an entirely new industry. New industries are created only by the development of what is called a radical innovation. Radical innovations are innovations of magnitude; they have not existed before; they are the solutions. Generally, inventions are gradual improvements on existing techniques, processes, or products, and only in some cases very dramatic ones. The radical innovation, however, is the creation of an entirely new technology to solve a problem or improve a situation by means that have never been in practice before. For example, the Xerox copy machine is not a radical innovation; it is merely an improvement over a wet process of duplicating.

Radical innovations have historically been characterized by slow adoption by the user, as in the cases of the steamboat and wireless radio. There is always a period during which the radical innovation has to prove beyond any reasonable doubt that it is an acceptable technique and technology to replace previously accepted means of providing a product or service.

In the early 1960s it became apparent to Arthur Minasy, during the course of his work with the New York City Police Department, that the problem of pilferage, shoplifting, and unauthorized movement of personnel and merchandise was becoming an increasingly costly factor to American industry, equaling and sometimes exceeding net profits. This was commonly known as "daylight theft," or "walking away." Historically, the means to control such unauthorized egress was through some manifestation of eye contact. High technology, at that time, consisted of closed-circuit television

cameras and monitors, just another extension of the eye. In the case of shoplifting and pilferage, the most common combatant was the utilization of personnel observing occurrences directly on the floor or from hidden "peepholes." But all methods involved the necessity of very carefully watching to see the act in progress. To Minasy, this did not seem to be the most logical or cost-effective method of controlling the movement of merchandise or personnel, and he decided that the ideal solution to control this movement would be to make each item self protected and automatically observed without the necessity of one-on-one visual contact.

The method he conceived was to attach some form of responsive target to the merchandise to be protected and then to establish remote sensing devices at the various exits and control points necessary for the detection, at the appropriate time, of the movement of each article.

Such a device had to be a very positive indicator, particularly in the cases of shoplifting or pilferage, which are criminal offenses and therefore rather serious in terms of making an accusation. It was also discovered by Minasy that, to be most effective, the devices had to be passive; that is, the targets attached to the merchandise could not contain active elements such as a battery. This was not only for cost-conserving reasons but assured a long life with no need for concern on the part of the user that perhaps the active device had gone dead, leaving his merchandise unprotected. It was also absolutely necessary for the items to be small and innocuous, and, of course, inexpensive. Other technical problems were the fact that the sensing equipment had to be very sensitive and yet low pow-

Arthur J. Minasy, founder and president.

ered, since all devices of that nature are regulated by governmental agencies and are legally restricted in their ability to radiate.

Once the principle and concept were established, Minasy proceeded to test various basic technologies to determine the most viable means of accomplishing his goals. These technologies ranged from the detection of innocuous nuclear isotopes placed on price tags, through radio frequency, micro-

The first Knogo radio-frequency electronic article surveillance system was installed during the 1960s.

wave detection, and magnetics. After several years of development, it was determined that for certain applications radio-frequency systems were the most flexible. It was at this point that the strongest patent in the industry was created, providing the unique characteristic of using radio frequency to sweep through a spectrum so that the target on the merchandise was not electronically observed just once, but 500 to 1,000 times a second. An alarm would be sounded only after a multiplicity of signals, each with exactly the same characteristics, were consecutively received. There could be no false alarms or false indications by innocent objects, or the purpose of the application would be defeated.

Since 1960 the electronic article surveillance (EAS) industry created by Minasy has soared to new heights as an internationally accepted method for the control of shoplifting and pilferage. Revenues generated by the EAS industry are several hundred million dollars per year and growing at an annual rate of 20 to 25 percent.

Despite new arrivals to the industry, Knogo Corporation remains the industry innovator and world product leader. New, imaginative ideas continue to come from Knogo, which remains the only company in the industry to create new products with its own engineering staff.

The Long Island engineer's farsighted dream was realized, an entire industry was created, and retailers were provided with an effective means with which to protect their merchandise.

EXECUTONE inc., THE NATIONWIDE BUSINESS PHONE COMPANY

In 1936 three unique men with varied backgrounds converged in Brooklyn with an idea for a business office intercom as unique as the Depression-era entrepreneurs themselves. Philip Seaman advanced $36,000 in working capital, N.A. Karr provided marketing creativity, and engineer Allan Bernstein provided an innovative loudspeaker system based on reversing electric current to an ordinary microphone.

Registering "Executone" with the Brooklyn County Clerk in August 1936, they commenced development of product models, hired a salesman and an installer, and made the rounds of business offices in the New York area. Their sales plan was called the "1 and 1 system," based on belief that the sale of one master station and one staff station would lead quickly to an order for an expanded system.

They were right. Today the $192-million Executone inc. is among the largest independent designers and marketers of business telephone systems, and the only one offering sales and service in

One of the earliest Executone office intercoms from the 1930s.

fifty states. Headquartered at 2 Jericho Plaza in Jericho, New York, Executone inc. is a wholly owned subsidiary of Atlanta-based Continental Telecom, Inc.

The founders sought expansion beyond New York but lacked capital. Thus, they created a system of nonfranchise distributorships responsible for their own operations. The first two opened in Philadelphia and Newark, and as the 1930s drew to a close, New England and other regions were targeted for an Executone national network.

By 1939 Executone had placed a variety of speakers and intercoms

in schools and hospitals. Yet, with the median annual office worker's salary at $1,400, many in the business world viewed a convenience for that employee, which cost $49, as superfluous.

World War II provided another obstacle since increased military demands on the nation made it difficult for Executone inc. to obtain material priorities. Then a company salesman visited Brooklyn Navy Yard with the idea of marketing intercoms there.

The Navy liked the premise and ordered research and development for products that would meet wartime specifications. This was difficult, but by 1943 the firm had achieved a successful pilot run on a destroyer, and the Navy proceeded with orders for as many intercoms as Executone could produce for the fighting fleet. The great success of these systems resulted in Executone inc. being awarded the prestigious Navy "E" Award.

Toward the end of the war Executone inc. made a breakthrough by marketing voice paging/music systems to industrial plants. In 1946 Dun & Bradstreet reported that in ten years the Executone network had installed 135,000 systems in forty-five product models, ranging in price to a high of $40,000 per system. The company showed a $179,304 net worth and was becoming the standard in an increasingly accepted industry.

Executone equipment was taken by the U.S. Navy on its post-World War II polar expeditions, was installed in the famed Palomar Observatory, and became the Sugar Bowl stadium sound system at Tulane University.

In 1948 an inquiry arrived from a Reading, Pennsylvania, hospital administrator who wanted a two-way nurse-to-patient intercom system. Executone inc. developed it, and the country's first such patient/nurse communication system was installed there, while a standard business intercom was placed in the administrator's office.

The stature of Executone products grew with large-scale projects such as tollbooth installation for the 1951 New Jersey Turnpike opening, while its domestic hospital market grew. The Korean War duplicated World War II's overseas demand for nurse call systems. Meanwhile, in April 1953 Executone inc. sold its one-millionth business system.

By the mid-1950s public relations gained by American GIs' wartime familiarity with the Executone name, plus growing business and industry acceptance, solidified the company's reputation. Executone systems found their way to such varied locations as Manhattan's Latin Quarter night club, the world's first atomic submarines, *Nautilus* and *Sea Wolf,* and Gary Moore's popular radio show.

In the late 1950s Executone public address and classroom-to-home systems had been installed in schools across forty-six states. At this time Allan Bernstein introduced the Executone seventy-watt speaker/booster hi-fi, which allowed playing of music behind voices over school and office intercom systems.

Also during the late 1950s longtime employee Edward Brody developed the Executone hand-held phone speaker as a solution to Woolworth restaurant waitresses' inability to make their kitchen orders heard over the din of store activities. This simple hand-held

mouthpiece was not yet a portable intercom, but the firm's technology advanced with transistorization in 1958 and miniaturized transistors two years later.

The company made a public offering of 136,000 shares at eleven dollars each in 1959, raising $1.3 million. At this time Bernstein was chairman, Seaman was president, and Karr was treasurer, with Brody as vice-president and general sales manager.

Executone intercoms were now the secret of the "Candid Camera" television show's talking litter basket episodes, part of California Institute of Technology's tracking station network, and the official system in terminals of American

This Executone business phone system shows the technology and design strides achieved by 1985.

Airlines in New York and Delta in Houston, among others.

During the 1960s Executone inc. created a strong presence in nursing homes spurred by federal seed money. In the late 1960s the firm installed an $85,000 system in TWA's terminal at Long Island's JFK airport.

In 1970, after the FCC Carterfone decision that opened up the telephone interconnect industry to independents, Executone inc. began serious incorporation of telephone technology in its product line.

But it was apparent in the early 1970s that Executone inc. needed greater resources to continue expanding its technology and evolving as a competitive force in the telecommunications industry. Thus, the firm engineered its successful acquisition in 1979 by the $4-billion Continental Telecom under whose umbrella Executone inc. was now part of a *Forbes* 500 corporation.

At this juncture of the mid-1970s Brody, who had played a significant role in the Contel negotiations, succeeded Karr as chairman of the board. Before retiring in 1980, Brody handled preparations for the 1981 headquarters move to Jericho, Long Island.

With warehouse/repair facilities still situated in Long Island City and in San Diego, California, the firm's 7,500-employee national network is now distributed among 250 independent and company-operated sales/service locations throughout the United States and Canada. Some of the cities in its growing company-owned segment are New York, Boston, Dallas, Los Angeles, Philadelphia, Newark, Seattle, San Francisco, Memphis, Chicago, Milwaukee, Davenport, San Diego, and Baltimore/Washington, D.C.

Executone inc. markets microcomputer-controlled intercom and sound systems and is the nation's leader in specialized health care communications systems. But the bulk of its telephony market is America's small to mid-size business segment using five- to 5,000-line phone systems.

EATON CORPORATION

By October 1940 more than 350,000 tons of Allied shipping were being sunk with virtual impunity by German U-boats. In response, a small group of MIT engineers at a Rhode Island naval air station in 1941 developed an airborne magnetic submarine detector under government grants through Columbia University. This group was Airborne Instruments Laboratory, the Long Island roots of Eaton Corporation.

This group, expanding from five to twenty-five members by January 1942, moved three months later to the TWA hangar at LaGuardia Field. By September AIL occupied buildings at 92 and 150 Old Country Road in Mineola, with 160 employees by the end of 1942 and 350 a year later. By mid-1944 over 400 aircraft installations of AIL submarine detectors had been made.

Meanwhile, toward the end of World War II, AIL worked on several electronic countermeasures and jamming devices against the Germans' radio command guided missiles and V-2 ballistic missiles.

Then, during the summer of 1945, a nucleus of AIL personnel huddled with personnel of the Radio Research Lab of Harvard, with whom they had worked on the submarine detectors. On September 1, 1945, these joint forces started operations as Airborne Instruments Laboratory, Inc., at 160 Old Country Road in Mineola. Hector R. Skifter was AIL's first president.

With one million dollars in government contracts as a base, AIL planned to translate wartime navigation and signaling solutions into the creation of safety factors that civil aviation would need to succeed on a common carrier basis. American Airlines provided working capital, and a holding company

was formed to purchase AIL stock for the major airlines.

Still, the firm's main effort between 1945 and 1950 was the completion of electronic countermeasure and moving target indicator contracts left over from the war. In 1946 AIL was joined by MIT Radiation Laboratory personnel, and created the technical ancestor to many intercept receivers still used by the U.S. Navy.

Under commercial airline sponsorship AIL performed landmark studies and experiments in ground radar use for air traffic control, air traffic delay causes, aircraft collision prevention, and airborne radar use in communications.

Sales reached $3.8 million in 1950 with 432 employees on the payroll. By this time several other Mineola buildings were leased, including AIL's first production shop, which opened in 1950 in an old icehouse on Second Street.

That same year AIL released the definitive Air Transport Association microwave search radar study of air traffic density in the Manhattan area. This study led to the "moving target indication" technique for discriminating between moving objects and stationary background.

In 1950 the commercial airline industry withdrew from AIL ownership, replaced by Laurance Rockefeller & Associates, American Research and Development Corporation, and a group of AIL employees. The resulting transition to a more financially stable, multi-market management permitted AIL's further evolution as a special hardware technology producer.

Ground was broken on August 31, 1951, at Stewart Avenue in Garden City for AIL's first owned facility. At the same time, in Huntington Station, AIL created an apparatus division that was the

During the Berlin Airlift (1948-1949) the United States and Great Britain airlifted 2,325,000 tons of coal, food, and medical supplies to the beleaguered citizens of West Berlin. The operation's phenomenal success was due in part to radar equipment for air traffic control produced by the Eaton Corporation.

nucleus of subsequent industrial electronics and microwave instruments divisions.

In 1954 President Dwight D. Eisenhower called for a study of America's airways predicting their development during the next twenty years; AIL authored this landmark study. In 1955 sales had climbed to $9.5 million, and there were 900 employees.

In 1957 AIL was located in seventeen buildings, most of them leased. The firm then received its first major aerospace contract and further expansion ensued. Construction was started on a Melville facility at which all AIL sites were to be consolidated by 1959.

During this period the company changed to a designer and manufacturer of complete systems, aided greatly by its 1958 acquisition by Milwaukee-based electrical and motor controls giant Cutler-Hammer. Almost immediately AIL received a $40-million government contract to develop airborne reconnaissance equipment, and at the same time managed a national team of major electronics firms in the project.

Growth was phenomenal in the late 1950s, and it became clear that the new Melville facility would not solve AIL's problem of available space. Thus, Cutler-Hammer purchased a 493,000-square-foot Deer Park aerospace building for the AIL Division. Meanwhile, the firm began building NASA's Topside Sounder satellite (launched in 1965), which was used to test the upper ionosphere via radio

AIR TRAFFIC CONTROL FOR THE BERLIN AIRLIFT 1949

ARRIDOR CONTROLLERS SCOPE

APPROACH CONTROLLERS SCO

AIRLIFT MAP

TRAFFIC CONTROL ROOM

soundings.

By 1960 sales were at $94 million, and AIL had over 4,000 employees. During the mid-1960s the Deer Park facility was expanded to 643,000 square feet. The former Jasik Laboratories was acquired for an antenna systems division, and a Farmingdale facility at Republic Airport was leased and served as the transportation systems division.

Skifter, who had guided AIL through its first two decades, died in July 1964, and was succeeded by a fellow AIL founder, Donald M. Miller, who also would become president of Cutler-Hammer.

During the late 1960s AIL was in need of specialized test equipment, and for this an internal department was spun off as the Electronic Instrumentation Division and located in Ronkonkoma.

Meanwhile, a great deal of consolidation was under way. By 1968 the employee base had shrunk to 3,500, and two years later there were 3,200 AIL employees. The firm was now a diverse, entrepreneurial entity in which all division heads were responsible for individual division growth. By this time another original AIL engineer, John N. Dyer, was AIL Division president. Winfield E. Fromm, who had been a member of the original Columbia University group, was executive vice-president, and was to follow Dyer as AIL Division president.

In 1978 Cutler-Hammer, including the AIL Division, was acquired by the advanced technology conglomerate, Eaton Corporation, based in Cleveland, Ohio. Fromm moved up in the Eaton corporate structure, to be replaced as presi-

dent of the AIL Division by John P. Clarke. The division remains a part of the Eaton corporate network today.

Besides its facility on Commack Road in Deer Park, Eaton maintains major facilities on Walt Whitman Road in Melville, on Broad Hollow Road in Farmingdale, on Fifth Avenue in Ronkonkoma, and in the Hauppauge Industrial Center. The reins of the AIL Division and its 4,000 employees are today in the hands of Michael J. Philbin, who was appointed president in 1984.

AIL Division continues to lead the international market in advanced aerospace and aviation technology. Current projects include its development of a defensive avionics system for the B1B bomber, and a tactical jamming system installed in the U.S. Air Force EF-111 and in the Navy EA-6B Prowler.

Eaton is responsible for the NASA Space Shuttle landing system and for most of the world's vessel traffic and air traffic control systems, almost 500 of which are operating today. Viewing its major potential market to be command control communications and intelligence, AIL Division created an important Command Systems Division at the Farmingdale facility in 1984.

A small, 25-member group of senior-level Eaton executives form the Government Systems Operation, which maintains an office at 1 Huntington Quadrangle in Melville. This group plans and oversees all of Command Systems and AIL Division's programs and strategies. As did AIL's founding group of MIT, Harvard, and Columbia engineers, this 25-member body works closely with the government and in direct response to its advanced technology needs.

LUNDY ELECTRONICS & SYSTEMS, INC.

The roots of Lundy Electronics & Systems, Inc., go back more than fifty years. But its real growth, through diversification, began in a vital post-World War II period of defense and aerospace technology development launched by former company salesman Robert Barbato, who bought the business in 1949.

Today Lundy is a $43-million, 700-employee high-technology researcher/developer with headquarters at 1 Robert Lane in Glen Head, and with major facilities in Pompano Beach, Florida, and Charlotte, North Carolina. Lundy has achieved status as one of two designated suppliers of radar-countermeasures chaff materials to the U.S. Defense Department.

But Lundy is also an innovator of data entry systems such as teller terminal and check-processing systems for the financial industry and computer-aided design (CAD) graphics work stations for automakers such as Ford and American Motors.

When engineer Elmer A. Lundy founded the E.A. Lundy Company on April 9, 1934, in New York City, rail transportation was its only market. During this time Lundy primarily manufactured hydraulic devices for trains.

During the early 1940s the firm took its first tentative step toward diversification with production of customized hydraulic actuators and air control "iris" valves for aircraft. Increasing emphasis on aircraft controls and systems led Lundy to the development of electronic submarine countermeasure buoys by the war's end.

While building this important reputation as a defense industry subcontractor, the firm changed its name to Lundy Manufacturing Corporation in 1946. Several years later Lundy developed one of the world's first digital compasses.

Lundy died in 1949, and when Robert Barbato bought the firm from Lundy's widow there were roughly twelve employees. Within a year Barbato had moved out of Manhattan to larger manufacturing quarters in Long Island City. A key force behind Lundy's wartime growth with defense contracts, Barbato wanted to expand that market.

Barbato's ability to encourage research and development of special products and product applications before their need was recognized by potential customers and competitors. This was a creative catalyst in the firm as the 1950s began. It was during this period that research and development for important radar countermeasures was well under way.

In 1957 Lundy Manufacturing introduced a radar countermeasures system for use in the B-52 bomber and was named subsystem supplier for the entire program.

During the late 1950s the firm developed missile penetration aid systems such as digital programmers for satellites and drones for prevention of premature missile triggering. Lundy again moved to larger manufacturing and development facilities, this time to the Glen Head site.

The 1960s dawned with Lundy positioned for even more aggressive product and market diversification and structural transition. The firm went public and changed its name to Lundy Electronics & Systems, Inc., in 1961. Lundy was first listed on the American Stock Exchange in March 1962.

During the same year Lundy also began advanced studies of penetration aid systems for the Minuteman InterContinental Ballistic Missile program, in 1967, and developed a waste management

Robert C. Barbato, whose foresight and managerial ability helped shape Lundy Electronics into a multimillion-dollar corporation.

system for the NASA Lunar Module and Apollo spacecraft.

In 1963 the firm acquired the rights to a proprietary method of metallizing glass fibers called the Bjorksten process. This acquisition would make Lundy virtually the single most important supplier in the world of radar-confusing chaff materials. The following year the Lundy Technical Center was opened on a 25-acre site at Pompano Beach for exploratory development of new chaff materials based on the Bjorksten process.

By mid-decade Lundy had successfully introduced the first low-cost Magnetic Ink Character Recognition reader-sorter, a development for automating various bank operations that led to contracts from IBM and NCR Corporation.

A Ford Motor Company representative demonstrates the Lundy UltraGraf® at a recent auto show. Major automobile manufacturers employ the Lundy UltraGraf® for more productive engineering design.

Thus, with its automation business well launched in banking markets, Lundy opened its 100,000-square-foot Charlotte facility for production of reader-sorters and other computer peripheral products. Lundy then developed its Remote Entry Bank Data System for data collection at branch offices and transmission to central pro-

cessing computers.

As the 1960s ended Lundy continued substantial gains in space, defense, and oceanographic contracts while further diversification in high-tech areas was accomplished as the 1970s began.

The innovative MICR Auto-Encoder (MAE)® check reject repair system was unveiled for banks in 1970.

In 1971 the System 32 high-performance interactive graphics display for CAD marked Lundy's

entry into the important field of computer-aided design. Major automotive designers became important users of System 32.

Lundy also strengthened its international position by establishing Lundy-Farrington Ltd., a United Kingdom subsidiary for sales and servicing of its commercial equipment in Europe.

Lundy began direct marketing and distribution organization for its new data entry systems in 1972. One year later Lundy introduced a new, low-cost Optical Character Recognition (OCR) system called System 8000. This was followed by the System 8700 line of highly advanced OCRs in 1975. The following year the L9700 Item Processing System and the L7200 OCR Data Entry System were introduced to financial markets.

The L470 Stripette® low-cost check reject repair device for small to mid-size banks was announced in 1977, as was Lundy's patented RhoMHOglas® metallized glass fiber. The firm immediately explored market potential for the latter product in textiles, carpets, and transformer filament windings. Also during this year Lundy introduced its second generation graphics design product—HyperGraf®.

In 1978 Lundy began installation of a $10-million data-entry and -processing system for the British Post Office National GIRO Bank. Two years later, as Lundy's annual revenues continued to climb, Barbato died.

The early 1980s were years of product and market refinement for the firm, which improved its MAE® system with in-line microfilming and matrix endorsing capabilities and a third-generation sophisticated 3-D interactive graphics display system now called UltraGraf®.

Lundy Electronics & Systems' sales reached twenty-eight million dollars by 1982. Product improvement continued with entry into front office banking markets through development of the FMS Series of financial management centers for tellers, administrators, and signature capture and verification, the first such systems to employ bubble memory technology for low-cost speed and reliability.

STATE UNIVERSITY OF NEW YORK AT STONY BROOK
BROOKHAVEN NATIONAL LABORATORY

State University of New York at Stony Brook

SUNY at Stony Brook, the system's most sophisticated campus, was chartered in 1957 as a science education center at Oyster Bay. In 1960 a gubernatorial commission mandated that the Stony Brook site become a comprehensive university center, and two years later the institution moved east to Suffolk County.

Since 1962 SUNY at Stony Brook has grown to ninety-eight buildings on 1,100 acres. With an internationally distinguished faculty, Stony Brook offers more than 100 undergraduate, graduate, and professional degree programs in the arts and sciences, engineering, policy analysis and public management, and marine sciences, as well as in the Health Sciences Center's schools of medicine, dental medicine, nursing, allied health professions, and social welfare. With research support from federal and other sources totaling over forty-five million dollars in 1984, Stony Brook is the state's leading public research university. It is also Long Island's fifth-largest employer.

The university enriches the region through the cultural presentations of its Fine Arts Center, Long Island's most comprehensive arts complex. The center includes a main theater, three experimental theaters, a recital hall, and an art gallery. More than 300 programs are presented each year.

University Hospital, Suffolk County's only tertiary care hospital, opened its doors in 1980 and has a planned capacity of 540 beds. It is a specialized referral center providing state-of-the-art patient care, instruction, and research.

Brookhaven National Laboratory

Brookhaven National Laboratory is an independently managed, fed-

The Earth and Space Sciences Building, State University of New York at Stony Brook. The oldest of the moon rocks brought back by the NASA Apollo mission, over four billion years old, was dated here.

erally supported, multidisciplinary research laboratory formed in 1946 by nine prominent universities in the Northeast. It presented a new approach to management of fundamental research with federal support, and focused on large-scale scientific enterprises beyond the reach of individual academic institutions.

Occupying more than 5,000 acres in Upton, Brookhaven National Laboratory employs over 3,000

An aerial view, looking north, of the Brookhaven National Laboratory site.

people while attracting the research of some 1,500 scientists and students from universities and other institutions annually.

To carry forth its founders' mission, Brookhaven designs, builds, and operates its own large facilities. The Alternating Gradient Synchrotron particle accelerator continues to be one of the nation's primary devices for high-energy physics research. The High Flux Beam Reactor provides intense beams of neutrons for fundamental experiments in nuclear and solid-state physics, chemistry, and biology.

Brookhaven's newest major research facility is the innovative National Synchrotron Light

Source. This provides beams of vacuum ultraviolet light and X-rays at levels of intensity never before achieved.

Brookhaven National Laboratory has led the country in the development of nuclear medicine, and its Medical Research Reactor is used for various activation analyses and medical dosimetry studies. The laboratory also conducts many programs in energy technology and applied sciences, and provides various forms of technical support for agencies such as the U.S. Department of Energy and the Nuclear Regulatory Commission.

DIONICS, INC.

During the mid-1960s Bernard Kravitz and Sherman Gross found an innovative technology for the manufacture of high-voltage integrated circuit components. "Dielectric Isolation" was an important factor in Minuteman ICBM circuits, but Kravitz and Gross saw potential for DI circuits in commercial and industrial markets.

On December 19, 1968, they formed Dionics, Inc., in Westbury to exploit that potential. Originally financed at under $500,000 by some twenty-four investors, Dionics opened in an 11,000-square-foot office/plant at 65 Rushmore Street. There were just two employees in addition to president Kravitz and vice-president Gross.

As a leading national exponent of DI technology, Dionics is now a $3.5-million, fifty-employee firm, expanding into an 8,000-square-foot building next door to its original plant. Dionics has a diversified commercial and industrial business, serving a wide range of major subcontractors to, or subsidiaries of, Exxon, General Electric, and the U.S. government.

All of this began some twenty years before when DI component technology was found to give superior performance in circuits under extremely high radiation, temperature, frequency, and voltage conditions.

In electronics, isolation refers to the requirement of integrated circuits to operate at different voltage levels while at close proximity. Higher voltage, or other stressful circuit conditions, makes traditional junction isolation impractical. The DI insulation of circuit components with a glass-like quartz provides the extra performance level needed under stress.

Almost immediately Kravitz and Gross found that their technology was successful in digital display products. A few good commercial and industrial contracts made Dionics self-supporting in the first eighteen months of its existence, although a limited capital base prevented any major market risks.

In the summer of 1973 Dionics filed with the SEC as a public company. Two years later Dionics found itself correctly positioned to take advantage of a sudden boom in digital watches. By late 1975 about 80 percent of the firm's shipping was funneled into the electronic watch market.

Suddenly, in January 1976 Texas Instruments announced the imminent release of a semiconduc-

A Dionics technician monitors a vacuum-metallizing process for the firm's integrated circuit wafers.

tor-based nineteen-dollar digital that would undercut even the cheapest of competitors, including the fifty-dollar models for which Dionics had geared nearly all of its production.

Kravitz and Gross spent the next several years refining Dionics inroads to the microprocessing industry. In 1981 a major contract arrived from an Exxon subsidiary for digital display driver circuits to be used in retail gas station pumps on a national basis.

This time success failed to entice Dionics into overemphasis on one market. Several other industrial inroads made during 1980 were expanded the following years, and by 1984 new market penetration had succeeded well enough that Dionics' largest customer represented only 20 percent of its total sales.

Dionics, Inc., now reaches many consumer products and industrial markets using digital display, customized circuitry markets including military and "safe-and-secure" applications, and a variety of telecommunications and power switching markets for its solid-state relays. Dionics also supplies ship products (diodes, resistors, and capacitors) to a growing list of hybrid circuit manufacturers internationally as well as on Long Island.

Dionics circuit wafers undergoing a process of high-temperature diffusion of selected atoms.

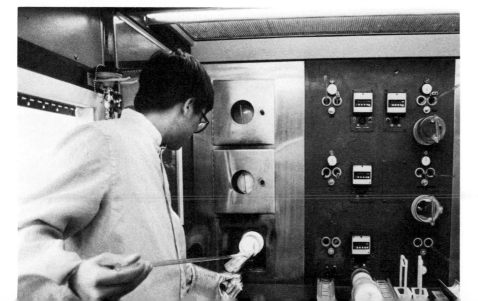

FAIRCHILD WESTON SYSTEMS INC.

Fairchild Weston Systems Inc., the product of corporate expansions, consolidations, and acquisitions, has had a sixty-year history begun by Sherman Mills Fairchild. His reputation for technical advances in aerial photography, imaging, and other aviation-associated technologies is exemplified by Fairchild Weston Systems, today among the world's leading high-technology firms.

A descendant of the former Fairchild Camera & Instrument Corporation, Fairchild Weston is a 3,000-employee company that is part of Schlumberger, Ltd., an international conglomerate. Headquartered at 300 Robbins Lane in Syosset, under its president Louis H. Pighi, Fairchild Weston has divisions and facilities in Archbald and Horsham, Pennsylvania, Sarasota, Florida, and regional offices in Dayton, Ohio, and in the Washington, D.C., area.

In 1919 Sherman Fairchild was in his early twenties and already a millionaire as a result of his father's business interests, which the elder Fairchild would consolidate as IBM in 1923. Sherman Fairchild's invention of a between-the-

Sherman Mills Fairchild, circa 1919, with one of his earliest cameras.

lens "rapidyne" shutter and timing device simultaneously made high-acuity aerial photography possible, and created a career for himself.

Since airplanes of the day weren't sophisticated enough to take full advantage of Fairchild's invention, he designed planes of his own after founding the Fairchild Aerial Camera Corporation in 1920. The Fairchild Aviation Corporation was incorporated in 1927. In 1936 Sherman Fairchild separated his aircraft manufacturing from his camera operations by creating Fairchild Engine & Airplane Corporation in Maryland.

The photography segment remained in New York, and in 1944 adopted the name Fairchild Camera & Instrument Corporation. During World War II this firm designed and manufactured 90 percent of the aerial cameras used by all Allied forces.

In 1957 Fairchild Semiconductor Corporation was formed in Palo Alto, California, and created an entirely new market. The small concern, which designed the world's first silicon diffused transistors and other semiconductor devices, became a wholly owned Fairchild Camera & Instrument subsidiary in 1959.

With this, Fairchild had created yet another new business. By the mid-1970s Fairchild was the third-largest U.S. supplier of semiconductors; 70 percent of its corporate revenues were derived from sales of these components. Meanwhile, Fairchild introduced a panoramic aerial camera with a patented rotating optical prism, making possible the first 180-degree, horizon-to-horizon aerial photographs.

Seeking to acquire a major semiconductor manufacturer, Schlumberger purchased Fairchild Camera & Instrument for $425 million in 1979. Under the Schlumberger um-

Astronaut Bruce McCandless II, floating free in space, operates a helmet-mounted television camera and lens system developed for NASA by Fairchild Weston.

brella, Fairchild Weston Systems has continued to carry the mantle of the original camera operation and to expand its technology base into a variety of aerospace- and defense-related areas.

A current technological advance

A Fairchild Weston solid-state TV camera, mounted on a satellite, captured this view of NASA's Space Shuttle Challenger 1 *in orbit.*

is Fairchild's development of miniature solid-state color and black-and-white TV cameras for the NASA Space Shuttle program. The color camera, mounted on a pallet satellite, captured pictures of *Challenger 7,* the first ever taken of a shuttle in orbit.

LONG ISLAND UNIVERSITY

The B. Davis Schwartz Memorial Library on Long Island University's C.W. Post Campus in Greenvale.

No history of Long Island, particularly one that delves into its explosive population growth in the years since World War II, could be complete without relating the substantial contributions of Long Island University, the region's largest private institution of higher learning.

For more than thirty years Long Island University, an institution founded in Brooklyn in 1925, has served the educational, cultural, and economic needs of the Nassau-Suffolk area.

Its pervasiveness stems from the fact that Long Island University since 1954 has established three campuses—LIU-C.W. Post, LIU-Brentwood and LIU-Southampton—to serve the growing populations of Nassau and Suffolk counties. While each of these units has a distinct character and curriculum, they at the same time give Long Island one of the most diverse private institutions in America. At present, the three campuses have enrollments totaling more than 15,000 undergraduate and graduate students.

Long Island University takes pride in knowing that through the past three decades it has educated a vast majority of Long Island's teachers, librarians, and public servants; it has at the same time prepared countless men and women for entry into professional schools of law, medicine, and dentistry. Its programs in business and accounting, as well as its offerings in the arts, communications, humanities, and the sciences—including marine science—are respected nationally for the quality of the men and women who are its alumni.

The university has been a pioneer in the creation of educational opportunities. Its expansion into Nassau County after World War II was, at first, a response to the needs of returning veterans. The establishment of the C.W. Post Campus in Greenvale in 1954 met the needs of the first wave of post-war population growth. The Suffolk "branch"—now located in Brentwood—was further commitment to an expanding suburban population. The Southampton Campus, founded in 1963, was a response to a community's desire for a college.

Since its earliest days on Long Island, the university has extended its services, both educational and cultural, to the entire community. It was the first institution in the region to open its regularly scheduled classes to adults—a policy that paved the way for the establishment of one of the nation's first "Weekend Colleges" for men and women who could attend classes at no other time.

As a cultural center, Long Island University is a recognized leader. The Concert Theater on the C.W. Post Campus ranks among the most acoustically perfect halls in America. Its subscription series, which brings the world's greatest orchestras and artists to Long Island, are usually sold out well in advance of performances. In addition to concerts and performances, the university offers a wide range of lectures, art shows, and seminars for the benefit of the entire community.

In its three decades of service to suburban Long Island, Long Island University has established an enviable record. Its more than 85,000 alumni, the majority of them living in the region, are a testimonial to its excellence and its value to Long Island.

The physical ambience of the university's Southampton Campus is symbolized by the evocative colonial windmill that stands on one of the site's rolling hills.

MARINE MIDLAND BANK

By 1919 the focus of the nation's energies and resources had turned entirely from the war effort to the pursuit of prosperity at home. From the creaking ships on the Great Lakes, to the shouting dealers on the floor of the stock exchange, the sounds that would make the 1920s "roar" in New York State were growing in number and intensity.

Long Island was not exempt from this war-spawned craving for peace and affluence. Its agricultural industry continued to reap the rewards of the growing urban population of New York City, while city residents flocked to its beaches on the north and south shores, creating a tidal wave of business for its tourist industry. At the same time local entrepreneurs began establishing businesses to serve the indigenous population expanding in a postwar "baby boom."

In East Setauket a group of prosperous residents led by Edward L. Tinker, son of a well-respected Manhattan banker, saw the aesthetic as well as financial development of their community as a way to help it thrive. They raised funds to fill in a marshy area and create a park. They also acquired a nearby dilapidated clapboard house, a former saloon, and turned it into a bank.

That decision was greeted with skepticism by other East Setauket residents, who pointed out that the village already had three banks and that the likelihood of getting a charter for a fourth was slim. To

improve the group's chances, Tinker led a delegation to Washington to plead his case to the Comptroller of the Currency.

Impressed with their community involvement and the financial potential of East Setauket, the Comptroller approved a charter. The result: Tinker National Bank opened its doors on August 28,

Edward L. Tinker, founder of Tinker National Bank, which later merged with Marine Midland Bank. Courtesy, Three Village Historical Society

1920, with capital of $37,500. During its first day of operation directors and principals of the institution, including Tinker, stood outside the door inviting customers in to open an account. The bank had nearly $85,000 in deposits by day's end.

At about the same time, the seed of an idea was sprouting some 450 miles away in Buffalo, New York. Since the mid-nineteenth century Marine Midland Trust Company had fueled its growth largely by financing shipping along the Great Lakes and Erie Canal.

As its business moved inland, principals of the bank saw an opportunity to enhance their market penetration and financial clout through confederation with other institutions. Over the next several years seventeen different banks joined the Marine Midland group. They were united in a single holding company incorporated in 1929.

At one point as many as sixty separate institutions were members of the Marine Midland group. Consolidations reduced the number of individual banks in the group, but as a whole Marine Midland grew. By 1968 there were eleven Marine Midland banks from Buffalo to New York City, and the

The original Tinker National Bank Building was constructed in 1919 on the site of this wood-frame saloon and general store in East Setauket. This 1890 photograph shows that the location was a popular meeting place before the turn of the century. Courtesy, Three Village Historical Society

The Tinker National Bank, chartered in 1919, became Marine Midland's cornerstone on Long Island in 1969. Tinker National's main office served as headquarters for the merged institution—Marine Midland Tinker National Bank—and is still one of Marine Midland's most successful Long Island branches. Courtesy, Three Village Historical Society

holding company was poised to enter a new market—Long Island.

While the Marine Midland system was established in 1929, many institutions and corporations did not fare as well that year under the shadow of the stock market crash. But despite financial reverses overall, communities and businesses on Long Island, including Tinker National Bank, more than survived since much of the population was relatively wealthy.

The industrial development that preceded World War II would provide impetus for Long Island's economic development in the 1940s, which served to strengthen and expand Tinker's customer base. That base grew even further in the 1950s as New York City residents, eager to escape the rigors of postwar urban life, established new homes in the suburbs.

By the 1960s the economic complexion of Long Island had changed. Both industry and individuals began seeking a broader range of financial services, and banks were eager to provide them. The Marine Midland holding company, now

known as Marine Midland Banks, Inc., took a first step east of New York City in March 1969, when Marine Midland Grace Trust Company, the holding company's Manhattan affiliate, opened a Jericho office.

Even as that move was being made, Marine Midland was exploring the possibility of acquiring an institution with a firm Long Island foothold. Tinker National, by then Suffolk County's second-largest commercial bank, was approached by Marine Midland.

Tinker's management, recognizing its need for greater resources to meet the increasingly sophisticated needs of its customers, was receptive to the idea of a merger. In May 1969 Tinker National

Bank became Marine Midland Tinker. Marine's Long Island expansion continued the following year, when it acquired the Community Bank of Lynbrook.

In 1976 Marine Midland Tinker as well as the Community Bank of Lynbrook and the other Marine Midland banks were merged into a single statewide institution. In this way Marine became one of the largest commercial banks in the United States.

Today Long Island's established industrial base, blossoming high-technology companies, and middle-market firms combined with a large and stable population make it a market of opportunity for Marine Midland.

Through a network of thirty offices, including commercial banking centers in Carle Place, Melville, and Centereach, Marine Midland provides state-of-the-art financial services, ranging from traditional consumer and small business banking products to sophisticated international services demanded by the growing number of Long Island-based companies seeking to expand their exports. Marine Midland's international capabilities are enhanced by those of its partner, the Hong Kong and Shanghai Banking Corporation, one of the largest financial institutions in the world.

Both Long Island and Marine Midland have grown since Tinker and his associates built a bank on the site of a rundown saloon. Yet the original Tinker National building still reflects their community spirit. Today Marine Midland provides free space in the building to the East Setauket Chamber of Commerce and the Suffolk County Office of the Aging—two groups that share Marine Midland's concern for the community and its residents.

GENERAL AERO PRODUCTS CORP.

Eli Reiter, co-founder and president.

Stanley Cohen, co-founder and executive vice-president.

In 1969 two young engineers from Philadelphia discovered a tiny manufacturing company in Tunkhannock, Pennsylvania, on the banks of the Susquehanna River. The young men pooled their resources and bought their way into the four-year-old firm, which went by the rather grand name of General Aero Products Corp. (GAP).

The two newcomers, Eli Reiter and Stan Cohen, became president and executive vice-president, respectively, and set about to make the little company grow. Both men, though only in their early thirties, possessed impressive qualifications for the job.

Reiter had been chief engineer for Kollsman Motor Corporation in Pennsylvania, where he was responsible for engineering of motors, synchros, and aircraft instrumentation. As an RCA project engineer before that, he had overseen electronic development of airborne digital data-link systems.

Cohen, as vice-president of engineering at Kollsman Motor Corporation, had been responsible for the design and development of advanced instrumentation components for the F-110 and F-111 fighters and for nuclear submarines. He was an expert in all phases of electromechanical products.

Putting this background to work in their own venture, the partners began making significant aircraft instrumentation research and development progress. Then, in 1972, disastrous floods along the Susquehanna resulting from Hurricane Agnes destroyed their Pennsylvania facility. With five employees, Reiter and Cohen moved to Long Island and set up shop in Copiague.

While success in the market for aircraft instruments had seemed imminent when the firm was in Pennsylvania, that success was realized after the move to Long Island. Within two years GAP boasted sixty employees. Two years after that, the employee roll topped 100.

In 1983 GAP bought controlling interest in a Pennsylvania-based

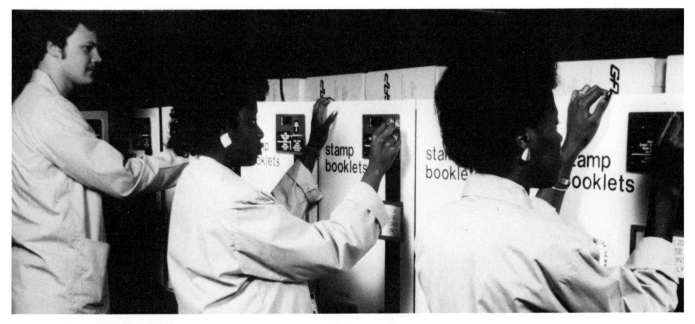

General Aero Products Corp. employees work on the firm's latest product, postage stamp vending machines.

wire distribution firm named Interstate Wire & Cable Corporation.

General Aero Products' sales more than tripled, from under $2.5 million in 1977 to $8 million in 1982. Sales reached $10 million in 1983 and had averaged a healthy 23 percent annual sales growth rate from 1978 to 1983.

In November 1984, with the guidance of company controller Chris Christoforou who joined the firm in 1980, General Aero Products became a public corporation, with Reiter and Cohen remaining its principal stockholders.

Today General Aero Products is located at 11 Lincoln Street in Copiague in three contiguous buildings totaling 50,000 square feet of manufacturing and office space. A 250-employee firm, which did more than $11 million in business during 1984, General Aero Products operates in the three major markets of airborne instrumentation, defense systems, and commercial vending.

Projecting 1985 as a $14-million year, the corporation ranks fourteenth among Long Island's top twenty defense contractors and does significant business under ongoing United States Army, Air Force, and Navy contracts.

GAP maintains a unique position in its marketplaces by surpassing the technological and production capabilities of competitive small technology firms, while providing speed of manufacture and service that equally capable larger technology firms find difficult to match.

The company produces more than thirty devices in the aircraft instrument category. All of these are U.S. government or customer "Qualified Product Listed" for military applications. The instruments and transmitters are utilized on a varied range of high-performance supersonic military jet aircraft such as the F100 series, F4, F5, F15, and F16 fighter aircraft, the C130, C135, C141, and B52 multiengined transport planes and bombers, as well as various helicopters such as the Huey Cobra and the CH47.

General Aero Products is an engineering-oriented manufacturing firm with special emphasis on electromechanical design. The production for both military and commercial products makes it a unique enterprise. About 85 percent of the materials, component parts, and tooling used in fabrication are produced internally.

Eli Reiter remains in the president's chair, while his longtime colleague and GAP co-founder, Stanley Cohen, remains executive vice-president. A substantial part of the Long Island community now, General Aero Products Corp. takes part in several vital regional activities, including employee blood donor programs and charitable campaigns such as the United Way.

Major product markets for GAP, besides aircraft instrumentation, include postage stamp vending machines and dollar changers, defense systems, wind-measuring systems, wire and cable products, integrated avionics, solid-state retransmission units, and various new products developed under government contract.

ENTENMANN'S, INC.

As recently as twenty-five years ago Entenmann's, Inc., was one of the best-kept secrets on Long Island. Those who knew of its line of top-quality, fresh baked goods had stumbled on the fact almost accidentally—they had heard about it by word of mouth, or had been served an Entenmann's product after dinner at a friend's house. One taste was usually enough to make a new customer. It was Entenmann's only form of advertising, and had been for a long time.

The family-run business was started back in 1898, when William Entenmann, a German immigrant, opened a bakery in Flatbush, Brooklyn, and began making local house-to-house deliveries of breads, rolls, and cakes in a horse-drawn buggy. He soon acquired a reputation for quality baked goods and had to increase the number of delivery routes.

In the early 1900s William's young son, William Jr., developed rheumatic fever, and the doctor advised the family to move to the country. They settled in Bay Shore, Long Island. William Jr. followed in his father's footsteps and became a baker. He quickly

took hold of the growing operation and moved the business to Bay Shore's Main Street, where he operated a retail shop and home and delicatessen delivery routes. Eventually horse-drawn carriages were replaced by motorized vans.

William Jr. married one of his employees, Martha Schneider, and they had three sons—Robert, Charles, and William—all of whom would eventually work in the busi-

William Entenmann, Jr., in Bay Shore with his new fleet of motorized delivery trucks. Photo circa 1935

ness. (Charles retired in 1979; Robert and William remained active in Entenmann's as chairman and vice-chairman, respectively until 1985.)

The business prospered through the Depression and World War II

William Entenmann's wife, Bertha, with their children, Bertha Lillian (left) and William Jr., in front of their Brooklyn bakery during the early 1900s.

on its reputation for fine quality products. There was no need to advertise—Entenmann's had all the customers it could handle. The secret of its quality products had even reached some of the most wealthy residents of the island, including the Morgans and Vanderbilts. But tragedy struck in 1951, when William Jr. suffered a fatal heart attack. All three sons, upon returning from service during the Korean Conflict, met with their mother to decide what to do with the business.

Some tough decisions had to be made because of changing market conditions and consumer lifestyles. Post-World War II America was characterized by the rapid growth of suburbs, and on Long Island the archetypical suburban enclave of Levittown had led the way. By the mid-1950s suburban towns were sprouting up all over the island, and in them were people who sought more casual living. They felt, for example, that there was no need to have fresh milk and bread delivered. It was simpler and cheaper to run down to the supermarket once a week and then store goods in a refrigerator.

As a result, home deliveries of

Entenmann's products, which had been the backbone of the business, were lagging. The family, therefore, made two important decisions. If customers preferred to shop for baked goods in supermarkets, Entenmann's would bring the bakery to the supermarket. Also, it would stop making bread and rolls and concentrate on the more popular cakes, pies, Danish, and doughnuts. The last decision prompted William Sr. to protest, "How can you not make bread in a bakery?" To this Robert replied forthrightly, "Grandfather, we

don't have the room for both, and cake is selling better."

In 1957 Entenmann's products were introduced in one of the largest supermarket chains in New York—Food Fair Stores. It proved so successful that home deliveries were dropped in favor of store deliveries.

Now in supermarkets, Entenmann's became one of the worst-kept secrets on the island. Sales moved across the Hudson River into New Jersey. In quick time, the secret of Long Island became the secret of New Jersey, and it spread north and south into Connecticut and Pennsylvania. By 1961 so many people knew of and were buying Entenmann's goodies that a new, modern bakery had to be built to handle the demand. And in 1975, with so many loyal New York area customers living in

An award-winning photo of the famed 1948 Entenmann's fire. This photo, taken by former East Islip fire chief Sid Parkan, ran in several New York area newspapers.

retirement in Florida, Entenmann's opened a bakery in Miami.

Word of mouth was still the only "advertising" used by the company, and the Miami operation helped boost total sales from $74 million in 1975 to $168 million three years later.

While the Miami bakery was expanding its delivery routes to service most of Florida, the Bay Shore facility was making daily deliveries as far north as Massachusetts and as far south as Maryland.

The secret might have remained on the East Coast but for Entenmann's being purchased in 1978 by the Warner-Lambert Company, a New Jersey-based health care and pharmaceutical firm. Entenmann's now had the financial wherewithal of the parent organization to expand its markets.

Warner-Lambert was quick to recognize the phenomenal success of Entenmann's products in Florida. Within months of the acquisition, a new 120,000-square-foot plant was opened in Miami that made it possible to expand Entenmann's Southeast market into Alabama, Georgia, Virginia, and the Carolinas. In Albany, New York, a processing center was built in the heart of New York State's apple-producing region to service upstate customers. The facility also produces approximately half the sliced apples used annually in the company's pies and pastries.

The Midwest was the next target market. Under the direction of David W. Johnson, then president of Warner-Lambert's Specialty Foods Division, Entenmann's opened a 320,000-square-foot bakery in the Chicago suburb of Northlake in 1979. Although some advertising was used to share the secret of its quality baked goods with midwesterners, word-of-mouth endorsements still stimulat-

ed sales growth, much as it did in the early days on Long Island. During the next two years the Chicago region was expanded from thirty to sixty routes, and depots were set up in St. Louis, Indianapolis, Detroit, Cleveland, Pittsburgh, and Cincinnati. By 1981 the company was serving approximately 30 percent of the U.S. population.

_____

William Entenmann, Sr., founder.

The next milestone in Entenmann's history came about in 1982, when General Foods Corporation acquired the company from Warner-Lambert. General Foods manufactures such well-known brand products as Maxwell House coffee, Oscar Mayer meats, Jell-O

gelatins and puddings, Post cereals, Birds Eye frozen foods, and Kool-Aid soft drink mixes. This huge, diverse food business resulted from the joining of forces of a number of different companies, each of which, like Entenmann's has a history and origin of its own.

In commenting on the acquisition, General Foods chairman and chief executive James L. Ferguson said, "We know of no investment opportunity of comparable size that would offer similar potential. . . . We think Entenmann's represents an opportunity to expand into a national business from its present 36 percent to at least 60 percent of the U.S. population."

When General Foods acquired Entenmann's, David Johnson remained as the firm's president and chief executive officer. He was elected a vice-president of the parent organization in 1983.

According to Johnson, under the General Foods' ownership Entenmann's recipe for success has been retained, and the company has continued to be run like a family business, with the same high

_____

William Entenmann, Jr., proudly shows off the motorized vans that replaced horse-drawn buggies for home deliveries.

standards and tradition of quality set by its founder, William Entenmann, Sr., in the 1890s. All the original recipes have been preserved, and Entenmann's product line continues to contain ingredients from America's premier suppliers, including Smucker's jams, Chiquita bananas, Diamond Sunsweet walnuts, Sun Maid raisins, Grade A butter, and Dole pineapple. Entenmann's even makes its own chocolate from imported chocolate liquor.

"General Foods' prime focus has been to provide funds for expansion and for refining Entenmann's marketing and strategic planning skills," Johnson explains. "By concentrating on these areas, General Foods has aided Entenmann's immeasurably."

In 1984 General Foods acquired the Oroweat Foods Company from the Continental Grain Company. Oroweat, a leading regional baker of premium variety breads, has a strong market presence in the West. The Oroweat connection provided the key for Entenmann's to expand distribution of its high-quality, freshly baked goods into the western part of the United States.

Entenmann's and Oroweat fit together like pieces of the same jigsaw puzzle. Both companies have a proud heritage, and both are firmly committed to supplying high-quality, premium products. Also, delivery systems are almost identical—company-employed route sales representatives deliver directly to retail outlets and return unsold products with expired code dates to a network of thrift shops.

Johnson is the architect of Entenmann's expansion to the West

Bakery Production and Marketing maga-zine designated Entenmann's "Baker of the Year" in 1981 in recognition of "the high-quality standards of the bakery food it produces, of the excellence of its operations as a large-volume bakery, and of the bakery industry leadership it has demonstrated."

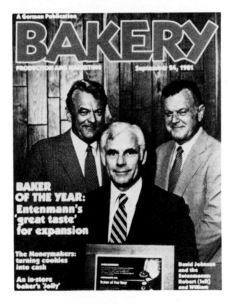

Coast, which began in October 1984 when products were introduced in the San Diego area. In early 1985 distribution was expanded into Orange County.

"In order to assure that our baked goods continue to live up to their reputation for freshness and high quality," Johnson says, "we are moving slowly, on a city-by-city basis, with a goal of reaching the entire greater Los Angeles area by the end of 1985."

According to company officials,

A computer operator monitors the Bay Shore plant's computer-controlled ingredient-handling system.

Entenmann's experienced tremendous consumer acceptance on the West Coast, confirming expectations that Californians desire high-quality, freshly baked goods.

The products are delivered daily by driver-salesmen from the Oroweat bakery in Montebello, California, one of eight bakery facilities in the western part of the United States that Entenmann's acquired with the purchase of the Oroweat Foods Company.

All that marked the beginning of Entenmann's in 1898 was one man, a small bakery, and a horse-drawn wagon that made house-to-house deliveries. Today—eighty-seven years later—as part of General Foods, Entenmann's employs approximately 7,000 people and, with Oroweat, has annual combined sales in excess of $600 million. From modest beginnings it has become one of the largest U.S. purveyors of fresh-baked goods.

Entenmann's is, indeed, an American success story of a family-operated business that has stuck to the basics of offering superior products at an affordable price. Entenmann's has proved that quality is synonymous with success.

At its Long Island headquarters in Bay Shore, Entenmann's operates a 550,000-square-foot facility that is one of the largest and most automated bakeries in the country. However, there are a few operations, such as frosting, that automated machinery can't perform to the company's satisfaction, so to this day they are done by hand. The personal touch and specially formulated brand ingredients assure that Entenmann's products maintain their "homemade" quality and high standard of excellence that have made Entenmann's "the upper crust" of all the baking companies.

CHYRON CORPORATION

Chyron founder Leon Weissman with computer-graphics equipment his company has made famous.

In 1966, when Leon Weissman founded a small Manhattan-based company to sell and lease used computers, he couldn't have known he was putting in motion a series of events that would result in the formation of Chyron Corporation nearly ten years later. But that's what happened.

Today Chyron is a $22-million, 275-employee corporation headquartered at 265 Spagnoli Road, Melville, New York. It is a world leader in the manufacture of computer-graphics equipment for television. Chyron's $4,000 to $100,000 graphics systems are used by major networks and independents, religious networks, production facilities that serve broadcasters, and a growing industrial video market.

In 1966 Weissman was heading a two-employee firm called The Computer Exchange, located in one room at 663 Fifth Avenue. Financed at a mere $20,000, this company traded in "second-generation" IBM equipment which then commanded selling prices of $200,000 to one million dollars.

Weissman found the market responsive, and in 1968 The Computer Exchange became a public company. And after several years of growth, the used-computer market became increasingly competitive. Soon Weissman was on the lookout for a more proprietary product to market.

In 1973 he became aware of Systems Resources Corporation in Plainview. This firm had developed a prototype electronic television title and graphics system called CHIRON. The system was not well understood by the television industry, but Weissman viewed the product as the kind he'd been seeking even though SRC was in financial trouble.

After loans of nearly $500,000 to the failing SRC, Weissman's firm exercised an option to buy it and its valuable product in 1975. Noting that The Computer Exchange no longer expressed his firm's future or even current identity, Weissman changed its name to Chyron Corporation. In 1976 the firm moved to the Newtown Road, Plainview, quarters formerly occupied by SRC.

Within a year the used-computer sales business was all but phased out in favor of serious concentration on television graphics. Though the prevailing wisdom in broadcasting still viewed electronic graphics as an interesting, but limited, capability, Weissman and his sales representatives trained in selling sophisticated computer systems quickly proved that television was ready for Chyron products.

In 1978 Chyron's sales were $3.2 million. That same year the firm moved to its current 20,000-square-foot Spagnoli Road headquarters. Sales escalated strongly on an annual basis, and reached $16.9 million by 1983.

That same year Weissman stepped down as chairman/chief executive officer in favor of Alfred O.P. Leubert. However, Weissman remains as vice-chairman and very much a part of Chyron's executive team.

The industrial video market is Chyron's brave new world, a market which could soon account for as much as 50 percent of its annual revenues. General Motors, IBM, the Nassau County Police Department, and several colleges are already Chyron video graphics customers. An office in London was recently established as an outpost from which to assess the overseas market.

About 40 percent of Chyron Corporation's employees are trained engineers or technicians. The firm competes favorably in a world market that now includes the 3M and Robert Bosch companies but which was virtually started by Chyron in 1975. Since that time, its products have evolved from simple titling capability into systems capable of animation, original artwork, thousands of colors, and almost limitless flexibility.

REPUBLIC
ELECTRONICS
COMPANY

Republic Electronics is a high-technology engineering and manufacturing firm specializing in radar environment simulators and navigation test equipment. Since its founding in April 1951 as the TLG Electric Company, the firm has enjoyed an excellent reputation as a domestic and international producer of high-quality electronics equipment for military and commercial markets.

The firm has well-established Long Island roots. In 1961 it moved from its original Farmingdale location near Republic Airport to its present location at 575 Broad Hollow Road in Melville. The next year that facility was expanded to 34,000 square feet to accommodate the demands of Republic's move into manufacturing Tactical Air Navigation airborne transmitter receivers for the U.S. Air Force.

By the late 1960s, with Republic acknowledged as the world's leading AN/ARN-52 airborne TACAN equipment producer, this expertise and experience in radio frequency engineering was combined to develop a new product: TACAN Beacon Simulators. This simulator enabled maintenance technicians to simulate the TACAN ground station signals for test and maintenance of airborne equipment.

Republic's resources and capabilities were further strengthened through its 1969 acquisition by Criton Technologies, a diversified manufacturing firm with electronics and defense, architectural, and air transportation product lines.

On the night of June 12, 1974, a devastating fire nearly destroyed the plant. Soon after, a major reconstruction effort began, and by April 1975 a 34,000-square-foot headquarters with new plant equipment was ready to open. Meanwhile, the TACAN test

Three Republic systems engineers look over radar simulator circuitry.

equipment business remained strong, and in 1978 Republic introduced a new related product: a hand-held TACAN flight line test set. This small battery-powered unit was an instant success, and Republic's stature in the TACAN industry was even further enhanced.

At the same time, with sizable resources committed to entering the radar environment simulator market, Republic was awarded its first such contract by the U.S. Air Force.

Then, in 1980 Johns Hopkins University/Applied Physics Laboratory contracted with Republic to develop a multiple-radar environment simulator for design testing of new radar systems in the U.S. Navy's New Threat Upgrade program.

The resulting simulator (REES-201) worked with shipboard radars at the radio frequency level to simulate not only realistic missile and aircraft targets, but also electronic countermeasures jamming, chaff, weather, and sea clutter. The simulator interfaced with two- and three-dimensional radars, IFF, and was later used with fire control radars.

This seagoing success led to development of ground-based radar simulators. In 1982, under contract

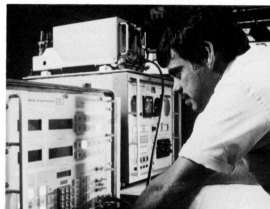

Republic's TACAN Beacon Simulator in test on the production line.

with the Royal Norwegian Air Force, Republic produced its first air defense radar environment simulator designed especially for air interceptor controller training.

In 1984 and 1985 the Naval Sea Systems Command funded production of AN/USQ-93(V) simulators developed by Republic to meet new requirements for on-board training, testing, and performance monitoring. At the same time the firm developed a new simulator for AN/SPS-48C three-dimensional shipboard radars.

With over 100 employees, Republic Electronics is known worldwide for the synergism of its radio frequency engineered products, which include development of electronic warfare simulators and microwave landing system test equipment.

DATABIT, INC.

With a patented time division multiplexer (TDM) technique, Long Island engineer Peter J. Cohen revolutionized telex transmission, since TDM allowed a much greater number of telex channels on a single transmission line than the number allowed by older techniques. To market this revolutionary application, Cohen and partner Philip Ackerman founded Databit in November 1969.

The new firm opened its first small office at 93 Marcus Boulevard in Hauppauge. Within a short time Databit was serving the United States international record-carrier market with top clients such as ITT, RCA, Western Union, TRT, and Western Union International. Virtually overnight, Databit had become *the* name in telex transmission.

Today, with over 500 employees and headquarters at 110 Ricefield Lane in Hauppauge, Databit is a world leader in advanced telecommunication networks. As a wholly owned subsidiary of Siemens AG, West Germany's largest electronics company and one of the world's largest, Databit is part of a legendary communications firm dating back to 1847. It was then that the famed Siemens family founded Siemens & Halske.

When Siemens & Halske was incorporated as Siemens AG in 1897,

The data-communications network control center installed by Databit at NETECH Communications, a division of US West, in Denver, Colorado. This state-of-the-art packet-switching system is typical of those provided by Databit to customers throughout the United States.

it had already become famous for its 1875 laying of the first transatlantic cable from Ireland to the United States. Siemens Communication Systems, Inc., today headquartered in Iselin, New Jersey, is Databit's direct corporate parent.

During the early 1970s, however, Databit was still a small independent firm, making a big mark in United States telecommunications. International marketing was initiated in 1973, when Databit quickly penetrated the Post, Telephone, and Telegraph (PTT) market. These overseas PTTs—

government agencies that provide telecommunications service—became such a responsive market for Databit that by the late 1970s they represented 70 percent of the firm's annual production.

Meanwhile, as international stature grew, Databit introduced its second major product line during 1976: concentrators for telex and data. Then, in October of that year, an international standard based on Databit's time division multiplexer was ratified by the CCITT in Geneva, Switzerland. Throughout the rest of the decade Databit maintained its prominence in the field of telex switching and transmission.

Siemens AG acquired Databit in 1979, with Cohen remaining in the president's suite. The important element in the acquisition agreement was the provision, of equal importance to Siemens and Databit, that the new subsidiary operate independently from the parent. This meant that Databit would maintain its own product development, manufacturing, and sales groups.

The Model 920 Time Division Multiplexer was the first product manufactured and sold by Databit back in 1970. Many of these TDMs are still in service, carrying domestic and international telex traffic.

Databit corporate headquarters, 110 Ricefield Lane, Hauppauge, New York.

The year 1981 was eventful for the Databit division of Siemens AG. In February the firm moved to its new quarters in the Hauppauge Industrial Park. Soon there were three Databit buildings there: 110 Ricefield Lane, 135 Ricefield Lane, and 50 Davids Drive. In October Siemens AG transferred a substantial amount of sales and customer technical support responsibility to Databit for certain Siemens telecommunications products.

By the end of 1981 Databit founder and president Peter Cohen had left the company. He was succeeded by Systems Division vice-president John P. Scheiwe.

In 1982 Databit entered its present major marketplace: packet-switched data communications. This was a vital move for the firm because the traditional telex market, which had made its name and its fortune, was mature and declining.

The 1982 Databit-Siemens packet-switching market entry began with sales of a national packet network to Western Union for that company's EasyLink data-transport system, which operates in major cities from Boston to San Francisco.

This market foresight also prepared Databit-Siemens for the imminent breakup of American

Databit manufacturing facility, 50 Davids Drive, Hauppauge, New York.

Telephone & Telegraph Company and the resulting transformation of the entire United States communications market.

When AT&T officially divested itself of twenty-two wholly owned telephone companies on January 1, 1984, these entities were suddenly free to compete in the large-scale data-communications market as something more than simply phone companies. They very quickly focused on packet switching as the best technology with which to do this. Databit-Siemens was poised to serve these new needs.

As a matter of fact, Databit-Siemens had already scored its first victory in the new and highly competitive Bell Operating Company market in 1983. New York Telephone had selected Databit-Siemens equipment for its new data-network service. Following this agreement, Southern New England Telephone picked Databit-Siemens as the supplier of its public data network in Connecticut.

During 1984 Databit-Siemens packet networks were chosen by Indiana Bell, Wisconsin Bell, New England Telephone, Bell Atlantic (representing seven local Bell Operating Companies), and the NETECH division of the US West regional holding company. By the end of 1984 Databit was the leading supplier of packet-switching network products to the new Bell Operating Companies.

In addition to this, corporate packet-switching networks proved to be another responsive and promising sector in the United States market in 1984. Databit-Siemens signed two contracts that year with Boeing: One was delivered to Boeing's network development center in Seattle, Washington, and the other is the backbone for a switched network for the Commonwealth of Pennsylvania.

SPERRY CORPORATION

On April 19, 1910, Elmer A. Sperry formally incorporated a new firm, the Sperry Gyroscope Company, in a Manhattan office building. He had no product to sell—only an idea for a compass that used a gyroscope instead of magnetic forces to guide ships. His firm had one employee, several gyro models, and no capital.

In the summer of 1911 the U.S. Navy gave this new gyrocompass a sea trial on the USS *Delaware.* The test was successful, and the Navy ordered eight gyrocompasses.

From this modest start, Sperry Corporation has grown into a $5-billion company with a major facility at Lake Success. It ranks among the top 100 industrial corporations in the country and has more than 70,000 employees worldwide. Sperry's business areas now include information processing systems and services, electronic systems for defense and aerospace, and specialized farm equipment.

In seventy-five years Sperry Corporation has been responsible for an impressive list of technological "firsts": the first successful gyrocompass, first airplane stabilizer and autopilot, first gunfire control systems, and first artificial horizon and turn-and-bank indicators for aircraft.

Other Sperry firsts were the first guided missile, gyrostabilized bombsight, automatic radio navigation system, klystron tube, electronic computer, and automatic aircraft direction finder and approach control. The Sperry inertial navigation system for ships made possible the first trip under the North Pole by the nuclear-powered submarine USS *Nautilus.*

Sperry's involvement with Long Island began in 1942, when it moved into its current Lake Success quarters. During World War II the firm employed more than

Sperry Corporation's Long Island headquarters in Lake Success.

18,000 people at its two-million-square-foot Long Island facility.

During the war years Sperry was heavily involved in the development and production of bombsights, naval fire control systems, radar, navigation systems, and various aviation systems. The firm also established a separate 2,000-employee research laboratory in Garden City that produced many radar and electronics advances.

On Long Island Sperry continues its leadership role in the design, development, and production of electronic systems for defense. The firm is responsible for advanced systems such as the navigation system for the *Polaris, Poseiden,* and *Trident* submarines; the combat systems for the FFG-7 class guided missile frigates; the next generation of automated test equipment for the U.S. Air Force; and various radar, sonar, and fire control systems for naval vessels. Sperry is also involved in state-of-the-art directed energy systems and such practical, yet complex, systems as computer-controlled warehouses.

Today, with facilities in Lake Success and Ronkonkoma, Sperry

Elmer A. Sperry, founder of the Sperry Gyroscope Company, was the first to demonstrate practical uses for the gyroscope with his successful development of the gyrocompass for ship navigation.

Corporation employs about 6,000 people on Long Island, making it the region's sixth-largest employer. Primarily involved in defense projects, its Systems Management Group is headquartered at Lake Success. A major division of the Defense Products Group also shares those quarters.

KULKA CONSTRUCTION MANAGEMENT CORP.

With seventy-five buildings to his credit by 1975, Jack H. Kulka was the fabled Marcus Organization's most productive construction superintendent. But six years with Marcus, and several years as an electrical contractor, had convinced this NYU and Polytechnic Institute of New York graduate engineer that many developers and general contractors didn't provide building owners the best construction value on the fastest schedule. Kulka formed his own company to prove that conviction.

Kulka Construction Management Corp. began in 1976 in the basement of its founder's Smithtown home. At the time the company included Kulka, a secretary, and a $100 phone-answering system. Jeffrey Greenberg joined the firm one year later and later became a partner. His outstanding administrative abilities are no small part of its success. Today the business is a 52-employee entity with six project managers and a two-million-square-foot annual construction rate. It is now located on Oser Avenue in the heart of Hauppauge's industrial center.

Having started as a "fast track"

industrial construction manager, the Kulka firm has now diversified into overall project development of office buildings, college campuses, hotels, condominiums, hospitals, and multiplex theaters throughout the Long Island and New York metropolitan region. The opening of Kulka branches in Westchester, New York, and in Connecticut and New Jersey is imminent, with national expansion as the ultimate goal.

Kulka's first job under his own sails was a 70,000-square-foot Hempstead building for Global Equipment, a project Kulka literally talked his way into as the prospective client was about to sign with a competitive builder. There were three projects the first year, totaling 165,000 square feet of space. In successive years that performance has increased, and from 1982 on Kulka has averaged over two million square feet annually and has created more than 30,000 jobs.

The firm is responsible for many of Long Island's more innovative and architecturally impressive structures for local clients as well as national and international firms, including Avant-Garde Optics in Port Washington, Narda Microwave and Standard Microsystems in Hauppauge, and Frequency Electronics at Mitchel Field.

Kulka recently concluded the first stage in converting the former

Central Islip Psychiatric Center into New York Institute of Technology's new, 520-acre engineering campus. The firm is also developing a new, $35-million, 306-room hotel at Exit 52 of the Long Island Expressway in Smithtown.

The Kulka organization executes a variety of jobs and job descriptions through the pooling of manpower and computerization. It was Kulka Construction Management Corp. that familiarized Long Island with such terms as "fast track" and "project team" construction.

Active in various community organizations, Kulka is the Long Island chairman of the New York State Committee for Jobs and Energy Independence, founder/vice-president of the Hauppauge Industrial Association, board member of the United Way, founder/president of the Suffolk County YM-YWHA, founder and former president of the SUNY Farmingdale Foundation, former chairman of the American Cancer Society Fundraising Ball, a member of the New York State Business Development Council and New York State Economical Council, a member of the Suffolk County Economic Council, former president of the Commack Jewish Center, member of the board of directors of LIMBA and Route 110 Action, vice-chairman of the Long Island Political Action Committee, member of the board of directors of B'nai B'rith and American Jewish Congress, and chairman of the Israel State Bonds and many other civic and religious organizations.

An artist's rendering of the $35-million, 234-room hotel now under development by Kulka Construction Management Corp. in Smithtown.

The Avant-Garde Optics Building in Port Washington is an example of the quality of work performed by Kulka Construction Management Corp.

LINOTYPE

Ottmar Mergenthaler arrived in Baltimore from Germany in 1872. He was eighteen years old, had thirty-six dollars in his pocket, and carried a vague idea of being an engineer. What he did instead was go to work in a cousin's electrical shop, and within twelve years he invented the world's first automatic typesetting machine.

He revolutionized the ancient art of printing and influenced the history and technology of mass communications. Thomas Edison termed his invention the "Eighth Wonder of the World" and called Mergenthaler a genius.

The Mergenthaler typesetting machine and its successors also gave birth to a successful internationally based company that today is a subsidiary of the $10-billion Allied Corporation of Morristown, New Jersey. Known for nearly a century as the Mergenthaler Linotype Company of Brooklyn, it is now part of the Industrial and Technology Sector of Allied Corporation and known simply as Linotype.

With some 500 United States employees, about 300 working on Long Island, Linotype is now in the process of consolidating its Long Island operations from Melville, Bay Shore, and Plainview to its new 20,000-square-foot headquarters at 425 Oser Avenue in Hauppauge.

Linotype is one of the largest manufacturers and distributors of typesetting systems in the world. Linotype also maintains a strong position in the phototypesetting equipment market. Major customers for its products are newspapers, printers, publishers, commercial typographers, and the growing in-plant market.

But if Linotype is today's leader in the technological revolution of computerized typesetting and pho-

totypesetting, this is within the Mergenthaler tradition. Mergenthaler's activities 100 years ago were literally as earthshaking as the invention of the printing press itself by Gutenberg in 1450.

Prior to Mergenthaler's invention, printers set type in the manner first developed by Gutenberg, picking up letters one at a time, tediously forming words, then sentences, and so on. This process took so many men so much time

that the largest daily newspapers of the 1880s were barely eight pages long. Magazines were few, thin, and costly, and only seventy-six libraries in America had more than 300 volumes.

But with the Mergenthaler typesetting machine, individual characters engraved in brass matrices could be selected and arranged at the touch of a button on a typewriter-like keyboard. Molten lead, poured into molds formed in part by the matrices, cooled to form type in precise lines ready for printing.

Mergenthaler first demonstrated his new composing machine in 1884 to a group of investors in the offices of National Typographic Company on Bank Lane in Baltimore. At the time many inventors

with millions of dollars in backing were competing to create a viable automatic typesetting apparatus. However, the successful operation of Mergenthaler's "band" typesetting machine would go on to change the world of printing.

In 1885 Mergenthaler invented

In 1884 Ottmar Mergenthaler's invention of an automatic typesetting machine revolutionized mass communications.

Linotype's new Long Island headquarters in Hauppauge.

an improved band automatic type-setter. This machine was exhibited at the Chamberlain Hotel in Washington, D.C., and Mergenthaler was praised by President Chester A. Arthur at a banquet in the inventor's honor.

An even further-improved "blower" typesetter was introduced in 1886. This machine derived its name from an ingenious system in which compressed air created the pressure to compose lines of type from circulating matrices.

Its first commercial use occurred on July 1 of that year, when it typeset the *New York Tribune.* Famed publisher Whitelaw Reid was the first to dub the term "Linotype," and it stuck. Meanwhile, the Mergenthaler Printing Company had been formed in Baltimore to succeed National Typographic.

By February 1888 some fifty

Mergenthaler Linotypes had been sold. Two years later the Mergenthaler Linotype Company was founded in Brooklyn. A division was also formed in England. By December 1892 about 1,000 Linotypes had been sold or rented. Most important, a mass communications revolution had begun. All major American newspapers, and many throughout the world, were equipping their plants with Mergenthaler Linotypes.

Tragically, Ottmar Mergenthaler died on October 28, 1899. He was just forty-five years old. Still, in the last six years of his life he had seen his Linotype become the sensation of the great Chicago World Exposition of 1893, had overseen the first European commercial use of his invention for a major newspaper in Holland, and had seen the formation of the Mergenthaler GMBH company in his native Germany.

During the early decades of the twentieth century Mergenthaler Linotype Company continued to lead the industry its namesake and founder had literally invented. The Mergenthaler Linotype trademark was represented in all principal cities of the world and was headquartered in Brooklyn, with offices in San Francisco, Chicago, and New Orleans.

The name Mergenthaler created an identity as a leading product manufacturer and distributor and as a driving force in stretching the industry's technological limits. This identity is maintained by Lino-

Linotype products are as technologically advanced in today's market as Mergenthaler's first typesetter was during the Industrial Revolution.

type, which today still directs 8 percent of its annual revenues into research and development.

In the 1950s Mergenthaler Linotype produced the world's first tape-oriented phototypesetter—LINOFILM. In the 1960s Mergenthaler Linotype engineers made the phototypesetter compatible with the digital computer for the first time. The result was LINOTRON 1010, the first 1,000-line-per-minute, cathode-ray tube typesetter, another technological breakthrough.

Linotype made further technological advances in the 1970s with the introduction of its now-classic VIP typesetter, which established new criteria for typographic quality. That decade also saw introduction of LINOTRON 202, which soon became the world's most popular typesetter.

On July 1, 1979, Allied Corporation acquired the Eltra Corporation, of which Mergenthaler Linotype Company was then part, for nearly $600 million.

Linotype has continued to lead its industry in technological innovation during the 1980s. One example has been a new system generation called the CRTronic family, which includes the first tabletop digital CRT typesetters.

To honor the tremendous contribution of Ottmar Mergenthaler to the graphic arts industry, the renowned Stemple Haas Mergenthaler Type Library has been renamed the Mergenthaler Library. Meanwhile, by January 1985 Linotype was announcing shipment of its 7,000th CRTronic typesetter. With the increasing acceptance of personal computers, Linotype has now incorporated them into its Series 100 and 200 systems.

THE LONG ISLAND SAVINGS BANK, FSB

In 1870 several small villages at Long Island's westernmost shore, Hunter's Point, Astoria, Ravenswood, and others in the borough of Queens, were incorporated by statute as Long Island City. As the size of Long Island City continued to grow several local businessmen, led by Sylvester Gray, decided that a good local bank was needed to ensure the growth of Long Island City, serving the community as a depository of funds and a source of home mortgage loans. Hence, the Long Island City Savings Bank was organized for that purpose on April 18, 1876.

Two months later, on June 19, the institution received its charter from New York State and opened its first office, a mere storefront, in lower Long Island City on Jackson Avenue. Its rapid growth made it necessary for the bank to move to larger quarters in December 1876, 1891, and again in 1912. Providing Long Island City residents with a good return of interest on their savings, as well as providing them with mortgage financing, proved to be the key to success for the Long Island City Savings Bank. By 1920 the bank had grown large enough to construct its first building at Queens Plaza, not too far from the Queensborough Bridge. This landmark structure, with its four Doric columns, remains in service today as a functional office—the Long Island City Branch. Expansion was necessary to continue to serve the increasing number of Long Island City depositors.

Back in the early days, carrying the full name of its birthplace, Long Island City Savings Bank served a single community. Gradually its stature in that community became matched by its growing reputation. For example, in 1885 a prominent Belgian-born bank member named Jean Henri Thiry

established the country's first automated school savings program together with Long Island City Savings Bank. This national program still operates today.

With the bank's continued growth and expansion, a new office was opened in 1924, at Thirtieth Avenue in Astoria. By 1926 its assets were over $36 million. As time progressed, the needs of the community encouraged the bank to open ten additional branches from 1946 to 1978. During this 32-year period the institution continued to grow and expand. By 1951 its assets exceeded $176 million. The bank started its move east when it opened its first Nassau County branch at Syosset in 1962.

On September 1, 1966, the name was legally changed to The Long Island Savings Bank, a fitting name for a savings bank with branches in Queens and Nassau counties and future thoughts of expansion.

By June 1976, its "100th year of serving the community," the institution had nine branches and its asset size had grown to well over $962 million. In addition, the

James J. Conway, Jr., chairman of the board and chief executive officer.

bank's new corporate headquarters was completed in Syosset. As part of the 100th-anniversary celebration, the bank created a scholarship program that was in effect for seven years, providing $4,000 college scholarships to outstanding local high school students. More than seventy-five students were awarded these scholarships during this period of time.

The institution continued its eastward expansion in 1978, establishing a branch in West Islip, Suffolk County. In order for it to continue to serve its customers in the very best way, The Long Island Savings Bank became federally chartered in 1982. This change would enable the bank to expand its services.

One of the bank's largest undertakings occurred on August 17, 1983, when it acquired the Suffolk County Federal Savings and Loan Association. After this date, The

J. Harvey Smedley was chairman of the board of the Long Island City Savings Bank in 1923, when the first automated school stamp machine was installed at the Third Ward School, P.S. #4, in Long Island.

Long Island Savings Bank name appeared on branches throughout Queens, Nassau, Suffolk, Brooklyn, New York City, Herkimer, Utica, and Whitesboro. The branch asset size ranged from $13 million to $241 million. The downstate branches cover Long Island from the Queensborough Bridge to Southampton.

Today known as The Long Island Savings Bank, FSB, it is headquartered at 50 Jackson Avenue in Syosset, with forty-eight branches and over 1,500 employees. But even at this expanded size, the institution still remains dedicated to its original mission as a source of various savings plans and home mortgage loans.

James J. Conway, Jr., chairman of the board and chief executive officer, states that in addition to a proud tradition of personal and professional service, The Long Island Savings Bank remains committed to the future. As Long Island prospers, so does Long Island's strong bank. Conway is convinced that "together we can move forward as partners in prosperity."

In 1984 the bank purchased the 87,000-square-foot former Mergenthaler Linotype building on Old

Country Road in Melville, with plans to convert the structure to an administrative headquarters. That same year The Long Island Savings Bank made banking history by combining low-cost, one-year adjustable-rate mortgages with free name-brand gifts, such as television sets, stereos, and computers.

Mortgage loans still remain as one of Long Island Savings' prime businesses, especially in one- to four-family houses as well as in condominiums and cooperative loans with adjustable and fixed-rate mortgages. However, the

---

The southwest corner of Jackson Avenue and Third Street was the site of the bank's original office—1876.

institution also maintains strong activity in auto and boat loans, home improvement and personal loans, as well as time deposit certificates, NOW/checking accounts, pension plans, and money market accounts. The Long Island Savings Bank is also expanding its services in commercial lending.

The bank's 1984 statement of condition proudly showed an asset size of over $4 billion dollars with a net income for that year of $24.4 million. This represented an overwhelming increase of 154.5 percent over the 1983 income of $9.6 million.

The bank's continued strength can be attributed to a combination of competitive savings rates and a

strong mortgage program. Its multifaceted mortgage programs and competitive rates have made the institution one of the largest mortgage lenders in New York State.

One can look at The Long Island Savings Bank's record for the past 109 years with great admiration. With such a solid foundation, the future can only be one of continued strength.

The corporate headquarters of The Long Island Savings Bank is located at 50 Jackson Avenue in Syosset.

NEW YORK INSTITUTE OF TECHNOLOGY

The history of New York Institute of Technology points with particular interest to its mission-oriented beliefs. Although substantial information is contained in its many publications, this synopsis is intended to pinpoint and highlight certain outstanding specifics.

Fully accredited, NYIT is a personalized independent college where career education has been the mainstay since its inception in 1955. Thirty years later over 14,000 students attended campuses in mid-Manhattan near Lincoln Center, and on Long Island in Old Westbury, Central Islip, and Commack. An alumni roster of more than 25,000 are engaged in all phases of business, industry, and the professions, or are enrolled in postgraduate institutions all over the globe.

An open-access college, New York Institute of Technology has been able to provide education and training for men and women of all ages and from all walks of life who may not otherwise have been able to obtain higher-education advantages. In addition, low, affordable tuition rates and fees have been available to all NYIT students over the years and until current time.

The college offers a variety of curriculums ranging from associate through baccalaureate and master's degrees in many disciplines

The Harry J. Schure Science and Technology Center in Old Westbury. One of the first buildings to be erected, part of the academic complex includes a quadrangle, two classroom buildings, the library, labs, and faculty and staff offices.

and to the doctorate in osteopathic medicine through its medical school, New York College of Osteopathic Medicine. Located in Old Westbury, the medical college is the only one of its kind in New York State and the only medical school in Nassau County. Its beginnings were made possible through the efforts of former Governor and Vice-President Nelson A. Rockefeller, former Secretary of State Henry Kissinger, and the Rockefeller Foundation.

Career-oriented programs include accounting, engineering, architecture (four- and five-year programs), business administration, computer science, hotel/restaurant administration, general studies, communication arts, behavioral sciences, technological management, life sciences, fine arts, design graphics, physics, political science, osteopathic medicine (combined BS/DO seven-year program), preprofessional, interior design, labor management, technical writing, and teacher/occupational education.

With origins that date back to a predecessor school founded in

1910, New York Institute of Technology has a continuous history of providing quality education in specialized areas. Grants of equipment and property by the Schure family led to the founding of the present college at its original location in Brooklyn. In 1955 New York Institute of Technology was chartered by the State of New York as a two-year college granting the associate in applied science degree. In 1958 a Manhattan facility was purchased to house an expanded program. The college continued this growth and expansion pattern by purchasing portions of the former Cornelius Vanderbilt Whitney estate in Old Westbury. The additional purchase of other estate properties—that once were part of the famed North Shore Gold Coast—now comprise the Dorothy Schure Old Westbury Campus, a scenic sprawling and contiguous 750 acres. Included is a 100-acre estate and mansion that once belonged to the late Winston Guest and which is now known as the NYIT deSeversky Conference Center. The center serves both the academic and the business community. The college's most recent acquisition is the Central Islip

Education Hall on the Dorothy Schure Old Westbury Campus. Formerly part of the Whitney Estate, and used as stables for prized horses and cattle, the building on the outside still serves as a landmark of years gone by but now houses ultramodern architecture and TV/radio broadcast laboratories, among others, on the inside.

Campus in Suffolk County—a recycled former state hospital property—where NYIT students began classes in the fall of 1984. This campus contains dormitories, the first on-campus accommodations as such for NYIT students. Over 400 students enrolled in the first class, 300 of them dormitory residents. Future plans at Central Islip call for a high-technology park as well as sophisticated movie and television broadcast studios of the futuristic kind. Over the past few years the college had purchased three former elementary schools on Long Island, refurbishing them for use as classrooms, offices, state-of-the-art labs, and more.

New York Institute of Technology bears the imprimatur of national and regional accrediting agencies such as the Middle States Association of Colleges and Secondary Schools; the Accreditation Board for Engineering and Technology, Inc., for the bachelor of technology; the National Architectural Accrediting Board for the bachelor of architecture; the Foundation for Interior Design Education Research for interior design programs; and the American Osteopathic Association for the New York College of Osteopathic Medicine of NYIT.

The college is affiliated with its sister institution, Nova University, in Fort Lauderdale, Florida. NYIT is also capable of offering—through its distant learning arm, the American Open University—computer

teleconferencing programs that lead to degrees in various disciplines. AOU/NYIT computer networks are available to students nationwide for communication with faculty and each other.

New York Institute of Technology is especially renowned for its outstanding research efforts and accomplishments in the fields of computer graphics, lasers and holography, robotics, biomechanics, medical electronics, ultrasonics, telecommunications, and high-definition television. The college's Computer Graphics Laboratory in Old Westbury has received worldwide recognition; it contains some of the foremost technical equipment possible in addition to a cadre of senior scientists who have been recipients of such honors as Emmy awards, numerous "Best in Computer Animation" citations, and much more.

NYIT has been successful over the years in bringing to the communities where it has settled a sense of permanence, an economic contribution, and an overall long-term social contribution. The college enjoys a prestigious reputation

The student activities center at NYIT's Central Islip campus in Suffolk County opened in the fall of 1984. This sprawling scenic campus was formerly the site of a state hospital.

for certain aspects of technology amid sister institutions known and admired for their expertise.

Truly steeped in the knowledge business, New York Institute of Technology is a multifaceted institution much in keeping with the challenge of the 1980s. A steady progression of achievements make up the history of NYIT. Much has come to pass—all adding up to the major milestones recorded for an institution still young in years. Recent evaluations of the college by Middle States teams have been most favorable, citing New York Institute of Technology as "... one of the most dynamic and interesting institutes of higher education in America."

A typical laboratory scene depicting students and equipment at NYIT.

DOWLING COLLEGE

Dowling College is an educational bridge between the needs of its students and those of their communities. From its 1958 birth through the present, Dowling's partnership of students, faculty, and trustees has served this mission. Dowling now has an enrollment of more than 2,550 full- and part-time undergraduate and graduate students in liberal arts, sciences, and professional programs. Served by a board of trustees chosen from America's business, financial, and professional worlds, the college flourishes on more than seventy acres of a former Vanderbilt estate in Oakdale. Dr. Victor P. Meskill is president of Dowling College.

In 1958 Port Jefferson newspaper publisher Stuart Gracey and Tinker National Bank chairman Cecil Hall first attracted Adelphi University president Paul Dawson Eddy to consider establishing a college in Suffolk County. Adelphi courses were already being offered in high schools in Riverhead, Sayville, and Port Jefferson.

The following year full-time classes for eighty students were consolidated in a surplus Sayville school known as "Old 88," named for the year it was built. This Dowling predecessor—Adelphi Suffolk—was the county's first four-year, coeducational liberal arts college.

Two years later "Old 88" was outgrown, and a search committee investigated new locations in Port Jefferson, Stony Brook, and Patchogue. In 1962 the committee chose William K. Vanderbilt's century-old Idle Hour estate, then owned by National Dairy Research Labs.

The estate, located in Oakdale, was a ready-made campus along the banks of the Connetquot River at the mouth of the Great South

Bay. It featured Vanderbilt's stately and still-functional 110-room, red-brick mansion, and its previous owners had already added a complete science wing.

In 1965 Allyn P. Robinson was Adelphi Suffolk dean. William Condon, also from Adelphi, joined him as dean of the college's 300 students. Then, in 1968, endowed by Manhattan financier Robert Dowling, the college became independent of Adelphi and was named for its benefactor. Robinson was named its first president.

By 1970, when its last Adelphi degrees were awarded, Dowling College had enrolled 1,500 students. Most of them represented the first college generation in their families from the nearby communities of Oakdale, Sayville, Islip, Patchogue, Bay Shore, and Brentwood.

Meanwhile, in August 1969 Dowling began a unique relationship with the Federal Aviation Administration (FAA), when a contract was signed at MacArthur Airport calling for 4,000 hours of FAA-approved flight training for Dowling students. In the following years the college produced the first graduates from these bachelor degree programs in aeronautics, aeronautics and applied math, and aeronautics and management. Dowling remains New York State's only college offering such degrees.

In 1972, before federal or state law mandated educational opportunities for the physically handicapped, the Peter Hausman Resource Center was established to commemorate the disabled brother

Dr. Victor P. Meskill (left), president of Dowling College, greets president emeritus Allyn P. Robinson during June 1984 commencement exercises.

of former Dowling board chairman Richard Hausman. Today it serves some sixty physically handicapped students. The Hausman Center is located in the Learning Resource Center, a modern four-story complex in which is also housed the college's 100,000-volume library, an auditorium for large gatherings, and a media resource center. The Student Computer Center and the Academic Support Services Center are also located in this building. In 1973 the college opened an innovative 51-unit apartment-style dormitory for over 200 resident students.

In 1974 a fire caused extensive damage to the Vanderbilt mansion. A four-year restoration was led by the trustees who also modernized the mansion with an elevator, new lighting, a new entranceway, an exterior courtyard, and physically handicapped student amenities.

Dr. Meskill was named president of Dowling College in 1977. During his first full year he officiated at the dedication renaming the mansion as the Max and Clara Fortunoff Hall, in honor of its benefactors.

In 1981 the first phase of a project to restore a very unique section of the mansion, the William K. Vanderbilt Palm House Conservatory, was begun. Now renamed the Marjorie Fortunoff Mayrock Conservatory, it is a prominent feature of the "Idle Hour" estate and is believed by historians to be one of the very few cast-iron buildings on Long Island. The board of trustees in 1985 appointed a special committee, chaired by trustee Doris Pike, to begin a $500,000 campaign to complete the restoration. When finished, the Marjorie Fortunoff Mayrock Conservatory will serve as a cultural center for Dowling College, to be used by its students and faculty, as well as the Long Island community at large, for such functions as chamber music concerts, art exhibits, and lectures.

In 1982 Dr. Meskill and Joseph M. Del Balzo, director of the FAA's Eastern Region, established a cooperative education program through which students planning to become air traffic controllers are able to make up to $14,000 while earning a Dowling bachelor of science degree.

In May 1985 Long Island Association and Long Island Builders Institute director John Racanelli succeeded Dale Carnegie & Associates vice-president and senior operating officer Stuart R. Levine as chairman of Dowling's board of trustees. Racanelli, partner and general counsel of commercial real estate developers N. Racanelli Associates, is also a prominent member of the Long Island business community.

Academically, Dowling's four-year bachelor of science degrees in computer information systems and computer science, amplified by high-technology internships in Long Island firms, exemplify its commitment to the community's business needs. Similarly, the growth in stature of the Dowling MBA, tailored to accommodate the working professional, reflects the college's continuing effort to involve that community in its programs.

Dowling recognizes the central role science and technology play in modern society, and is aware of the responsibility of an institution of higher education to expand its thinking to meet new challenges. To address this critical need, Dowling has developed "the concept of partnerships." One of the most recent developments at Dowling, and an example of this approach, is an agreement signed in January 1985 with Suffolk County to increase educational opportunities for county employees and their families. Dowling also strives to involve area businesses in its activities and through these efforts has developed the "Partners in Education" program, a tri-partnership involving the college, the student, and the student's employer.

The Dowling teacher education program averages an 86-percent success rate in placing its graduates in teaching positions. The college also offers master of science in education degrees.

Dowling has also expanded its concept of community to the national and international levels, as evidenced by the recently established Study Center in Manhattan where full-time undergraduate students have an opportunity to become familiar with the extraordinary vocational, cultural, and recreational resources available in New York City. Dowling is also exploring a cooperative reading/teaching program with the government of Puerto Rico. The program would provide that area with needed educational resources. The college also founded and organized an International and Mediterranean Studies Group Conference Series in which, along with more than thirty-five other member colleges and universities, it has been an active participant for the past eight years. These conferences, unique in the Mediterranean academic world, serve as a valuable forum for scholars to present their latest research in particular specialties and interests.

On the campus itself, Dowling College's community concept is evidenced by twenty-seven clubs and organizations run autonomously by the student government; eight intercollegiate sports programs, projects, and scholarships directly sponsored by trustees; and Dr. Meskill's every-other-Wednesday ritual brown-bag lunches with students.

The key to "the Dowling experience," as described by Dr. Meskill, "is helping students become aware of their own personal strengths and enjoy the college's unique qualities which are a highly personalized learning environment characterized by friendly informality and academic excellence." Dowling provides both the choice and quality that allows it to meet the needs of today and the promise of tomorrow.

An aerial view of Dowling College's lovely campus shows its location along the banks of the Connetquot River in Oakdale, Long Island, on Suffolk's south shore.

PALL CORPORATION

In retrospect, it was fortunate for the Pall Corporation that its founder and chairman, Dr. David Pall, met resistance to a new porous stainless steel material he invented and attempted to market in the mid-1940s. Incorporated in New York on July 31, 1946, as Micro Metallic Corporation, Dr. Pall's firm sought to exploit his invention.

But the filtering companies this McGill and Brown University-educated chemist targeted as his market remained uninterested. As a result, Dr. Pall began developing his own process filter business. Over the next 40 years this fledgling idea grew to a more than $250-million, 4,600-employee firm.

But in 1944 the idea that would become the Pall Corporation was still a single individual with one product—an ingenious way of making process metal sheets through sintering fine stainless steel powder by heating it in a furnace with a controlled atmosphere at just below the melting point.

Canadian-born Dr. Pall saw a need in the chemical industry for filter elements that could withstand high pressures, temperatures, and corrosive conditions. But the initial rejection by traditional filter manufacturers led him to develop and manufacture his own line of filters in a Brooklyn basement.

The products sold well, and as demand increased, the company expanded in 1950 to its present Long Island headquarters on Sea Cliff Avenue in Glen Cove.

In 1954 the firm became aware of a serious problem in the hydraulic systems of Boeing 707 commercial jets, the Century series fighters, and other aircraft. Newly sophisticated hydraulic systems in these planes were contamination sensitive, and the filters then in

Pall's management team (from left to right): Maurice G. Hardy, executive vice-president and chief operating officer; Dr. David B. Pall, founder and chairman; Henry Petronis, executive vice-president; and Abraham Krasnoff, president and chief executive officer.

use were inadequate to protect engine and system components.

Over the next ten years the firm grew as a custom metal filter producer for the aerospace industry as well as for small portions of the process filter market. In this decade the company developed disposable fiberglass filters and the first paper-made disposables. Pall Corporation became a public company in 1957.

From the time of its inception in 1946 through 1964, Pall Corporation enjoyed an extended period of growth. However, after 1964 both the military and commercial aerospace industries declined substantially.

The company decided that its correct direction was in the development of proprietary disposable filters designed for large market distribution. A number of years were spent on diversification. At-

tempts in a number of areas outside of fluid clarification proved unsuccessful and were dropped.

Then in 1969 an important new disposable filter technology was developed. Pall undertook considerable retooling, new market development, field testing, and the refinement of new manufacturing

Some of Pall Corporation's modern bacteria grade filters and filter discs for pharmaceutical and other critical applications.

capabilities. By 1972 all of this was substantially completed, and by 1973 Pall Corporation had made a successful metamorphosis into a very different kind of company. Over the next decade Pall sales grew at more than 20 percent annually.

Today the Pall Corporation is the leading supplier of ultrafine filters with the broadest range of proprietary filter media and hardware in the world.

Pall Corporation has principal plants in Glen Cove and East Hills on Long Island, in Cortland, New York, in four Florida locations, and in California, Connecticut, and Puerto Rico. There is at least one Pall subsidiary in Austria, Canada, France, Germany, Great Britain, Italy, Japan, and Switzerland.

The company's basic business remains fluid clarification. Its filters, air cleaners, compressed air dryers, and fluid purifiers protect people and equipment through the capture and removal of contaminants in a wide variety of critical applications in four broad markets: fluid processing, aerospace, fluid power, and biomedical.

Pall's fluid processing market includes a wide range of customers who process fluids to produce chemicals, pharmaceuticals, electronic components, magnetic tape, film, beverages, electric power, and oil. New fields such as enhanced oil recovery, containment of radioactive and chemical wastes, and biotechnology fall into this market.

Pall has long been the leader in the supply of hydraulic and lubricating oil filters for military and commercial applications and has been increasing its aerospace applications in fuel filtration. The company remains the leader in centrifugal separators which, for example, protect helicopter engines from ingested dirt. Military ma-

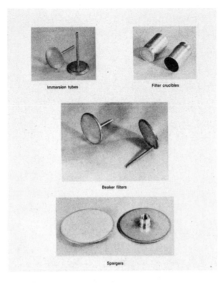

Some of Pall's earliest laboratory filters made from Dr. Pall's initial invention of porous stainless steel.

rine, military mobile, and aircraft ground support equipment continue as substantial markets for the firm.

The fluid power market includes a broad array of customers in applications where hydraulic oil under pressure is used as a motive force. These include producers of electric power, steel, paper, automobiles, earth-moving equipment, and oil well equipment, as well as users of heavy equipment in construction, mining, materials handling, and manufacturing. More recently Pall has introduced sophisticated lubricating oil filters to this market.

In the biomedical field, Pall Corporation supplies filters for direct use with hospital patients to protect them against the intrusion of bacterial or particulate contaminants during the administration of blood, breathing gases, and intravenous fluids. These prevent infection and postoperative damage to vital organs.

The Pall Corporation Conference Center in Glen Cove, the former Woolworth estate, serves as an employee and customer training center.

Patrons

The following individuals, companies, and organizations have made a valuable commitment to the quality of this publication. Windsor Publications, the Society for the Preservation of Long Island Antiquities, and the Long Island Association gratefully acknowledge their participation in *Between Ocean and Empire: An Illustrated History of Long Island.*

AABBACCO Equipment Leasing Corporation
Accurate Chemical & Scientific Corp.
Adelphi University*
AETNA Life & Casualty
Alexander & Alexander*
Allstate Insurance Company*
APOCA Industries*
Austin Travel*
Avis Rent A Car System*
Howard Blankman Incorporated
Boardroom Planning & Consulting Group, Inc.
Brookhaven National Laboratory*
J.A. Brudermann & Son, Inc.
Cablevision of Long Island*
Dale Carnegie & Associates, Inc.*
Chemical Bank*
The Church Charity Foundation of Long Island
Chyron Corporation*
Computer Terminal Systems, Inc.*
Cosgrove Aircraft Service, Inc.
Databit, Inc.*
Dionics, Inc.*
Dowling College*
Eaton Corporation*
E.I.L. Petroleum, Inc.
Entenmann's, Inc.*
Executone inc.
The Nationwide Business Phone Company*
Fairchild Weston Systems Inc.*
General Aero Products Corp.*
Grumman Corporation*
Hartman Systems/A Figgie International Company*
Hazeltine Corporation*
HNL Distributors
Hoffman, Dilworth, Barrese & Baron
Hofstra University*
Huntington Personnel Consultants
Huntington Personnel Temps
Knogo Corporation*
Peter F. Korpacz

Kuehnel Sheet Metal Co., Inc.
Kulka Construction Management Corp.*
Linotype*
Long Island Marriott Hotel
The Long Island Savings Bank, FSB*
Long Island Trust Company, N.A.*
Long Island University*
Lundy Electronics & Systems, Inc.*
Margolin, Winer & Evens, C.P.A.'s
Marine Midland Bank*
Marine Midland Bank, N.A.
Miltope Corporation*
Molloy College
Monitor Aerospace Corporation*
National Coverage Corp.
National Westminster Bank USA*
NEC America, Inc.*
New York Institute of Technology*
New York Islanders*
Norstar Bank of Long Island
Old Westbury Gardens
Pall Corporation*
Rains & Pogrebin, P.C.
Raymond Buick, Inc.
Reckson Associates*
Republic Electronics Company*
Russell Plastics Tech. Co. Inc.
Sill Oil Service
Smithtown Library
Spartan Concrete Corp.
Sperry Corporation*
State University of New York at Stony Brook*
Tambrands Inc.*
Tempus Fugit
Howard E. Thompson
Thomson Industries, Inc.*
Touche Ross*
Underwriters Laboratories, Inc.*
Mr. and Mrs. William S. Winters

*Partners in Progress of *Between Ocean and Empire: An Illustrated History of Long Island.* The histories of these companies and organizations appear in Chapter Ten, beginning on page 220.

Bibliography

Bailey, Paul. *Long Island, A History of Two Great Counties, Nassau and Suffolk.* New York: Lewis Historical Publishing Co., 1949.

Bangs, Charlotte. *Reminiscences of Old New Utrecht and Gowanus.* Brooklyn, 1912.

Barber, John. *Historical Collections of the State of New York.* New York: Tuttle, 1841.

Barck, Dorothy, ed. "Papers of the Lloyd Family of the Manor of Queens Village, Lloyds Neck 1654-1826." *Collections of the New-York Historical Society.* New York: 1926.

Bassett, Preston. *Long Island: Cradle of Aviation.* Amityville: Long Island Forum, 1950.

Brasser, T.J.C. "The Coastal Algonkians: People of the First Frontiers." In Eleanor Leacock and Nancy Lurie, eds., *North American Indians in Historical Perspective.* New York: Random House, 1971.

Carpenter, James. *The Mineola Fair.* Uniondale: Agricultural Society of Queens, Nassau, and Suffolk County, 1965.

Ceci, Lynn. "The Effect of European Contact and Trade on the Settlement Pattern of Indians in Coastal New York, 1524-1664." Doctoral dissertation, CUNY, 1977.

_____ . "Method and Theory in Coastal New York Archaeology: Paradigms of Settlement Pattern." *North American Archaeologist* 3(1982):5-36.

Christ Church Parish Records. Oyster Bay, New York.

Clark, Stephen. "Gabriel Furman: Brooklyn's First Historian." *Journal of Long Island History* 10(Spring 1974):21-32.

Colonel Josiah Smith Account Book for 1776. Society for the Preservation of Long Island Antiquities, Setauket, New York.

Conkey, Laura, E. Boissevian, and I. Goddard. "Indians of Southern New England and Long Island: Late Period." In Bruce Trigger, ed., *Handbook of the North American Indians, Vol. 15: The Northeast.* Washington: Smithsonian Institution, 1978.

Cory, David M. "Brooklyn and the Civil War." *Journal of Long Island History* 2(Spring 1962):1-15.

Cummings, John. "The Dorflinger Glass Works." *New York History* 34(October 1953):468-74.

Daggett, Marguerite. *Long Island Printing 1791-1830.* Brooklyn: Long Island Historical Society, 1979.

Dankers, Jasper, and Peter Sluyter. *Journal of a Voyage to New York* (1679-80). Translation by H.C. Murphy, 1867. Reprint. Ann Arbor: University Microfilms, 1966.

DeLeat, John. "Extracts from the New World: A Description of the West Indies" (1625). In H.C. Murphy, ed., *Collections of the New-York Historical Society.* 2nd Series, Vol. 1. New York: H. Ludwig, 1841.

Denton, Daniel. *A Brief Description of New York: Formerly Called New Netherland* (1670). Ann Arbor: University Microfilms, 1966.

DeVerazzano, John. "The Voyage of John DeVerazzano Along the Coast of North America" (1524). In H.C. Murphy, ed., *Collections of the New-York Historical Society.* 2nd Series, Vol. 1. New York: H. Ludwig, 1841.

Dillard, Maud. *Old Houses of Brooklyn.* New York: Richard R. Smith, 1945.

Dobriner, William. *Class in Suburbia.* New York: Prentice Hall, 1963.

Dunn, Richard. "John Winthrop, Jr., Connecticut Expansionist, The Failure of his Designs on Long Island 1663-1675." *New England Quarterly* XIX (1956).

Dwight, Timothy. *Travels in New England and New York.* New Haven: S. Converse, 1823.

Eberlein, Harold. *Manor Houses and Historic Homes of Long Island and Staten Island.* Philadelphia: J.B. Lippincott, 1928.

Failey, Dean. *Edward Lange's Long Island.* Setauket: Society for the Preservation of Long Island Antiquities, 1979.

_____ . *Long Island is My Nation.* Setauket: Society for the Preservation of Long Island Antiquities, 1976.

Flick, Alexander. *Loyalism in New York During the American Revolution.* New York: Arno Press, 1964.

Floyd Family Papers. Society for the Preservation of Long Island Antiquities, Setauket, New York.

Fullerton, Edith. *History of Long Island Agriculture.* Jamaica: Long Island Rail Road, 1929.

Gabriel, Ralph. *The Evolution of Long Island.* New Haven: Yale University Press, 1921.

George Weekes Day Book. Raynham Hall Museum, Oyster Bay, New York.

Gibbs, Alonzo. "New Year's Calling." *New York Folklore Quarterly* 16:295-97.

Gosnell, Harold. *Boss Platt and his New York Machine.* Chicago, 1924.

Gwynne, Gretchen. "The Late Archaic Archaeology of Mount Sinai Harbor, New York." Doctoral dissertation, SUNY-Stony Brook, 1982.

_____ . "Pipestave Hollow Ideography." *Expedition* 24(1982):14-19.

Hammack, David C. *Participation in Major Decisions in New York City, 1890-1900: The Creation of Greater New York and the Centralization of the Public School System.* Ann Arbor, 1973, 1975.

_____ . *Power and Society: Greater New York at the Turn of the Century.* New York, 1982.

Hazelton, Henry. *The Boroughs of Brooklyn and Queens, Counties of Nassau and Suffolk, N.Y., 1609-1924.* 7 vols. New York: Lewis Historical Publishing Co., 1925.

Hedges Family Papers and Account Books. East Hampton Public Library.

Hofstra University Yearbook of Business.

Horne, Field, ed. *The Diary of Mary Cooper.* Oyster Bay: Oyster Bay Historical Society, 1981.

Horton, Azariah. "Azariah Horton's Letters to the Scots Mission" (1742). *Christian History* V:21-67.

Howell, George. *History of Southhampton.* New York: J.N. Hallock, 1866.

Huntington Town Meeting Records. Office of the Town Historian, Huntington, New York.

Idzerda, Stanley J. "Walt Whitman, Politician." *New York History* 37:171-184.

Jacob, Albert C. "Schooldays in Brooklyn in the Early 1900s." *Journal of Long Island History* 8(Summer-Fall 1968):30-38.

Jameson, J. Franklin, ed. *Narratives of New Netherlands.* New York: Charles Scribner's Sons, 1909.

Jaray, Cornell, ed. *Historical Chronicles of New Amsterdam, Colonial New York, and Early Long Island.* Port Washington: Ira J. Friedman, 1968.

Johnson, Henry. *The Campaign of 1776 Around New York and Brooklyn.* New York: De Capo Press, 1971.

Jones, Thomas. *History of New York During the Revolutionary War.* New-York Historical Society, 1879.

Judd, Jacob. "The Administrative Organization of the City of Brooklyn, 1834-1855." *Journal of Long Island History* 5 (Spring 1965):39-50.

_____ . "The Administrative Organization of the City of Brooklyn, Part II." *Journal of Long Island History* 5(Fall 1965):39-49.

_____ . "Brooklyn's Changing Population in the Pre-Civil War Era." *Journal of Long Island History* 2(Spring 1964):9-18.

_____ . "Brooklyn's Volunteer Fire Department." *Journal of Long Island*

BETWEEN OCEAN AND EMPIRE

History 6(Summer 1966):29-34.

_____ . "Brooklyn's Health and Sanitation, 1834-1855." *Journal of Long Island History* 7(Winter-Spring 1967): 40-52.

_____ . "A City's Streets: A Case Study of Brooklyn, 1834-1855." *Journal of Long Island History* 9 (Winter-Spring 1969):32-43.

_____ . "Policing the City of Brooklyn in the 1840s and 1850s." *Journal of Long Island History* 6(Spring 1966):13-22.

_____ . "Water for Brooklyn." *New York History* 47(October 1966):362-71.

Juet, Robert. "Extract from the Journal of the Voyage of the Half-Moon, Henry Hudson, Master, from the Netherlands to the Coast of North America" (1609). In H.C. Murphy, ed., *Collections of the New-York Historical Society.* 2nd series, Vol. 1. New York: H. Ludwig, 1841.

Kaiser, William, and Charles Stonier, eds. *The Development of the Aerospace Industry on Long Island.* Hempstead: Hofstra University, 1968.

Kurland, Gerald. *Seth Low: The Reformer in an Industrial Age.* New York, 1971.

LeBoeuf, Randall J., Jr. "Fulton's Ferry." *Journal of Long Island History* 10(Spring 1974):7-20.

Leiter, Samuel L. "Brooklyn as an American Theatre City." *Journal of Long Island History* 8(Winter-Spring 1968):1-11.

Log of the Schooner *Bayles.* Society for the Preservation of Long Island Antiquities, Setauket, New York.

Log of the Whaleship *Ontario.* Society for the Preservation of Long Island Antiquities, Setauket, New York.

Long Island: America and Sunrise Land. New York: Long Island Rail Road, 1933.

Long Island Directory of Manufacturers. New York: Nassau Department of Commerce and Industry/Suffolk County Office of Economic Development, 1981.

Long Island Fact Book of Nassau and Suffolk Counties. Garden City: Long Island Association of Commerce and Industry, 1965.

Mabee, Carleton. "Brooklyn's Black Public Schools: Why Did Blacks Have Unusual Control Over Them?" *Journal of Long Island History* 11(Spring 1975):23-36.

_____ . "Charity in Travail: Two Orphan Asylums for Blacks." *New York History* 55(January 1974):55-77.

McCullough, David. *The Great Bridge.* New York, 1972.

Ment, David, et. al. *Building Blocks of Brooklyn: A Study of Urban Growth.* Brooklyn, 1979.

_____ . *The Shaping of a City: A Brief History of Brooklyn.* Brooklyn, 1979.

Nassau County Historical Journal.

O'Callaghan, Edmund. *The Documentary History of the State of New York.* Albany, 1849.

Occum, Samson. "An Account of the Montauk Indians, on Long Island" (1761). *Collections of the Massachusetts Historical Society.* Vol. IX. Boston: Hall & Hiller, 1804.

Onderdonk, Henry. *Hempstead Annals 1643-1832.* Hempstead: L. Van De Water, 1878.

_____ . *Revolutionary Incidents of Queens County.* New York: Leavitt and Co., 1884.

_____ . *Revolutionary Incidents of Suffolk and Kings Counties.* New York: Leavitt and Co., 1849.

Orderly Book of the Three Battalions of Loyalists. Baltimore: Geneological Publishing Co., 1972.

Ostrander, Stephen M. *A History of the City of Brooklyn and Kings County.* Brooklyn, 1894.

Papers relating to the Sag Harbor Custom House. Society for the Preservation of Long Island Antiquities, Setauket, New York.

Pelletreau, William. *A History of Long Island.* New York: Lewis Historical Publishing Co., 1903.

Pomerantz, Stanley T. "The Press of A Greater New York, 1798-1893." *New York History* 39(January 1958):50-66.

Prime, Ebenizer. *Records of the First Church in Huntington, Long Island, 1723-1779.* New York: Scribner's, 1899.

Prime, Nathaniel. *History of Long Island to 1845.* New York: Carter, 1845.

Proceedings of the New York State Agricultural Society 1848-1869. Nassau County Research Library, East Meadow, New York.

Proceedings of the Queens County Agricultural Society 1842-1860. Nassau County Research Library, East Meadow, New York.

Queens County Wills. Surrogate Court, Jamaica, New York.

Randall, Monica. *The Mansions of Long Island's Gold Coast.* New York: Hastings House, 1979.

Rattray, Jeannette. *East Hampton History and Geneology.* Garden City: Country Life Press, 1953.

Roff, Sandra Shoiock. "The California Gold Miners from Brooklyn: As Viewed by the Local Press." *Journal of Long Island History* 9(Spring 1973):7-22.

Rossano, Geoffrey. "Suburbia Armed." In Roger Lotchin, ed., *The Martial Metropolis: American Cities in Peace and War.* New York: Praeger, 1984.

Salwen, Bert. "Indians of Southern New England and Long Island: Early Period." In Bruce Trigger, ed., *Handbook of the North American Indians, Vol. 15: The Northeast.* Washington: Smithsonian Institution, 1978.

Sclare, Donald, and Lisa Sclare. *Beaux Atres Estates.* New York: Viking Press, 1975.

Seyfried, Vincent. *The Long Island Railroad: A Comprehensive History.* Garden City: Privately Printed, 1961-1971.

Simon, Donald E. "Brooklyn in the Election of 1860." *New York History* 51(July 1967):248-262.

Slave Manumission Records 1793-1827. Office of the Huntington Town Historian.

Smith, Robert P. "Heroes and Hurrahs: Sports in Brooklyn, 1890-1898." *Journal of Long Island History* 11(Spring 1975):7-18.

Smits, Edward. *The Creation of Nassau County.* Mineola: Nassau County, 1962.

_____ . *Nassau-Suburbia U.S.A.* Garden City: Doubleday, 1974.

Statistical Abstract of Nassau and Suffolk Counties. Garden City: Franklin National Bank, 1962.

Statistical Reports on Age, Marital Status, Housing, School District Populations, Land Use, Farmland, Manufacturing, and Office Space. Hauppauge: Long Island Regional Planning Board, 1976-1982.

Statistical Reports on Social, Economic, and Housing Characteristics. Mineola: Nassau County Planning Commission, 1963.

Stiles, Henry. *History of the City of Brooklyn.* Brooklyn, 1867-1870.

_____ . *History of the Kings County Including the City of Brooklyn.* New York: Munsell, 1884.

_____ . et. al. *The Civil, Political, Professional and Ecclesiastical History and Commercial and Industrial Record of the County of Kings and the City of Brooklyn.* New York, 1884.

Stone, Gaynell, ed. *Readings in Long Island Archaeology and Ethnohistory.* 7 vols. Stony Brook: Suffolk County Archaeological Association, 1977-1984.

Stoutenburgh, Henry. *A Documentary History of the Dutch Congregation of Oyster Bay.* New York: 1902.

Syrett, Harold C. *The City of Brooklyn, 1865-1898: A Political History.* New York and London, 1944.

The Airplane Industry of the New York Metropolitan District. New York: Mer-

298

chants Association of New York, 1920.

The Beauties of Long Island. New York: Long Island Rail Road, 1895.

The Corrector. 1826. East Hampton Public Library.

The Future of Nassau County. New York: Regional Plan Association, 1969.

The Long Islander. 1839-1841. Huntington Historical Society.

The Portico. 1826-1828. Huntington Historical Society.

Thomas, Samuel. *Nassau County: Its Governments and Their Expenditure Patterns.* New York: City College Press, 1960.

Thompson, Benjamin. *History of Long Island.* New York: E. French, 1849.

Townsend Family Papers. East Hampton Public Library.

Townsend Family Papers. New-York Historical Society.

Townsend Family Papers. Raynham Hall Museum, Oyster Bay, New York.

Tredwell, Daniel M. *Men and Things on Long Island, Part I* (1839). Brooklyn: C.A. Ditmas, 1912.

United States Census Returns, 1800-1860. Nassau County Research Library, East Meadow, New York.

Vagts, Christopher. *Suffolk: A Pictorial History.* Huntington: Huntington Historical Society, 1983.

Van Der Donck, Adriaen. "A Description of the New Netherlands" (1656). In H.C. Murphy, ed., *Collections of the New-York Historical Society.* 2nd Series, Vol. 1. New York: H. Ludwig, 1841.

Vanderzee, Barbara and Henri. *A Sweet and Alien Land.* New York: Viking Press, 1878.

Van Pelt, Daniel. *Leslie's Illustrated History of Greater New York.* New York: Arkell Publishing Co., 1901.

Vogel, Virgil. *American Indian Medicine.* Norman: University of Oklahoma Press, 1970.

Waller, Henry. *History of Flushing.* Flushing: J.H. Ridenour, 1899.

Ward, William. J. and Margaret C. "The Green-Wood Cemetery." *Journal of Long Island History* 12(Fall 1975):23-34.

Wassenaer, Nicholas. "First Settlement of New York by the Dutch" (1621-1632). In Edmund O'Callaghan, ed., *Documentary History of the State of New York.* Vols. 1-3. Albany: Weed, Parsons, 1850-1851.

Watson, Edward H. "One Hundred Years of Street Railways in Brooklyn." *E.R.A. Headlights* 16(July 1954):1-5.

Weld, Ralph. *Brooklyn Village, 1816-1834.* New York: 1938.

Winsche, Richard. "Echoes of Belmont Park." *Nassau County Historical Journal* XX(Spring 1964):15-33.

Wood, Silas. *A Sketch of the First Settlement of the Several Towns on Long Island.* Brooklyn: Alden Spooner, 1828.

Wyatt, Ronald J. "The Archaic on Long Island." In Walter Newman and Bert Salwen, eds., "Amerinds and Their Paleoenvironments in Northeastern North America." *Annals of the New York Academy of Sciences* 228(1977):400-410.

Index